The Foundations of Modern International Law on Indigenous and Tribal Peoples

Volume 1: Basic Policy and Land Rights

The Travaux Préparatoires of Multilateral Treaties

VOLUME 3

The titles published in this series are listed at *brill.com/tpmt*

The Foundations of Modern International Law on Indigenous and Tribal Peoples

The Preparatory Documents of the Indigenous and Tribal Peoples Convention, and Its Development through Supervision

Volume 1: Basic Policy and Land Rights

By

Lee Swepston

BRILL
NIJHOFF

LEIDEN | BOSTON

Library of Congress Cataloging-in-Publication Data

Swepston, Lee, author.
 The foundations of modern international law on indigenous and tribal peoples: The preparatory documents of the Indigenous and Tribal Peoples Convention, and its development through supervision. Volume 1: Basic Policy and Land Rights / by Lee Swepston.
   pages cm. -- (The travaux preparatoires of multilateral treaties ; v. 3)
   ISBN 978-90-04-28905-5 (hardback : alk. paper) -- ISBN 978-90-04-28906-2 (e-book) 1. Indigenous peoples (International law) 2. Indigenous peoples--Legal status, laws, etc. 3. Indigenous and Tribal Peoples Convention (1989) I. Title.

K3247.S94 2015
341.4'852--dc23

2015013595

This publication has been typeset in the multilingual "Brill" typeface. With over 5,100 characters covering Latin, IPA, Greek, and Cyrillic, this typeface is especially suitable for use in the humanities. For more information, please see www.brill.com/brill-typeface.

ISSN 1875-9807
ISBN 978-90-04-28905-5 (hardback)
ISBN 978-90-04-28906-2 (e-book)

Copyright 2015 by Koninklijke Brill NV, Leiden, The Netherlands.
Koninklijke Brill NV incorporates the imprints Brill, Brill Hes & De Graaf, Brill Nijhoff, Brill Rodopi and Hotei Publishing.
All rights reserved. No part of this publication may be reproduced, translated, stored in a retrieval system, or transmitted in any form or by any means, electronic, mechanical, photocopying, recording or otherwise, without prior written permission from the publisher.
Authorization to photocopy items for internal or personal use is granted by Koninklijke Brill NV provided that the appropriate fees are paid directly to The Copyright Clearance Center, 222 Rosewood Drive, Suite 910, Danvers, MA 01923, USA.
Fees are subject to change.

This book is printed on acid-free paper.

Contents

Introduction   1

PART 1
Introductory Materials

   A   Contents of This Volume   5
   B   How the ILO Adopts Standards   5
        1   *Tripartism*   6
        2   *Adoption Process*   6
        3   *Voting in the ILO Conference*   7
   C   Supervision of the Application of ILO Standards   8
        1   *Regular Supervisory Mechanism*   8
        2   *Complaint Procedures*   9
   D   Citation of Materials in This Volume   10
        1   *Supervisory Comments*   11
        2   *Preparatory Materials*   11

PART 2
Adoption of the Articles of the Convention

1   Why the ILO? The Motivation, Mandate and Competence of the ILO   15
    1   Adoption of Convention No. 107   17
    2   Adoption of Convention No. 169   38
    3   Concluding Remarks on the ILO's Mandate and Motivation   41

2   Article 1 of Convention No. 169 – Coverage   43
   A   Before Conventions Nos. 107 and 169   43
   B   Article 1 of Convention No. 107   45
   C   Article 1 of Convention No. 169   57
       a   *The 1986 Meeting of Experts*   57
          i   Peoples or Populations   57
          ii   Indigenous and Tribal   59
          iii   Tribal and Semi-tribal   60
       b   *The International Labour Conference*   61
          i   1988 Session   61
          ii   1989 Session   76

    D   Development through Supervision   89
        a   *Interpretation Requested by Switzerland*   90
        b   *How to Identify Who is Covered*   91
        c   *The Importance of having a Legal Personality*   96
        d   *The Importance of Self-identification*   99
        e   *Coverage beyond 'Indigenous'*   102
        f   *Changes in Governments' Manner of Identification*   104

3 Article 2 of Convention No. 169 – Basic Policy and Orientation   107
    A   Convention No. 107   107
    B   Convention No. 169 – A New Approach   117
        i   *The Meeting of Experts*   117
        ii   *The 1988 Discussion*   120
        iii   *The 1989 Discussion*   133
    C   Development through Supervision   137

4 Article 6 – Consultation   148
    A   Convention No. 107   149
    B   Convention No. 169   154
        i   *The Meeting of Experts*   154
        ii   *The 1988 Discussion*   161
        iii   *The 1989 Discussion*   172
    C   Development through Supervision   182

5 Article 7 of Convention No. 169 – Participation, Development and the Environment   195
    1   The Meeting of Experts   196
    2   The 1988 Discussion   197
    3   The 1989 Discussion   205
    4   Development through Supervision   210

6 Articles 13 to 19 of Convention No. 169 – Land Rights   219
    A   Introduction   221
    B   Before the Standards   222
    C   Convention No. 107 – Introduction   224
    D   From C. 107 to C. 169   229
        1   *Article 13 of Convention No. 169: Lands and Territories and the Spiritual Relationship*   229
        2   *Article 14 of Convention No. 169: Rights of Ownership and Possession*   237

		a	Article 11 of C. 107 237
		b	Adoption of Article 14 of Convention No. 169 243
			i *Multiple Use and Nomads* 253
			ii *Adequate Procedures to Resolve Land Claims* 255
			iii *Adoption of Article 14 as a Whole* 261
	3	*Article 15 of Convention No. 169: Natural Resources* 266
	4	*Article 16 of Convention No. 169: Removal from Their Lands* 280
		a	Article 12 of Convention No. 107 281
		b	Adoption of Article 16 of Convention No. 169 286
	5	*Article 17 of Convention No. 169: Transmission of rights* 301
		a	Adoption of Article 13 of Convention No. 107 301
		b	Adoption of Article 17 of Convention No. 169 310
	6	*Article 18 of Convention No. 169: Penalties for Unauthorized Intrusion* 322
	7	*Article 19 of Convention No. 169: National Agrarian Programmes* 325
		a	Adoption of Article 14 of Convention No. 107 326
		b	Adoption of Article 19 of Convention No. 169 330
E	Development of the Land Rights Provisions through Supervision 333
	1	*Information Gathering* 333
	2	*Consultation over Land Rights* 334
	3	*Invasions of Indigenous Territory* 338
	4	*Demarcation of Territories* 339
	5	*Natural Resources* 340
	6	*The Involvement of Religious Institutions* 341

Appendices

I	*Indigenous and Tribal Peoples Convention, 1989 (No. 169)* 345
II	*Indigenous and Tribal Populations Convention, 1957 (No. 107)* 359
III	*How the ILO Adopts Standards* 370
IV	*Major Documents Consulted and Citation in this Volume* 380
V	*Interpretation of Convention No. 169* 383

Index   390

Introduction

The International Labour Organization is responsible for the only two international Conventions ever adopted for the protection of the rights and cultures of indigenous and tribal peoples. The Indigenous and Tribal Populations Convention, 1957 (No. 107) and the Indigenous and Tribal Peoples Convention, 1989 (No. 169) that revised and replaced Convention No. 107, are the only international Conventions ever adopted on the subject, and Convention No. 169 is the only one that can now be ratified. It will become evident in perusing this volume and the second one to be published at a later date, that the basic concepts and the very vocabulary of international human rights on indigenous and tribal peoples derives from these two Conventions.

The adoption in 2007 of the UN Declaration on the Rights Of Indigenous Peoples (UNDRIP), and the discussions going on in the international human rights community about the relative merits, impact and legal validity of the UN and ILO instruments, make it all the more important to understand how C. 169 was adopted.

The author of this volume was responsible for many years for the supervision of both these Conventions in the ILO's supervisory machinery, and was intimately involved in the adoption of the 1989 instrument, as well as in international discussions on the subject of indigenous and tribal peoples.

In writing this study, I shall go beyond a strict "travaux" approach, and discuss the organizational precedents and the subsequent practice under these instruments. Indeed, to explore the preparation of C. 169, we must also explore to an extent the drafting of C. 107, and some of the ILO instruments that preceded it. In addition, the supervision of the application of these Conventions is very largely unknown in the wider human rights community, and even in the more specialized "indigenous community" that forms a special subset of human rights activists. This guide may be of some help in redressing that situation.

PART 1

Introductory Materials

∴

A   Contents of This Volume

It is intended to present the *travaux* in two volumes. The present volume examines the background to the ILO's interest in this subject, and the adoption and meaning of a first selection of provisions of Convention No. 169: the provisions on coverage of the instrument, its basic orientation, the provisions on consultation and participation, and the land rights provisions. A second volume will cover all the rest of the Convention, dealing with a number of other subjects such as basic human rights, respect for culture and traditional structures, traditional economic activities, rights at work, education, health and administration.

This is done for two reasons. First, interest will be higher in this first volume at an initial stage, and too many years have passed since the Convention was adopted to delay its issuance any further. Second, the complexity of the discussions and issues will benefit from a more detached discussion of the very diverse subjects covered by the two volumes. Finally, there is a considerable amount of material to cover, and it will fit well into two volumes.

B   How the ILO Adopts Standards

As the ILO follows a different standard setting process from that of other international organizations, it is worth detailing it, with some indication also of how indigenous and tribal peoples' own representatives participated in the adoption of C. 169. The full explanation of the ILO procedures for adoption of standards is long and complex, and is contained in an Appendix. The following brief explanation may serve for the general reader.

The ILO is the most prolific standard-setting body among the universal organizations that form the United Nations system. It was established for the purpose of setting standards in 1919,[1] when it was founded together with the League of Nations, and from that time has steadily adopted Conventions and Recommendations on a regular basis. Over the nearly 100 years of its existence, the ILO has adopted 189 Conventions, 6 Protocols and 203 Recommendations, as of 2014. It has also taken measures to consolidate and regularly update these standards.

---

1 The preamble to the ILO Constitution makes it clear that the Peace Conference in Versailles considered it necessary to regulate conditions of work to prevent social injustice, and the adoption and supervision of Conventions and Recommendations are referred to extensively throughout the text.

1   *Tripartism*

The ILO is the only *tripartite* inter-governmental organization. The participants in ILO standard setting are governments and representatives of employers' and workers' organizations, thus going beyond the purely intergovernmental process in all other international organizations. The non-governmental constituents often consult other non-governmental organizations – in the case of the adoption of Convention No. 169, various indigenous and human rights organizations – which may take part in the discussions as observers but have no formal role to play. This corresponds in most respects to general international treaty making procedures, except for the participation of employers' and workers' representatives in addition to governments.

2   *Adoption Process*

The ILO process follows well-defined steps and takes place within a strict time frame.

Discussion of a proposed instrument is included on the agenda of a forthcoming Conference session by the ILO Governing Body, for a double discussion (occasionally a single discussion, not applicable here). In the case of the adoption of Convention No. 169, the Governing Body first called a Meeting of Experts in 1986 to advise it – an increasingly popular procedure in the ILO – and then decided later in 1986 to include the subject on the agendas of the 1988 and 1989 Sessions of the International Labour Conference.

The International Labour Office (hereinafter referred to as 'the Office') then prepares a Law and Practice report, examining the background to the question, and sends this to Governments along with a set of questions as to what they wish to include in the new instrument. (In this case this step happened in late 1987.) Governments consult their organizations of employers and workers, and all parties may reply to the ILO with proposals for draft conclusions based on these questions.[2] The Office then consolidates these replies and observations in a second report, makes any comments on them that appear necessary, and draws up a set of proposed conclusions for the first Conference discussion on the basis of these replies. (This report was sent to ILO constituents in early 1988.)

At each session of the Conference it establishes a tripartite committee (Government, employer and worker representatives) to consider the proposed

---

2   As will be seen from the materials relating to the adoption of Convention No. 107, at the time that instrument was adopted in the 1950s employers' and workers' organizations did not have the right to submit their own comments, and very few references are found to consultations with them having taken place.

conclusions and amend them as necessary. In the case of this discussion, special arrangements were made to allow a significant, if limited, right to speak for indigenous and other NGOs who attended the Conference. The Conference met for this first discussion in June 1988 and adopted an amended version of the conclusions.

It is important to know how the amendment process works in the ILO Conference, to make the proceedings clearer. The text submitted to the Committee is that contained in the Office report. When this is to be discussed, all committee members may offer *amendments*, which are submitted ahead of time and circulated in writing in English, French and Spanish. These are considered in an order approved by the Chair of the Committee. When they come before the Committee for discussion, they are subject to proposed *subamendments*, submitted orally as each proposed amendment comes before the Committee, and which are either adopted, withdrawn or rejected in turn.

Immediately following the Conference, the Office translates the conclusions into the form of a draft Convention or Recommendation, which in this case was sent to constituents in late 1988 for their comments. In the light of the comments received, in early 1989 the Office issued a revised draft Convention, together with explanations for any modifications it proposed on the basis of these proposals or on the basis of the discussion in the Conference the previous year. This revised draft is then submitted to the Conference for a second discussion and adoption, which in this case took place in June 1989. The new Convention was then opened for ratification.

The proposals for each word of an ILO Convention are spelled out in the reports submitted to the Conference, and in the reports of the Conference sessions. It will be seen below that on this occasion some of the provisions were negotiated behind the scenes and returned to the Conference for further deliberations, so the line of reasoning occasionally was hidden, but this happened only in a few cases and is historically rare in the ILO context.

3   *Voting in the ILO Conference*

In view of the brief time available for consultation and discussion in the ILO, the Conference fairly often resorts to voting to decide disputed points, and the results of these votes sometimes appear in the accounts below of how specific provisions were adopted. The results require some explanation. In view of its tripartite nature – i.e., the fact that employers' and workers' representatives as well as governments vote – the Conference has a 'weighted voting' procedure. At the committee level, the government group, the employers' group and the workers' group each have equal voting power. That is, all the employers together have the same number of votes as all the governments, and as all the workers.

This can result in apparently impossible results for votes, which those new to the ILO need to understand. The Conference calculates the lowest common denominator which will allow each delegate to contribute the correct amount to his or her group's votes. To take the simplest example, if there are 10 governments, 5 employers and 4 workers on a committee, then each government has 2 votes, each employer 4 votes and each worker 5 votes. But ILO Conference committees frequently have several hundred members, making the lowest common denominator very large. It is common to find that the results of votes are expressed as 2,523 in favour, 3,308 against, and 1,050 abstentions (not actual numbers from a real vote). This does not mean that there were nearly 6,000 members of a committee.

C Supervision of the Application of ILO Standards

The different Articles of Convention No. 169 are examined below not only for how they were adopted, but to explore how their meaning has been developed through supervision. It is therefore necessary to include here some basic notions of how the ILO carries out this supervision.

Supervision is carried out mainly by two ILO bodies, the *Committee of Experts on the Application of Conventions and Recommendations* and the *Conference Committee on the Application of Standards,* both created in 1926, which are supplemented by complaints procedures. The complaints procedures are important but relatively little used, except – as it happens – for Convention No. 169.

1 *Regular Supervisory Mechanism*

ILO supervision functions mainly on the basis of regular reporting and examination by the Committee of Experts. When a government ratifies an ILO Convention, it is required to submit regular reports on its implementation in law and in practice. Reports on some more important conventions are required on a three-year basis, and those on all others – including Convention No. 169 – are due at five-year intervals. The ILO supervisory bodies can also call for more frequent reports if needed, for instance when violations are noted or suspected, or when a government consistently fails to provide full information. This has fairly frequently been the case for Convention No. 169.

An additional feature of ILO supervision arises from its tripartite nature. Unlike all other international procedures, the ILO's non-governmental partners – organizations of employers and of workers – have a right under Article 23 of the ILO Constitution to submit their own reports on governments' performance under a ratified Convention, and these comments form an important part of the supervisory process. This is done on Convention No. 169 with even greater frequency than for most other Conventions.

The *Committee of Experts on the Application of Conventions and Recommendations* is the main supervisory body. It is composed of 20 independent experts on labour law and social questions, appointed by the Director-General with the approval of the Governing Body. It meets annually to examine reports received from governments. If the Committee notes problems in the application of ratified Conventions, it may respond in two ways. In most cases it makes 'direct requests', which are sent directly to governments and to workers' and employers' organizations in the countries concerned, to seek corrective measures or simply to ask for more information. These are not immediately published, and if governments furnish the information or take the measures requested, the matter goes no further. For more serious or persistent problems, the Committee of Experts makes 'observations', which, in addition to being sent to governments, are published as part of the Committee's annual report to the International Labour Conference.

The *Conference Committee on the Application of Conventions and Recommendations* is the next level of supervision. Established each year by the International Labour Conference, it reflects the ILO's tripartite structure of governments and of workers' and employers' representatives. On the basis of the report of the Committee of Experts, the Conference Committee selects about 25 especially important or persistent cases and requests the governments concerned to appear before it and explain the reasons for the situations commented on by the Committee of Experts. The Committee then reports to the full Conference on the problems governments are encountering in fulfilling their obligations under the ILO Constitution or in complying with conventions they have ratified. The Conference Committee's report is published in the *Proceedings of the International Labour Conference* each year, along with the Conference's discussion of the Committee's report.

2   *Complaint Procedures*

The supervisory mechanism described above is generally an effective way of ensuring that ratified Conventions are implemented. However, the ILO Constitution also provides for two procedures to consider complaints that ILO Conventions are not being adequately applied.

Representations under Article 24 of the ILO Constitution. Under Article 24 of the ILO Constitution, a representation may be filed if a country 'has failed to secure in any respect the effective observance within its jurisdiction of any

Convention to which it is a party'. A representation thus may be filed only against a state that has ratified the Convention concerned. The state must be a member of the ILO. A representation may be submitted by 'an industrial association of employers or of workers', that is, a trade union or an employers' organization. They may be local or national organizations, or regional or international confederations.

After a representation has been declared receivable, a special tripartite committee appointed by the Governing Body from among its members examines the substance of the representation. The committee communicates with the filing organization and with the government concerned. The government is asked to comment on the allegations and to 'make such statement on the subject as it may think fit'. When all the information from both parties has been received, or if no reply is received within the time limits set, the committee makes its recommendations to the Governing Body. The Governing Body decides whether or not it accepts the government's explanations, if any, of the allegations. If the Governing Body decides that the government's explanations are not satisfactory, it may decide to publish the representation and the government's reply, along with its own discussion of the case – *i.e.*, to give it wider publicity than simply including the case in its records.

Whether or not the Governing Body decides that it is satisfied with the government's explanations, the questions raised in the representation are normally followed up by the ILO's regular supervisory machinery, *i.e.*, by the Committee of Experts and the Conference Committee on the Application of Conventions and Recommendations. Even if the Governing Body is satisfied with the government's explanations, these committees may raise questions that they feel require further examination.

An unusually high number of representations have been made on Convention No. 169 compared to other Conventions.

It is also possible to make *complaints under article 26 of the ILO Constitution*, which would give rise to the establishment of a commission of inquiry. However, this procedure has not been used for Convention No. 169, and therefore is only mentioned here.

D   Citation of Materials in This Volume

Most citations will be in short form, without the full information each time. The principal citations are from preparatory materials and from supervisory comments. A more complete indication of the materials concerned is found in Appendix II.

1   *Supervisory Comments*

In this volume the comments of the ILO's principal supervisory body, the Committee of Experts on the Application of Conventions and Recommendations, will be cited in the form '*Peru observation 1998*' or '*Bolivia direct request 2000*.'

The Committee of Experts makes two kinds of comments on the application of Conventions: *Observations* are published originally in Report III (Part 1A) submitted to each session of the International Labour Conference, and this report is posted on line usually around February following the Committee's session in November/December the previous year. *Direct requests* are not published in print, but about six months after they are adopted they can be found on the ILO web site.

Comments of the Committee of Experts are cited in the year in which they were adopted, and not in the year of publication – the two are always different.

All supervisory comments by the ILO bodies – both the comments of the Committee of Experts and the representations – can be found on the ILO web site in the NORMLEX data base, which is available at www.ilo.org, under 'Labour Standards'.

2   *Preparatory Materials*

This volume will cite preparatory materials for both the adoption of Convention No. 107 in 1957, and for the adoption of Convention No. 169 in 1989. There are two kinds of preparatory materials cited below.

a.   *Reports to the Conference*: The Conference that adopts standards works on the basis of reports submitted to it by the International Labour Office ('the Office').

> Before each first discussion in the Conference the Office submits a 'law and practice report' including a questionnaire:
> 1956: cited as Report VIII (1)
> 1988: cited as Report VI (1)
> The responses to the questionnaire are reported and analysed in a second report that also includes a set of 'Proposed conclusions' for Conference discussion.
> 1956: cited as Report VIII (2)
> 1988: cited as Report VI (2)
> After the first Conference discussion the Office circulates a third report summarizing the Conference discussion, and adapting the conclusions the Conference adopted into a draft Convention.
> 1957: Report V (1)

1989: Report IV (1)
Once comments have been received from the ILO constituents the Office prepares a fourth report summarizing and analysing the comments and submitting a final draft of the Convention for consideration and adoption.
1957: Report V (2)
1989: Report IV (2A) (containing summaries and analysis) and Report IV (2B) (containing the draft Convention).

b.   Reports of discussions in the International Labour Conference

When a Convention is adopted, this is done in the International Labour Conference, which appoints a specific committee for the purpose, and then discusses and adopts the report in the plenary of the Conference. These are all reported in extensive detail in the Proceedings of the International Labour Conference, which are available on line on the ILO web site.

The Proceedings relating to the adoption of Convention No. 107 are cited simply as *Proceedings 1956* and *Proceedings 1957*, in each case followed by a page number for the specific citation.

Before the 1988 and 1989 Sessions of the Conference the method of citation changed. The reports of the Conference proceedings are produced and posted on the ILO web site within a few days of each report or discussion. These are issued in 'Provisional Records' which are numbered, and in publishing the final version of the Proceedings the Provisional Record number is conserved and page numbers are counted inside these PRs. The pagination is now in the following form:

Proceedings 1989, p. 32/6.

PART 2

Adoption of the Articles of the Convention

CHAPTER 1

Why the ILO? The Motivation, Mandate and Competence of the ILO

The International Labour Organization may appear to be a strange locus for the adoption of the only two Conventions ever adopted specifically on indigenous and tribal peoples – and not just once, but twice, in 1957 and in 1989 – but in both cases it was the only possible organization to undertake this work.

The reasons the ILO moved to revise Convention No. 107 and to adopt Convention No. 169 are summarized in the following extract from an ILO publication:

> The implementation of Convention No. 107 was not supervised seriously for over a decade. The end of the AIP[1] in 1972 meant, in practice, the end of the Organization's indigenous policy and the dismantling of internal structures that were responsible for the subject, and the 1957 instruments on indigenous and tribal peoples were very close to being consigned to history. In addition, the integrationist focus of Convention No. 107 ran afoul of other developments.
>
> The emergence of the international indigenous movement in the mid-1970s, and the first institutional moves in this realm by the United Nations Centre for Human Rights, suddenly reawakened the ILO's indigenous policy from its state of lethargy. Convention No. 107 was rediscovered as being the only international instrument dealing with indigenous and tribal peoples, and started being targeted by newly established indigenous groups and activists as the embodiment of the assimilation policies they sought to reverse. The Office began to review this Convention, and to take an active part in the emerging discussions at the international level.
>
> Rodriguez-Pinero, who is practically alone in researching this period of the ILO involvement with the subject, has written that the Office was essentially reacting to a perceived threat to its primacy from the sudden interest of the UN in the subject, and that subsequent ILO work was intended to pre-empt UN action on it.[2] The recollection of the author of

---

1 Andean Indian Programme – see *infra*.
2 This refers to a doctoral thesis that examined the ILO's work on this subject: L. Rodriguez-Pinero: *Indigenous peoples, post-colonialism and international law: The ILO regime (1919–1989)* (Oxford, Oxford University Press, 2005).

this chapter (who as a junior official was the only ILO staff member working on the subject from the early 1970s until the mid-1980s) is that the revival of the ILO's interest paralleled that of the UN in reacting to a change in the international climate and to the criticism of Convention No. 107. The Convention was recognized as having the wrong focus, and even as being destructive to the aspirations of the emerging indigenous movement. There was also a concern that the UN's intention to adopt new standards could encounter political obstacles with which the ILO's tripartite processes might be able to deal better – which proved prescient. Francis Blanchard, Director-General throughout this period, had been closely involved with the AIP, and allowed the work to proceed. That being said, inter-organizational rivalry might have played a role.

Reacting to severe criticism from the emerging indigenous movement and from other observers of the integrationist and colonialist orientation of Convention No. 107, as well as to pressure on Director-General Blanchard from Jef Rens, the former ILO Deputy Director-General, who had been responsible for much of the ILO's work on this subject during the 1950s and 1960s, the Office proposed to the Governing Body a Meeting of Experts to consider revising the Convention.

This colourful meeting in 1986 was the first exposure of the emerging international indigenous community to the ILO, as the usual tripartite participants were supplemented by indigenous members of trade unions, employers' organizations and government ministries, and by a selection of concerned NGOs. The Meeting of Experts concluded that the Convention should be revised to remove its integrationist tone – although positions differed on how far the revision should go. The Governing Body decided to place the item on the Conference agenda for 1988 and 1989, and, after a decidedly unusual ILO Conference discussion that included delegates on all benches who had never encountered the ILO before, the Indigenous and Tribal Peoples Convention (No. 169) was adopted.[3]

The ILO's motivation for undertaking this standard setting both in the 1950s and in the 1980s was directly derived from its history with the subject. As is outlined below, the adoption of Convention No. 107 was a codification of a long history of technical and conceptual work to improve the living and working conditions of indigenous and tribal peoples – originally in the overseas colonies of the European powers, and later applying to these peoples inside national

---

3 Rodgers, Lee, Swepston and van Daele, *The ILO and the quest for social justice, 1919–2009*, ILO, 2009, pp. 87 and 88.

borders – and was carried out with the full support and encouragement of the rest of the new UN system.

By the mid-1980s, the ILO was acting to preserve both its own sense of its responsibility for this subject, and to respond to criticism of C. 107, which the Office accepted as being justified. The recollection of the author of this book – who was the junior official referred to above and was the official responsible for the subject in the ILO – is also that there was a sense that the UN was the more natural venue for standard setting but that the UN was far from being ready to shoulder this work. All of us thought that the ILO was filling a gap that would eventually be filled by the UN. However, a quarter century after the adoption of Convention No. 169 there is scant evidence that any other international Conventions will be adopted on this subject to supplement C. 169 and the UN Declaration on the Rights of Indigenous Peoples.

1 Adoption of Convention No. 107

The adoption of Convention No. 107 by the ILO in 1957 is easier to explain than that of C. 169. In the first place, the ILO had a long history by this time of dealing with indigenous and tribal peoples. It had begun already in the 1920s to work for the improvement of the life and work of 'native' workers in overseas territories of colonial powers, which resulted in the adoption of a series of Conventions. As the ILO reported in reviewing the antecedents of Convention No. 107,

> …in April of (1926) the Governing Body of the I.L.O., at its 31st Session, set up a committee of experts to frame international standards for the protection of indigenous workers. The work of this committee served as a basis for a number of Conventions including the Forced Labour Convention, 1930, the Recruiting of Indigenous Workers Convention, 1936, the Contracts of Employment (Indigenous Workers) Convention, 1939, the Penal Sanctions (Indigenous Workers) Convention, 1939 and a number of other Conventions and Recommendations. Some of these are applicable not only to indigenous workers in non-metropolitan territories but also to certain classes of workers known as indigenous in the independent countries where they exist.[4]

---

4 Report VIII (1), p. 5. Much of the information on the work leading up to the decision to adopt Convention No. 107 is detailed in this report, which is available on the ILO's web site, and unless stated otherwise the information below is drawn from Chapter 1 of that report.

After World War II, the ILO was the most senior and most experienced part of the new United Nations system, as it had been established in 1919. It took up its work on indigenous peoples once again, in the first instance focusing on Asia:

> In 1947 the Preparatory Asian Regional Conference of the I.L.O. (New Delhi, October-November 1947) adopted a number of resolutions advocating economic and social development among the rural populations of the Asian countries. Three of these resolutions were directly concerned with the position of the indigenous peoples and untouchable castes. The Conference called the attention of the governments of the Asian countries concerned to the urgent need for taking action to improve conditions among these sections of their peoples and requested the Governing Body to instruct the International Labour Office to give assistance to these governments in studying the problems.[5]

It also worked on the situation in the Americas, as the countries of the American region followed the Asian example and asked that the ILO examine their situation as well.[6] As a result of its Asian and American regional conferences, the ILO established a Committee of Experts on Indigenous Labour, which met in 1951 and 1954. In 1953 after considerable research the Office published an examination of the living and working conditions of these peoples around the world: *Indigenous Peoples*.[7]

Beginning in 1952, the 'Joint Technical Assistance for the Peoples of the Andean High Plateau', which was to be known more popularly as the *Andean Indian Programme*, was launched. The plan, which was 'prepared by the I.L.O. in consultation with the United Nations, U.N.E.S.C.O., the F.A.O., and the W.H.O., was approved by the United Nations Technical Assistance Board which also allocated the funds for its execution.'[8] The Organization of American States also took part. This large joint effort led by the ILO lasted until 1972.

The exploration of the ILO's work in this area – sometimes together with other parts of the UN system, but most often as part of its own mission – led in the early 1950s to the conviction that the many problems raised had to be

---

5 Ibid., p. 7.
6 See, e.g., *Conditions of Life and Work of Indigenous Populations of Latin American Countries*, Report II, Fourth Conference of American States Members of the International Labour Organisation, Montevideo, April 1949 (Geneva, I.L.O., 1949).
7 *Indigenous Peoples – Living and Working Conditions of Aboriginal Populations in Independent Countries*, Studies and Reports, New Series, No. 35 (Geneva, I.L.O., 1953).
8 Report VIII (1), p. 44.

tackled in a systematic way. As the Law and Practice Report that launched the standard-setting process for C. 107 stated:

> 17. The studies carried out by the International Labour Office and the activities of the I.L.O. Committee of Experts on Indigenous Labour have now reached a stage where the matter is ripe for discussion by the International Labour Conference with a view to the possible adoption of an appropriate instrument dealing with the protection and integration of indigenous peoples in independent countries. This instrument could contain a number of general provisions based mainly upon an analysis of national law and practice, the recommendations of I.L.O. regional conferences and the I.L.O. Committee of Experts on Indigenous Labour, and the principles and experience of other international organisations. These provisions should be applicable both to countries where the indigenous peoples have a special legal status and to those where they are covered by general legislation appropriately adapted to the special conditions in which these peoples live.
>
> 18. Some of the problems arising out of these conditions have already been treated in a more or less fragmentary manner in existing or proposed instruments. However, the work of the I.L.O. Committee of Experts on Indigenous Labour, together with the information given in the present report, and in the publication *Indigenous Peoples*, clearly demonstrates the advisability of treating these problems in a systematic and co-ordinated fashion and in relation to other important problems not dealt with by such instruments. This would provide a balanced set of principles which would greatly facilitate practical action at both the national and international levels for the benefit of indigenous populations in independent countries.[9]

The standard-setting aspect of the question was thus seen by the ILO simply as a means of putting its many activities in this area into a coherent framework, and it considered that it was acting on behalf of the entire UN system, which indeed it was. At that time the other parts of the UN system had not yet started adopting international conventions, another reason for the ILO to undertake this work.

The question of the ILO's competence and mandate was raised squarely during the first discussion of what was to become Convention No. 107, in 1956, and occupied an inordinate amount of time and energy during the deliberations.

---

9 Ibid., p. 174.

The following long extract from the report of the Committee formed to consider this subject, lays out the concerns and the responses:

> 13. The Portuguese, Australian and Canadian Government members stated that the proposed Conclusions covered a wide range of subjects, many of which might fall outside the constitutional or traditional field of competence of the I.L.O. One or two Government members, while not questioning the constitutional competence of the Organisation, were doubtful whether some of the subjects covered in the proposed Conclusions might not fall outside its traditional field of action. The Australian Government member stated further that in presenting the proposed Conclusions in a way mainly directed towards the protection and integration of indigenous populations in independent countries, the Office had not complied strictly with its terms of reference as they had been laid down by the Governing Body and had been cited in the Introduction to Report VIII (1). He considered that in asking the Office to prepare an instrument on the living and working conditions of indigenous peoples the Governing Body had treated protection and integration as secondary matters to be considered only in connection with such conditions. He did not believe that the Office was right in assuming that protection and integration were the only means of solving the problems facing indigenous populations in independent countries.
> 14. ...the Representative of the Secretary-General said that the terms of reference given to the Office by the Governing Body had been strictly observed with respect to both form and substance. The Governing Body had based its decision on a document which contained a description of all the aspects of the problem dealt with in the proposed Conclusions. The Governing Body's instructions regarding concerted action with the other international organisations had been duly followed by the Director-General, who, from the beginning of the work, had kept these organisations fully informed and had received their generous co-operation. Report VIII (1) containing the questionnaire had been duly circulated to all member States and none of the 45 governments which had replied to it had raised an objection on the ground of constitutional competence.
> 15. The Peruvian Employers' member stated that it was the opinion of the majority of the Employers' group of the Committee that the improvement of living and working conditions of indigenous peoples was a direct contribution to the well-being of their respective countries. To raise the standards of living of those peoples meant to increase the number of consumers and hence assisted in the expansion of industry. A higher educational

level meant greater individual responsibility and a higher *per capita* output. The nature of the problem demanded that governments should treat it as a whole and not in a fragmentary way. The South African Employers' member, while associating himself with these general views, indicated that he personally supported the point of view expressed by the Australian Government member and outlined in paragraph 13 above.

16. It was the opinion of the Workers' group that the problem of the living and working conditions of indigenous populations was a broad and complex one. It was impossible to consider its various aspects separately as if they were in watertight compartments. If the over-all scope of the problem went outside the limits of competence of the I.L.O. it was inevitable that the solutions proposed should also go beyond those strict limits. The I.L.O. had therefore approached this matter in the only way possible.

17. The Brazilian Government member, in common with several other Government representatives, stated that the I.L.O. was justified in treating this problem in a comprehensive way. The Brazilian Government member added that if, in the course of the detailed discussion, it were to be found that any particular point fell clearly outside the scope of the subject as laid down by the Governing Body, the possibility would always be open to recommend that appropriate action should be taken.

18. The Egyptian Government member considered that the mandate as laid down by the Governing Body of the I.L.O. specifically stated that the international instrument should contain general provisions for the protection and integration of indigenous peoples, based on the previous work of the Organisation carried out in consultation with other international agencies.

19. The representative of the United Nations referred to the different stages of consultation that had taken place in the preparation of the Office reports, and stated that the proposed Conclusions had been drawn up by the Office in agreement with the United Nations, in accordance with the policy of close collaboration followed by the two Secretariats in this as well as in other spheres of common interest.

20. The representative of U.N.E.S.C.O. said that his Organisation was in complete agreement with the statement made by the Representative of the Secretary-General that the problem was a comprehensive one, its educational and anthropological aspects could not be artificially separated from the general scope of the instrument merely on the ground that they fell within the purview of U.N.E.S.C.O. His Organisation was glad to have been associated with the I.L.O. in the preparation of the two reports and the proposed Conclusions. He informed the Committee

that the Executive Board of his Organisation, at its meeting in April 1956, had taken note of these texts with satisfaction and had instructed the Director-General of U.N.E.S.C.O. to continue his collaboration with the I.L.O. on this subject.

21. The representative of the World Health Organisation stated that his Organisation had been very happy to collaborate at the secretariat level with the I.L.O. in the preparation of the reports and the proposed Conclusions. Health was an indispensable part of the measures which had to be taken to increase the well-being of indigenous populations. Disease was often linked to ignorance and poverty; it was therefore necessary to attack educational, social, economic and health problems in a comprehensive manner.

22. The representative of the Food and Agriculture Organisation expressed the satisfaction of his Organisation at having cooperated with the I.L.O. in drafting the chapter of the proposed Conclusions concerning land: Emphasis should be placed on the developmental aspects of the problem under discussion, including that of land settlement, and every possible measure should be taken in order progressively to integrate the indigenous populations in the processes of national development. The primary rights of these populations in respect of land should be firmly protected during the period of transition preceding that of development. No policy could be considered adequate if it merely preserved the rights of tribal communities as they stood, since this would be tantamount to economic and social stagnation and would mean that economic development would pass tribal areas by.

23. The majority of the Committee were agreed that the conditions of life and work of indigenous populations in independent countries had to be conceived as constituting an integral problem, which of necessity called for a broad and comprehensive approach. The majority did not dispute the contention that the Office had rightly followed its terms of reference in assuming that this problem should be studied with a view to the protection of those populations and to their progressive integration into their respective national communities.

24. The question described in the preceding paragraphs was, at least by implication, put to the test when the Committee took up a formal amendment moved by the Australian Government member. The amendment was designed to revise the Conclusions proposed by the Office in order to exclude provisions relating to other than labour and social security matters and thus to conform more strictly with the view which the Australian Government member had expressed relating to the Governing

Body's decision. The amendment was rejected by 4 votes to 64, with 8 abstentions.[10]

There are several points of interest here. First, of course, was the concern that the ILO was attempting something beyond its competence, in both the constitutional and ordinary senses of the term. The doubt over whether the ILO had sufficient experience and knowledge to do this was contradicted both by its long experience in the field, and by the rather enthusiastic endorsements of the UN, UNESCO, WHO and FAO.

Second is the fact that this approach of dealing with the question on this broad basis was not simply an emerging consensus – always open to interpretation – but was actually confirmed by a vote with a very large majority approving this course of action.

Finally, the reaction of the Employers' members is worth at least a wry glance, with the statement that the ILO was helping to create millions of potential new consumers.

The question was not, however, settled by the Committee's decisions. When the report was discussed in the plenary of the Conference there were several voices still challenging the ILO's competence. The most comprehensive statement, of which a part is reproduced below, was made on behalf of the Employers' group (contradicting the position of their members in the Committee who had stated their approval of the ILO's approach):

> Mr. BURNE (*Employers' delegate, Australia*) – A substantial number of the Employers' delegates to this Conference regret that they cannot accept the Conclusions set out in the Committee's report. In our opinion, the Committee in its Conclusions has far exceeded the competence of this Organisation. No doubt they have done so from extremely laudable motives, but we hesitate to think what would happen if each of the specialised agencies started to deal in this manner with the field of competence of the others. We do not believe that the Conference as a whole has yet realised the far-reaching effects which would result from our straying into the fields of competence of other international organisations. That is the aspect which we wish to pinpoint now, so that everyone may have a chance of reflecting seriously on this question between now and next June.
>
> ...It is rather strange, and in fact, significant, that the Committee deliberately decided not to include the text of this mandate in its report.

---

10   Proceedings 1956, pp. 737 and 738.

Instead of dealing with the living and working conditions of indigenous populations in independent countries, which was the question on the agenda, they have changed the title of the Conclusions and, more importantly still, the substance, to the "protection and integration of indigenous and other tribal and semi-tribal populations in independent countries". In other words, they have gone far beyond living and working conditions. Moreover, they have introduced tribal and semi-tribal populations, whether they are indigenous or not. In doing so, they have altered the whole approach and character of the discussion and have dealt with detailed instead of general provisions in connection with the question of protection and integration of indigenous peoples.

The proposed instrument consists of 14 Parts.

Of these, three, that is, Parts IV, General Policy, V, Rights and Duties, and XIV, Administration, are solely the responsibility of governments. Another four, that is, Parts VI, Land, XI, Health, XII and XIII, Education and Means of Communication, are the joint responsibilities of governments and of one or other of the specialised agencies, namely the Food and Agriculture Organisation, the World Health Organisation and U.N.E.S.C.O. respectively, as well as the United Nations itself.

If the I.L.O. were operating as an intergovernmental agency, much of what has been included in this document would be appropriate, but it is not. It is a tripartite organisation, and only some of the introductory clauses and Parts VII, VIII, IX and X, that is those parts dealing with recruitment and conditions of employment, vocational training, handicrafts and rural industries and social security, ought to have been included in this document.

Let me give you just three or four examples of points which, however important they are, go outside the competence of the I.L.O.

Point 15 deals with the administration of law and the relationship between customary law and national law. Point 20 deals with the possible removal of indigenous peoples from their habitual territories. Point 38 stresses the need to ensure a progressive transition from the mother tongue to the national tongue. Point 41 urges governments to bring to the notice of these peoples their constitutional rights and duties. I could give you more, but I will not waste your time. Of course, these matters are indeed important but they are not matters on which we here can usefully pronounce.

We realise it is pointless at this stage solemnly to go through the Conclusions one by one and try to get them amended so as to bring them within the competence of this Organisation. Because we do realise the importance of the question to the peoples concerned and that there is an urgent need for their problems to be solved, and because we really do feel that the I.L.O. has within its own sphere an effective part to play, we shall not go against the Conclusions but we shall abstain in the hope that within the next 12 months the matter can be more fully examined.[11]

This intervention was remarkable because of its concern more with the good of the ILO than with the approach taken. It was contradicted a bit later in the discussion by the following intervention, which according to the speaker was decided upon only once he heard what the Australian Employer was saying. It will be recalled that this discussion was taking place relatively early in the life of the United Nations system, when the relations among its constituent parts were still being worked out:

> Mr. HAUCK (*Government delegate, France*) – I asked to speak when Mr. Burne was telling the Conference of his scruples regarding the competence of the I.L.O. in a number of questions dealt with by the Committee on Indigenous Populations and figuring in the report we are now examining. The question of the competence of the I.L.O. and more generally the question of the competence of each of the international organisations, the problem of how their jurisdictions should be interlocked, and the question of how the agencies should mutually co-operate, is indeed a question of great importance. Since the war we have seen the birth and development not only of the great United Nations Organisation but also of a number of specialised agencies – U.N.E.S.C.O., F.A.O., W.H.O., etc. – and it is inevitable that the borders between these agencies are not always very clearly marked, and there may be what may be called duplication and overlapping between them. Consequently, it is extremely important that the problems of co-ordination of the work of these institutions should be settled with the greatest care and in a spirit of cordial co-operation between all parties. These international agencies are linked to the United Nations, as the I.L.O. is, by agreements which define their respective competence and field of action and respecting the autonomy of each. It is indeed very important, as Mr. Burne rightly says, that each of these agencies should scrupulously keep to its own field and avoid impinging on those of others. They should not try to occupy fields reserved for other international agencies.
>
> It is precisely because my Government is profoundly convinced of this fact that it was rather doubtful regarding the wisdom of including in a

---

11   Ibid., pp. 531 and 532.

text on forced labour considerations such as those put forward in the Danish and Swedish Government amendments, which seemed to exceed to some extent the competence of the I.L.O.[12] But though there may be doubt in the case of forced labour, there is certainly no doubt at all in the case of the problem of indigenous populations. One should remember that this is an entirely special case. The text before us today is the result of long and practical action undertaken by the I.L.O., the United Nations and other international agencies, with a view to giving practical help and useful technical assistance to the Andean Indians and to the countries which have to face the problems of indigenous populations.

I would like to take this opportunity of saying how important it is that practical technical assistance should have produced a proposed international labour Convention. Today we have seen a combination of the two complementary forms of action which the I.L.O. should undertake – its practical and technical action on the one hand and its legislative action on the other hand – which we do not wish to have it abandon.

This practical action, which has been going on for some years, was a perfect example of collaboration between several international agencies. In this programme of aid for the Andean Indians it was the I.L.O. which took the lead and which acted as guide, and the other agencies willingly grouped themselves around the I.L.O. in this matter. When the question arose of producing a text for a Convention, which had to be a general comprehensive text, the other international agencies – the United Nations, W.H.O., F.A.O., and U.N.E.S.C.O. – agreed to co-operate with the I.L.O. and their representatives at the Committee on this subject said they were in full agreement with the arrangements made with the I.L.O. and the provisions which it wished to have introduced in the proposed text. There has, therefore, been no infringement by the I.L.O. of the jurisdiction and functions of other international agencies.

I think that I will by now have appeased the legitimate scruples of Mr. Burne and I think that this remarkable example of coordination and cooperation between international agencies with due respect for the autonomy of each, thanks to the guiding role played by the I.L.O., will be a model for future action at the international level and that our Organisation will be able to continue to cooperate in the same spirit with other agencies

---

12 In the same Conference sessions that the ILO was adopting Convention No. 107, it was also discussing what became the Abolition of Forced Labour Convention, 1957 (No. 105).

with a view to performing as useful a job as that done in regard to the indigenous populations.[13]

The discussion continued at great length in the plenary of the Conference,[14] and not all the statements need to be reproduced here as they repeat points made by those already quoted, but the statement of the Workers' member of the United Kingdom deserves to be quoted both because of its eloquence and the telling details included:

> Sir Alfred ROBERTS (*Workers' delegate, United Kingdom*) – I want to deal with the question of competence, which was raised by Mr. Burne...I think it is important that the Conference should understand just how far the field of competence of the I.L.O. covers the points dealt with in this report. I do not want to quote the Declaration of Philadelphia,[15] but I hope you will read that Declaration, for you will then see how wide is the field of competence of the I.L.O. In fact the field of competence, and the comprehensive character of this competence, has been recognised by the Permanent Court of International Justice on several occasions. In its Advisory Opinion No. 2 the Court referred to the draft of the Constitution defining this competence and said that "language could hardly be more comprehensive".
>
> Now, it is not the first time that this Conference has dealt with particular problems of social policy applicable to indigenous populations. For example, in 1947 the Conference adopted a Convention concerning social policy in non-metropolitan territories.[16] That was adopted by 103 votes to

---

13 Ibid., pp. 533 and 534.
14 While most of the discussion was related to the ILO's competence, the discussion also covered the decision taken in the Committee to consider a Recommendation in addition to the Convention, and to transfer some of the detailed considerations to this instrument which would be discussed in the second discussion in 1957. This was, and would remain, an unusual procedure to decide only during a Conference discussion to adopt a second instrument. It will not be discussed here, but did occupy considerable attention during the Conference discussions. This eventually resulted in the adoption of the Indigenous and Tribal Populations Recommendation (No. 104), 1957.
15 This Declaration was adopted in 1944, precisely to redefine the ILO's competence in preparation for the post-World War II situation, and to adapt it to new realities. The Declaration was incorporated into the ILO Constitution in 1946, and at the time of the 1956 discussion the Organization was still exploring all its implications.
16 The speaker was referring to the Social Policy (Non-Metropolitan Territories) Convention, 1947 (No. 82).

1 against. No question of competence was raised in connection with the adoption of that Convention at that time, although it contained parts analogous to those contained in the proposed Conclusions which are now before the Conference appended to this report. For example, there is a section on the improvement of standards of living and a section on education and training. Article 8 of the 1947 Convention, for example, provides that: "The measures to be considered by the competent authorities for the promotion of productive capacity and the improvement of standards of living of agricultural producers shall include…the control, by the enforcement of adequate laws or regulations, of the ownership and use of land and resources to ensure that they are used, with due regard to customary rights, in the best interests of the inhabitants of the territory". Again, in Article 19 provision is made for the "progressive development of broad systems of education, vocational training and apprenticeship". That Convention is now in force and, in fact, it has been ratified by such countries as Belgium, France, New Zealand and the United Kingdom.

It should be recalled, I think, that in 1946 also, during the first discussion on this subject of non-metropolitan territories, the Conference unanimously adopted a resolution stating that the conditions of life of indigenous populations in independent territories presented special problems which should receive prompt and careful consideration, and requested the Governing Body to consider the desirability of placing this as an item on the agenda of a forthcoming session of the Conference.

The Conference, having in the Convention of 1947 interpreted in a comprehensive manner – and I emphasise that word "comprehensive" – the whole question of social policy in nonmetropolitan territories, felt that the problems in independent territories should also be examined in a similarly comprehensive manner. I believe that the Committee has done just that.

In paragraph 14 of the report of the Committee it is stated that when the Governing Body decided to place this question on the agenda it "based its decision on the document which contained a description of all the aspects of the problem dealt with in the proposed Conclusions" – and I have that document here. It is a very comprehensive document, which mentions every item contained in the report. It was pointed out in this document that the problems arising out of the conditions of life and work of indigenous populations in independent countries must be viewed within the wider context of economic, social and cultural development, in some aspects of which – let me admit this, as Mr. Hauck has said – other international organisations may have a primary or a concurrent interest. The Governing Body, in deciding to place this item on the agenda, noted that the other organisations concerned would have to be fully consulted with a view to reaching agreement concerning the way in which those aspects which do come within their competence to some extent could be effectively dealt with in an international instrument. The Committee's report clearly indicates that the consultation took place at all stages in the preparation of the Office reports and the preparation of the proposed Conclusions. This procedure is, of course, laid down in article 39 *bis* of the Standing Orders of the Conference, which provides for consultation with the United Nations and the other specialised agencies. This article in itself is, to my mind, sufficient proof that the Conference may include in its decision concerning labour problems related matters which are of interest to other international organisations, provided that that consultation is properly observed and carried out.

My final point on this is that of the 45 governments which replied to the questionnaire on indigenous populations, not one raised an objection to the comprehensive character of the questionnaire on the grounds of constitutional competence.

In view of the above facts it is clear to me – and I hope it is clear to everybody else – that the proposed Conclusions fall within the competence of the I.L.O. as set forth in the Declaration of Philadelphia and as demonstrated by the past action of this Conference.[17]

Following this long discussion and the doubts raised and contradicted, the Office report that communicated a draft Convention to the constituents in preparation for the second discussion reported:

> Finally, the Conference adopted the proposed Conclusions as a whole by 140 votes to 1, with 32 abstentions. Mr. Barltrop, Government adviser, United Kingdom, announced that, despite his earlier statement, in view of the danger that the quorum might not be reached the United Kingdom Government delegation had voted for the proposed Conclusions. The Conference, on a record vote, then adopted by 154 votes to 0, with 25 abstentions, the resolution concerning the placing on the agenda of the next general session of the Conference of the question of the protection and integration of indigenous and other tribal and semi-tribal populations in independent countries.[18]

---

17   Ibid., pp. 535 and 536.
18   Report VI (1), p. 43.

There was only one reference in governments' 1957 submissions on the proposed Convention to the broad question of ILO competence that had been discussed so extensively in the Conference in 1956. Israel stated that:

> Before the 40th Session of the International Labour Conference, i.e. before the final adoption of the instruments concerning the protection and integration of indigenous and tribal and semi-tribal populations in independent countries, the I.L.O. should try to consult representatives of these populations with regard to the proposed instruments.[19]

In the 1957 Conference discussion the question of competence again arose in the responsible committee:

> 8. The Employers' member of the Union of South Africa stated that there was an apparent conflict between the position taken by the Director-General of the International Labour Office with regard to the competence of the Organisation in the question before the Committee, and that taken with regard to the question of forced labour. In the latter case, some points had been excluded on the grounds that they fell outside the purview of the I.L.O., while in the proposed Convention and Recommendation on indigenous and other tribal and semi-tribal populations the opposite tendency was being followed. Employers in South Africa doubted the ability or the suitability of an organisation like the I.L.O. to formulate a comprehensive instrument for universal adoption, in a field in which there was considerable heterogeneity of cases and circumstances.
>
> 9. The Government member of Portugal expressed the view that some of the provisions included in the proposed Convention did not fall within the competence of the I.L.O. Those concerning the ownership of land, in particular, lay exclusively within the ambit of national legislation. He reserved the position of his Government.
>
> 10. The Employers' member of the United States expressed concern that a unilateral determination of competence on the part of the I.L.O. might open the possibility of practically unlimited jurisdiction; any instrument on this subject emanating from the I.L.O. should be confined to broad general principles and should refrain from dealing with details.
>
> 11. The Representative of the Secretary-General explained that, in approaching the question of indigenous and other tribal and semi-tribal populations, the I.L.O. had been faced with a highly complex problem. It

---

19   Report VI (2), pp. 4 and 5.

had soon become apparent that comprehensive and simultaneous action was required over the whole field of the living and working conditions of such populations if substantive improvements were to be obtained. The United Nations, F.A.O., U.N.E.S.C.O. and W.H.O. had fully recognised the validity of this conclusion. They had agreed to concert their action under the initiative of the I.L.O., recognising the fact that this Organisation had made a start with the examination of aspects of the problem some 20 years previously. The principle of concerted action under the initiative of the I.L.O. had met with the approval of the United Nations Administrative Committee on Co-ordination. The United Nations and the other organisations concerned had been closely associated with the I.L.O. throughout the different stages of the elaboration of the texts before the Committee and they would continue to co-operate in the process of applying the standards which the International Labour Conference might adopt. The Tenth World Health Assembly and the Executive Board of U.N.E.S.C.O. had already expressed full approval of the action taken by their respective secretariats in the establishment of the proposed texts and had agreed to continued cooperation with the I.L.O. It was expected that the appropriate bodies of the United Nations and F.A.O. would take similar action in the near future. Collaboration between the secretariats had not been merely at the level of the technical services but had involved an agreement between the executive heads of the organisations both directly and through the Administrative Committee on Co-ordination. To affirm that the I.L.O. was including in the proposed instruments aspects which fell somewhat outside its purview was admissible only from a strictly legal point of view. There had been no unilateral extension of the competence of the I.L.O., nor had the participating agencies relinquished their own competence. While the initiative of the I.L.O. had been accepted and welcomed, the other organisations had had, and would continue to have, their rightful share in the work undertaken.

12. The representative of the United Nations informed the Committee that the need for concerted action by the United Nations and the specialised agencies in the social field was of constant concern to the respective organisations and that the possibilities for such concerted action had considerably increased, particularly since the Economic and Social Council, in recent years, had laid special emphasis on over-all development problems, including the social components of economic development plans. The draft texts before the Committee dealt with subjects which were of interest to several international organisations, and various provisions of the proposed instruments touched more or

less closely upon the activity of the United Nations, e.g. projects concerning social welfare in general, social services and land reform. The United Nations secretariat had accordingly co-operated closely with the I.L.O. in their preparation, as well as in other projects concerning the well-being of certain indigenous populations. The United Nations was also prepared to co-operate fully in furthering the application of the proposed instruments, after their adoption.

13. The representatives of F.A.O., W.H.O. and U.N.E.S.C.O. associated themselves with these views, and outlined the steps which the secretariats of their organisations had taken to assist in the preparation of the texts. The representatives of W.H.O. and U.N.E.S.C.O. confirmed that the appropriate governing bodies of their organisations had recently adopted resolutions relating to the texts. The Tenth World Health Assembly had specifically endorsed the actions taken by the Director-General of W.H.O. in co-operation with the I.L.O., had formally approved the provisions of the proposed Convention and Recommendation which related to health matters, and had approved the methods which it was proposed to adopt to ensure the continued association of the two organisations in promoting the application of those provisions. The Executive Board of U.N.E.S.C.O., after recalling its previous decisions concerning cooperation with the I.L.O. in this field and approving the steps taken by the Director-General of U.N.E.S.C.O., had taken note of the provisions in the proposed texts relating to questions falling within U.N.E.S.C.O.'s purview, and had approved the procedure proposed by the I.L.O. for continued association in promoting their application. The representative of F.A.O. stated that his organisation would be happy to continue to co-operate with the I.L.O. when the instruments became operative.

14. Workers' members of the Committee expressed the view of their group that the approach taken by the I.L.O. in dealing with the problems of integration and protection of indigenous and other tribal populations was commensurate with the needs and requirements of the situation. The question of competence had in their opinion been dealt with once and for all at the 39th Session of the Conference. The discussions in the Committee should accordingly be limited to the proposed texts themselves.

15. The Government member of Egypt observed that the question of competence had been dealt with at length in the first discussion, as described in Report VI (1). He could not see any point in raising this question again, when the international organisations concerned had not raised it themselves.

16. The Employers' member of Mexico stated that human problems could not be treated by thinking in terms of separate watertight compartments. The basic remedy to the problem of indigenous and other tribal populations was to be found in an integral approach. Without raising the question of competence, however, he wished to recall that there was an Agreement between the United Nations and the I.L.O., regulating their mutual relations. Moreover, to discuss some of the provisions included in the proposed texts which were not within the normal purview of the I.L.O., one needed the necessary knowledge, which not every member of the Committee possessed. He wondered whether the proposed instruments did not imply an element of discrimination by making a distinction between integrated and non-integrated sectors of a national community. There was, too, an apparent opposition between the notions of integration into the national community and of the conservation of the cultural traits and traditional ways of life of the indigenous populations. It did not seem that the texts before the Committee offered a solution to this dilemma. Practical general standards should be fixed, taking account of the heterogeneity of conditions in various regions of the world and avoiding as far as possible the inclusion of matters extraneous to I.L.O. instruments.

17. The Employers' member of Peru stated that...(t)he I.L.O.'s competence in this sense was not open to question and it had been bolstered by the agreement of the other international organisations to contribute their efforts to this common task.

18. The Government member of the U.S.S.R. stated that the attitude of his Government had not changed since the first discussion. It was necessary to discuss the problem on a comprehensive basis and in the same atmosphere of collaboration as had existed the previous year. The indigenous populations were no longer satisfied with their way of life. The dilemma which some members felt had been left unsolved in the text of the proposed Convention disappeared if integration was rightly understood as the removal of social and economic barriers, and of discrimination, without unduly upsetting the cultural personality and the traditional ways of life of indigenous populations. Not only the provisions regarding the ownership of land but all other provisions of the proposed instruments were the concern of national legislation; Conventions and Recommendations could only be applied through the medium of national laws.

19. The Government member of Mexico stressed that the concept of competence should be interpreted in its wider sense of ability to deal with a problem. The I.L.O. had been faced with a problem which by necessity required an integral approach, and it had rightly provided for such an

approach by taking the initiative and enlisting the active co-operation of the other international organisations concerned. Considerations of formal competence had been obviated by the agreement between the organisations.

20. The Government member of the United Kingdom stated that...(t)he question of competence had been decided by last year's vote; it should be borne in mind, nevertheless, that the proposed Convention and Recommendation dealt at some points with complex and difficult issues. He wondered whether it was right for particular groups to receive special treatment by scaling down general standards set in other I.L.O. instruments to deal with particular situations.

21. The Employers' members of Brazil, Ghana and Pakistan declared themselves in general agreement with the proposed texts. ...

22. At the close of the general discussion, the Chairman observed that a substantial majority of the Committee appeared to agree that the question of competence had been settled by the Conference at its 39th Session.[20]

This did not put the subject entirely to rest, however. Once the Committee had completed its work and the proposed Convention and Recommendation were submitted to the plenary for discussion and approval, some members maintained the previous objections, though sometimes with a different emphasis. For instance Mr. Yllanes Ramos, Employer member from Mexico,[21] had the following to say, in a statement that contained several internal contradictions:

> I am not raising the problem of competence, but what I am talking about is my concern that the instrument should have the greatest possible support. If a Convention is adopted presently, then many governments will not be able to apply it or to ratify it. They will agree with the principles in it, but they will not be able to agree with the actual terms of the Convention and consequently they will not be able to ratify it. Why is that? Because in this instrument there is included a whole series of factors which are not within the real purview of the I.L.O. If you would be so good as to look at paragraph 11 of the report you will see that the representative of the Secretary-General recognised in a critical and objective spirit, completely clearly, that from a strictly legal point of view the I.L.O. does not have the possibility of studying the fields which are properly

---

20   Proceedings 1957, pp. 722 to 724.
21   Who would, incidentally, serve also as the employers' representative from Mexico at the Meeting of Experts on this subject 29 years later.

those of the agencies mentioned in paragraph 4 of the report, that is to say, F.A.O., U.N.E.S.C.O. and W.H.O. If you read the last paragraph of the Preamble you will see that it is recognised and expressly stated that the standards have been framed with the co-operation of these organisations at appropriate levels, and that each remains competent in its respective field.

Now, you will see that this document causes a dilemma. It covers the indigenous field – I say "indigenous", meaning tribal, semi-tribal and so on – but if it dealt with the indigenous problem in the light of the strict competence of the I.L.O. then it would not be possible to cover all that is necessary for integration. If it dealt with the problem as a whole, however, we would have to enter fields which are not our own, that is to say, we should be encroaching on the fields of other organisations laid down in the Agreement between the United Nations and the I.L.O. Article XVI of the Agreement provides that the Economic and Social Council shall be informed of inter- agency agreements. The proposed instrument is not within the competence of the I.L.O. and will have to be harmonised with the other agencies and the Economic and Social Council. For that reason we believe that it is not possible to have a Convention. There is not the technical possibility of doing so; it does not fulfil the requirements of a Convention established by the Constitution, and this is one of the cases which really is a matter for a Recommendation. This is our reason for opposing a Convention.

As regards the first instrument, I can sum up. There is opposition on the part of some delegates who believe that technically there are reasons why it cannot be a Convention, for reasons of international law. On the other hand, we agree with the principles included in it in general except for those parts where we think that the I.L.O. is incompetent, because we say that we – I myself for instance – have not the training to study land problems in all countries. Educational problems and administrative problems are subjects for examination by other international agencies. We have not the necessary personal competence to deal with them. We think that it is unfortunate to try and go into these problems. How can we deal with land questions, which is something for the sovereignty of each country and varies very greatly? In some countries the land belongs to the State by constitutional rule, as in the U.S.S.R., for instance. There it is impossible to apply the principle of personal ownership referred to in Part II of the proposed instrument. In other directions we find that we are looking at the land problem in the light of principles which we cannot consider, we who come (from) free enterprise countries, countries where there is freedom of press, freedom of property, within a social function which is the only way we can explain property. There are some things we cannot agree with and here we have the difficulty of approving the document as it is, as a Convention. We do not believe it should be a Convention. We think that it goes beyond the purview of the I.L.O. I do not raise the problem of competence: I simply say that we are not able to deal with the subject.[22]

The Government representative of New Zealand contributed another way of looking at the question:

> As to the question of competence, which is dealt with at some length in the report and which has been referred to by several previous speakers, I want to say only this. My Government considers that the problem is one which needed to be tackled and that it could not have been dealt with adequately on anything less than a comprehensive basis. The New Zealand Government believes that the provisions of the Convention and the Recommendation, once they are adopted, will be more and more widely applied, and that the number of ratifications secured over the next few years should be satisfactory. The exercise on which we are now engaged does not end with the adoption of the text; in some senses, perhaps, this is only the beginning.[23]

The Employer member of Peru gave another perspective:

> ...those who raise a plea of incompetence in a lawsuit are precisely those who consider that their field of competence has been encroached upon by an outsider. But the funny thing about this case is that those who might have felt their sphere of competence was challenged have not raised any pleas of incompetence, have made no protests, and have not called in question the competence of the International Labour Organisation. Those who should have done so in this case, supposing there were incompetence, are the other United Nations specialised agencies or governments, but neither governments nor the other specialised agencies of the United Nations have objected on this score at all. As I said in the Committee itself, if we dwelt on this we should be contradicting ourselves, because we would have been working for two years on something we feel to be outside our province; and yet we are demonstrating by

---

22 Ibid., pp. 400 and 401.
23 Ibid., p. 403.

our physical presence, by our endeavours and by our enthusiasm in trying to solve this problem, that in practice we do not really consider this problem to be outside our competence. And in reality it is not, because in this case the fact that a number of international agencies have been involved with the indigenous problem, and have dealt with it, is not due to bureaucratic "empire-building" on the part of the international agencies but is due solely to the nature of the indigenous problem itself.

It is an extremely complex problem and partial solutions of it would undoubtedly make its solution more difficult, because, when facts are complex, if you look at them one-sidedly, from one facet only, you will never get a complete solution. The economic, legal, sociological, ethnographic, ethnological, psychological reality is such in the case of the indigenous problem that in fact it is not only a question of living conditions but of human attitudes; not only a problem of housing and health but a problem of education, culture and way of life. It needs to be approached comprehensively and integrally, and just because of that it is for the international agencies specialising in economics, health and culture to assist each other and make possible an integrated approach to the indigenous problem. That is a necessary condition for the integral, effective and practical solution of the indigenous problem.

Thus by choosing the I.L.O. as the coordinating agency, the other international agencies and the United Nations gave the I.L.O. the responsibility of co-ordinating all these efforts in order to put forward, as a result of the perspicacious investigation carried out, the instrument submitted to the tripartite Committee; and I must associate myself with what has been said about the way in which the Committee worked. Everybody brought his contribution, his knowledge and his experience with a view to helping to solve this problem.[24]

The Conference did adopt the Convention and the Recommendation, but some delegates continued to feel that in doing so the ILO had gone beyond its competence. There were other arguments for and against, but a thoughtful comment by the representative of the Government of Australia should be reproduced:

Many of the subjects covered by these two instruments lack special labour content and it follows that the Conference as a whole cannot bring to them its special expertness. In fact, the proposed Convention dealing with very important subjects was approved by the Committee on

---

24   Ibid., pp. 403 and 404.

> Indigenous Populations by a very small vote. It was approved on the affirmative votes of nine member Governments, two Employers' members and eight Workers' members. In our opinion much of the subject matter of the Convention goes beyond what is regarded as the traditional field of competence of the I.L.O., although it is not our intention to press the reservation on competence to the point of opposition to these instruments. But we have felt that we should express the view that the practice of adopting Conventions of this nature might lead to a lessening of the authority of both past and future Conventions formulated by the Organisation.[25]

While the Conference had to debate at some length the question of the ILO's competence to deal with this question, the reservations expressed almost all related to a concern about the ability of the Conference to discuss the subject fully, and in only a few cases reflected a conviction that there were any problems with the standards themselves. What was never mentioned explicitly was the fact that no other international organization was capable of adopting these standards, and even those delegates who were opposed to the ILO's adopting them did not maintain that they should not have been adopted.

2   Adoption of Convention No. 169

When the revision of Convention No. 107 was proposed, the ILO called a Meeting of Experts in 1986 to consider the possibility. The report of the Meeting included the following:

> 40. The issue of the ILO's competence to deal with the subject occasioned very little discussion. The Meeting feels that this issue was resolved at the time of the original discussion of the issue, and notes the opinion of the other organisations attending the Meeting that the ILO should revise the Convention. Note was taken of the broad mandate of the ILO in dealing with economic, social and cultural questions, of the ILO's long involvement with the question, and of the need for a comprehensive approach to the problems raised. It was essential, however, that in revising the Convention the ILO should work closely with the other international organisations involved in the subject. The importance of close collaboration on this subject between the ILO and the United Nations was stressed. Reference was made to the standard-setting activities of the United Nations Working Group on Indigenous Populations, established by the

---

25   Ibid., p. 407.

Economic and Social Council in 1982 within the Sub-Commission on the Prevention of Discrimination and Protection of Minorities. The greatest effort must be made so that the draft texts being considered by the United Nations would contain no provisions which would contradict or conflict with those adopted by the ILO. One of the surest ways to avoid this situation would be to organise constant consultations between the bodies concerned, and between the secretariats of the two organisations. The Meeting welcomes the positive approach taken by these other organisations to collaborating with the ILO in the present discussions.[26]

In the replies to the questionnaire about the possible revision of C. 107, there were a few replies to the basic question '*Do you consider that the International Labour Conference should undertake a partial revision of the Indigenous and Tribal Populations Convention, 1957 (No. 107)?*' that touched on this point. The Government of Bolivia raised it in the following terms:

> The possibility of exceeding the ILO's competence should be kept in mind, since some of these questions are covered by other bodies in the United Nations system.[27]

Two employers' organizations also expressed opinions on this. The Brazilian employers stated:

> *Brazil.* National Confederation of Industry (CNI): Yes, as long as the partial revision does not go beyond the ILO's competence, and provided the principles of universality and flexibility are observed.[28]

The Netherlands employers' organization did not agree that the ILO was competent, and said so in relation to specific subjects that might be covered. As concerns the basic orientation:

> A positive answer to the first part of question 3 does not require that the orientation of integration be abolished. The ILO is not in a position to judge if the concept of integration should be abolished. This should be left to national circumstances and goes beyond the ILO's field of competence.[29]

---

26 Report of the Meeting of Experts, reproduced in Report VI(1), p. 106.
27 Report VI (2), p. 5.
28 Ibid.
29 Ibid., p. 10.

This organization also stated more generally that 'The ILO went beyond its competence when Convention No. 107 was adopted.'³⁰

On one particular issue the ILO itself stated that an aspect of the subject would exceed the ILO's competence:

> The Office does not propose that the revised Convention should provide a complete definition of the term "peoples", but it would be advisable to clarify that the use of the term in this Convention should not be taken to imply the right to political self-determination, since this issue is clearly beyond the competence of the ILO.³¹

When the Conference convened in 1988 to discuss the adoption of the Convention, there was again some discussion of the question of the ILO's competence and mandate, but far less than with regard to Convention No. 107. In the report of the Committee, we find only the following:

> 8. One Employers' member considered that the revision of Convention No. 107 presupposed that there was a sufficient body of experience with such an instrument. However, given the low level of ratification, he considered that there was no basis in fact for the view that Convention No. 107 was outdated. Moreover, he considered that a number of the changes which were being proposed, including changes to certain terminologies, were beyond the competence of the ILO. He suggested that a working party of legal advisers be set up to study the matter. In questioning the reasons behind the decision to revise Convention No. 107, he felt that the existing text adequately respected the culture and customs of indigenous and tribal populations and that it upheld a policy of spontaneous, rather than compulsory integration.
>
> 11. Many Government members expressed their support for the decision to undertake a partial revision of Convention No. 107 along the lines that had been proposed by the Meeting of Experts....
>
> 12. The Government member of India expressed reservations on a number of the conclusions of the report of the Meeting of Experts which, in his view, did not represent any degree of consensus. For this reason, his Government considered that the draft amendments to some of the Articles of Convention No. 107 were invalid. The Government member of France

---

30 Ibid., p. 11. This particular organization maintained its vocal opposition to the ILO's dealing with this subject throughout the process.

31 Ibid., p. 13. See *infra.*, concerning the adoption of Article 1 of Convention No. 169.

supported the view expressed by an Employers' member that the proposed revision of Convention No. 107 should not go beyond the competence of the ILO. He felt that the partial revision should focus on working conditions and social security, leaving standards setting on other issues to the United Nations. The Government member of the Netherlands agreed that the Committee should deal with matters within its competence.[32]

Apart from the long discussion on the term 'peoples' that is reported elsewhere in this volume, these were the only mentions of the question of the ILO's competence and mandate during the Committee session. There was a general acceptance that the ILO could and should proceed with the revision. And in the 1988 discussion in the Conference's plenary session of the Committee's report, unlike the situation in 1956 and 1957, the ILO's competence and mandate were never mentioned.

In the constituents' comments preceding the second discussion, there were only two instances in which objections were raised to the ILO's competence, and then only with regard to specific subjects. The Employers' Confederation of Gabon considered that 'violations of human rights and questions relating to land rights are not within the ILO's competence.'[33] This sentiment was echoed by the Brazilian National Confederation of Industry, with regard to respect for customary law.[34]

When the Conference met to discuss the revision for the second and final time, this question had practically disappeared except in relation to the broad question of 'peoples' and the related questions of self-determination. The same applied to the discussion in the plenary session of the Conference when the proposed new Convention was discussed. At the conclusion of this session the Convention was adopted by 328 votes in favour, 1 against, with 49 abstentions,[35] which sealed the question of whether the member States and the representatives of employers and of workers considered that this subject was within the ILO's competence and mandate.

3   Concluding Remarks on the ILO's Mandate and Motivation

The significant internal opposition to the ILO's treatment of this issue, especially in the 1957 discussions and to a lesser extent in 1989, reflects a long

---

32   Proceedings 1988, pp. 32/2 and 32/3.
33   Report IV (2A), p. 4.
34   Ibid., p. 24, 26, 28 and 29.
35   Proceedings 1989, p. 32/6.

struggle in the ILO between those who believe that the ILO should be concentrating strictly on industrial relations and world of work questions, and those who see the ILO in a larger framework. The ILO's structure reinforces this conflict, with its tripartite structure of employers' and workers' representatives, and government participation mostly through ministries of labour, meaning that discussions beyond the comfort zone of these participants are likely to be difficult.

In fact, this kind of dispute had been taken to the Permanent Court of International Justice in 1922 by the Government of France to consider the capacity of ILO to regulate conditions of work of agricultural workers, because they were not the industrial workers the French thought should be the exclusive concern of the ILO.[36] The PCIJ endorsed the broader view of the ILO's mandate, and those who have argued for a wider scope of ILO operations have usually prevailed ever since. This wider view of the ILO's responsibilities was reinforced in the expansive and comprehensive Declaration of Philadelphia adopted in 1944 and incorporated in the ILO's Constitution in 1946.

In addition, though the term was not in use at the time, Convention No. 169 may be seen as the international instrument best adapted to dealing with the *informal economy* in which many indigenous and tribal peoples live and work. A large proportion of the world's work force does not operate in the so-called formal economy, subject to labour law and regulations, minimum wages and hours of work. Thus in many ways – and without having intended it explicitly – Convention No. 169 was prescient in setting standards for what was to become a major preoccupation of the ILO and the international development community over the following decades.

---

36   Competence of the Int'l Labour Org. in regard to Int'l Regulation of Conditions of Labour of Persons Employed in Agriculture, Advisory Opinion, 1922 P.C.I.J. (ser. B) No. 2 (Aug. 12).

CHAPTER 2

Article 1 of Convention No. 169 – Coverage

Article 1 of Convention No. 169 lays out the coverage of the Convention, without providing a definition in the strict sense.

> 1. This Convention applies to:
> (a) tribal peoples in independent countries whose social, cultural and economic conditions distinguish them from other sections of the national community, and whose status is regulated wholly or partially by their own customs or traditions or by special laws or regulations;
> (b) peoples in independent countries who are regarded as indigenous on account of their descent from the populations which inhabited the country, or a geographical region to which the country belongs, at the time of conquest or colonisation or the establishment of present state boundaries and who, irrespective of their legal status, retain some or all of their own social, economic, cultural and political institutions.
> 2. Self-identification as indigenous or tribal shall be regarded as a fundamental criterion for determining the groups to which the provisions of this Convention apply.
> 3. The use of the term peoples in this Convention shall not be construed as having any implications as regards the rights which may attach to the term under international law.

A   Before Conventions Nos. 107 and 169

The ILO's first use of the term "indigenous" in an international standard was in the Recruiting of Indigenous Workers Convention, 1936 (No. 50). This was the second of a series of Conventions that came to be known as the "Native Labour Code", to regulate the conditions of native, or indigenous, workers in member States.[1] Convention No. 50 was focused on the conditions of work of indigenous

---

1   The first Convention in the Native Labour Code was the Forced Labour Convention, 1930 (No. 29), which is still in force as a general instrument to prohibit forced labour – but only a few Articles of that instrument are still in use. The Convention's provisions on regulation of

workers, and did not attempt the much broader approach to the question used in the later Conventions Nos. 107 and 169. It contained the following provisions:

> *Article 1*
> Each Member of the International Labour Organisation which ratifies this Convention undertakes to regulate in accordance with the following provisions the recruiting of indigenous workers in each of its territories in which such recruiting exists or may hereafter exist.
>
> *Article 2*
> For the purposes of this Convention –
> …
> (b) the term *indigenous workers* includes workers belonging to or assimilated to the indigenous populations of the dependent territories of Members of the Organisation and workers belonging to or assimilated to the dependent indigenous populations of the home territories of Members of the Organisation.

It will be seen that this definition referred to indigenous workers in both dependent territories and in the home territories of member States, though it was actually aimed more at the dependent territories – i.e., colonies.

The short series of indigenous workers' instruments included also the Contracts of Employment (Indigenous Workers) Convention, 1939 (No. 64), the Penal Sanctions (Indigenous Workers) Convention, 1939 (No. 65), and the Contracts of Employment (Indigenous Workers) Convention, 1947 (No. 86). These later instruments relied on the definition in C. 50. Art. 1(a) of C. 64 provided that:

> For the purpose of this Convention –
> (a) the term *worker* means an indigenous worker, that is to say a worker belonging to or assimilated to the indigenous population of a dependent territory of a Member of the Organisation or belonging to or assimilated to the dependent indigenous population of the home territory of a Member of the Organisation;

Convention No. 65 used almost exactly the same language in its Article 1(1), but the last in the series, C. 86, provided the following definition in Article 1(a): "the

---

the use of forced labour, at a time when it was in general use in overseas colonies of European nations, have been deemed completely outdated, and have been declared to be 'deleted' by Article 7 of the 2014 Protocol to Convention No. 29.

term *worker* means an indigenous worker, that is to say a worker belonging to or assimilated to the indigenous population of a non-metropolitan territory". C. 86 is thus the only one of this series that is restricted by its terms to dependent or 'non-metropolitan' territories.

These three Conventions are now considered by the ILO to be 'shelved', that is they are no longer actively supervised as they are considered to have been replaced by more modern Conventions.

B   Article 1 of Convention No. 107

After World War II the ILO returned to the subject with some adjustments to its programme. It convened a *Committee of Experts on Indigenous Labour* for two sessions, during which the subject of coverage of the concept was of course discussed. The conclusions of the two sessions of the Committee of Experts on Indigenous Labour were submitted to the Governing Body at its 114th and 125th Sessions (Geneva, March 1951 and May 1954).

In 1953, the ILO published the results of extended research into this subject: *Indigenous Peoples – Living and Working Conditions of Aboriginal Populations in Independent Countries.*[2] This book contained an extended section on the difficulties of defining the term "indigenous", and as reported in Report VIII (1)[3] it concluded:

> The difficulties encountered by the International Labour Office in attempting to determine what groups might be considered as indigenous are of the same order as those that national administrations have had to face. The Office has sought to formulate a practical definition suited to its own objectives, without neglecting the ethnological and cultural implications of the problem as a whole. In this spirit it has suggested that the following description might constitute a practical means of identifying indigenous peoples in independent countries:
>
> Indigenous persons are descendants of the aboriginal population living in a given country at the time of the settlement or conquest (or of successive waves of conquest) by some of the ancestors of the non-indig-

---

2   *Indigenous Peoples—Living and Working Conditions of Aboriginal Populations in Independent Countries,* Studies and Reports, New Series, No. 35 (Geneva, I.L.O., 1953).

3   This was the first of two reports prepared by the International Labour Office to lay the groundwork for the first of two discussions in the International Labour Conference of what became Convention No. 107. See the section on the adoption of ILO standards.

enous groups in whose hands political and economic power at present lies. In general these descendants tend to live more in conformity with the social, economic and cultural institutions which existed before colonisation or conquest (combined in some countries with a semi-feudal system of land tenure) than with the culture of the nation to which they belong; they do not fully share in national economy and culture owing to barriers of language, customs, creed, prejudice and often to an out-of-date and unjust system of worker-employer relationships and other social and political factors. When their full participation in national life is not hindered by one of the obstacles mentioned above, it is restricted by historical influences producing in them an attitude of overriding loyalty to their position as members of a given tribe; in the case of marginal indigenous persons or groups, the problem arises from the fact that they are not accepted into, or cannot or will not participate in, the organised life of either the nation or the indigenous society.[4]

The Office then went on in this first preparatory Report to the 1956 Session of the Conference to make what came to be a very important distinction between the eventual ILO standards and other international standards on indigenous peoples, with the following passage:

For purposes of eventual action by the International Labour Conference, a formula which is more condensed and broader at the same time may be suggested, which defines indigenous persons as –
   (*a*)   descendants of peoples who inhabited the country at the time of conquest or colonisation, who lead a tribal or semi-tribal existence more in conformity with the social, economic and cultural institutions of the period before conquest or colonisation than with the institutions of the nation to which they belong, or who are governed by special legislation; and
   (*b*)   peoples with a tribal or semi-tribal structure whose social and economic conditions are similar to those of the peoples defined under (*a*).
The latter part of the formula makes it possible to extend the scope of any international instrument which the Conference may adopt to tribal groups which, while they are not indigenous in the historical sense, nevertheless live under similar social and economic conditions.[5]

---

4   Report VIII (1), Chapter 2, quoting *Indigenous Peoples,* op. cit., p. 26.
5   Ibid., p. 48.

The Office's proposal thus went well beyond the strict notion of "indigenous" by extending the coverage to those parts of the population who were living under similar conditions, preemptively avoiding the bitter discussions on who should be considered indigenous that marked much of the UN's discussion of this concept years afterwards. It went on to lay the foundation for the idea, now generally accepted, that it is impossible to adopt an actual definition of these terms at the international level, and that all that can be done is to indicate the coverage of international standards and related development efforts. Referring to the discussion that had taken place during the adoption of Convention No. 64 referred to above, Report VIII (1) stated:

> The discussion which took place at the session of the International Labour Conference during which the Convention was adopted showed that it was impossible to draw up a list of the States to which the expression "workers belonging to or assimilated to the dependent indigenous populations of the home territories of Members of the Organisation" would be applicable, because of the judgment as to the status of indigenous populations in such States which such a list would imply. A judgment of this kind could not possibly be formed in the absence of more complete and reliable information; accordingly it was decided that it should be in the first instance for States Members ratifying the Convention to decide which indigenous groups on their home territories its provisions should apply to.[6]

The questionnaire in Report VIII (1) of 1955 put the following question to the constituents:

> 3. Do you consider that the peoples to be covered by the instrument would be sufficiently described if they were defined as follows:
> (a) descendants of peoples who inhabited the country at the time of conquest or colonisation, who lead a tribal or semi-tribal existence more in conformity with the social, economic and cultural institutions of the period before conquest or colonisation than with the institutions of the nation to which they belong; or who are governed by special legislation; and
> (b) peoples with a tribal or semi-tribal structure whose social and economic conditions are similar to those of the peoples defined under (a)?
> 4. If not, do you have any suggestions for improving this definition?[7]

---

6   Ibid., p. 48.
7   Ibid., p. 175.

Sixteen governments replied to this question, some with specific suggestions for redrafting. The Office commented on these suggestions with the following analysis. The selection from the report is long, but it demonstrates the care with which both the constituents and the Office were exploring the problem:

> ...it has been deemed expedient not to limit the scope of the instrument to the tribal or semi-tribal groups which in many countries are considered indigenous by virtue of their historical antecedents (clause (*a*) of the suggested definition) but to extend it to other tribal or semi-tribal groups as well who, without being "indigenous" in the historical sense, live in social and economic conditions comparable to those of the former category (clause (*b*)). On the other hand, care has been taken to avoid using a formula so broad that it would apply also to other sectors of the population who, although they may not lead a tribal or semi-tribal existence, have nevertheless not achieved a sufficient degree of integration into the economic, social or cultural life of the nation. In spite of its relativity, the "tribal or semi-tribal" criterion appears to be decisive since, in its absence, the proposed instrument would be so all-embracing that it would lose much of its effectiveness in a large number of countries where, either in law or in practice, the integration of tribal or semi-tribal communities is a problem *sui generis* quite different from that of other unintegrated groups. Were this criterion not embodied in the definition, the scope of the instrument would become so vast and indefinite that it might in a number of countries cover the majority of the rural population and even certain non-indigenous urban groups. The instrument would cease to be one designed for the protection of the population groups dealt with in Report VIII (1), but would cover all groups who are "underdeveloped" either from the socio-economic or from the cultural point of view. ...with a view to avoiding difficulties of interpretation, clause (*a*) of the definition has been amended in the proposed Conclusions in a manner which would seem to meet the preoccupation expressed by the Government of Brazil.[8]

---

[8] The Government of Brazil had stated, among other things, that 'descent from people who inhabited the country at the time of conquest or colonisation would constitute too restrictive a criterion, as it would be practically impossible, owing to the mobility of tribal groups, to determine in the case of large areas which groups were living within the present-day boundaries of a given country at the time of conquest or colonisation'. (Report VIII (2), pp. 103 and 104.)

In recognition of the obvious difficulty (pointed out by the Government of Brazil) of determining, in the case of large areas, which tribal groups were living within the present-day boundaries of a country at the time of conquest or colonisation, the suggested definition has been altered through the introduction in the proposed Conclusions of the phrase "(or a geographical region to which the country belongs)" after the words "inhabited the country" in clause (a). Moreover, it should be pointed out that such exceptional cases as might still not be covered by clause (a), as now drafted, would fall within the terms of clause (b) of the definition.

The criterion of ethnic consciousness as embodied in the definition suggested by the Government of Brazil would appear to be covered by the concept of greater conformity with tribal or semi-tribal institutions contained in clause (a) as now proposed.[9]

The inclusion of the words "or semi-tribal" in the definition would appear to meet the preoccupation expressed by the Government of Ceylon that the instrument should cover also peoples who have lost their main tribal characteristics but whose socio-economic status is low, and who continue to live in conditions of geographical or social isolation. For the sake of clarity, however, a sentence has been added to the proposed definition, indicating the latitude with which the term "semi-tribal" should be interpreted.

The definition suggested by the Government of Iran, according to which the instrument would apply to the inhabitants of a country who lead an existence more in conformity with "ancient" customs, traditions and social, economic and cultural institutions than with those of the present, could be extremely useful, if it did not in turn entail the need for laying down an objective and universally valid criterion for defining the scope of the word "ancient" within the context of the present study. Moreover, in various parts of the world customs, traditions and institutions dating back to antiquity have survived in a number of non-tribal population groups.

The new wording suggested by the Government of Egypt for clause (b), while it undoubtedly contributes to clarifying the definition suggested by the Office, might raise difficulties of interpretation, in that the words "early stage of human progress" imply a value judgment for which it would

---

9 Note that this prefigures the phrase eventually included in Art. 1 of C. 169 according to which self-identification is a fundamental criterion. The idea was thus fully recognized in adopting the 1957 Convention, but it was assumed the wording covered the idea without having to make it explicit.

be very difficult to find an objective criterion applicable to all tribal groups to be covered by the text. It may be added that, taken as a whole, the proposed new wording might apply also to some groups already covered by clause (*a*) of the text suggested in the questionnaire, e.g. forest-dwelling tribes. Thus, it would blur the distinction which the latter seeks to establish between the groups described in each of the two clauses. It seems important that this distinction be preserved since, in many countries, particularly in Latin America, the various indigenous groups are commonly identified in administrative practice (and sometimes in the law), as well as by the public, by reference to their historical origin. Moreover, elimination of this criterion might have the effect of minimising certain rights and titles which such peoples often enjoy in the territories which they inhabit, precisely because of that origin. The same argument seems to be applicable to the reply of the Government of Honduras, which has suggested basing the definition on the present living conditions of indigenous peoples without any reference to the historical element.

As regards the suggestion made by the Government of Lebanon, it must be explained that the reason why the word "cultural" has been used in clause (*a*) and not in clause (*b*) is that – as mentioned on page 49 of Report VIII (1) – while the way of life of nomadic desert tribes in the Near and Middle East may occasionally bear resemblances to that of forest-dwelling peoples in other parts of the world, the former populations differ from the latter through "their close cultural kinship with the sedentary populations in the countries to which they belong". This kinship "is due primarily to the influence exerted on them by the Moslem religion".

The clarification urged by the Government of New Zealand in regard to the scope of the instrument in cases where the bulk of the indigenous population has already reached an advanced stage of integration, would appear to be covered by the principle embodied in clause (*b*) of question 7, which contemplates that special protective measures would be continued only so long as there were indigenous groups which needed special protection and in accordance with the extent to which they needed it.

With respect to the suggestion of the Belgian Government that clause (*a*) of the definition should contain a reference to the groups which conquered or colonised the country, it might be suggested that, while such a reference appears to be appropriate in a descriptive monograph, it seems less suitable for inclusion in a concise regulatory text. As regards the suggestion by the same Government that the word "State" be substituted for "nation", this might have the effect of limiting the scope of integration to the field of political, legal and administrative institutions of which the

State is the embodiment *par excellence*. It should be recalled, however, that integration, as understood in various I.L.O. studies and by the Committee of Experts on Indigenous Labour, implies adaptation of the indigenous population not only to the institutional standards and practices which properly fall within the sphere of state action but also to the socio-economic and cultural values and institutions which the social sciences associate preferably with the "nation" concept.

In view of the foregoing considerations it has been felt advisable to draft the corresponding point of the proposed Conclusions on the basis of the question and in the light of the observations of the Government of Brazil concerning legal status and territorial occupation. (*Point 3.*)[10]

The following revised formulation of the proposed conclusions regarding this point was therefore put to the Conference for the first discussion[11] in Report VIII (2). Note that references to indigenous and tribal 'peoples' had been replaced by references to 'groups' – of considerably less relevance to the discussion in 1956 than a similar amendment would have been when Convention No. 169 was being discussed, because the human rights Covenants had not yet been adopted:[12]

> 3. The instrument should apply to –
> (a) members of tribal or semi-tribal groups who are descendants of the population which inhabited the country (or a geographical region to which the country belongs) at the time of conquest or colonisation and who, irrespective of their legal status, live more in conformity with the social, economic and cultural institutions of that time than with the institutions of the nation to which they belong;
> (b) members of tribal or semi-tribal groups whose social and economic conditions are similar to those of the groups described under (a).
> In this definition the term "semi-tribal" should include groups which, while at an advanced stage in the process of losing their tribal characteristics, are not yet integrated into the national community.

---

10   Report VIII (2), pp. 105 to 108.
11   It is made clear in the portion of this study on adoption of ILO standards that in adopting Conventions, the ILO holds two discussions in successive years, interlaced with various written consultations. The 'first discussion' therefore refers to the Conference session in 1956.
12   As will be discussed below, this is because the Covenants' common Article 1 provides that all peoples have the right to self-determination, a discussion that did not arise at this point.

It will be noted that the word 'members' had appeared in the text at this point, without any reason having been evoked. There is no indication that the Office wished to undercut the collective nature of the references to indigenous and tribal populations, as would be a point at issue when this Convention's revision was discussed 30 years later – it appears to have been a simple drafting device that nevertheless did diminish the collective nature of rights under this instrument.

When the Conference held its first discussion of the proposed new Convention in 1956, the question of coverage was raised not only directly in relation to specific proposed conclusions, but also in the general discussion. A very revealing set of comments was made at this point:

> 25. The Indonesian Government member informed the Committee that the policy of his country was to abolish all differentiation between the various elements in its population. Moreover, all the national laws of his country applied to all the sectors of the population. In these conditions, it was not appropriate to consider that certain tribal or semi-tribal groups were indigenous, as the Office had done in the descriptive part of Report VIII (1).
> 26. A broadly similar point was made by other speakers among the Government group, including those of Egypt, Syria and Liberia, who explained that the term "indigenous" itself could have an undesirable connotation in certain areas. The subsequent discussion raised the whole problem of the extent to which the proposed instrument should be considered to apply to various categories of countries.
> 27. The work of the I.L.O. in this field had begun with special reference to a situation existing in many of the countries in Latin America. There was no doubt in the minds of the Committee that the proposed Conclusions should apply equally to other independent countries where two or more different peoples lived side by side as the result of conquest or colonisation. Moreover, several Government members representing countries where similar situations did not exist but where tribal or semi-tribal groups were still to be found expressed their governments' view that the proposed Conclusions should apply in their case also, provided that a form of words could be found which did not imply that any difference existed between the tribal or semi-tribal groups and the rest of the population except that of the level of their general social and economic development.

28. With these points in mind the Committee devoted special attention to the drafting of point 3 of the proposed Conclusions, which appears as point 4 of the text appended to this report. The formula appearing in the title of the proposed Conclusions – " Indigenous and Other Tribal or Semi-Tribal Populations " – was discussed with particular care. This wording was subsequently adopted in the Committee by 44 votes to 0, with 24 abstentions.[13]

This is particularly interesting in view of the battle some of these countries fought in later years *not* to be included in the United Nations' discussions of indigenous peoples, though they had readily accepted and even solicited the ILO's inclusion of their countries as having as indigenous *or tribal* populations.

The report of the Conference Committee discussing this report in 1956 referred to the discussion and decisions on the proposed conclusions as follows:

44. Point 3 of the text, relating to the population groups in regard to which the instrument should be applied, was adopted as follows: the opening phrase of the point and clause (*a*) were adopted unanimously, with the insertion of the words "in independent countries" after the words "tribal or semi-tribal groups", in accordance with an amendment moved by the Employers' members. A new text proposed for clause (*b*) by the Government members of Egypt, Indonesia and Syria was adopted by 78 votes to 1, with no abstentions, the words "in independent countries" again being inserted as proposed by the Employers' members. The final paragraph of the text under consideration was retained after a lengthy exchange of views. Several members, however, felt that the scope of this paragraph as worded would be very difficult to determine and it was generally agreed that further study would be given to this section during the second discussion.

45. Point 3, as amended, was adopted by 65 votes to 0, with 1 abstention.[14]

The text of the conclusions adopted on this point read as follows:

4. The instrument should apply to –

---

[13] Proceedings 1956, pp. 738 and 739.
[14] Ibid, p. 740.

(a) members of tribal or semi-tribal groups in independent countries who are descendants of the population which inhabited the country (or a geographical region to which the country belongs) at the time of conquest or colonisation and who, irrespective of their legal status, live more in conformity with the social, economic and cultural institutions of that time than with the institutions of the nation to which they belong;

(b) members of tribal or semi-tribal groups in independent countries whose social and economic conditions are at a less advanced stage in relation to the general development of the country, and who are governed totally or partially by customs or traditions or by special legislation. In this definition the term "semi-tribal" should include groups which, while at an advanced stage in the process of losing their tribal characteristics, are not yet integrated into the national community.

There are several points to be noted in this text. First, the 'final paragraph' to which reference is made in para. 44 of the Conference Committee's report was integrated by the Conference drafting committee[15] into sub-paragraph (b), beginning with 'In this definition ...'. Second, though it is not detailed in the report, the addition to sub-paragraph (b) of the reference to groups 'whose social and economic conditions are at a less advanced stage in relation to the general development of the country' contradicts the concern of the Office in the draft conclusions submitted to the Conference not to include judgements on the relative advancement of the groups concerned – this judgemental aspect was inserted into the text in a number of places by the constituents. The third thing to remark is the emphasis in the same sub-paragraph on the objective of integration into the national community, a concern that was inherent but not explicit in the draft presented by the Office.

The only comments of substance made on this point in the written consultations between the two discussions were made by the United Kingdom:

United Kingdom: It is doubtful whether the concept of detribalisation is sufficiently explicit for the purposes of this definition. Moreover, indigenous

---

15   Note that after a committee adopts a text, it is sent to a drafting committee consisting of representatives of the employers' and workers' groups and of governments, supported by the ILO Legal Adviser and other members of the secretariat. The purpose of the drafting committee is to ensure consistency between the English and French versions of the proposed text, as well as to make other minor drafting changes that do not change the meaning of the text adopted by the committee. The revised text is then submitted to the plenary session of the Conference.

people more often than not become an integral part of the society to which they belong as persons rather than as members of a tribe. Again, the expression "time of conquest or colonisation" is vague since conquest or colonisation may have taken place on a number of occasions. The reference to conquest or colonisation does not, in any case, appear to be necessary.

The following redraft is suggested for consideration:
1. This Convention applies to indigenous peoples in independent countries who retain their separate identities either by virtue of custom or tradition or as a result of special laws and regulations, and whose social, cultural and economic conditions are in consequence substantially behind those of the rest of the population.
2. For the purpose of this Convention the term "indigenous peoples" includes immigrants whose social and economic conditions are comparable to those referred to above.

Various references are made throughout the Convention to "indigenous peoples" or "non-integrated indigenous peoples" or "non-integrated indigenous groups", etc. Special reference has not been made below to the numerous occasions where these occur in the draft but it is suggested that either "non-integrated indigenous peoples" or "peoples to which this Convention applies" should be used consistently throughout. In the former case the following words might with advantage be inserted at the end of paragraph 1 of the proposed Article 1: "and the expression 'non-integrated indigenous peoples', wherever it occurs, shall be construed accordingly."[16]

The Office did not accept any of these suggestions, which the Government could have made again at the Conference in 1957 but did not. They are reproduced here largely to indicate that still at this time even a very careful government such as that of the United Kingdom was using the term 'peoples' without any thought for its meaning beyond the Convention itself.

In 1957, the discussion of this point was much briefer. The Office had proposed the following as the text of this Article:

Article 1
1. This Convention applies to –
   (a) members of tribal or semi-tribal populations in independent countries whose social and economic conditions are at a less advanced stage than the stage reached by the other sectors of

---

16   Report VI (2), pp. 10 and 11.

the national community, and whose status is regulated wholly or partially by their own customs or traditions or by special laws or regulations;

(*b*) members of tribal or semi-tribal populations in independent countries which are regarded as indigenous on account of their descent from the populations which inhabited the country, or a geographical region to which the country belongs, at the time of conquest or colonisation and which, irrespective of their legal status, live more in conformity with the social, economic and cultural institutions of that time than with the institutions of the nation to which they belong.

2. For the purposes of this Convention, the term "semi-tribal" includes groups and persons who, although they are in the process of losing their tribal characteristics, are not yet integrated into the national community.

3. The indigenous and other tribal or semi-tribal populations mentioned in paragraphs 1 and 2 of this Article are referred to hereinafter as "the populations concerned".[17]

The very brief discussion in the 1957 Conference Committee is reported in the Committee's report as follows:

37. An amendment moved by the Government member of the United States to simplify the definition contained in this Article was withdrawn after detailed discussion, the majority of the Committee agreeing that the proposed text met the situation existing in the various countries as adequately as possible. The Committee then adopted the text of Article 1.[18]

When the report of the Committee was submitted to the plenary of the Conference, there was no further discussion of Article 1, and the Convention was adopted with the following wording for this Article:

Article 1
1. This Convention applies to –

---

17   Ibid., pp. 50 and 52. (The proposed Convention was presented in both English and French on alternating pages for each section, accounting for the non-consecutive page numbering.)
18   Proceedings 1957, p. 726.

(a) members of tribal or semi-tribal populations in independent countries whose social and economic conditions are at a less advanced stage than the stage reached by the other sections of the national community, and whose status is regulated wholly or partially by their own customs or traditions or by special laws or regulations;

(b) members of tribal or semi-tribal populations in independent countries which are regarded as indigenous on account of their descent from the populations which inhabited the country, or a geographical region to which the country belongs, at the time of conquest or colonisation and which, irrespective of their legal status, live more in conformity with the social, economic and cultural institutions of that time than with the institutions of the nation to which they belong.

2. For the purposes of this Convention, the term semi-tribal includes groups and persons who, although they are in the process of losing their tribal characteristics, are not yet integrated into the national community.

3. The indigenous and other tribal or semi-tribal populations mentioned in paragraphs 1 and 2 of this Article are referred to hereinafter as "the populations concerned".

C Article 1 of Convention No. 169

a *The 1986 Meeting of Experts*

Several of the points raised in the 1956 and 1957 discussions were to be raised again in 1988 and 1989, though in the end the Conference chose to keep the same general approach as had been used in Convention No. 107. There were, however, significant differences in several respects.

Various aspects of definition and coverage were discussed in the Meeting of Experts that preceded the beginning of the Conference discussions, and were later taken up by the Conference. The additional element of the significance of the term 'peoples', which had been treated rather casually in 1956 and 1957, now took on enormous significance.

1 Peoples or Populations

The discussion on this point began in the Meeting of Experts, and it would consume a great deal of the Conference's attention over the two following years. The Experts' report stated:

Terminology

30. There was a long discussion over the terminology which should be used in the revised Convention to designate those covered by it. Several of the experts, supported by all the indigenous and tribal representatives present, thought that the term "populations" used in Convention No. 107, should be replaced by "peoples". The latter term indicated that these groups had an identity of their own, and a right to self-determination. It better reflected the view these groups had of themselves, and was not degrading as was the term "populations" which implied merely a grouping. It was noted that several countries already used the term in internal legislation, and that its use had become accepted in discussions in the United Nations and other international forums.

31. Others felt that it was precisely because of the implications of the term that its use in a revised Convention raised difficult questions. They respected the wishes of the indigenous and tribal representatives to be referred to as peoples, but felt that to incorporate such a term in an ILO Convention might imply a degree of recognition to these groups which went beyond the ILO's competence and was in conflict with the practices in a large number of countries which might otherwise be able to ratify the Convention. On the other hand, they agreed that it was a legitimate point which should be carefully considered by the Conference in revising the instrument.[19]

This concept was closely tied to that of self-determination, which was discussed more thoroughly under Article 2 of the Convention at this stage, and the reader is referred to the discussion of that point below. While eventually the Conference adopted the term "peoples" in Convention No. 169, this was far from easy and was fraught with difficulty.

It is worth recalling that when Convention No. 107 was adopted in 1956 and 1957, the terminology was not felt to be constraining, and different terms were used indiscriminately. See for instance the text adopted by the Conference in its first discussion of what would become Article 2:

> Governments should have the primary responsibility in developing co-ordinated and systematic action aimed at the protection of indigenous populations and progressive integration of indigenous peoples into the life of their respective countries.[20]

---

[19] Report of the Meeting of Experts, reproduced in Appendix I of Report VI (1), pp. 104 and 105.
[20] Proceedings 1956, p. 748.

The terms 'peoples' and 'populations' clearly were regarded as synonymous at the time, and would not acquire special significance until the Human Rights Covenants were adopted a decade later, with the provision that all peoples have the right to self-determination.

ii   Indigenous and Tribal

As noted above under Convention No. 107, the ILO had early on adopted an approach that favoured references to social situation rather than ancestry or historical precedence, and this continued thereafter to distinguish the ILO position from that adopted in the United Nations. As the Meeting of Experts' report noted:

> 33. The Meeting notes that the working document before it made it clear that Convention No. 107 is intended to apply to a wide variety of indigenous and tribal peoples in all parts of the world, and that it has been so applied in the past. For instance, it applies to Indians in the Americas, whatever may be their degree of integration into the national cultures, to different extents depending on their needs and circumstances. It also applies to tribal peoples in Asia, such as in Bangladesh, India and Pakistan which have ratified the Convention, and a number of other countries which have not. It has been considered applicable also to nomadic populations in desert and other regions. All of these groups share certain characteristics such as being relatively isolated and less economically developed than the rest of the national community. This wide degree of coverage should not be modified, although it does make it more difficult to adopt language which is sufficiently flexible to cover all these situations.
>
> 34. Especially difficult problems were noted as concerns sub-Saharan Africa, where the entire population had tribal links and all were indigenous. The experts from Africa shared the opinion that the Convention is applicable in Africa, while referring to particular difficulties of application which arise. It is clear that the present Convention applies to such relatively isolated groups in this continent as the San or Bushmen, the Pygmies and the Bedouin and other nomadic populations. Other groups share many of the characteristics of these peoples, and would also be covered. These experts cited the basic principles of consent, consultation and participation applied in their countries for activities affecting the entire national population and not simply these groups. The Meeting was informed of a recent comment by the Committee of Experts regarding one African country, in which it stated that the fact that the national legislation made

no distinction between different population groups was not in itself a sufficient reason for deciding that the Convention is not applicable to a country, but that it was also necessary to examine whether different ethnic groups appeared to be isolated from the national community or to be in a relatively less advantaged position.

35. As concerns nomadic populations in particular, the representative of the FAO referred to the special problems of establishing the rights and guarantees which should be recognised for them, especially since they often share the use of territories with other population groups. This problem is dealt with more fully in the section of this report on land rights.[21]

With this endorsement of the ILO's long-standing approach by the Meeting of Experts, the ILO avoided many of the discussions of coverage and inclusion that would plague the United Nations in the adoption of the Declaration.

iii   Tribal and Semi-tribal

Finally, the Meeting of Experts discussed some of the other terminology in Convention No. 107 that was considered outdated and patronizing. The report of the Experts stated in this regard:

> *Article 1 – Definition*
> 88. Reference to the concepts of a "less-advanced stage" of development, and "of that time" in paragraph 1 were not considered acceptable, since they reflect a notion of cultural inferiority. Use of the term "regarded as indigenous" in paragraph 1 (*b*) was taken to imply that these groups had no right to define themselves. Several speakers thought that some language should express the notion that these peoples were disadvantaged in relation to the national community, whether economically or in other fields. One of the experts offered the following language as a possible replacement:
>
>> Indigenous and tribal peoples, individually and collectively, in independent countries whose social, economic and cultural traditions and practices distinguish them from the national dominant society.
>
> 89. Some experts requested an explanation of the term "semi-tribal". It was stated that this term was meant to indicate that there could be

---

21   Ibid., p. 105.

different forms of social organisation among the groups covered by the Convention, and that they would continue to be covered to the extent appropriate in the situation. Reference was made in this connection to the flexibility required by Article 28 of Convention No. 107 and recognised by the supervisory bodies, to the effect that the Convention applied to the extent and under the conditions necessary in different situations. One expert suggested that the term "tribal and semi-tribal" should not be used in the revised Convention since it was not used in some countries and was not necessary to describe the peoples in question. Another expert suggested that reference be made to the draft working definition contained in the United Nations Sub-Commission study of this subject. A number of other experts felt, however, that the definition should remain in its present form in view of the wider coverage it allowed for groups in many parts of the world who lived in similar situations but who were defined in different ways in the context of different countries.[22]

b *The International Labour Conference*

All these points were then taken up in the Office reports and the discussions in the Conference that took place in 1988 and 1989.

i 1988 Session

The initial Office report to the Conference – the 'Law and Practice' report – contained the following passage on 'peoples' and 'populations':

> Convention No. 107 refers in its title and in a number of its Articles to indigenous and tribal *populations*. During the Meeting of Experts, the indigenous participants and a number of the experts considered that the Convention should be amended to refer to indigenous and tribal *peoples* (see paragraphs 30 to 32 of the report). The indigenous representatives stated that the term "peoples" indicated that these groups had an identity of their own, and better reflected the view they had of themselves, while "populations" implied merely a grouping. They also noted that several countries already used the term in internal legislation, and that its use had become accepted in discussions in the United Nations and other international forums.
>
> On the other hand, as the report of the Meeting of Experts noted in paragraph 31:

---

22   Ibid., p. 115.

> Others felt that it was precisely because of the implications of the term that its use in a revised Convention raised difficult questions. They respected the wishes of the indigenous and tribal representatives to be referred to as peoples, but felt that to incorporate such a term in an ILO Convention might imply a degree of recognition to these groups which went beyond the ILO's competence and was in conflict with the practices in a large number of countries which might otherwise be able to ratify the Convention. On the other hand, they agreed that it was a legitimate point which should be carefully considered by the Conference in revising the instrument.
>
> In ILO practice the terms have been used interchangeably in the past. The 1953 publication *Indigenous peoples: Living and working conditions of aboriginal populations in independent countries* used both terms in its English and Spanish titles, though the French version used "populations" in both parts of the title. In the United Nations, the recently completed major study by the Sub-Commission on Prevention of Discrimination and Protection of Minorities is entitled *Study of the problem of discrimination against indigenous populations,* and the name of the United Nations Sub-Commission Working Group on this question is the "Working Group on Indigenous Populations". On the other hand, most United Nations documentation and the Working Group itself in its documentation, often use the term "peoples". The Special Rapporteur appointed by the Sub-Commission to carry out the above-mentioned study expressed a preference for the term "peoples", and this is current usage also in other international forums.
>
> The concern of those who do not wish to use the term "peoples" is that it will imply recognition of a right to a degree of political autonomy which is unacceptable to many States. The Office considers that this implication can be avoided, if the Conference discussion makes it clear that the term is used to recognise that these groups have an identity of their own and consider themselves to be peoples, but that the implications of the term within the national context of ratifying States must be determined at the national level. Thus, in the present report the Office has followed the example of the Meeting of Experts in using the term "peoples", and proposes its use in a revised Convention.[23]

As the Law and Practice report began to consider specific provisions more closely, others of the concerns noted in the Meeting of Experts were taken up. On the question of *coverage* in Article 1 the report stated:

---

23   Report VI (1), p. 31.

This Article applies to "indigenous" as well as "tribal" populations in independent countries, and the Meeting of Experts concluded (see paragraphs 33 to 35 of its report) that this should not be modified. It may be noted that several countries that have tribal populations which are not considered as indigenous have ratified Convention No. 107; attempts to analyse the historical precedence of different parts of the national populations would detract from the need to protect vulnerable groups which in all other respects share many common characteristics, wherever they are found. While recent discussions in the United Nations Sub-Commission do not follow this example (see paragraph 89 of the report of the Meeting of Experts), there is no element of conflict with the draft working definition offered by the United Nations Special Rapporteur on this question, as the definition in Convention No. 107 simply allows for a wider coverage with a view to including all groups similarly situated.[24]

The question of cultural inferiority was also taken up in this report, as a consequence of some of the language used in Convention No. 107, and here was linked to the 'indigenous and tribal' usage:

> Paragraph 1 of this Article contains two subparagraphs, both of which include presumptions of the cultural inferiority of indigenous and tribal peoples.
>
> Subparagraph (*a*) refers to populations "whose social and economic conditions are at a less advanced stage than the stage reached by other sections of the national community". Subparagraph (*b*) speaks of populations regarded as indigenous because of their descent from populations present at the time of conquest or colonisation, which "live more in conformity with the social, economic and cultural institutions of that time than with the institutions of the nation to which they belong."
>
> Both of the phrases quoted above imply a lack of cultural development of indigenous or tribal peoples, and indeed, their cultural inferiority. Many such groups, however, have an unbroken cultural tradition and highly developed social structures which pre-date the cultures and institutions of the dominant societies of the countries in which they live. Others, of course, have much less well developed institutions and can be considered as "primitive" cultures, though this is a difficult concept to define since modern anthropological research has shown that many such cultures are extremely complex. Others still are descended from highly

---

24   Ibid., p. 32. The United Nations never took up this viewpoint, and continues today to use the term "indigenous" as its only point of reference.

developed cultures but have lost many of the characteristics of these cultures. This last category covers groups that were the dominant populations in their territories before colonisation but which are now in a culturally disadvantaged situation.

The assumption that the groups covered are culturally inferior and should be given the opportunity to benefit from the advantages offered them by superior cultures, should be deleted from the Convention. At the same time, it should remain clear that the revised instrument refers to groups that are marginal to the dominant societies, that have certain characteristics which distinguish them from these societies, and that are in need of special protection.

The question then arises of how to redraft this provision. Three basic ideas need to be included in paragraph 1 of Article 1. The first is that the groups covered may be indigenous in the anthropological sense of the term – i.e. that their ancestors occupied the area "at the time of conquest or colonisation", as Article 1 (*b*) of Convention No. 107 provides. The second is that they may be tribal, which is to say that they may share all of the characteristics of indigenous peoples except for the descent from groups that inhabited the area before conquest or colonisation. The third concept is that these groups retain their own traditional social, economic, cultural and political institutions, without, however, characterising these institutions as less developed or primitive.[25]

In a section entitled "Other problems", the Office wraps up the above-mentioned points while adding other considerations as well:

> The wording of paragraph 2 of this Article also raises problems owing to the integrationist approach of the Convention. It applies the term "semi-tribal", used in the title and elsewhere in Article 1, to "groups and persons who, although they are in the process of losing their tribal characteristics, are not yet integrated into the national community".
>
> There are two problems with this paragraph. The first is that it assumes a process ("not *yet* integrated") whereby these groups will inevitably lose their tribal characteristics and be fully integrated into the national community. If the basic argument made above concerning the integrationist approach of the Convention is accepted, this assumption should be removed.
>
> The second problem is the term "semi-tribal". The intention is clear: the Convention's applicability should not be subject to calculations of

---

25   Ibid., pp. 32 and 33.

the degree to which the indigenous or tribal groups concerned retain their traditional characteristics. The approach which has always been taken by the Committee of Experts, in the light of this provision and the flexibility required by Article 28, is that the Convention is applicable in different ways depending on the extent to which the groups covered still require protection.

In the light of these considerations, this Article might be revised in the following ways.

First, all occurrences of the term "semi-tribal" should be deleted; the idea contained in paragraph 2 of this Article should be incorporated in the body of paragraph 1.

Second, paragraph 1 (*a*) of Article 1 should be redrafted to refer to peoples in independent countries whose social and economic conditions distinguish them from other sectors of the community, and whose status is regulated wholly or partially by their own customs or traditions or by special laws and regulations.

Third, paragraph 1 (*b*) of Article 1 should be redrafted to refer to peoples in independent countries who are regarded as indigenous on account of their descent from the populations which inhabited the country, or a geographical region to which the country belongs, at the time of conquest or colonisation and which, irrespective of their legal status, retain some or all of their traditional social, economic, cultural and political institutions.

Lastly, paragraph 3 of this Article, which would become paragraph 2, would state that the indigenous and other tribal peoples mentioned in paragraph 1 of this Article are referred to in the remainder of the Convention as "the peoples concerned".[26]

As a consequence of this discussion, the questionnaire sent to the constituents contained the following questions on these points:

6. Do you consider that the revised Convention should replace the term "populations" with the term "peoples" in order to reflect the terminology used in other international organisations and by these groups themselves?

7. Do you consider that Article 1, paragraph 1 (a), should be amended to refer to tribal peoples in independent countries whose social, cultural and economic conditions distinguish them from other sections of the

---

[26] Ibid., pp. 33 and 34.

national community, and whose status is regulated wholly or partially by their own customs or traditions or by special laws and regulations?

8. Do you consider that Article 1, paragraph 1 (b), should be amended to refer to peoples in independent countries who are regarded as indigenous on account of their descent from the populations which inhabited the country, or a geographical region to which the country belongs, at the time of conquest or colonisation and which, irrespective of their legal status, retain some or all of their traditional social, economic, cultural and political institutions?

9. Do you consider that paragraph 2 of Article 1 should be omitted from the revised instrument, and that other references in the Convention to "semi-tribal populations" should also be omitted?[27]

The replies of the constituents were examined point by point in the second Office report. On *question 6*, the report stated the following:

> The vast majority of replies were affirmative. The few negative replies expressed concern that the word "peoples" has a political connotation which does not belong in an ILO Convention, and raises the issue of political self-determination. It was also stated that the term "peoples" does not have a clear meaning in international law. Notwithstanding these important considerations, there appears to be general agreement that the term "peoples" better reflects the distinctive identity that a revised Convention should aim to recognise for these population groups; moreover, it has been pointed out that the term "peoples" is sometimes used in domestic legislation dealing with these groups.
>
> Reference is made to the reply of the Government of Australia. It is for the reasons indicated in that reply that the Office suggested, in Report VI (1), that the Conference discussion should make it clear that the implications of the term within the national context of ratifying States must be determined at the national level.
>
> The Office does not propose that the revised Convention should provide a complete definition of the term "peoples", but it would be advisable to clarify that the use of the term in this Convention should not be taken to imply the right to political self-determination, since this issue is clearly beyond the competence of the ILO. This is reflected in the Proposed Conclusions, in the form of a new paragraph of a revised Article 1 of the Convention.[28]

---

27 Ibid., pp. 93 and 94.
28 Report VI (2), pp. 13 and 14.

The concerns expressed by the Government of Australia, referred to above, were the following, and neatly encapsulated the discussions that would continue in the Conference until the very last moment:

> Such a change would be consistent with the rejection of the integrationist approach, and would more appropriately convey the notion of distinctive identity on which the revision is based. It is significant that the term "peoples" or its equivalent is already used by many countries in their internal legislation dealing with indigenous affairs. However, Australia also recognises that in the context of the United Nations, the term "peoples" has a particular meaning which would be out of place in a Convention intended to cover indigenous peoples with a high degree of political autonomy, even a right to political self-determination and independence, as well as indigenous peoples which are part of a larger nation. Careful consideration should be given to how the meaning of "peoples" can be defined so as to include indigenous groups whose political status may vary widely from country to country.[29]

The replies to *questions 7 and 8* were considered together in the Office analysis of replies:

> The substantial majority of replies to these questions were affirmative. However, additional points were also proposed. First, the Governments of Argentina and Australia and the CLC[30] of Canada have proposed that the concept of self-identification be included. The Government of Mexico has mentioned the aspect of ethnic identity. This concept is also important to all indigenous organisations from which information is available.
>
> It would seem useful to incorporate the concept of self-identification of indigenous or tribal communities as one important criterion for determining the population groups to which the provisions of the present Convention apply.
>
> This is reflected in the Proposed Conclusions. An indigenous organisation has stated that indigenous peoples may, through no fault of their own, no longer possess their traditional institutions, and that for this reason the words "retain some or all of their traditional institutions" may be an unjustifiable criterion. It has therefore proposed the deletion of all the words after "colonisation". It would seem inappropriate to delete all the words after "colonisation" because some reference to social, economic

---

29   Ibid., p. 13.
30   The Canadian Labour Congress, a trade union organization.

and cultural institutions different from those of other sectors of the national population appears necessary. The Office also considers that the term "some or all" is sufficiently flexible that it covers a very wide range of degrees of retention of these institutions.[31]

The replies to *question 9* were practically unanimous, and this point thereafter disappeared from further consideration:

> With one exception, there was unanimous agreement that this paragraph should be omitted from a revised instrument. It is therefore proposed to delete this paragraph and all other uses of the term "semi-tribal".[32]

The conclusions proposed to the Conference for its first discussion were worded as follows (noting that in points 2 to 4, as in other instances, wording that would be new or different compared to C. 107 figured in italics):

> 1. The revised Convention should replace the term "populations" with the term "peoples" in order to be consistent with the terminology used in other international organisations and by these groups themselves.
> 2. The revised Convention should apply to –
> (a) tribal *peoples* in independent countries whose social, *cultural* and economic conditions *distinguish them from* other sections of the national community, and whose status is regulated wholly or partially by their own customs or traditions or by special laws or regulations;
> (b) *peoples* in independent countries *who* are regarded as indigenous on account of their descent from the populations which inhabited the country, or a geographical region to which the country belongs, at the time of conquest or colonisation and *who,* irrespective of their legal status, *retain some or all of their traditional* social, economic, cultural *and political* institutions.
> 3. *Self-identification as indigenous or tribal should be considered as an important criterion for determining the population groups to which the provisions of the revised Convention should apply.*
> 4. The indigenous and other tribal *peoples* mentioned above should be referred to in the revised Convention as "the *peoples* concerned".[33]

---

31 Ibid., p. 16.
32 Ibid., p. 17.
33 Ibid., p. 105.

In the first Conference discussion of the proposed revised Convention in 1988, debate on most points, including terminology and coverage, was ardent and sometimes very contentious. Before individual points were discussed, a number of interventions in the general discussion already raised points that would be considered in more detail under each point of the proposed conclusions.

> 15. A number of Government members expressed the view that when considering changing the term "populations" to the term "peoples" it should be borne in mind that, in an international context, the meaning of the term " peoples " was unclear and in some cases had political connotations. The Government members of Canada and France considered that its use could imply rights which went beyond the scope of Convention No. 107, such as the right to self-determination. The Government member of India felt that replacing the term "populations" by the term "peoples" could inhibit the number of ratifications of the revised Convention. The Government member of Argentina considered that while replacing the word "populations" by "peoples" might create difficulties for some States, not including the word "peoples" could disappoint indigenous communities and cast doubt on the nature of the Committee's work. He therefore supported a solution which would specify that the term should not be interpreted as it was in international law.[34]

In summarizing interventions by a number of indigenous representatives during the general discussion, the Conference Committee report stated the following:

> Several of the representatives of the non-governmental organisations affirmed their strong preference for the use of the term "peoples" rather than "populations" in the revised Convention, stating in particular that it reflected better their view of themselves. They stressed the view that the revised Convention would be limited to social, economic, environmental and cultural considerations, and thus that political issues such as self-governance and other political aspects of self-determination would be beyond its scope.[35]

It should be noted that the repeated statements throughout the rest of the proceedings by indigenous representatives that the use of the term "peoples", and complications raised by its association with self-determination, should not be

---

[34] Proceedings 1988, p. 32/3.
[35] Ibid., p. 32/4.

understood to imply any intention to declare political self-determination, were not taken into account by the delegates. They no doubt felt that intentions stated during these deliberations could not necessarily be maintained once a text was adopted.

Point 1 naturally was discussed at length, and the Committee report on this point is reproduced *in extenso* because of its importance:

> 30. The Committee had before it four amendments on the question of replacing the term " populations" in Convention No. 107, by the term "peoples" in the revised Convention. Amendments submitted by the Employers' members and by the Government member of Canada proposed using the term "populations" in the revised text. The Government member of Bolivia proposed an amendment to use the term "populations" in its generic meaning which included tribal peoples and indigenous populations. The Government member of Canada proposed an additional amendment to the effect that, if the Committee should decide to use the term "peoples", the use of that term in the revised Convention would "not imply the right to self-determination as that term is understood in international law". The Government member of Norway offered a sub-amendment to the Canadian amendment, providing that the term "peoples" as used in the revised Convention would "not address the question of national self-determination as this term is understood in international law".
>
> 31. The Employers' members indicated in respect of their amendment that the use of the term "peoples" could create difficulties for ratification of the revised Convention, as it might be taken as a synonym for self-determination, and might have different meanings in different countries. The Workers' members strongly supported the use of "peoples" as proposed in the Office text, in particular as it correctly reflected the view these peoples had of themselves. Moreover, they recalled that the great majority of governments which replied to the questionnaire had favoured using the term "peoples". The Government member of Canada stated that her Government felt that the term might have implications in international law that were different from its use in international legislation.
>
> 32. At several moments during the Committee's deliberations, when representatives of accredited non-governmental organisations spoke, they recalled the vital importance of this terminology for them. It reflected their own sense of who they were, and the use of the term "populations" in Convention No. 107 was degrading. They recognised that it

was not within the ILO's mandate to pronounce on issues of self-determination. They stressed that if the revised instrument did not use this term they would not be able to support its adoption or its ratification by States, regardless of the other provisions it might include.

33. The Legal Adviser was asked to provide clarification as to whether the use of the term "peoples" would have legal implications affecting the scope of the revised Convention. He indicated that the notion "people" had no legal definition as such, but that it did carry some political implications at the international level. The legal implications resulted first from Article 1, paragraph 2 of the United Nations Charter, and had subsequently been developed further in other instruments. The general view was that the notion of self-determination applied in principle to peoples under foreign colonial domination and not to peoples in independent States which were precisely those referred to in the Proposed Conclusions. The Committee might thus conclude that the use of the term "people" would therefore have no implications in this respect. It had, however, to be recognised at the same time that the notion was not fully established within the United Nations framework, and that its evolution was beyond the ILO's competence and control. The question thus remained as to the advantages of using the term in this revised Convention given its objectives. It would not appear to make more specific the identification if the groups were covered by the Convention. It would merely emphasise the sense of self-identification of these groups, an element which, however, was in any event included in the text. It was therefore ultimately for the Committee to decide, in the light of these considerations and of the concrete objective sought, which of these terms should be preferred.

34. Some Government members expressed continuing reservations over the use of the term "peoples"; some supported the use of the term and others expressed the conviction that a solution could be found which would allow its use. The Committee decided to refer the question to a Working Party which it created for that purpose, including four members of each group in the Committee.

35. When the Working Party had completed its deliberations, the Chairman informed the Committee of the results of its work in this respect. He stated that it had been clear there were firm positions on this matter, and many reservations over the Working Party had, however, been able to agree that the term "peoples" should be used instead of "populations", but that to allow this it would be necessary to make it perfectly clear that its use in the revised Convention would not imply

recognition of the right to self-determination as it is understood in international law. The Working Party had considered a number of different formulations and had decided to put before the Committee a text which might serve as a basis for further deliberations. This text was as follows: "The use of the term "peoples" in the present Convention shall not be taken to affect the interpretation given to this term in other international instruments or proceedings, in particular as concerns the question of self-determination." He emphasised that this was not a final text, and that no member of the Working Party considered it as such, and that it was put before the Committee as a basis for the next discussion as such, it should be included in the proposed revised Convention so that governments, employers and workers could react to it.

36. The Government member of Canada stated that her Government understood and sympathized with the feelings of the indigenous and tribal representatives on this point, and that Canada did use the term "peoples" in its internal legislation. However, she was not now in a position to express a final position on this text. She stated that if her Government's own proposal were not accepted, they would prefer another formulation offered during the working party's deliberations, which she read out : "Nothing in this Convention shall be taken to imply that the peoples concerned are, by the force of this Convention, being accorded the right of self-determination or other rights in international law or as understood in other international organisations."

37. The Government members of Brazil, France, India, Turkey and Venezuela stated that they had serious reservations about the use of "peoples", and felt that the text put before the Committee by the working party should not be used in the Committee's conclusions. The Government member of Japan requested a clarification of the text put before the Committee by the Working Party, and stated that it was not appropriate to use the text as a basis for the next discussion because its meaning was not clear. The Government members of Bolivia, Colombia, Norway and Portugal, as well as the Employers' and Workers' members, felt that the compromise text was a good basis for further deliberations, that it should be included in the Committee's conclusions, and that the term "peoples" should therefore be used in the draft Convention. It was also recalled that 26 of the 32 governments whose replies were reproduced in Report VI (2) had supported the use of the term "peoples".

38. The representative of the Secretary-General recalled that there had been an agreement within the working party to use the term "peoples",

subject to the reservation that a statement would have to be included limiting its implications so far as self-determination was concerned. He recalled that in any case, this was a first discussion, that no one could be committed by what was agreed this year, and that every element of the conclusions of the present Committee would be subject to review during the further consultations.

39. As the Committee was unable to achieve consensus on this Point, it was decided that the expression "(peoples/populations)" should be used in its conclusions and in the proposed revised Convention, and that further deliberations would have to be held on it next year.[36]

The passage above is reproduced in this detail to demonstrate that there was a very serious discussion going on, and that most of the participants were attempting to find a way to respect the feelings of the indigenous representatives while preserving the position in international law. The formula that had been on the table since even earlier, of using the term "peoples" with a phrase limiting its meaning for the purposes of the Convention, continued to be obvious as the way forward. The opinion by the Legal Adviser to the Conference (paragraph 33 in the Committee's report above) reinforced the notion that the term could be used, but that the meanings of both peoples and self-determination were not settled in international law, thus emphasizing the need for care.

The discussion of *point 2* had more facets, but they were dealt with more expeditiously. The first to be considered was whether the Convention should apply only to independent countries, as Convention No. 107 had.

40. The Committee had three amendments before it. First, the Workers' members proposed an amendment to delete the words "in independent countries" in Point 2(a), in order to enable better coverage of all governmental situations. The Employers' members opposed the amendment since independent countries were already referred to in Article 1 of the Convention. A representative of the Secretary-General recalled that the 1986 Meeting of Experts had recommended that the revised Convention should apply to independent countries, and stated that a change could affect a number of other Conventions which dealt with indigenous populations in dependent territories. In view of the complications referred to, the Workers' members withdrew the amendment, with the proviso that they

---

[36] Ibid., pp. 32/5 and 32/6.

> would review their position in a year's time. (In their second amendment, the Worker's members had proposed a similar deletion in Point 2(b), which was also withdrawn.)[37]

A second question discussed was how to define the areas covered. Although the proposal before the Committee did not gain acceptance at this Session of the Conference, another version of it was to be agreed upon before the revision was complete.

> Another amendment presented by the Workers' members called for the insertion of the words "or the establishment of state supremacy" after the word "colonisation", in order to make the revised Convention apply to situations in which there had been neither conquest nor colonisation. The Employers' members believed that, because the phrase was a legally indeterminate expression, it could lead to difficulties in implementation. They opposed both remaining proposals. A number of Government members supported the amendment since it closed a potential loophole or mirrored national experience. After further discussion, the question was referred to the Working Party, which reported to the Committee that the amendment had been considered and then withdrawn.[38]

The final question under this point carried unstated implications for whether the Convention was to apply only to a limited portion of territories occupied by indigenous and tribal peoples, and the quality of their rights over these territories.

> 41. The Workers' members had also proposed deletion of the word "traditional", which the Employers' members and some Government members opposed. The Employers' members felt it was against the sense of Convention No. 107. The Workers' members then sub-amended their amendment to substitute the word "own" for "traditional". The Employers' members felt that this formulation would lead to the Convention being interpreted as referring to both traditional and non-traditional institutions,

---

37 Ibid., pp. 32/5 and 32/6.
38 Ibid., p. 32/6. This proposal was in fact the brainchild of the Sami representatives present, who maintained that they had neither been conquered nor colonized, though they were within the boundaries of States established including their territories. This is not referenced in the reports.

which was not its intention. The proposal to replace the word "traditional" by the word "own" was adopted by 8,840 votes in favour, 7,237 against, with 680 abstentions.

42. Point 2, as amended, was adopted.[39]

Point 3 occasioned the following discussion and decisions:

43. The Employers' members introduced an amendment intended to permit the governments concerned to have an option, not an obligation, whether to consider self-identification in determining the population groups to which the Convention would apply. The Workers' members opposed the amendment, since it would weaken the text and self-identification was very important. A number of Government members expressed their views, most of which were opposed to the amendment. The amendment was withdrawn by the Employers' members. The Workers' members submitted an amendment to replace the word "important" by the word "fundamental", which they felt better reflected the approach of the Proposed Conclusions, and to delete the word "population" which they felt was superfluous. The Employers' members opposed the amendment, stating that the Office text already went quite far and that the proposed amendment would make implementation more difficult. The Government member of the United States considered that while either term in the first part of the amendment was satisfactory, he wanted to ensure the maximum number of ratifications. The Government members of Brazil and India opposed the first part of the amendment. The Government member of Colombia expressed support for it. The first part of the amendment (to replace "important" by "fundamental") was adopted by 9,505 votes in favour, 1,190 against, with 7,820 abstentions. The second part of the amendment was referred to the Drafting Committee.[40]

44. Point 3, as amended, was adopted.[41]

---

[39] Ibid. The implications of this discussion would reappear in the discussion of land rights.

[40] It will be recalled that the Drafting Committee is an institution in ILO standard setting whereby minor drafting or vocabulary questions are referred to a linguistically oriented group from within the committee to sort out small differences, including questions of coherence between languages. It is to be distinguished from the use of a Working Party. The Drafting Committee is not empowered to take decisions that affect meaning, but rather to render clarity of expression.

[41] Ibid.

Point 4 was amended and adopted in a very brief discussion:

> 45. The Government member of the USSR introduced an amendment which would avoid ambiguity in the text by removing the word "other" before "tribal", and this was adopted.
> 46. Point 4, as amended, was adopted.[42]

The amended version of the conclusions on points 1 to 4 that emerged from this discussion in 1988 was as follows:

> 1. The term "(peoples/populations)" should be used in the proposed Convention, pending a final decision by the Conference at its 76th Session.
>   I.   SCOPE OF THE REVISED CONVENTION AND DEFINITIONS
> 2. The revised Convention should apply to:
>   (*a*) tribal (peoples/populations) in independent countries whose social, cultural and economic conditions distinguish them from other sections of the national community, and whose status is regulated wholly or partially by their own customs or traditions or by special laws or regulations;
>   (*b*) (peoples/populations) in independent countries who are regarded as indigenous on account of their descent from the populations which inhabited the country, or a geographical region to which the country belongs, at the time of conquest or colonisation and who, irrespective of their legal status, retain some or all of their own social, economic, cultural and political institutions.
> 3. Self-identification as indigenous or tribal should be regarded as a fundamental criterion for determining the groups which the provisions of the revised Convention should apply.
> 4. The indigenous and tribal (peoples/populations) mentioned above should be referred to in the revised Convention as "the (peoples/populations) concerned".[43]

ii   1989 Discussion

When these conclusions were rendered into a draft Convention in Report IV (1) for the 1989 discussion, and circulated to the membership for comments, the question of terminology was referred to in the following passage:

---

42   Ibid.
43   Ibid., p. 32/24.

The use of the term "(peoples/populations)" reflects an agreement in the Committee that the question could not be satisfactorily resolved during the 75th Session; reference is made to paragraphs 30 to 39 of the report of the Committee. There did appear to be widespread, though not universal, agreement that the term "peoples" should be used if an acceptable formula could be found to ensure that it did not imply rights beyond the scope of the revised Convention, in particular with regard to self-determination in the sense of separation from the State.[44]

Draft Article 1 circulated for comments read as follows:

Article 1
1. This Convention applies to:
   (*a*) tribal (peoples/populations) in independent countries whose social, cultural and economic conditions distinguish them from other sections of the national community, and whose status is regulated wholly or partially by their own customs or traditions or by special laws or regulations;
   (*b*) (peoples/populations) in independent countries who are regarded as indigenous on account of their descent from the populations which inhabited the country, or a geographical region to which the country belongs, at the time of conquest or colonisation and who, irrespective of their legal status, retain some or all of their own social, economic, cultural and political institutions.
2. Self-identification as indigenous or tribal shall be regarded as a fundamental criterion for determining the groups to which the provisions of this Convention apply.
3. The indigenous and tribal (peoples/populations) mentioned above are referred to hereinafter as "the (peoples/populations) concerned".[45]

Most of the constituents' comments on the proposed text of Article 1, predictably enough, concerned the proposed use of the term "peoples". The Office summary and analysis of these replies was as follows:

The majority of replies favour the use of "peoples", as was also the case in Report VI (2) before the first discussion. However, in the first discussion and in the replies received, serious reservations have been expressed

---
44 Report IV (1), p. 3.
45 Ibid., p. 6.

concerning the implications of using this term, at least if used without an appropriate qualifying clause. While a few of the respondents are opposed to the use of "peoples" under any circumstances, most have indicated that they could accept it if the meaning of the term could be suitably qualified; various formulations were put forward for a qualifying clause, both during the first discussion and in the replies received. Essentially, these proposals fall into two categories. The first provides that the use of the term "peoples" should not imply or provide for any rights additional to those provided for in the revised Convention. The second provides more specifically that the use of the term should not imply the right to self-determination, some going on to mention specifically the right to secession. The reasons for favouring the use of "peoples" are detailed by Canada (IPWG), and have been discussed in earlier reports. They consist essentially in the idea that its use is necessary to reinforce the recognition of the right of these groups to their identity and as an essential aspect of the change of orientation toward increased respect for their cultures and ways of life. As concerns the implications in international law of the use of the term, it may be noted in particular that Article 1 of the International Covenants on Civil and Political Rights and on Economic, Social and Cultural Rights, provides that "All peoples have the right of self-determination". However, the meaning of "peoples" is evolving in international law, in particular as it relates to the right of self-determination; and the meaning of "self-determination" is likewise an evolving concept, as to both its content and beneficiaries. There has been no decision by the deliberative bodies of the United Nations as to whether and to what degree the right of self-determination attaches to indigenous and tribal peoples, nor in what circumstances. It is clearly outside the ILO's mandate to assign meaning to these terms until these questions have been decided in more appropriate spheres of the United Nations system – where indeed such deliberations are taking place.

Equally important, the ILO must be careful not to adopt language which would in any way limit those other deliberations. It would be contrary to the intention and spirit of the present revision process to adopt terminology which would embody a lower standard than that already recognised, or which would go against recent trends.

The trend toward the use of "peoples" is apparent in other parts of the United Nations system, though no uniform common language has been established. A recent example is its increasing use in United Nations documentation and deliberative bodies (e.g. the resolution mentioned by Switzerland (SGB)). UNESCO and World Bank documentation use the term – albeit inconsistently – as does the Inter-American Indian Institute. While due weight has been given to the arguments against using it, the term "peoples" has been used in the proposed text. This reflects the position expressed in a majority of replies that the term can be used on condition that a suitable qualifying clause is adopted, the effect of which would be to ensure that the term did not imply rights beyond the scope of the revised Convention. In proposing the qualifying phrase no specific reference has been made to self-determination because this might present an obstacle to further evolution of the concept with regard to these peoples. It would, in particular, involve the ILO in assigning a meaning to a term which all concerned agree should not be determined by the ILO. The Office considers that the concerns voiced can be covered by providing unambiguously that the use of the term "peoples" does not imply any other rights than those provided for in the revised Convention, and that it does not affect the meaning of other international instruments.

The proposal to use "nations" has not been retained.[46]

While nothing new emerged from these exchanges, the trend toward acceptance of a qualified consensus was clear. In the draft of the proposed Convention forwarded to the Conference for final discussion, the following text was used as paragraph 3 of Article 1 to respond to this discussion:

> 2. The use of the term "peoples" in this Convention shall not be construed as having any implications as regards the rights which may attach to the term under other international instruments.[47]

The observations by the constituents and the Office commentary on them were very much shorter, most of the outstanding points having been settled in the first Conference discussion:

> The proposal made by the Government of Norway concerning paragraph 1 (b)[48] has been retained; it also covers the use of "contact" suggested by Canada (IPWG).
>
> Self-identification would not appear to be the sole criterion applied to coverage by the Convention, as suggested by the Government of Sweden. As concerns the observation by the Government of Japan, the question of whether to attempt to adopt a detailed definition was considered at the earlier stages of discussion and it was decided not to do so in view of the

---

46 Report IV (2A), pp. 11 and 12.
47 Report IV (2B), p. 6.
48 Norway proposed: In paragraph 1 (b), after "colonisation", add "or establishment of state boundaries".

flexible nature of this instrument, the difficulties of adopting such a definition, and the fact that few problems in this respect have arisen in supervising the application of a similar provision in Convention No. 107.

The proposal by the Government of Colombia would remove any reference to tribal peoples, thereby narrowing the scope of the Convention and preventing its application to several countries which have ratified Convention No. 107. A proposal to this effect in the first discussion was not accepted.[49]

Paragraphs 1 and 2 of Article 1 of the proposed Convention (see above for paragraph 3) was forwarded to the second Conference discussion in the following form:

> *Article 1*
> 1. This Convention applies to:
>   (*a*) tribal peoples in independent countries whose social, cultural and economic conditions distinguish them from other sections of the national community, and whose status is regulated wholly or partially by their own customs or traditions or by special laws or regulations;
>   (*b*) peoples in independent countries who are regarded as indigenous on account of their descent from the populations which inhabited the country, or a geographical region to which the country belongs, at the time of conquest or colonisation or the establishment of present state boundaries and who, irrespective of their legal status, retain some or all of their own social, economic, cultural and political institutions.
> 2. Self-identification as indigenous or tribal shall be regarded as a fundamental criterion for determining the groups to which the provisions of this Convention apply.[50]

As the 1989 Session of the Conference opened discussion for the adoption of the final text, the representative of the Secretary-General of the Conference made a preliminary statement to the Committee in which he referred to the peoples/populations controversy:

> Turning to items on which no agreement had been reached, the representative of the Secretary-General cited the use of the term "peoples" or "populations". He noted that despite the difference of opinion, both sides

---

49   Report IV (2A), p. 13.
50   Report IV (2B), p. 6.

agreed that political separatism – which could be implied by the use of "peoples" – should not in any way be promoted by the Convention. Moreover, both sides had agreed that the communities concerned should retain their identities and should not be reduced to ciphers – which was the concern surrounding the use of "populations". He referred the Committee to a formula which had been suggested in Article 1, paragraph 3, of the proposed text as a means to assist in reaching an agreement.[51]

The general discussion that preceded a point-by-point discussion also occasioned some discussion of this topic:

> 13. In a preliminary exchange of views concerning terminology, the Government members of Argentina and Venezuela expressed a strong preference for the use of the term "populations" rather than "peoples" in order to avoid possible erroneous interpretation of the latter in the context of self-determination under international law. A similar concern on the possible interpretation of the term "peoples" in international law was expressed by the Government member of Canada. A number of other Government members expressed similar views but were prepared to consider a suitable qualifying clause to the term "peoples". The Government member of Ecuador noted that the term "indigenous nationalities" was used in his country. The Government member of India felt that the Committee should carefully consider the impact that the use of "peoples" could have in countries beset with the problems of integration. Moreover, he did not consider the term "peoples" to be relevant to the tribal situation in his country. The Government member of Australia noted in regard to the choice of term that his Government wished to explore further the application of Article 1 of the draft Convention. The Government member of Nicaragua said that the use of the term "peoples" did not imply the recognition of a State within a State. The Workers' members and a number of other Government members supported the use of the term "peoples" without any qualifying phrase, while the Employers' members expressed serious reservations.[52]

The Employers' members also referred to this question in their introductory comments:

---

[51] Proceedings 1989, pp. 25/1 and 25/2.
[52] Ibid., p. 25/3.

> The use of the term "peoples" presented problems regarding its political interpretation, and had connotations of social and national self-determination. The Employers' members expressed surprise that, notwithstanding agreement on the term "peoples/populations" at the first discussion, "peoples" had been used in the text proposed to the Conference. They could only accept "peoples" if it was clearly defined and if its use respected the identity, national unity and laws of each country. The use of the term should also be consistent with its use in other international instruments. For this reason, it needed to be reviewed in the preamble as well as in the relevant Articles of the draft Convention.[53]

The Workers' members' opening comments on this question were even more succinct: "The Workers' members unreservedly supported the use of the term 'peoples' throughout the Convention."[54]

As should be expected, the representatives of indigenous organizations that spoke were also unanimous in the introductory discussion of this point:

> 19. The Committee also heard statements from international non-governmental organisations which were attending the Conference in accordance with article 56, paragraph 9, of the Standing Orders of the International Labour Conference. ...The organisations themselves had been active in the past year canvassing their members and making their views and concerns known to relevant governments and employers' and workers' organisations. ...All of the representatives strongly supported the use of the term "peoples" without any prejudicial qualifications, comments or conditions. The representative of the Four Direction Council noted that it was increasingly the terminology of preference in the United Nations and it constituted a determination to deal with peoples as organised groups, not as aggregations of individuals. In seeking the use of "peoples", indigenous and tribal peoples were not advocating secession. ...
>
> 21. The representative of the International Organization of Indigenous Resource Development...believed that the failure to recognise the unanimous request of the indigenous peoples' organisations for the use of the term "peoples" would perpetuate the philosophy of racism which all participants were determined to eliminate.[55]

---

53 Ibid., p. 25/4.
54 Ibid.
55 Ibid., p. 25/5.

Other indigenous representatives returned to this question in their statements on the section entitled General Policy:

> 26. The representative of the Inuit Circumpolar Conference recalled that a majority of governments making comments on the proposed text circulated by the Office, following the first discussion, had supported the use of the term "peoples". She expressed the conviction that there were no legal grounds to governments' opposition to the term on the basis that its use accorded the right to self-determination as understood in international law. She referred to a number of United Nations instruments in support of her contention, including General Assembly resolution 1514(XV), and quoted from the Declaration on the Granting of Independence to Colonial Countries and Peoples in support of her position that a recognition of the right to self-determination would not lead to the dissolution of States. She also stated that any questions concerning political self-determination were outside both the scope of the revised Convention and the competence of the ILO. She noted that the draft the preamble adequately addressed the concerns felt by some governments, by indicating that the Convention would be applicable within the framework of the States in which the peoples lived. The speaker underlined that many peoples could enjoy collective rights. The Inuit Circumpolar Conference was seeking the right of indigenous and tribal peoples to control their own lives, cultures and territories. For this reason, it could not accept any qualification of the term "peoples" in the Convention. No other peoples were discriminated against in this way and such efforts to diminish the basic human rights of indigenous and tribal peoples would be contrary to the Constitution of the ILO among other instruments; the unqualified term "peoples" should be used throughout the Convention.
>
> 27. The Co-ordinator for Indigenous Organisations of the Amazon Basin strongly advocated the use of the term "peoples" in the Convention. He stressed the need to understand the position of indigenous and tribal peoples which stemmed from centuries-old history of settlement on territories which resulted in specific languages, customs and histories which no authority could force them to abandon. He stressed that indigenous and tribal peoples had never expressed the wish to create a state within a state. They were a true part of the country to which they belonged and has amply demonstrated that they had not and would not undertake the action regarding self-determination which some governments feared.

> 28. The representative of the Indian Council of South America emphasised that indigenous and tribal peoples had considered themselves peoples since before colonisation. The threat to political sovereignty which governments perceived from the use of the term "peoples" was being used to discriminate against them, to undermine their fundamental human rights and to deprive them of the natural resources on which their survival depended. Self-determination was a universal concept which was used to determine membership in a particular group. The speaker considered that the term "peoples" should not be qualified under any circumstances. He stressed that a Convention was necessary to take care of indigenous and tribal peoples' needs since there were no adequate means to implement the existing laws. If these peoples' rights were ignored again, it would result in the continuation of discrimination against them.[56]

These interventions reflected the growing frustration of the indigenous representatives in these discussions, because decisions were being taken concerning their status in international law which they could not influence in the way they preferred. These frustrations would boil over in their statements to the plenary of the Conference in the final adoption session – see below. It should be noted that in the ILO discussions they had the same quality of right to participation that they had in other international fora – the right to speak but not to vote – but this did not assuage the frustration felt by many of them.

The controversy over the terminology was the only question discussed in the Committee in 1989 as regards Article 1. The discussion was long, but consisted almost entirely of accepting a proposed consensus while reserving positions. The Chairman took a very daring step by forestalling further amendments and proposing a compromise that ended up being accepted. This report of this long discussion is reproduced *in extenso* here (though considerably condensed from the actual – and fruitless – discussion in the Committee itself). In the end it concluded with one amendment to the text proposed to the Conference:

> Article 1. After some discussion the Chairman noted that three options had emerged regarding the terms used in Article 1 and in consequence throughout the Convention. These were "populations", "peoples", and "peoples" plus a wording for paragraph 3 of this Article stating that the use of this term had a specific meaning in the Convention. After each amendment had been introduced by its sponsor there was a lengthy

---

56   Ibid., pp. 25/5 and 25/6.

discussion, plus consultations outside the meetings, in an attempt to obtain an acceptable text for paragraph 3 of Article 1.

30. The Chairman believed that an effort should be made to accept the text as drafted by the Office in order to retain the essence of the meaning of the Article. As a result of the foregoing discussions he suggested that paragraph 3 be amended by replacing the words "other international instruments" by "international law". In addition to adopting this change, he proposed that the Committee approve the text of an explanatory statement which would be included in its report. The text of the statement would serve as an instrument of clarification for the interpretation of the meaning of the Convention.

31. This statement read as follows:

> It is understood by the Committee that the use of the term "peoples" in this Convention has no implication as regards the right to self-determination as understood in international law.

32. The Chairman believed that, with the amendment and the explanatory statement in the report, the Committee could reach an understanding which covered the need expressed by several Government members for the term "peoples" to be accompanied by a clarification as to the impact of its use. Speaking in his own name, he considered that the clarification would imply that, among many other rights, indigenous and tribal peoples had the right to a large degree of self-determination within the framework of national States, but that any implications regarding self-determination in international law were outside the area of competence of the ILO.

33. The Chairman considered that the inclusion of the term "peoples" in the Convention represented substantial progress. He felt that it expressed recognition of the rights of these peoples to their culture, respect and self-determination which were needed by all the peoples of the world. He believed that the proposed text and clarifying statement, which were arrived at after intense consultations, would serve as a good basis for understanding the Convention's intent.

34. The Workers' members supported the amendment to paragraph 3 and associated themselves with the explanatory statement. They were, however, not fully satisfied with the compromise which had emerged, and they reserved the right to explain their position during the discussion of the report in the plenary.

35. The Employers' members had discussed the proposals extensively and had concluded that in the spirit and tradition of the ILO they should support them. They expressed full support for the amendment to paragraph 3, and for the explanatory text. They believed that reaching an acceptable compromise was a notable achievement with respect to the ability of the Committee properly to complete its task. The Employers' members, like the Workers' members, were not entirely satisfied with the outcome of the discussions and felt that many of the elements in the Convention did not fit within the framework of the ILO. While they reserved their right to present their point of view during the plenary discussion, the Employers' members, in the spirit of consensus, offered their full support for the two proposals.

36. The Government member of Portugal supported the proposed amendment to paragraph 3. She expressed her Government's reservations over the explanatory text and stated that it was not for the ILO to address the question of self-determination. This was a basic human right that could not be taken away and she considered that it should not be referred to in the Convention. Her Government interpreted the text as having no implications for the universal right to self-determination. She would, however, respect the consensus which had been achieved. The Government member of Peru stated that while his delegation preferred the term "peoples" it was concerned about the links between this term and the right to self-determination. He suggested that if governments did not wish to provide self-determination to peoples, another term should be used. Alternatively, a footnote could be inserted in the text of the Convention to the effect that use of the terms "peoples" did not connote any right to self-determination. He considered, however, that a Convention with such a footnote would not be ratifiable. What had occurred was the settlement of an important point in international law in a bureaucratic manner. His delegation would accept the proposed amendment and the inclusion of an explanatory text in the report in the spirit of consensus, but he expressed his Government's serious reservations. The Government member of Ecuador supported the views of the Government members of Portugal and Peru. He noted that the text contained no implications regarding the right to self-determination as understood in international law and he pointed out that this did not diminish the impact of the term in other international instruments. He regretted that since his Government had not had the opportunity to participate in the consultations concerning the proposed text, he would have to explain his delegation's position at a later stage.

37. The Government member of the USSR expressed satisfaction with the proposed amendment to paragraph 3 and appreciated the efforts made to achieve consensus. He was concerned about the proposed explanatory statement and was unsure of its appropriateness in an ILO document. He would, however, support the consensus. The Government member of India appreciated the efforts involved in the discussions. He noted that a number of governments had voiced genuine reservations about the proposed text, and further noted that his country, with a large tribal population, had the most cause of any to be concerned about this matter. His delegation would, however, abide by the consensus.

38. The Government member of Argentina stated that while his Government was not in favour of the use of the term "peoples" it would have been able to accept its use, provided that a clause was included in the text of the Convention itself which indicated clearly that there would be no implications for self-determination under international law. His delegation would not obstruct the consensus on the amendment and the proposed text for the report but it was not satisfied and expressed its reservations. The Government member of Venezuela expressed his appreciation of the efforts made by many governments in accepting the proposals. He appreciated that the Workers' members had made significant concessions. His delegation could not support the consensus which had been reached but it would not oppose it. The Government member of Brazil joined in acknowledging the efforts of all who took part in attempting to find a solution to this issue. His delegation, which had made strenuous efforts to accept the compromise, joined in the spirit of the consensus.

39. The Government member of Canada acknowledged the efforts of all involved in achieving an acceptable solution and appreciated the statement made by the Workers' members. He recognised the difficulties which they had overcome in order to reach a consensus. His delegation supported, without reservation, the amendment and the text for inclusion in the report. The Government members of Australia, Honduras, New Zealand and the United States made similar statements of support.

40. The Government member of Norway welcomed the use of the term "peoples". While he did not see the need for a qualifying statement, since the notion of peoples had no clear legal definition, he welcomed and accepted the compromise. This view was shared by the Government member of Denmark.

41. The Government member of Colombia stated that, while he would have preferred a clause which referred to all of the terms included in the draft Convention, he would support the consensus.

42. During his summary of the discussion on the amendment to Article 1, paragraph 3, the Chairman referred to the remarks of the Government member of Ecuador who had said that there was no reference in the Convention to any limitation on self-determination. The Chairman considered that the text was distancing itself to a certain extent from a subject which was outside the competence of the ILO. In his opinion, no position for or against self-determination was or could be expressed in the Convention, nor could any restrictions be expressed in the context of international law.

43. The text of paragraph 3, as amended, together with the inclusion in the report of the explanatory statement, which appears in paragraph 31 above, was adopted by consensus.

44. The Employers' and Workers' members considered that in the light of the agreement on the amended text, the remaining amendments to Article 1 should not be discussed. Several Government members supported this view. It was agreed to submit three amendments submitted by the Government members of Canada, Colombia and the USSR to the Drafting Committee.

46. Article 1, as amended, was adopted.[57]

It will be recalled that 18 years later, the Chairman of the UN Human Rights Council made a similar move by submitting the entire text of his own draft of the United Nations Declaration on the Rights of Indigenous Peoples to the Council, for an up or down decision. In that case, like this one, a peremptory move to challenge delegates to accept a consensus none of them fully supported, carried the day.

The text of this Article that emerged from the discussions was therefore the following:

Article 1
1. This Convention applies to:
    (*a*) tribal peoples in independent countries whose social, cultural and economic conditions distinguish them from other sections of the national community, and whose status is regulated wholly or partially by their own customs or traditions or by special laws or regulations;

---

57   Ibid., pp. 25/7 and 25/8.

(b) peoples in independent countries who are regarded as indigenous on account of their descent from the populations which inhabited the country, or a geographical region to which the country belongs, at the time of conquest or colonisation or the establishment of present state boundaries and who, irrespective of their legal status, retain some or all of their own social, economic, cultural and political institutions.

2. Self-identification as indigenous or tribal shall be regarded as a fundamental criterion for determining the groups to which the provisions of this Convention apply.

3. The use of the term "peoples" in this Convention shall not be construed as having any implications as regards the rights which may attach to the term under international law.[58]

It should be noted that, in spite of some of the language used during the discussions, the ILO supervisory bodies and technical advice since the Convention's adoption have insisted that this Article does not constitute a definition of indigenous and tribal peoples, which is impossible at the international level, but rather a statement of coverage.

D   Development through Supervision

The ILO has a detailed and uniquely thorough supervisory process, which is described in the introductory materials to the volume. While the ILO's supervisory bodies do not have the formal right to 'interpret' Conventions – a power reserved to the International Court of Justice – the Committee of Experts in particular does develop its understanding of the meaning of Conventions and offers both assessment of the degree to which a Convention is applied in ratifying States, and measures which are needed to apply it correctly.

In this and other passages on development through supervision, only illustrative examples are given. The supervisory comments are extensive and should be consulted on the ILO web site.

The Committee of Experts has pushed governments to identify what groups are covered under Convention No. 169. Although, as indicated already, there can be no globally-applicable definition of indigenous and tribal peoples, it is necessary that governments identify at the national level, in consultation with representatives of these peoples themselves, just who is covered in each

---

58   Ibid., p. 25/26.

country. This is needed for several reasons. First, it is tied into who benefits from the protections in the Convention. It is needed to determine, for example, who is entitled to land and resource rights and to the other protections provided especially for these peoples.

It also has emerged from the Convention's supervision that a large number of indigenous and tribal peoples do not have any legal identity at the national level and that without identification cards, registration, etc., it is impossible for them to have access to legal protection and social security in their countries. The measures stimulated by the Convention for governments to recognize the existence of these peoples has led also to ensuring that all their citizens do indeed have a legal personality.

Convention No. 169 entered into force in 1991 following the receipt of the second ratification (the usual arrangement for ILO Conventions), and the first comments of the Committee of Experts on governments' reports were made in 1993.[59]

a   *Interpretation Requested by Switzerland*

While the following is not really one of the ILO's supervisory procedures, it does inform supervision. One of the procedures available to the ILO on Conventions is a so-called 'interpretation' by the Office. Legally speaking this is not a formal interpretation – the right to interpret the meaning of Conventions is reserved by the ILO Constitution to the International Court of Justice – but rather an explanation of the Office's understanding of the terms of a Convention rendered when a government so requests.

There has been one of these 'interpretations' on Convention No. 169, requested by Switzerland in 2000 and published in 2001 – it is reproduced *in toto* in Appendix III. The request was based on the question of whether a ratifying country could decide definitively which groups are covered by the Convention, as well raising other questions. Without attempting to reproduce here all the explanations provided, the Office's memorandum stated that there were both objective and subjective criteria used in Article 1 of the Convention, and that the decision on coverage was not entirely to a ratifying country. In particular, while the 'traveller' community in Switzerland had not stated that it wished to be covered by the Convention (referring to the 'self-identification' criterion) they did meet the objective criteria for coverage and if they later

---

59   All comments by the Committee of Experts and other ILO supervisory bodies are available in full on the ILO web site under its NORMLEX data base. More detailed citations will not be provided to every comment in this text unless more information is needed to consult them. See the explanation of styles of citation in the introductory materials of this volume.

decided they should be covered this could not be excluded. Switzerland decided not to ratify the Convention.

b   *How to Identify Who is Covered*

The questions put by the Committee to the first two governments to report were typical of the large majority of comments to other countries in subsequent years on points of identification:

> *Direct Request, Norway, 1993*:
> 2. Article 1 of the Convention. The Committee notes that during the census of 1970 efforts were made to determine the size of the Sami population, which the Government estimates to be approximately 40,000. Please indicate whether there are any plans for a further census which would include a specific indigenous component.
> 3. The Committee also notes the Government's decision to identify the Sami as indigenous. Please provide information on the processes by which individuals express their self-identification as members of the Sami people.
>
> *Direct Request, Mexico, 1993:*
> 3. Article 1 of the Convention. The Committee notes the detailed census information provided on the indigenous population of the country. Noting that use of an indigenous language is the primary basis for deciding on whether an individual is counted as indigenous, the Committee would be grateful for information on how the requirement that self-identification be regarded as a fundamental criterion is implemented, in particular in a situation of conflict over whether an individual is to be included in an indigenous community.

After further exchanges, this was followed up in a 2009 Observation to Mexico:

> *Article 1 of the Convention.   Identification and self-identification of the peoples covered by the Convention.*   The Committee notes the Government's indication that there are approximately 10,103,571 indigenous persons living in Mexico, representing 9.8 per cent of the national population. With reference to its previous request concerning whether individuals belonging to indigenous groups who do not speak an indigenous language enjoy the protection of the Convention, the Committee notes the Government's statement that "even if indigenous persons lose their language, they do not lose their identity, nor, consequently, do they lose their specific rights deriving from their cultural difference and their

specific social, cultural, political and economic characteristics" and the criterion of voluntarily joining any group laid down in the Political Constitution remains the fundamental criterion for determining to whom the provisions relating to indigenous matters apply.

Thus, as it would many times in later years, the Committee was asking what criteria were used to determine that particular population groups were covered by the Convention, and how many people were included.

The Committee of Experts also began pressing governments to explain how the various criteria in Article 1 were being used to define those covered. This direct request to Costa Rica in 1997 illustrates this:

> 2. Article 1, paragraph 2, of the Convention. The Committee notes that the definition of the concept of "indigenous" contained in section 1 of the Indigenous Act, under which "persons are indigenous who constitute ethnic groups descended directly from pre-Columbian civilizations and who conserve their own identity", does not include self-identification as indigenous or tribal as one of the criteria for the definition of the peoples to which the Act applies. Please state how effect is given to this requirement of the Convention.

The Committee also began questioning whether the national coverage was as broad as the Convention contemplated. See the direct request to Honduras adopted in 1989:

> 2. Article 1 of the Convention. The Committee notes the Government's statement that the Convention covers those persons that are members of indigenous and tribal peoples, particularly those belonging to the Confederation of Autochthonous Peoples of Honduras (CONPAH). Please indicate whether and in what manner the Convention is applied to those indigenous and tribal peoples that are not affiliated with CONPAH, and how the self-identification criterion contained in Article 1(2) of the Convention is applied in practice. Please also supply copies of any judicial decrees or legislation relevant to the application of this Article.

Some years later the Committee raised related comments to Guatemala in a 2006 direct request:

> 1. *Article 1 of the Convention.* The Committee notes that according to the Government, no state bodies or indigenous organizations have statistical

information indicating the population covered by the Convention, as no distinction is made as to ethnic group in implementing public policies. The Government also indicates that it has not reached consensus with any indigenous organizations or institutions on the criteria for determining membership of an ethnic group. The Committee points out that since the Convention provides for the implementation of a series of public policies targeting indigenous peoples exclusively, it is important to set criteria for determining its coverage. *The Committee hopes that the Government will do its utmost, in consultation with the peoples concerned, to establish criteria for identifying peoples liable to be covered by the Convention, bearing in mind that paragraph 2 of this Article establishes that self-identification must be regarded as a fundamental criterion. Please report to the Committee on progress made in this regard, and specify whether the Convention applies to non-Garífuna peoples of African extraction indicating, if appropriate, how the latter's representation in Government institutions is secured.*

The comments of the Committee of Experts appear by this time to have been sparking more in-depth reflection at the national level, and even to begin involving courts. In 2000 the Committee's direct request to Costa Rica included the following:

3. *Article 1(2) of the Convention.* The Committee notes that section 4(a) of Bill No. 12032 provides that each indigenous people will define autonomously who they recognize as indigenous. The Committee hopes that the Government will provide additional information on the practical application of this provision once the Bill has been adopted. The Committee notes also that the Government's report refers to several criteria under Costa Rican law for defining "indigenous". First, section 1 of the Indigenous Act No. 6172 states that "persons are indigenous who constitute ethnic groups descended directly from pre-Columbian civilizations and who conserve their identity". Second, the criterion of self-identification found in *Article 1(2)* of the Convention is directly applicable, given that article 7 of the Constitution of Costa Rica conveys on international treaties ratified by that country a rank superior to its domestic laws. Lastly, the criteria formulated by the Republic's General Prosecutor in the Action of Unconstitutionality No. 6433–95, provides that the concept of identity is interrelated with that of "community". The Committee recalls that self-identification as indigenous shall be regarded as a fundamental criterion for determining the groups to which the provisions of the Convention

apply. The Committee requests the Government to indicate whether it plans to harmonize section 1 of the Indigenous Act No. 6172, the criteria formulated by the General Prosecutor and the Constitutional Court's Judgement No. 1786–93, which states that "it is the indigenous communities themselves that determine who are their members, applying their own criteria and not those followed by statutory law", with *Article 1(2)* of the Convention.

A direct request made to Peru in 2005 illustrates the way in which ratification of the Convention and its supervision have pushed some countries to re-examine the ways in which they define and interact with indigenous and tribal peoples:

> 1. *Article 1 of the Convention. Identification and self-identification.* The Committee notes that, according to the Government's report, Peru's population, estimated at around 24 million inhabitants, is mainly *mestizo* (of mixed extraction) and that over 9 million Peruvians are indigenous, principally *Quechua* and *Aymara*, living in the Andean region. There are 42 ethno-linguistic groups residing in the Amazonian region of Peru, which covers 62 per cent of the national territory. These populations have cultural, economic and political characteristics that are distinct from other sectors of the national population. The Indian population is made up, not only of rural and indigenous communities, but also of remote settlements: groups that are in a situation of voluntary isolation, or with which contact is sporadic. The official languages are Spanish, *Quechua* (spoken by more than 3 million people), *Aymara* (350,000 speakers) and in the Amazonian region 40 languages, belonging to 16 linguistic families, are spoken. According to the report, there is a need for greater recognition of the right to their own identity of all those communities that do not explicitly identify themselves as native, indigenous or members of a specific linguistic group, in addition to the 1,265 rural and indigenous communities included in the State's registers. In this regard, the Committee previously referred to the difficulties that arose from the various definitions and terms used to identify the populations covered by the provisions of the Convention: rural, indigenous and native populations and those living in the highlands, the forest and the edge of the forest. The Committee again suggests that the Government consider certain fundamental common criteria for the identification of the groups to which the Convention may apply, with an indication, for example, of the criteria used in the last census, and it requests information on the manner in which the criterion of "self-identification", set out in *paragraph 2* of this Article, is applied.

This comment was in turn followed up further by a 2012 direct request to Peru examining how the Government was defining who was covered:

> Article 1 of the Convention. Peoples covered by the Convention. In its previous comments, the Committee pointed out that all indigenous communities must be covered by the Convention, regardless of their designation. The Committee notes the criteria for the identification of indigenous or original peoples laid down in the Regulation which provides that the criteria established in section 7 of the Act on the right to prior consultation "should be interpreted within the framework of Article 1 of the Convention" (section 3(k) of the Regulation). Furthermore, Ministerial Resolution No. 202-2012-MC of 22 May 2012 approved a directive regulating the operation of the official database of indigenous or original peoples. The database is a declarative register and reference tool, not a constitutive register of rights. *The Committee invites the Government to indicate in its next report which indigenous peoples have been entered in the official database and to explain how the latter has been updated and evaluated.*

As governments continue to refine the way in which they deal with this part of their populations, the Committee of Experts continues to pose questions, intended largely to ensure that governments do not forget their obligations under the Convention. A 2013 direct request to Chile raised the following points:

> Article 1 of the Convention. Self-identification. In the report received in August 2012, the Government states that, since the Convention came into force, the term "ethnic group" has been replaced by the term "indigenous people". The 2011 National Socio-Economic Characterization Survey (CASEN) recognizes the existence of 1,369,563 indigenous persons in Chile, equivalent to 8.1 per cent of the estimated population of the country. In reply to the comments made in 2012, the Government indicates that sections 60 and 61 of the Indigenous Act recognize the indigenous status of the Huilliche and Pehuenche communities. Moreover, in the records of the sessions for the adoption of the Indigenous Act, note was made of the existence of communities who have little representation at present. *The Committee refers to the observations made by the indigenous organizations in 2010 and requests the Government to continue providing information on the steps taken to ensure that the Changa, Chono, Huilliche and Pehuenche peoples are protected by measures designed to give effect to the provisions of the Convention.*

c   *The Importance of having a Legal Personality*

The Committee also regularly poses questions about the consequences of identification as indigenous or tribal under the Convention, as in this direct request to Paraguay in 1995:

> 1. *Article 1 of the Convention.* The Committee notes the Government's reply in which it explains that the entry of indigenous persons into the Single National Register is no different from the entry of other rural workers. The Committee would be grateful if the Government would indicate the manner in which recognition is given to indigenous communities and individuals so that they can benefit from the legislation which applies to them. It also notes that a census is being undertaken with the assistance of the United Nations Development Programme and requests the Government to keep it informed of the results of the census.

In a 2003 direct request to Argentina, the Committee of Experts followed up comments by an Argentinian trade union on the question of identity:

> 2. The Committee notes that in September 2001, the Congress of Argentinian Workers (CTA) sent detailed observations on the application of the Convention ...
>
> 4. *Article 1 of the Convention.* With regard to the self-identification of indigenous peoples, the CTA indicates that both the national and the provincial legislation, including the census forms, contain criteria which are not in compliance with the Convention and calls for the indigenous peoples to be consulted for the formulation of questions which would provide guidance for the indigenous census. Please indicate when it is planned to undertake the indigenous census and the manner in which the peoples concerned are participating in its preparation.
>
> 5. The CTA alleges that many problems arise in the recognition of indigenous peoples, principally related to obtaining legal personality as a result of long and complex procedures which amount to "more to the granting than the recognition of such personality". It alleges that these have serious repercussions, as the peoples concerned cannot defend their rights in the courts or before the public administration if they have not first acquired legal personality. Of the 850 indigenous communities, it states that only 15 per cent have been recognized by the National Institute of Indigenous Affairs (INAI) and, according to the CTA, no consultations were held with the communities themselves on the criteria for such recognition. Moreover, the legal personality granted

at the provincial level has no value at the national level in the absence of special agreements, but only four of the 20 provinces in which indigenous peoples are located are reported to have concluded such agreements. Please indicate the manner in which the functions of the State and the provinces in relation to indigenous affairs are coordinated, and in particular the manner in which effect is given to article 75(17) *in fine* of the Constitution which, after determining the functions of the Congress with regard to recognition, lands and the management of resources in relation to indigenous affairs, provides that "the provinces may discharge these functions concurrently".

This began to reflect the concern that the question of coverage by the Convention was only one of the problems raised in relation to identity, and that the lack of identity under national legislation – which has a close relation to whether the Convention's coverage is as wide as the Convention would require – has serious legal consequences. This also invoked the general right to consultation in the application of the Convention required under Article 6. The above comment was followed up in 2005 in another direct request to Argentina:

4. *Indigenous identity.* In its previous comments the Committee noted the CTA's assertion that the peoples concerned are unable to defend their rights in the courts or before the public administration unless they are able to show that they have legal personality. The CTA further alleged that only 15 per cent of the 850 indigenous communities are recognized by the National Institute of Indigenous Affairs (INAI) and that no consultations were held with the communities themselves on the criteria for such recognition. Furthermore, legal personality granted by a province is not recognized at the national level unless there is a special agreement, and only four of the 20 provinces that have indigenous peoples have concluded such agreements. The Committee likewise noted that pursuant to the constitutional reform of 1994, a resolution was passed (No. 4811/96) establishing requirements for the registration of indigenous communities, the requirements have been simplified, and account is taken of self-identification as a fundamental right. The Committee takes notes of the information supplied by the Government in its report to the effect that in registering at national level the legal personality of indigenous communities, the latter's customs and forms of organization are respected and that in the provinces agreements to this effect are concluded. The Committee requests the Government to provide information on the application of resolution

No. 4811/96 in the various provinces, particularly in Neuquén and the provinces which have no agreement with the nation. Please also indicate how central authority and provincial authority in this matter are coordinated. Please provide information on the manner in which it is ensured that indigenous communities participate in, or are consulted on, the formulation of procedures for recognition of legal personality, at both national and provincial levels.

5. The Committee notes with interest the information supplied by the Government that in the province of Río Negro an agreement has been signed with the *Mapuche* community for recognition of the legal personality of the various communities. The Committee requests the Government to provide information in its next report on the number of indigenous communities that have acquired legal personality since the signing of the abovementioned agreement.

The wider consequences, particularly in relation to land rights which often are intimately connected to identity, of whether a part of the population was recognized as falling under these criteria was also invoked in a 2009 direct request to Bolivia:

Article 1 of the Convention. Recognition and identification of indigenous peoples. In its previous comments, the Committee requested the Government to state whether procedures or registers of indigenous peoples exist for the purposes of determining the peoples covered by the Convention. The Committee notes that, according to the Government's report, the register of indigenous peoples is directly connected with community lands of origin (TCO), which represents a specific type of property linked to the pre-existence of a territory which is imprescriptible, non-seizable and inalienable. The register of identity of indigenous peoples is part of the procedure to restructure community lands of origin, and one of the key requirements which has been laid down is the drawing up of a Register of Identity of Indigenous and Original Peoples (RIPIO). The Under-Ministry of Land Affairs is the public authority responsible for RIPIO and its report enables the competent state institution to "register" the declaration of identity of the indigenous or original people concerned. The report states that there is no administrative entity that performs the task of legal registration or recognition of new indigenous peoples. The Committee notes that the Government is making a major effort to guarantee indigenous peoples' land rights, something which is fundamental for the application of the Convention and in general terms for their survival and development. The Committee understands that, in this context, the Government has linked recognition to the land restructuring process. The Committee would point out, however, that even though land rights are fundamental, the rights in relation to the Convention (including rights in relation to education, health and work) are wider in scope than land rights alone. The Committee considers that recognition should also be given to indigenous peoples who, for various reasons, did not occupy traditional lands or were nomadic but who could enjoy other rights laid down in the Convention. *The Committee requests the Government to indicate the manner in which it gives recognition to, or guarantees the rights afforded by the Convention to indigenous and original peoples, or sections thereof, who for various reasons did not have a link to the land (for example, because of being nomadic or because of leaving for various reasons the lands which they traditionally occupied). Furthermore, referring once again to the Government's previous report, which indicated the existence of persons of African extraction and that there had been significant intermingling with original or indigenous persons or groups, particularly the Aymara, the Committee recalls that, since those groups display the features set forth in paragraph 1(a) or (b), they are covered by the provisions thereof, and it requests the Government to indicate: (i) whether it considers that such communities of African extraction are covered by Article 1, paragraph 1(a) or (b); (ii) if so, the way in which it secures the rights of the Convention to those communities; and (iii) if not, to state the reasons why.*

d   *The Importance of Self-identification*

The criterion of 'self-identification' was developed in a direct request addressed to Paraguay in 2006:

> 1. *Article 1 of the Convention.* The Committee notes the statistical data provided by the Government from the 2002 census carried out by the Directorate of Statistics, Surveys and Census, indicating the number of indigenous persons in the country by region and by ethnic group. It also notes that the Government has not modified the Indigenous Communities Charter, adopted by Act No. 904/81 for the reasons indicated in the observation, and thus, self identification as a criterion for defining indigenous peoples as provided for by the Convention has not been incorporated. *The Committee, recalling that under paragraph 2 of this Article of the Convention, self-identification as indigenous or tribal shall be regarded*

as a fundamental criterion for determining the groups to which the provisions of this Convention apply, requests the Government to incorporate this criterion in its next report and to give legislative expression to it in consultation with indigenous people.

And the self-identification criterion was again examined in an observation made to Brazil in 2008:

Article 1(2). Undermining of the application of the criterion of self-identification. The CUT[60] also states that the criterion of self-identification established in *Article 1(2)* of the Convention was incorporated in national law by means of Decree No. 4887/2003, which regulates the procedure for granting titles regarding lands occupied by the remaining Quilombola communities. Nevertheless, the Government is allegedly undermining self-identification by means of subsequent legislation (Decree No. 98/2007), thereby preventing issues regarding land titles from being settled since doing so depends on registration of communities. It is, according to the trade union, more and more difficult to obtain registration and thus secure the application of other rights, in particular with regard to land. The violation of the criterion of self-identification is also visible in the dispute between the Quilombola community of Isla de Marambai and the Navy. The communities identify themselves as indigenous and claim the protection afforded by the Convention. Although occurring less frequently, the indigenous identity of the Indians of the North-East is sometimes not recognized either, and this makes the recognition of their rights to the lands they have traditionally occupied more difficult. In the light of the information received, the Committee considers that the Quilombola communities appear to meet the requirements laid down by *Article 1(1)(a)* of the Convention, according to which the Convention applies to "tribal peoples in independent countries whose social, cultural and economic conditions distinguish them from other sections of the national community, and whose status is regulated wholly or partially by their own customs or traditions or by special laws or regulations". *Article 1(2)* states that "self-identification as indigenous or tribal shall be regarded as a fundamental criterion for determining the groups for which the provisions of this Convention apply". ***The Committee requests the Government to provide information on the application of the Convention***

---

60   This observation was based on information received from the Single Confederation of Workers (CUT) under article 23 of the ILO Constitution.

to the Quilombola communities, and should the Government consider that these communities do not constitute tribal peoples within the meaning of the Convention, the Committee requests the Government to state the reasons for its viewpoint.

The complexity of definitions, and the close link between definition and coverage and other aspects of the Convention, are illustrated in a 2009 Observation to Peru:

> *Article 1 of the Convention. Peoples covered by the Convention.* The Committee notes that in its report the Government states, as it did during the discussion in the Conference Committee, that a draft Framework Act on Indigenous or Original Peoples of Peru has been prepared, which sets out a definition of indigenous or original peoples, with a view to removing ambiguities from the national legislation regarding identification of the peoples covered. The Committee notes that section 3 of the draft contains such a definition, whereas section 2 states that indigenous or original peoples of Peru include "the so-called peasant communities and native communities; as well as indigenous people in a situation of isolation and a situation of initial contact; it likewise applies to those who identify themselves as descendants of the ancestral cultures settled in Peru's coastal, mountain and rainforest areas". The Committee notes that, although the definition in section 3 of the draft reproduces the objective elements of the Convention's definition, it makes no reference, unlike section 2, to the fundamental criterion of self-identification. The Committee also notes that the objective elements of the definition in the abovementioned draft include the criterion that these peoples "are in possession of an area of land", which does not appear in the Convention. The Committee would point out in this connection that *Article 13* of the Convention stresses the special importance for these peoples of the cultures and spiritual values of "their relationship with the lands or territories, or both as applicable, which they occupy or otherwise use". The Committee also draws the Government's attention to the fact that *Article 14(1)* of the Convention, and in particular the expression "the lands which they traditionally occupy", has to be read in conjunction with *Article 14(3)* on land claims, in that the Convention likewise covers situations in which indigenous and tribal peoples have recently lost occupation of their lands or have been recently expelled from them. ***The Committee accordingly urges the Government, in consultation with the indigenous peoples, to align the definition in the draft Framework Law on Indigenous or***

> *Original Peoples of Peru with the Convention. Please also supply information on the manner in which effective consultation and participation is ensured with indigenous peoples in the preparation of the abovementioned draft. Furthermore, the Committee again asks the Government to provide information on the measures taken to ensure that all those covered by Article 1 of the Convention are likewise covered by all provisions of the new legislation and enjoy the rights set forth therein on an equal footing.*

e   *Coverage beyond 'Indigenous'*

The question of just which population groups are covered by the Convention arose in a direct request made to Bolivia in 2005:

> The Government also indicates that, although there is a minority population of persons of African extraction, and that there has been significant interbreeding with persons from indigenous groups and groups of origin, and particularly the Aymara, they are not included in the category of indigenous groups or groups of origin. The Committee considers that, if such groups show the characteristics set out in *Article 1, paragraph 1(a) or (b)*, of the Convention and identify themselves as indigenous or tribal peoples, they are covered by the provisions of the Convention.

A related question was put to Guatemala in a direct request in 2006:

> Please report to the Committee on progress made in this regard, and specify whether the Convention applies to non-Garífuna peoples of African extraction indicating, if appropriate, how the latter's representation in Government institutions is secured.

The broad coverage of the Convention in relation to non-indigenous peoples was made even clearer in an observation to Colombia in 2006:

> 2. *Article 1 of the Convention. Coverage.* In 2005, the Committee expressed the view that in the light of the information sent by the USO, the black communities of Curbaradó and Jiguamiandó appeared to fulfil the requirements set in *Article 1, paragraph 1(a)*, of the Convention, according to which the Convention applies to "tribal peoples in independent countries whose social, cultural and economic conditions distinguish them from other sections of the national community, and whose status is

regulated wholly or partially by their own customs or traditions or by special laws or regulations". Furthermore, from the information provided in the communication, the representatives of the community councils of the Curbaradó and the Jiguamiandó had participated in preparing the USO's observations, and it appeared that in seeking application of the Convention to their communities, these peoples identify themselves as being tribal. The Committee further noted that the definition of "black community" in Act No. 70 appeared to coincide with the definition of tribal peoples in the Convention. It accordingly asked the Government and the USO to specify whether these communities identify themselves as tribal within the meaning of *Article 1, paragraph 1(a)*, and requested the Government to give its reasons if it deems that these communities are not tribal peoples within the meaning of the Convention. The Committee notes that the USO confirmed that the communities identify themselves as tribal. It also notes with satisfaction the Government's statement that the Curbaradó and Jiguamiandó communities, which are of African extraction, are covered by the Convention. ***The Committee requests the Government to state whether all the communities of African extraction recognized by Act No. 70 of 1993 are covered by the Convention.***

This approach is confirmed by a report from Honduras, of which note was taken in a 2008 Observation to Honduras:

Article 1 of the Convention. The Committee notes that according to the Government, the Convention covers the various ethnic groups that lived in Honduras before colonization and also those known as "pueblos negros" (which include, among others, Afro-Hondurans and the Garifuna), who, though not originally from Honduras, live in much the same social, economic, ecological and geographical conditions. The 2001 census recorded 493,146 indigenous peoples and "pueblos negros", accounting for 6.33 per cent of the population of Honduras. They currently account for an estimated 15.7 per cent according to the Strategic Plan for the Comprehensive Development of Indigenous Peoples. The Government indicates that the indigenous and "pueblos negros" of Honduras are: (1) Miskito; (2) Garifuna; (3) Pech; (4) Tolupan; (5) Lenca; (6) Tawahka; (7) Nahoa/Nahualt; (8) Maya Chorti; and (9) English-speaking black peoples.

A similar approach has been demonstrated by Brazil, according to a 2008 observation by the Committee of Experts:

Article 1(1)(a) of the Convention. Scope of application. Black rural Quilombola communities. Both communications refer to the Quilombola communities and maintain that the remaining Quilombola communities constitute tribal peoples within the meaning of *Article 1(1)(a)* of the Convention. They indicate that these are social groups whose origins lie in the resistance movement to slavery in Brazil and to racial discrimination, and whose ethnic identity is based on common ancestry and a differentiated way of life. The Brazilian Constitution of 1988 guarantees to Quilombola communities their right to ownership of their lands and recognizes the importance of such communities for the cultural heritage of Brazil. The CUT indicates that, even though the executive and judicial authorities have recognized in documents or rulings that the Convention applies to the Quilombola communities, the Government merely provides information in its report on the situation of the indigenous peoples covered by *Article 1(1)(b)* of the Convention. The CUT claims that there is a pressing need to include information on the realities of life for the Quilombola communities in the Government's report with reference to *Article 1(1)(a)* of the Convention and guarantee the effective application of the Convention to these communities. The General Land Registry of the Remaining Quilombola Communities, under the responsibility of the Palmares Cultural Foundation, has registered the existence of 1,228 Quilombola communities, but the National Coordinating Committee of the Black Rural Quilombola Communities, indicates the existence of more than 3,000 communities scattered over all the regions of the country.

f   Changes in Governments' Manner of Identification

The fact of the Convention requiring governments to re-examine the way they deal with the question of identity is highlighted in the immediately preceding observation to Peru. It was also taken up in 2005 also in a direct request to Mexico:

> 1. *Article 1 of the Convention. Identification and self-identification. Linguistic requirements and physical location.* In its previous comments, the Committee noted that article 2 of the constitutional reform provides that awareness of indigenous identity shall be a fundamental criterion in determining the persons to whom the provisions on indigenous peoples apply. It also noted that according to article 2, paragraph 5, "recognition of indigenous peoples and communities shall be provided for in the constitutions

and laws of the federative entities which shall take into account ethno-linguistic criteria and physical location, in addition to the general principles set out in the previous paragraphs of this article". The Committee notes that, according to the Government's report, Mexico's indigenous population is numerically the largest in Latin America, that the National Population Council (CONAPO) estimated the size of the indigenous population to be 12.7 million in 2000 and that it is made up of 62 indigenous peoples. The CONAPO survey included questions about the indigenous languages spoken and membership of indigenous groups of at least one member of the household. The Committee notes that according to Annex 16 of the Government's report (Socio-economic indicators for indigenous peoples of Mexico, 2002), "the 'de-indianization' process led many indigenous persons to abandon their communities of origin, contributing to a significant loss in their indigenous languages and their ethnic identities". It also notes that in the above annex, there are six categories in answer to the questions on language and membership of an indigenous group, the fourth of which is "Do not speak an indigenous language and belong to an indigenous group". The Committee further notes that, since formal censuses were first introduced in 1895, language has been the main criterion used for identifying the indigenous population. Since, as noted in the annex sent by the Government, "de-indianization" has led to many indigenous people losing their language, the Committee would be grateful if the Government would state whether the persons in the fourth category ("Do not speak an indigenous language and belong to an indigenous group") enjoy the protection afforded by the Convention, so that the application of *Article 1* is not limited, as it does not include language as a criterion for defining the peoples protected by the Convention. With regard to paragraph 5 of article 2 of the constitutional reform, which makes the federative entities responsible for the recognition of indigenous peoples and communities, taking into account ethno-linguistic criteria and physical location, the Committee would be grateful for information on the manner in which these entities apply such criteria.

In sum, the decisions taken at the national level on the coverage of Convention No. 169 have consequences that go well beyond the content of reports to the ILO on its application. The ways in which different countries interact with the indigenous and tribal peoples living in their territories are intimately related to identification, including self-identification, of indigenous and tribal peoples. Ratification of the Convention has prompted re-examination of this relation in all the countries cited above, and in a number of cases the establishment for the first time of clear and detailed criteria of identification. As seen above it has also prompted several governments to take measures that have resulted in the recognition for the first time of the actual legal existence of parts of their own populations.

The extracts of comments of the Committee of Experts' comments listed above are only examples that are part of a rich and ongoing exchange on these questions, and are worth examining in greater depth through the reports of the Committee, and the measures taken at the national level by a large number of governments.

CHAPTER 3

Article 2 of Convention No. 169 – Basic Policy and Orientation

A   Convention No. 107

Since Article 2 of Convention No. 169 was closely based on Article 2 of Convention No. 107 – even though its meaning was radically different – it is useful to see how the C. 107 approach was developed. The basic approach of Convention No. 107 has universally been characterized as integrationist, which finds its most succinct statement in Article 2 of that Convention:

> 1. Governments shall have the primary responsibility for developing co-ordinated and systematic action for the protection of the populations concerned and their progressive integration into the life of their respective countries.
> 2. Such action shall include measures for –
> (*a*) enabling the said populations to benefit on an equal footing from the rights and opportunities which national laws or regulations grant to the other elements of the population;
> (*b*) promoting the social, economic and cultural development of these populations and raising their standard of living;
> (*c*) creating possibilities of national integration to the exclusion of measures tending towards the artificial assimilation of these populations.
> 3. The primary objective of all such action shall be the fostering of individual dignity, and the advancement of individual usefulness and initiative.
> 4. Recourse to force or coercion as a means of promoting the integration of these populations into the national community shall be excluded.

When the ILO drew up the Law and Practice Report in 1955 to begin preparing what was to become Convention No. 107, it looked back at its own previous work, examined the situation of indigenous and tribal peoples around the world, and undertook an exhaustive examination of policies and practices followed by States. The first part of the conclusions it expressed in this report was the following:

A study of the legislative, administrative and other measures adopted by the governments concerned, and of the current practice in various countries, leads to the following general observations:

1. It is now almost universally recognised that, left to their own resources, indigenous peoples would have difficulty in overcoming their inferior economic and social situation, which inevitably leaves them open to exploitation. Despite the national differences in the juridical treatment of indigenous groups, the policy of the great majority of governments is the same, namely to counteract the social, economic and cultural handicaps that prevent these groups from benefiting fully from the rights granted to them either explicitly or tacitly by law. In addition, the view has been gaining ground in one way or another, varying with the circumstances in each country, that it is no longer possible to ignore the special conditions and needs of tribal communities during their adaptation to the forms of life and work of the technologically more advanced societies to which they belong politically; and that special measures are therefore necessary, particularly during the initial phase of this process, to safeguard their institutions, persons and property.

2. The growing acceptance of this view has been accompanied by a recognition that, if they are to succeed, these measures should be maintained only as long and in so far as there are still indigenous communities which require special protection; and that the general rights of citizenship should not be denied to individuals belonging to a given tribal community or group merely because they are still protected by special safeguards. Experience has shown that a static system of protection, however well-meaning, may produce the opposite effect to that intended and contribute to maintaining indigenous communities in their situation of inferiority and prolonging a condition of segregation that may be harmful to the growth of democratic institutions and the consolidation of national unity. As the I.L.O. Committee of Experts on Indigenous Labour pointed out, the integration of indigenous communities into modern society must be looked upon as inescapable.

3. Experience has also demonstrated that, to be successful, integration must not involve the precipitate introduction of new forms of social and economic organisation in tribal communities before the latter have been prepared to accept these innovations freely and a rightful place has been secured for them within their respective national communities.

4. Lastly, experience has demonstrated that a certain amount of flexibility is needed in deciding upon the nature and extent of the special measures to be adopted for the protection and integration of indigenous

peoples. Depending on the circumstances of a given country or the features peculiar to an indigenous group or problem within that country, these measures may take the form of interim legislation applicable only to the indigenous population or certain of its groups, or of special administrative machinery set up to adapt general legislation to the conditions of life and cultural development of the groups concerned.

5. It seems clear that the foremost objective in planning the economic development of areas inhabited by indigenous peoples should be to improve their living and working conditions. Among the problems arising out of these conditions the following appear to be fundamental, with variations according to region or country: the precarious position of indigenous communities with regard to the ownership and use of the land; the absence or inadequacy of vocational training facilities for indigenous workers; the inefficient use of indigenous labour and the abuses arising out of its uncontrolled recruitment or the inadequate supervision of working conditions; the technical backwardness of certain indigenous homecrafts and rural industries, and the inadequacy of measures taken to protect and develop them; the absence or inadequacy of social assistance and health measures in many areas inhabited by indigenous peoples; and various special problems related to the educational needs of non-integrated indigenous groups and the part played by their vernacular languages in the process of integration.

Several observations result from reading this text. The first is the heavily patronizing but benevolent tone of these conclusions. A sincere conviction emerges of the cultural and economic inadequacy of these peoples, and of their total inability to help themselves. At the same time, there is an urgency to the expressions of the need to help them that is convincing, if depressing seen from today's perspective.

It should be kept in mind that at this point many indigenous cultures had indeed collapsed under the weight of government action and inaction, and that there was no spokesperson for them anywhere at the international level. This is not an excuse for such cultural arrogance, but may have been a contributing factor to these conclusions.

In addition, there is the conclusion at the end of the second paragraph above that "the integration of indigenous communities into modern society must be looked upon as inescapable". The drafters of this report obviously felt that if this approach was not taken, further misery and even extinction was to be the result.

The relevant questions in the questionnaire put to the constituents therefore consisted of the following:

5. Do you consider that governments have the primary responsibility in developing co-ordinated and systematic action aimed at the protection and progressive integration of indigenous peoples into their respective national communities?

6. Do you consider that there is a need for adopting special measures for the protection of the institutions, persons, property and labour of non-integrated indigenous peoples, so long as the inferior social, economic and cultural status of these peoples prevents them from enjoying the benefits of the general laws of the country?

7. Do you consider that it is necessary to ensure that such measures –
  (a) *will not be used as a means of prolonging a state of segregation?*
  (b) *will be continued only so long as there are indigenous groups which need special protection and in accordance with the extent to which they need it?*

...

10. Do you consider that, in any action undertaken with a view to promoting the integration of indigenous peoples into the national community, recourse to force or moral coercion should be excluded?[1]

Governments' replies occasionally took different points of view on whether special treatment was desirable and on the agencies that should be responsible, but a reading of the replies themselves shows that none of the replies contested the suggestion that the basic approach that integration, and protection until this had been achieved, were the correct paths to follow. In almost every case, with minor variations, the Office concluded its examination of these replies with the phrase 'The corresponding point in the proposed Conclusions is based on the wording of the question'.[2]

The draft conclusions proposed to the Conference for its first discussion therefore followed the questionnaire very closely:

4. Governments should have the primary responsibility in developing co-ordinated and systematic action aimed at the protection and progressive integration of indigenous peoples into their respective national communities.

5. Special measures should be adopted for the protection of the institutions, persons, property and labour of non-integrated indigenous peoples, so long as the social, economic and cultural status of these peoples

---

1 Ibid., pp. 175 and 176.
2 Report VIII (2), pp. 108 to 111.

prevents them from enjoying the benefits of the general laws of the country to which they belong.

6. Care should be taken to ensure that such measures –

(a) will not be used as a means of creating or prolonging a state of segregation; and

(b) will be continued only so long as there are indigenous groups which need special protection and to the extent to which they need it.

7. Any person belonging to an indigenous group benefiting by such special measures should enjoy the general rights of citizenship.

8. The nature and scope of the special measures provided for in point 5 should be determined in a flexible manner, having regard to the conditions characteristic of each country.

9. In any action undertaken with a view to promoting the integration of indigenous peoples into the national community, recourse to force or coercion should be excluded.[3]

The discussion of these points in the 1956 Session of the Conference reached consensus fairly easily that the principles proposed in the draft conclusions were shared by most members of the Committee:

Point 5
48. Point 4 of the text under consideration was approved in conformity with an amendment moved by the U.S.S.R. Government member, which described the principal elements that the concept of integration should encompass, taking into account a sub-amendment proposed by the Indian Workers' member which consisted in substituting the words "all measures aimed at enabling" for the words "all measures aimed at ensuring". The vote was 70 votes to 6, with 4 abstentions.

Point 6
49. Point 5 of the text under consideration, stating that special measures should be adopted for the protection of the institutions, persons, property and labour of non-integrated indigenous persons, so long as their situation prevented them from enjoying the benefits of general legislation, was adopted unanimously by 78 votes to 0, with no abstentions.

Point 7
50. Point 6 of the text under consideration, stressing the need to ensure that such special measures should not be used as a means of creating or prolonging a state of segregation and that they should be continued only

---

[3] Ibid., pp. 156 and 157.

so long as they were needed, was adopted without amendment by 72 votes to 6, with no abstentions.

Point 8

51. Point 7 of the text under consideration was the object of detailed discussion. An amendment by the Portuguese Government member proposing that it should be redrafted so as to state that any person belonging to an indigenous group should not be debarred from the general rights of citizenship because he belonged to such a group, was rejected by 24 votes to 37, with no abstentions. Finally, the text, stressing that any person belonging to an indigenous group benefiting by special measures of protection should enjoy the general rights of citizenship, was adopted with the addition of the words "without discrimination between him and the rest of the population", in accordance with an amendment moved by the Workers' members. The vote for adoption of the point, as amended, was 54 to 1, with 7 abstentions. An amendment moved by the Government member of Egypt with the object of clarifying the term "general rights of citizenship" was not adopted.

Point 9

52. Point 8 of the text under consideration, stating that the nature and scope of the special measures should be determined in a flexible manner, was adopted by 47 votes to 0, with 9 abstentions, following an amendment moved by the New Zealand Government member calling for the substitution of the words "measures provided for in this instrument" for the reference to point 5.

Point 10

53. The Committee then discussed point 9 of the text under consideration, stating that in any action undertaken with a view to promoting integration recourse to force or coercion should be excluded. An amendment moved by the Portuguese Government member, proposing to introduce the qualification "except in the case of practices repugnant to generally accepted moral principles", was withdrawn in view of the feeling in the Committee that the proposed qualification might be subject to differing interpretations and might unduly weaken the provision. This point was adopted by 51 votes to 0, with no abstentions.[4]

The conclusions adopted at the end of this discussion were:

---

4   Proceedings 1956, pp. 740 and 741.

5. Governments should have the primary responsibility in developing co-ordinated and systematic action aimed at the protection of indigenous populations and progressive integration of indigenous peoples into the life of their respective countries. This action should encompass all measures aimed –
   (a) at enabling indigenous populations to benefit on an equal footing from the rights and opportunities which national legislation grants to the other elements of the population, in all fields;
   (b) at promoting the social economic and cultural development of the indigenous populations and raising their standard of living;
   (c) at the creation of possibilities of national integration to the exclusion of any measures tending towards the forced or artificial assimilation of indigenous peoples.
6. Special measures should be adopted for the protection of the institutions, persons, property and labour of non-integrated indigenous peoples, so long as the social, economic and cultural status of these peoples prevents them from enjoying the benefits of the general laws of the country to which they belong.
7. Care should be taken to ensure that such measures –
   (a) will not be used as a means of creating or prolonging a state of segregation; and
   (b) will be continued only so long as there are indigenous groups which need special protection and to the extent to which they need it.
8. Any person belonging to an indigenous group benefiting by such measures should enjoy the general rights of citizenship without discrimination between him and the rest of the population.
9. The nature and scope of the special measures provided for in this instrument should be determined in a flexible manner, having regard to the conditions characteristic of each country.
10. In any action undertaken with a view to promoting the integration of indigenous peoples into the national community, recourse to force or coercion should be excluded.[5]

This was in turn translated into the form of a proposed Convention in the first of two reports to be submitted for the 1957 discussion:

---

5 Ibid., p. 748.

Article 2

1. Governments shall have the primary responsibility for developing co-ordinated and systematic action for the protection of indigenous peoples and their progressive integration into the life of their respective countries.

2. Such action shall include measures for –

(*a*) enabling indigenous peoples to benefit on an equal footing from the rights and opportunities which national laws or regulations grant to the other elements of the population;

(*b*) promoting the social, economic and cultural development of the indigenous peoples and raising their standard of living;

(*c*) creating possibilities of national integration to the exclusion of measures tending towards the artificial assimilation of indigenous peoples.

3. In any action undertaken with a view to promoting the integration of indigenous peoples into the national community, recourse to force or coercion shall be excluded.[6]

Points 7, 8 and 9 were moved elsewhere in the proposed new Convention.

The observations made on draft Article 2, reproduced and commented upon in the last report to go to the Conference, referred almost entirely to the question of force or compulsion, and the general orientation towards integration was never called into question:

> The suggestion made by the Government of the Philippines concerning the introduction of a provision specifying that no attempt should be made to interfere with the religious beliefs and practices of the populations concerned appears to be covered by the beginning of Article 4 (*a*), which stipulates that due account shall be taken of the cultural and religious values of such populations, and by subparagraph (*b*) of the same Article, which stresses the need for a recognition of the danger involved in disrupting their values and institutions.
>
> As regards the observation made by the Government of the United Kingdom,[7] it should be pointed out that Article 2 (3) excludes the use of force or coercion only in the case of action aimed at promoting integration. This paragraph thus supplements the principle laid down in paragraph 2 (*c*) of the same Article, which provides that action for the

---

6 Report VI (1), p. 46.

7 The United Kingdom stated: "As regards paragraph 3 it is suggested that government would be completely ineffective if it was unable to have recourse to compulsion in the last resort if that was clearly in the interest of the peoples concerned." Report VI (2), p. 12.

protection and integration of the populations to which the proposed Convention applies shall include measures for "creating possibilities of national integration to the exclusion of measures tending towards the artificial assimilation of indigenous people". In other cases governments are, of course, free to act without the consent of the populations concerned, when the measures are in the latters' interests: for instance, in the situation referred to in Article 12. However, this provision relates to a concrete and foreseeable eventuality and it does not seem that a general exception such as that suggested in the observation of the United Kingdom Government could be introduced in the proposed Convention without running the risk of weakening the provision considerably.

The proposal made by the Government of the U.S.S.R. to add a new sentence to paragraph 3 of Article 2 seems to be broadly met by the provisions of paragraph 2 (c) of Article 2 and by subparagraphs (a) and (b) of Article 5.[8] These provisions exclude all measures aimed at the artificial integration of the populations concerned and make it obligatory to seek the co-operation of the representatives of these populations as well as to give these populations the opportunity of developing their initiative fully. The same considerations appear to apply in regard to the suggestions made by the Government of the Philippines, to the effect that integration should take place mainly on the initiative of the populations covered by the proposed Convention.

It has seemed useful to modify slightly the wording of paragraph 3 in order to bring out more clearly the prohibition of the use of force or coercion as a means of promoting integration.[9]

The text forwarded to the Conference therefore read:

Article 2
1. Governments shall have the primary responsibility for developing co-ordinated and systematic action for the protection of the populations concerned and their progressive integration into the life of their respective countries.
2. Such action shall include measures for –
   (a) enabling the said populations to benefit on an equal footing from the rights and opportunities which national laws or regulations grant to the other elements of the population,

---

8 The USSR proposed to add to paragraph 3, "The proper conditions should be created for the development of indigenous populations according to their desires." Ibid.
9 Ibid., pp. 12 and 13.

(b) promoting the social, economic and cultural development of these populations and raising their standard of living;

(c) creating possibilities of national integration to the exclusion of measures tending towards the artificial assimilation of these populations.

3. Recourse to force or coercion as a means of promoting the integration of these populations into the national community shall be excluded.[10]

The rewording of paragraph 3, mentioned above, appears to have made no difference to the meaning. In the interim, however, reference to 'indigenous peoples' had been replaced by different variants of 'the populations concerned.'

The discussion of this Article in the 1957 Conference was brief, but it was amended and a statement was made to express an understanding of its meaning, neither of which impinged upon the orientation towards integration as the preferred outcome:

Article 2

38. An amendment to clause (a) of paragraph 2 moved by the Government members of Iran and Portugal, designed to introduce the notion of obligations alongside that of rights and opportunities, was withdrawn since the majority of the Committee felt that its main purpose was already covered in paragraph 3 of Article 7.

39. The Employers' member of the United States moved an amendment to include a new paragraph providing that a prime objective of the instrument should be the fostering of individual dignity and the advancement of individual usefulness and initiative among the populations concerned. The Committee adopted the amendment by 51 votes to 0, with 4 abstentions. It decided, by 30 votes to 23, with 2 abstentions, to place it as paragraph 3 of Article 2 and to renumber the subsequent paragraph.

40. It was understood that paragraph 3 of the proposed text did not aim at preventing governments from taking measures necessary in the interests of health and education or in cases like that mentioned in Article 7, paragraph 2. The Committee unanimously approved Article 2, as amended.[11]

---

10   Ibid., p. 52.
11   Proceedings 1957, p. 726.

There is no report of any discussion of the US Employer's amendment, or of its effect. The result of this change appears to be to have moved the instrument even further from any recognition of the collective rights nature of this Convention – understated as compared to Convention No. 169, but still present. In the absence of any reported discussion, it is not clear whether this result was a conscious decision.

As adopted, the Article read as follows:

> *Article 2*
> 1. Governments shall have the primary responsibility for developing co-ordinated and systematic action for the protection of the populations concerned and their progressive integration into the life of their respective countries.
> 2. Such action shall include measures for:
>   (*a*) enabling the said populations to benefit on an equal footing from the rights and opportunities which national laws or regulations grant to the other elements of the population;
>   (*b*) promoting the social, economic and cultural development of these populations and raising their standard of living;
>   (*c*) creating possibilities of national integration to the exclusion of measures tending towards the artificial assimilation of these populations.
> 3. All actions taken shall have as the prime objective the fostering of individual dignity, and the advancement of individual usefulness and initiative.
> 4. Recourse to force or coercion as a means of promoting the integration of these populations into the national community shall be excluded.[12]

B Convention No. 169 – A New Approach

It would not be an exaggeration to state that the principal purpose of the revision of Convention No. 107 was centred on the revision of Article 2, and the other provisions that flowed from it.

i *The Meeting of Experts*

As the 1986 Meeting of Experts' report stated:

---

12 Ibid., p. 734.

45. The Governing Body had noted when it convened the present Meeting of Experts that the Convention's basic orientation was towards integration as the fundamental objective of all activities undertaken by governments in relation to indigenous and tribal populations, and that it was necessary to re-examine this orientation to take into account different views and changed circumstances. In particular, it was necessary to revise the instrument in order to take account of the existence of organisations of indigenous and tribal peoples and of their capacity to express the views and to defend the interests of the groups they represented.

46. The Meeting is unanimous in concluding that the integrationist language of Convention No. 107 is outdated, and that the application of this principle is destructive in the modern world. In 1956 and 1957, when Convention No. 107 was being discussed, it was felt that integration into the dominant national society offered the best chance for these groups to be a part of the development process of the countries in which they live. This had, however, resulted in a number of undesirable consequences. It had become a destructive concept, in part at least because of the way it was understood by governments. In practice it had become a concept which meant the extinction of ways of life which are different from that of the dominant society. The inclusion of this idea in the text of the Convention has also impeded indigenous and tribal peoples from taking full advantage of the strong protections offered in some parts of the Convention, because of the distrust its use has created among them. In this regard, it was recalled that the Sub-Commission's Special Rapporteur had stressed in his study (see paragraph 19 above) the necessity of adopting an approach which took account of the claims of indigenous populations. In his opinion, the policies of pluralism, self-sufficiency, self-management and ethno-development appeared to be those which would give indigenous populations the best possibilities and means of participating directly in the formulation and implementation of official policies.[13]

The discussion in the Meeting of Experts was not neatly organized into what would become the Articles of Convention No. 169, and this discussion on orientation also included language that has been reported above in relation to Article 1 (particularly the concept of self-determination) and below in relation to Articles 6 and 7 on consultation and participation. It is impossible to

---

13   Report of the Meeting of Experts, reproduced in Report VI (1), p. 107.

separate these discussions, though aspects of them appeared in different Articles. As concerns what was to become Article 2 and the basic orientation, the Experts (or rather, the majority of them) produced the following:

> 54. After considerable discussion, a group of experts and observers offered the following text as an attempt to meet the objections which had been raised while reflecting the principles included in the concept of self-determination:
>
> *Replace the fourth preambular paragraph of Convention No. 107 with:*
> Considering that the International Covenant on Economic, Social and Cultural Rights affirms the fundamental importance of the right to self-determination, as well as the right of all human beings to pursue their material, cultural and spiritual development in conditions of freedom and dignity;
> Recognising that these rights are fundamental to the survival and future development of indigenous and tribal peoples as distinctive and viable societies;
> *Replace Articles 2 and 5 with*
> *Article 2*
> In co-operation with indigenous and tribal peoples, governments shall have the responsibility for developing co-ordinated and systematic action to ensure:
> (*a*) that indigenous and tribal peoples are able to enjoy the full measure of human rights and fundamental freedoms without hindrance or discrimination;
> (*b*) that indigenous and tribal peoples' territorial rights, economic rights, and political, social, cultural, and religious institutions are recognised and protected;
> (*c*) that indigenous and tribal peoples be accorded the respect of determining for themselves the process of development as it affects their lives and institutions.
>
> 55. This proposal received substantial general support among many experts, who endorsed the ideas contained in it. They felt that, while it was clear that the present Meeting had not been convened to offer specific amendments to the text of the present Convention, the text quoted above reflected many elements of consensus among them. All of the employer experts and some government experts, expressed reservations, however.[14]

---

14   Ibid., p. 109.

ii   *The 1988 Discussion*

In its Law and Practice report, outlining the kinds of changes that might be made, the Office reflected as follows on issues that would find their way into Article 2:

> ORIENTATION OF THE INSTRUMENT: BASIC PRINCIPLES
>
> As noted in the introduction to this chapter and elsewhere in this report, Convention No. 107 has been found by many commentators among academic writers, other international organisations and representatives of indigenous and tribal peoples, in particular, to reflect an integrationist approach which urgently needs to be modified. The first three conclusions adopted by the Meeting of Experts convened to advise the Governing Body on this subject read as follows:
>
> 1. The Convention's integrationist approach is inadequate and no longer reflects current thinking.
> 2. Indigenous and tribal peoples should enjoy as much control as possible over their own economic, social and cultural development.
> 3. The right of these peoples to interact with the national society on an equal footing through their own institutions should be recognised.
>
> In the opinion of the Meeting of Experts, the integrationist approach of the Convention manifested itself in two fundamental ways. In the first place, the 1957 Convention assumed that all government programmes should, for the ultimate benefit of the groups covered by the Convention, be directed toward their integration into national society. Safeguards were provided, as in Article 2, paragraph 4: "Recourse to force or coercion as a means of promoting the integration of these populations into the national community shall be excluded."
>
> This, however, is merely a restriction on the kinds of measures to be used, and does not change the basic orientation of the instrument, best expressed in Article 2, paragraph 1:
>
> "Governments shall have the primary responsibility for developing co-ordinated and systematic action for the protection of the populations concerned *and their progressive integration into the life of their respective countries.*" (emphasis added)
>
> The second aspect of the integrationist approach of the Convention is an inherent assumption of the cultural inferiority of the groups covered by the instrument. This, of course, is the justification of the basic impulse towards integration. An example of this assumption is found in Article 3, paragraph 1, of Convention No. 107:

"So long as the social, economic and cultural conditions of the populations concerned prevent them from enjoying the benefits of the general laws of the country to which they belong, special measures shall be adopted for the protection of the institutions, persons, property and labour of these populations." (emphasis added)

A number of similar references are found in the Convention, implying a lower stage, or degree, of cultural development of the populations covered. This approach can also be characterised as "paternalistic", with benevolent as well as harmful aspects. It is benevolent in its adoption of a protective attitude toward weaker elements of society – which the Meeting of Experts insisted should be maintained, as will be indicated below. It is harmful, however, in the sense that it assumes that governments can and should take measures for the benefit of these groups regardless of their wishes, since they are presumed to be incapable of expressing a valid opinion.[15]

When the Office offered its first suggestions for how Article 2 of C. 107 might be revised, it stated the following, which in large part predicted how the discussion would end up when the new Convention was adopted:

Article 2
Article 2 is the fundamental policy provision of Convention No. 107; it is the Article most frequently criticised for its integrationist approach. In considering the orientation of the revised Convention, and in the light of earlier discussions on the basic principles of respect and consultation, the Meeting of Experts suggested combining Articles 2 and 5 of the Convention into one provision containing these two fundamental policy points (see in particular paragraphs 54 to 60 of the report of the Meeting of Experts). While the experts did not recommend any specific wording, the Office considers the basic idea appropriate for revising the Convention's basic orientation.

In combining the basic principles of respect for these peoples, protection where needed, and effective participation in making decisions on matters which affect them, the basic obligation of governments might be defined as exercising primary responsibility for developing co-ordinated and systematic action, in co-operation with the peoples concerned, to ensure both their protection and their participation in the life of their

---

15 Report VI (1), pp. 27 and 28.

respective countries, with full respect for their social and cultural identity.

This Article might then go on to provide, as does the present Article 2, for the kinds of measures which governments should take. These should, of course, be stated in rather general terms in order to apply to a wide variety of circumstances.

The Office considers that subparagraph (*a*) of paragraph 2 retains its applicability. Paragraph 2 might go on to provide for measures to ensure that the economic and social rights, and the cultural, political, social and religious institutions of these peoples are recognised and protected (see paragraph (*b*) of the draft suggested during the Meeting of Experts, paragraph 54 of its report). It might then provide for measures for raising the standard of living of the peoples concerned (see Article 2, paragraph 2 (*b*), of Convention No. 107), but without implying, as does the present Article 2, that they are in need of social or cultural development.

The basic principle of consultation, contained in a weaker form in Article 5 of Convention No. 107, should be included in the Article that sets forth the basic orientation for governments' actions. Taking into account what has been said above, as well as the discussions of the Meeting of Experts, this Article might provide that governments should, whenever possible, undertake consultations with the peoples concerned, or with their representatives, whenever consideration is being given to measures or programmes which may affect them. It will also appear from what has been said above that such consultations should be carried out in such a way as to provide these peoples with an effective voice in the process of reaching decisions that affect them.

It would, of course, be necessary to retain one of the strongest protections offered in the present Convention, which is found in Article 2, paragraph 4.[16]

The questions put to the constituents were therefore as follows:

> *10. Do you consider that Article 2, paragraph 1, should be amended to provide that governments shall have the primary responsibility for developing co-ordinated and systematic action, in co-operation with the peoples concerned, to ensure both their protection and their participation in the life of their respective countries, with full respect for their social and cultural identity?*

---

16   Ibid., pp. 34 and 35.

> 11. Do you consider that paragraph 2 of Article 2 should be amended as follows:
> (a) subparagraph (a) should remain unchanged;
> (b) subparagraphs (b) and (c) should be replaced by a requirement that the action to be taken should include measures for –
> (i) ensuring that the economic and social rights, and the cultural, political, social and religious institutions of the said peoples are recognised and protected?
> (ii) raising the standard of living of the peoples concerned?
> 12. Do you consider that paragraph 3 of Article 2 should be omitted from the revised instrument?
> 13. Do you consider that paragraph 4 of Article 2 should remain unchanged?[17]

In their comments on the questionnaire, some governments made general observations before addressing specific questions, including on the basic orientation towards integration. Among these comments:

> *Australia.* It is no longer appropriate that the basic thrust of the Convention should be towards integration of indigenous and tribal peoples through government activities. The Preamble to the Convention should be amended to remove integrationist language and to acknowledge the rights of indigenous people to determine freely their own economic, social and cultural future.
> *India.* The Government agrees that presumptions of cultural inferiority should be removed from the Convention when it is revised. It further considers that it is necessary to examine closely the precise connotations of "integrationism/non-integrationism" and of concepts such as "as much control as is possible over economic, social and cultural development", "right to interact with national society", "self-determination", etc. It considers it necessary that the question of revising the basic orientation of the Convention be remitted to the International Labour Conference, which should decide whether or not such a change in orientation is necessary and, if so, define its conceptual foundations, especially with regard to the concepts mentioned above.[18]

The replies to such a complex set of questions were in themselves complex. On Question 10, the Office commented on the replies received as follows:

---

17 Ibid., p. 94.
18 Report VI (2), p. 4.

> As pointed out in Report VI (1), Article 2 is the fundamental policy provision of Convention No. 107, and has been heavily criticised for its integrationist approach. While the vast majority of replies to this question were affirmative, a number of suggestions have been made for rewording this Article.
>
> A number of indigenous organisations have expressed strong concern that the concept of participation may in itself be inadequate to ensure respect for their traditions, lifestyles and resources.[19] In this connection, they have also drawn attention to the formulation put forward during the Meeting of Experts and mentioned by the Government of Australia.
>
> The text proposed during the Meeting of Experts would appear to correspond to many of the proposals made in response to the questionnaire. First, it would replace the emphasis on protection of these peoples, which has been criticised as paternalistic, by the concept of recognition and protection of the fundamental rights established by international instruments since the adoption of Convention No. 107, thus responding to the concerns expressed in a number of replies. It would also provide that the peoples concerned would determine for themselves the process of development, and that it should not be imposed on them from outside. At the same time, it may be felt that certain parts of this proposed amendment (particularly its paragraph 2 (c)) belong more appropriately in another part of the Convention (see below under question 22).
>
> The Proposed Conclusions attempt to take into account the largely positive response to question 10, and the concerns and proposals mentioned above.[20]

As concerns question 11:

> While most replies to this question were affirmative, a number of specific proposals for amendments have been made.
>
> This Article – both in Convention No. 107 and in the proposed revision – covers a wide range of questions and it will prove difficult to reach agreement on its wording, but most of the suggestions made above do not vary greatly in their basic meanings. One point for discussion is whether the emphasis should indeed be on the concept of rights, as is proposed, or on the concept of development. As has been pointed out, Convention No. 107 was adopted before the adoption of the International

---

19 This was later moved to what became Article 7.
20 Ibid., p. 18.

Covenant on Economic, Social and Cultural Rights in 1966. In recent years, declarations adopted by the United Nations and in other forums on development and the right to development have increasingly stressed the notion that meaningful development involves the full realisation of all civil, political, economic, social and cultural rights. (It has in fact been proposed that the Preamble to the revised Convention should make specific reference to the Covenant.)

It should also be borne in mind that the rights to development, and to the benefits accruing from it, are inherent in the ILO's objectives and standards. If a specific reference is made to these rights here, it is to recall their relevance and to ensure that they form a part of national goals in connection with indigenous and tribal peoples.

With regard to the other proposals made, the word "elements" imparts the notion of rights pertaining to groups and thus is worth retaining (Argentina). The point made by the Governments of Australia,[21] Colombia and Mexico on the drafting of clause (*b*)(*ii*) is taken into consideration in the Proposed Conclusions. The United States' suggestion on shared responsibility coincides to a degree with indigenous groups' concern to be able to determine their own process of development, and has also been taken into account.

The questions of treaty rights and legislation granting special privileges are raised here for the first time, and by only one respondent (United States). As concerns treaty rights, the Office considers that additional work needs to be done before proposing concrete provisions on such a complicated and controversial issue, and one which affects very few States.[22] It notes, however, that work in this connection has recently begun in the United Nations. The question of legislation granting special privileges is inherent in the approach taken already in Convention No. 107, to the effect that special measures are called for to protect these specially vulnerable groups and to promote their interests. (See also Article 3 of Convention No. 107, and question 14 below.) In this connection, the Office notes that the replies received from several governments to the effect that the Convention does not apply to them because non-discrimination is provided for in their law, are inconsistent with the intention of the Conference and the comments of the ILO's supervisory bodies

---

21   Australia proposed: 'Add to the end of the suggested wording of paragraph 2 (*b*): "to that enjoyed by other elements of the national community".' Ibid., p. 20.

22   The United States stated that: '... these populations should share the responsibility with the government for raising their standard of living.' Ibid., p. 21.

concerning, inter alia, Conventions on equality of treatment and on indigenous and tribal populations. In the light of these considerations, a saving clause may be sufficient to meet the concerns of the Government of the United States.[23]

On Question 12 it is worthwhile to include here the Office's summary of the replies received as well as its analysis of them:

Replies:
Algeria. Paragraph 3 of Article 2 as presently formulated should be omitted. The notions to which it refers should be proclaimed in the fundamental texts of these countries and for all other populations inhabiting these territories.
Bulgaria. Yes, if the text proposed under question 11 is adopted.
Canada. The paragraph should be replaced by the following provision: "Such action shall aim at fostering respect for and observance of the human rights and fundamental freedoms of persons belonging to such populations". This would provide a more precise reference to the human rights and freedoms of the members of the populations concerned.
Peru. It should be replaced by the following provision: "The principal objective of these programmes should be promotion of ethnic dignity, social utility, and the associative and solidary tendencies of the population".
Sierra Leone. Yes, because it is already implied.
United Kingdom. TUC: No. It might be altered to read: "All such action should take into consideration the fostering of individual dignity".
United States. No. It should be amended to indicate that one objective of such action shall be the fostering of individual dignity, self-esteem and self-sufficiency.
Zambia. Yes. It implies that these peoples are inferior.[24]

Office analysis:
Most replies to this question were affirmative. However, a number of governments and other respondents have proposed that this provision be retained with certain amendments, though some of these points have already been taken into account in earlier Proposed Conclusions. The Office proposes two alternatives: either this paragraph might be reworded, in accordance with the recommendation made at the Meeting of Experts,

---

23 Ibid., pp. 20 and 21.
24 Ibid., pp. 22 and 23.

to read: "Indigenous and tribal peoples shall enjoy the full measure of human rights and fundamental freedoms without hindrance or discrimination", or the paragraph might be deleted altogether in accordance with the views expressed in the majority of replies to this question. The latter course would be better if it is considered that respect for human rights and fundamental freedoms is already sufficiently implied in the other paragraphs of Article 2, as reworded.

The discussion of the replies to question 13 was very brief:

While most replies to this question were affirmative, there were a number of suggestions for partial rewording which are almost all consistent with each other. In view of these suggestions, a partial rewording is suggested in the Proposed Conclusions.[25]

The proposed conclusions for this Article were presented as follows (with words and phrases that would differ from the text of Convention No. 107 in italics). Even though the quantum of change in terms of redrafting was not great, these amendments would effect a complete turnaround in the tone of the new instrument:

5. Governments should have the responsibility, *in co-operation with the peoples concerned,* for developing co-ordinated and systematic action for the protection of *these peoples and the promotion of their rights.*
6. Such action should include measures for:

(*a*) enabling the said *peoples* to benefit on an equal footing from the rights and opportunities which national laws or regulations grant to other *members* of the population
(*b*) *promoting the full realisation of the social, economic and cultural rights of these peoples, with respect for their social and cultural identity and institutions*;
(*c*) *raising the standard of living of the peoples concerned to that enjoyed by other members of the national community.*[26]

In the 1988 Session of the Conference, there was general but not unanimous approval of the decision to revise the Convention and of the direction of the proposed changes, and those who were reticent spoke very little except to

---

25   Ibid., p. 24.
26   Ibid., p. 106.

challenge the extent of the changes from time to time. In the general discussion in the Committee, however, there was one brave employers' representative (not named in the report) who stated:

> In questioning the reasons behind the decision to revise Convention No. 107, he felt that the existing text adequately respected the culture and customs of indigenous and tribal populations and that it upheld a policy of spontaneous, rather than compulsory integration. As for paternalism, he observed that it existed in all countries and that its desirability should be carefully examined before being condemned. He further observed that because of the difference between indigenous and tribal populations in developed and developing countries, it would be very difficult to treat them in a single instrument. For these reasons, he was opposed to the revision of Convention No. 107.[27]

He was not heard from again in the same terms, though there were some Government members who expressed themselves in broadly similar terms:

> The Government member of India expressed reservations on a number of the conclusions of the report of the Meeting of Experts which, in his view, did not represent any degree of consensus. For this reason, his Government considered that the draft amendments to some of the Articles of Convention No. 107 were invalid. The Government member of France supported the view expressed by an Employers' member that the proposed revision of Convention No. 107 should not go beyond the competence of the ILO. He felt that the partial revision should focus on working conditions and social security, leaving standards setting on other issues to the United Nations. The Government member of the Netherlands agreed that the Committee should deal with matters within its competence.[28]

As the discussion of point 5 got under way it became evident that not all the delegates were fully in accord on the direction the revised instrument would be going:

> 48. The Workers' members introduced a two-part amendment which they considered better reflected the new approach to be embodied in the revised Convention. First they proposed that the words "in co-operation with" be replaced by "with the full participation and consent of". The

---

27 Proceedings 1988, p. 32/2.
28 Ibid., pp. 32/2 and 33/3.

second proposal was to replace the words "for the protection of these peoples and the promotion of their rights" by the words "to guarantee respect for the integrity of these peoples and their rights". They considered that the amendment better reflected the aspirations of indigenous peoples. Concerning the first part of the amendment, the Employers' members and the Government members of Brazil, India and New Zealand considered that the original text was appropriate and opposed the amendment. The Government member of Argentina supported the expression "with the full participation", but opposed "with the full consent". The Government member of Venezuela stated that since the amendment was contrary to the Venezuelan Constitution, he opposed it. The Government member of the USSR supported it. The Workers' members suggested that the word "consent" be deleted from the amendment. This subamendment received broad support and the first part of the amendment as subamended was adopted by consensus. The Workers' members introduced the second part of the amendment and stated that the term "protection" had patronising overtones. They recognised the principle, however, and considered that it should be retained in the amended text. Several Government members supported this part of the amendment. The Employers' members did not consider that the term "protection" was derogatory and opposed the amendment, as did the Government members of Canada and the United States. The Government member of India added that less developed tribal populations were in considerable need of protection and that he also opposed the second part of the amendment. The second part of the amendment was adopted by 9,690 votes in favour, 8,330 votes against, with 1,020 abstentions.

49. In the light of this decision, an amendment to replace the word "co-operation" by the word "partnership" submitted by the Government member of New Zealand, was withdrawn.

50. The Employers' members introduced an amendment which that [sic] it made it clear that the rights invoked would be legally recognised. In reply to a question by the Government member of Venezuela, the Employers' members indicated that their amendment would not refer to laws adopted by indigenous institutions, but to those adopted by national governments. Several Government members and the Workers' members considered that the amendment would make this provision too restrictive. The Employers' members withdrew the amendment.

51. Point 5, as amended, was adopted.[29]

---

29   Ibid., pp. 32/7 and 32/8.

The point as amended therefore read:

> 5. Governments should have the responsibility for developing, with the full participation of the (peoples/populations) concerned, co-ordinated and systematic action to guarantee respect for the integrity of these (peoples/populations) and their rights.[30]

The amendments made left the principal responsibility for developing action to the governments, which did not constitute a change. They also changed the reference to 'full participation' to 'in cooperation with'. What would become Article 7 would require participation, so this emphasis was not lost, only moved; it added a requirement for cooperation, which in some ways is a stronger term than participation because it imposes a duty more active than simply allowing participation. The concept of consent could not be maintained, and was withdrawn. The most important change was to require respect for the integrity of these peoples – i.e., for their continued existence – in place of protection. This point had, in fact, been considerably strengthened.

The discussion of point 6 was more complicated. The first set of amendments raised the complicated question of collective and individual rights.

> 52. The Government member of the United States introduced an amendment to Points 6(a) and 6(b) to add references to individual members of these peoples. The Employers' members supported this view. The Government member of Australia submitted an amendment to Point 6(a) and 6(c) to use the term "members of the peoples". This amendment was supported by the Government members of France and the United States, who accepted it as a subamendment to the United States proposal, and by the Employers' members. The Workers' members recalled that Convention No. 107 did not contain any references to individual persons and suggested that the amendment be subamended to read "the said peoples and their members" instead of "the said peoples". The Government member of Australia explained that support for collective rights was still contained in his amendment, as well as rights which were accorded to members of populations. The Government member of the United States supported this position and withdrew the amendment to Point 6(b). The amendments to Point 6(a) were adopted, as amended, by consensus.[31]

---

30   Ibid., p. 32/34.
31   Ibid., p. 32/8.

Thus, while adding references to individual members of these peoples, which had not been included in Convention No. 107, these amendments ensured that Convention No. 169 would become one of the rare international conventions upholding collective rights.

As concerns point 6(b):

> 53. Five amendments to Point 6(b) had been submitted. The Workers' members tabled an amendment proposing the replacement of "promoting" by "ensuring", and the insertion of "custom and traditions" after "cultural identity" and "their" before "institutions". The Workers' members explained that the purpose of the amendment was to strengthen the Office text. A number of Government members, supported by the Employers' members, opposed part of the Workers' members' amendment, which called for the use of the word "ensuring" rather than the word "promoting". The Government member of Norway pointed out that the amendment would not be in accordance with other ILO Conventions. In the light of this view, the Workers' members withdrew it.
>
> 54. The Government member of Canada also introduced an amendment to include a reference to customs and traditions, explaining that this amendment had been specifically requested by Canadian indigenous groups. The Government member of New Zealand, who had submitted an amendment intended to insert the concept of spiritual well-being, noted that it was covered by both of the previous amendments and withdrew it. An amendment proposed by the Government member of the USSR, which proposed the inclusion of a provision for the protection of indigenous populations' way of life at the end of Point 6(b), was withdrawn in view of its similarity to the one which was being discussed. The Employers' members considered that the amendment was unnecessary in view of the fact that the original wording encompassed traditional considerations. Several Government members supported the amendment, which was adopted by consensus.[32]

Point 6(b) was therefore adopted with the following slightly amended text:

> promoting the full realisation of the social, economic and cultural rights of these (peoples/populations), with respect for their social and cultural identity, their customs and traditions, and their institutions;[33]

---

[32] Ibid.
[33] Ibid., p. 32/34.

The discussion of point 6(c) read as follows:

> 55. An amendment to Point 6(c) was introduced by the Government member of the United States, calling for its replacement by the words "assisting the members of the peoples concerned to raise their standard of living to that enjoyed by other members of the national community". The Workers' members agreed with the principle that people should have a higher standard of living but considered that indigenous peoples should decide the issue for themselves. They submitted an amendment to replace the text of Point 6(c) by "ensuring an adequate standard of living of the peoples concerned and a process of development compatible with their aspirations and way of life". The Employers' members said that the amendment submitted by the Government member of United States was more appropriate and supported it. The Workers' members proposed a subamendment to the amendment submitted by the Government member of the United States to include references to those peoples' aspirations and ways of life, and withdrew their amendment. The Government member of the United States and the Employers' members supported the subamendment. Point 6(c) as amended was adopted by consensus, with reservations expressed by the Government member of Venezuela.[34]

The amended text of point 6(c) was therefore:

> assisting the members of the (peoples/populations) concerned to raise their standard of living to that enjoyed by other members of the national community, in a manner compatible with the aspirations and ways of life of these (peoples/populations).[35]

An attempt to add another paragraph was not successful:

> 56. The Government members of Canada and the United States each proposed amendments calling for a new Point 6(d) which would address the encouragement of self-reliance and self-esteem. The Government of Canada supported the amendment of the Government member of the United States and withdrew her amendment. The Workers' members considered that the proposed new Point was paternalistic and superfluous in view of the agreement already reached on Point 6(a). The

---

34 Ibid., p. 32/8.
35 Ibid., p. 32/34.

ARTICLE 2 NO. 169 – BASIC POLICY AND ORIENTATION 133

Employers' members supported the amendment and stressed the importance of fostering individual dignity. They felt that for clarity, economic self-sufficiency should be included and proposed a subamendment to this effect. The Workers' members proposed subamendments which they considered would better protect individual rights. After further discussion, the Government member of the United States withdrew the amendment. The subamendments were subsequently also withdrawn.[36]

iii   *The 1989 Discussion*

When the Office issued the first report for the second discussion and circulated the draft Convention for comments, draft Article 2 read as follows:

Article 2

1. Governments shall have the responsibility for developing, with the full participation of the (peoples/populations) concerned, co-ordinated and systematic action to guarantee respect for the integrity of these (peoples/populations) and their rights.
2. Such action shall include measures for:
   (a) enabling members of these (peoples/populations) to benefit on an equal footing from the rights and opportunities which national laws and regulations grant to other members of the population;
   (*b*) promoting the full realisation of the social, economic and cultural rights of these (peoples/populations) with respect for their social and cultural identity, their customs and traditions and their institutions;
   (*c*) assisting the members of the (peoples/populations) concerned to raise their standard of living to that enjoyed by other members of the national community, in a manner compatible with the aspirations and ways of life of these (peoples/populations).[37]

The Office commentary on the replies received concerning draft Article 2 was the following:

The suggestion by the Government of Argentina to delete "members of the" would contradict a decision by the Conference in the first discussion, where these words were added with reference to the recognition of communal rights in paragraph 2 (*c*).

---

36   Ibid., p. 32/8.
37   Report IV (1), pp. 6 and 7.

The proposal of the Government of India would also contradict language adopted by the Conference, which decided to remove the original reference to protection on the grounds that it was patronising. In this respect, the Office considers that the Government has made an important point, and that a requirement to protect vulnerable population groups is in no way patronising.

On the other hand, the approach taken in the remainder of this Article would appear to be consistent with the Government's concern, if it is understood that all measures adopted under the revised Convention would be based on the assumption that respect for the integrity, rights, customs and other aspects of the ways of life of these peoples is in no way contradictory to their playing an active and constructive role in the life of the nation. A balance between protective action and measures to allow and encourage participation must therefore be sought. The proposal by the Government of Colombia on 2 (*b*) appears already to be implied in the existing wording. On 2 (*c*), the existing wording appears more suited to the sense of the provision.

The proposal by the Government of Japan[38] would remove any obligatory force whatsoever. Sufficient flexibility is provided for in Article 33 (Article 34 in the new text) to take account of the diversity of national situations. The point made by Brazil (CONTAG) appears to be covered by the final phrase of the sentence. The reference is to levels of living standards rather than to identical standards.

The point raised by the Government of the United States was clarified during the first discussion (see paragraph 47 of the Committee's report). In view of the above considerations, the proposal by the Government of Canada on paragraph 1 would meet most of the points raised. It would, however, omit the very important addition introduced at the first discussion of respect for the identity of these peoples, which would not appear to be a "vague objective" if understood to mean respect for their ability to retain their own identity consistent with the principles developed more fully in paragraph 2. This reference has therefore been retained.[39]

The proposed text that went to the Conference for the second discussion thus included some modifications in paragraph 1 and paragraph 2(c) from the version circulated for comments, though none appear to have changed the meaning of these provisions:

---

38 Japan proposed that 'the words "in a manner and to an extent depending on the situation of the country and of the (peoples/populations) concerned" should be added at the beginning of paragraph 1.' Report IV (2A), p. 15.

39 Ibid.

Article 2

1. Governments shall have the responsibility for developing, with the participation of the peoples concerned, co-ordinated and systematic action to protect the rights of these peoples and to guarantee respect for their integrity.

2. Such action shall include measures for:

(*a*) enabling members of these peoples to benefit on an equal footing from the rights and opportunities which national laws and regulations grant to other members of the population ;

(*b*) promoting the full realisation of the social, economic and cultural rights of these peoples with respect for their social and cultural identity, their customs and traditions and their institutions;

(*c*) assisting the members of the peoples concerned to raise their standard of living to that enjoyed by other members of the national community, in a manner compatible with their aspirations and ways of life.[40]

In the second discussion in the Conference in 1989, the basic principle that the revision had been intended to secure had been accepted. As the Committee's report stated in the part on the general discussion:

There was widespread support, also expressed during the first discussion, for the need to change the emphasis of the Convention from integration of indigenous and tribal peoples to respect for their cultures, traditions and unique circumstances. Several Government members referred to recent enactments of legislation on this subject in their countries and noted that their legislation went beyond the provisions contained in the proposed Convention.[41]

This basic orientation was never questioned again, and the discussion concerned finer points of wording, and was brief:

46. The Committee had six amendments before it. First, the Government member of Colombia introduced an amendment with the triple purpose of harmonizing the text of paragraph 1 of the Article in the three languages, of adding a requirement that the participation of indigenous peoples be "direct and authentic", and of substituting the word "safeguard" for "protect", which he felt was paternalistic. The Workers' members supported the amendment since it would strengthen the involvement of

---

40   Report IV (2B), pp. 6 and 8.
41   Proceedings 1989, p. 25/2.

these peoples and would assist them to safeguard their rights. This view was shared by the Government members of Ecuador and Nicaragua. The Employers' members preferred the Office text which offered adequate protection and avoided paternalism; they did not support the substantive part of the amendment. Several Government members expressed similar views. The Government member of Peru wished to subamend the Office text by adding the word "safeguarding", but the Government member of India questioned whether this proposal would add anything to the provisions already in the text. The proposed drafting changes were referred to the Drafting Committee and the rest of the amendment was not adopted. A second amendment to strengthen the text of paragraph 2(a) by replacing "enabling" with "ensuring that" was proposed by the Government member of Colombia. The amendment was supported by the Workers' members and by the Government members of Ecuador and Brazil and was adopted by consensus. An amendment proposed by the Government member of the USSR was not seconded. An amendment to paragraph 2(c), which would require governments to devise measures to eliminate social and economic gaps between indigenous and tribal peoples and other members of the community, was proposed by the Government member of New Zealand. The Workers' members supported the amendment and proposed a subamendment to restore the phrase "assisting the members of the peoples concerned". The Employers' members and several Government members supported the amendment as subamended and it was adopted. As a result, an amendment on the same subject proposed by the Government member of Colombia was not considered.

47. The Government member of Ecuador proposed an amendment to add a new paragraph 2(d) which would require measures to guarantee the territorial integrity of indigenous and tribal peoples. The Workers' members supported the amendment which recognised the strong ties between cultures and territories. On a suggestion of the Employers' members, supported by several Government members, it was decided to consider this amendment during discussion of Part II of the proposed Convention.

48. Article 2, as amended, was adopted.[42]

Article 2 was thus adopted in the following form:

Article 2

1. Governments shall have the responsibility for developing, with the participation of the peoples concerned, co-ordinated and systematic

---

42   Ibid., pp. 25/8 and 25/9.

action to protect the rights of these peoples and to guarantee respect for their integrity.
2. Such action shall include measures for:
(a) ensuring that members of these peoples benefit on an equal footing from the rights and opportunities which national laws and regulations grant to other members of the population;
(b) promoting the full realisation of the social, economic and cultural rights of these peoples with respect for their social and cultural identity, their customs and traditions and their institutions;
(c) assisting the members of the peoples concerned to eliminate socio-economic gaps that may exist between indigenous and other members of the national community, in a manner compatible with their aspirations and ways of life.
2. Such action shall include measures for:
(a) enabling members of these peoples to benefit on an equal footing from the rights and opportunities which national laws and regulations grant to other members of the population ;
(c) assisting the members of the peoples concerned to raise their standard of living to that enjoyed by other members of the national community, in a manner compatible with their aspirations and ways of life.[43]

C Development through Supervision

The impact of the supervision of Article 2 by the Committee of Experts has been focussed on administration, and not on the basic principles that were the focus of revising this provision, because it appears that governments have accepted the basic principle when ratifying the Convention. The focus of the Committee's questions and recommendations has been on Article 2(1), and specifically on the requirement for coordinated and systematic action.

The supervision of this Article has had a significant impact in focussing the attention of governments and of indigenous and tribal peoples on the need to have coordinated and systematic action in this area, and it is possible to see the development of these arrangements reflected in the Committee's comments.

In addition, the direct requests and observations of the Committee of Experts have become an excellent source for learning the administrative arrangements governments have made, with the more or less effective

---

[43] Ibid., pp. 25/26.

participation of representatives of indigenous and tribal peoples, for 'indigenous affairs', as it is called in many countries.

The following are representative of the majority of comments the Committee of Experts has made on this Article, and do not attempt to chronicle all the Committee's many comments under Article 2. Note that a number of the comments below reflect the fact that representatives of indigenous and tribal peoples are participating in these arrangements, as provided in Article 2, or that the Committee asks when and how this is to be arranged:

> *Norway, direct request 1993:*
> Article 2. The Committee notes the establishment of the Sami Development Fund (SDF) to promote the economic, social and cultural rights of the Sami. The Committee would appreciate further information regarding the structure and programme of action of the SDF, and the number of Sami who benefit from these projects.
>
> *Mexico, direct request 1993:*
> Article 2. Noting the detailed information communicated on the involvement of indigenous communities in decision-making and in consultations, the Committee would be grateful for information on the effect given to the proposal to include indigenous representatives on the Executive Committee of the National Indian Institute (INI).
>
> *Colombia, direct request 1994:*
> Article 2. The Committee recalls that due to the ratification of the Convention and the adaptation of legal and administrative provisions to a pluri-cultural framework in accordance with the provisions of the revised Constitution of 1991, the various state entities active in indigenous affairs are undergoing a transitional period, including among others the Department of Indigenous Affairs (DAI), the Colombian Institute for Agrarian Reform (INCORA) and the National Recovery Plan (NPR). It also recalls its previous comments under Convention No. 107 and in the observation made under the present Convention this year, that this has resulted in a reduced focus on the specific characteristics of indigenous communities; for instance, with the creation in 1991 of the National Agrarian Fund (FINAGRO) as the central agency responsible for agrarian development financing, special credit facilities for indigenous communities have been withdrawn. The Committee draws the Government's attention to its previous request under Convention No. 107 for further information on the mechanisms for inter-institutional coordination and collaboration, and any measures taken or envisaged to provide direct

development assistance specially adapted to the needs of indigenous communities.

The comments often track changes in the administrative arrangements as they occur:

Colombia, direct request, 1995
Article 2. The Committee notes the explanation of the Government regarding the adaptation of juridical and institutional provisions to the pluri-cultural framework of the new Constitution. It notes in this respect that the Department of Indigenous Affairs (DAI) has become the Directorate General of Indigenous Affairs attached to the Ministry of Government and that other organizational changes have taken place. It understands from these explanations that although institutions have changed, the focus of various programmes on the specific characteristics of indigenous communities is still in place. The Committee again requests information on the mechanisms for coordination among different institutions.

Another, more substantial example of this is found in the following comment, which like a number of other comments to countries that had already ratified Convention No. 107, refers to information previously communicated or requested in supervising that Convention:

Peru, direct request 1997:
3. Article 2. The Committee requests the Government to provide additional information on specific programmes for indigenous communities and their participation in the formulation of such programmes.
4. The Committee notes that the Peruvian Indigenous Institute (IIP) was described by the Government in its first report as the central organization for the coordination of government action in relation to indigenous peoples in the country. The Committee notes that the Institute has been abolished since the sending of the report and its staff is now part of an "indigenous unit" in the Ministry for the Promotion of Women and Human Development and it requests the Government to indicate whether the indigenous unit has assumed all the functions of the IIP and, if not, to specify the government body which is currently responsible for developing "coordinated and systematic action", as required by Article 2.

5. With regard to the Act respecting private investment in the development of economic activities on the lands of the national territory and of rural and native communities, which was enacted after the ratification of the Convention, the Committee requests the Government to inform it whether the peoples concerned participated in its formulation, as provided for by Article 2. Furthermore, the Committee would be grateful to be provided with information on the activities currently undertaken by the National Institute for Rural Development (INDEC). Moreover, in the context of a direct request in 1992 on Convention No. 107, the Committee recalled that the Government had proposed to undertake a study on the possibility of adopting measures to improve the situation of indigenous peoples living on marginal cultivable land in urban areas. Since no new information is provided in the current report on this study, the Committee requests the Government to provide information on any new measure which has been taken in this respect.

The comments on Article 2 are often paired with those on Article 33, which also applies to integrated management.[44] They may highlight problems in coordinated management of indigenous affairs, including by non-governmental entities such as the churches:

Paraguay, Direct Request 1998
4. Articles 2 and 33. The Committee notes that the Paraguayan Indigenous Institute (INDI) has created a directorate for projects and development with which it hopes to implement a development planning policy for indigenous communities on the basis of proposals stemming from the communities. The Government lists a number of projects which are

---

44 Article 33, the adoption of which will be examined in the second volume of this publication, provides:
Article 33
1. The governmental authority responsible for the matters covered in this Convention shall ensure that agencies or other appropriate mechanisms exist to administer the programmes affecting the peoples concerned, and shall ensure that they have the means necessary for the proper fulfilment of the functions assigned to them.
2. These programmes shall include:
   (a) the planning, co-ordination, execution and evaluation, in co-operation with the peoples concerned, of the measures provided for in this Convention;
   (b) the proposing of legislative and other measures to the competent authorities and supervision of the application of the measures taken, in co-operation with the peoples concerned.

being carried out by the INDI which is conducting consultations with the indigenous communities likely to be affected. The Committee requests the Government to keep it informed on the consultation procedure being carried out with the indigenous communities and how their opinions are being taken into account where they are contrary to a development project likely to affect them.

5. The Committee hopes that the Government will communicate the INDI reports for 1990, 1991 and 1992, and the most recent reports which have been published.

6. The Committee noted that private entities provided reports on their activities in indigenous communities to the INDI (Council resolution No. 36/89) and that their collaboration and cooperation with the INDI is secured. However, it also notes indications that the relationship between the INDI and the religious missions has not been free of conflict. The Committee requested more information on the mechanisms for interinstitutional collaboration and cooperation among the various governmental, non-governmental and religious entities active in indigenous affairs, including how the INDI has acted on the reports provided to it.

The concerns raised here were followed up as the situation developed, as the Committee often does:

Paraguay, direct request 2003
3. *Articles 2 and 33.* Noting that the executive authority has submitted to the Legislature a Bill envisaging the replacement of the INDI, the Committee refers to its comments in its observation with regard to the application of *Article 6* of the Convention prior to the adoption of any legislative or administrative measures which may directly affect the peoples concerned. It also recalls that, in accordance with *Articles 2 and 33* of the Convention, governments have the responsibility for developing, with the participation of the peoples concerned, coordinated and systematic action to protect the rights of these peoples and, to this effect, have to ensure the existence of agencies or other appropriate mechanisms. In this respect, the Committee notes that, according to the communication made by the National Federation of Workers (CNT), received in August 2001, the new entity which would replace INDI would have fewer powers than those currently entrusted to the INDI. Furthermore, according to this Bill, certain of the INDI's current powers would be decentralized and entrusted to non-specialized institutions. For example, the legal personality of indigenous communities is currently

administered by the INDI while, under the above Bill, their legal personality would be the responsibility of the governments. The current areas of competence of the INDI with regard to access to land would be similarly affected. These changes would appear to weaken the INDI and would significantly reduce the possibilities for the Government to develop a coordinated and systematic policy within the meaning of *Article 2* of the Convention. The Committee hopes that, in addition to consulting the peoples concerned prior to the adoption of legislative or administrative measures which may involve the replacement of the INDI, the Government will ensure that such modifications are compatible with *Articles 2 and 33* of the Convention, and it requests the Government to provide information in its next report on developments on this situation.

On occasion, the Committee has examined far-reaching arrangements under this Article:

Peru, direct request, 1999
3. Article 2. The Committee requests the Government to provide additional information on specific programmes for indigenous communities and their participation in the formulation of such programmes.
4. The Committee notes that the Peruvian Indigenous Institute (IIP) was described by the Government in its first report as the central organization for the coordination of government action in relation to indigenous peoples in the country. The Committee notes that the Institute has been abolished since the sending of the report and its staff is now part of an "indigenous unit" in the Ministry for the Promotion of Women and Human Development and it requests the Government to indicate whether the indigenous unit has assumed all the functions of the IIP and, if not, to specify the government body which is currently responsible for developing "coordinated and systematic action", as required by Article 2.
5. With regard to the Act respecting private investment in the development of economic activities on the lands of the national territory and of rural and native communities, which was enacted after the ratification of the Convention, the Committee requests the Government to inform it whether the peoples concerned participated in its formulation, as provided for by Article 2. Furthermore, the Committee would be grateful to be provided with information on the activities currently undertaken by the National Institute for Rural Development (INDEC). Moreover, in the context of a direct request in 1992 on Convention No. 107, the Committee

recalled that the Government had proposed to undertake a study on the possibility of adopting measures to improve the situation of indigenous peoples living on marginal cultivable land in urban areas. Since no new information is provided in the current report on this study, the Committee requests the Government to provide information on any new measure which has been taken in this respect.

Mexico, direct request 2001

4. The Committee notes the various legislative initiatives adopted during the period covered by the report, particularly the constitutional reforms on indigenous questions, published in the Official Bulletin of the Federation on 14 August 2001. An initial analysis of these reforms indicates that they cover a large part of the subjects covered by the Convention. Nevertheless, the Committee is aware that these reforms have generated a great deal of controversy and that some sections of Mexican society, including indigenous and workers' organizations, have expressed concern that these reforms will have a negative impact on the social, economic and legal situation of the indigenous peoples of Mexico.

5. The Committee is examining the constitutional reforms in a more detailed way in a request being sent directly to the Government, which raises the following questions.

...

Administration: How development of "coordinated and systematic action" for the protection of the integrity of the indigenous peoples of the country is assured (*Article 2*), in the light of the devolution to the constituent states of the power to legislate on a certain number of questions.

The Committee also sometimes asks quite pointed questions under this Article about whether the structures created to coordinate indigenous affairs are actually functioning:

Honduras, direct request, 1999:

3. Article 2. The Committee notes with interest the information contained in the Government's report on measures taken to implement the provisions of this Article, including the establishment of a bilateral commission composed of members of the Government and ethnic groups and the Accords of 19 April 1996 and 11 October 1996. The Accord of 19 April 1996 sets forth the Government's undertaking to carry out previous commitments it made in July 1994 and July 1995. Specific reference is made in this Accord to, among other things, work to be undertaken by the Inter-institutional Commission, composed of a number of governmental

agencies. Reference is also made to a transportation project and certain programmes intended to benefit the Chorti tribes. The report does not indicate how the 1994–95 undertakings, carried forward into the Accord of 19 April 1996, have been applied. The 11 October 1996 Accord supplied by the Government also refers to a number of commitments, including a programme which was initiated on 16 October 1996 entailing the granting of land to Garifuna communities and a National Agrarian Institute (INA) programme to provide agrarian technical assistance to indigenous communities.

4. The Committee requests the Government to provide, in its next report, copies of all Accords it has entered into with or on behalf of Honduran indigenous and tribal peoples and their representative organizations since the date the Convention entered into force, and to indicate the current status of the commitments undertaken in those Accords. The Government is further requested to provide information on the status of any activities undertaken by the Government-Ethnic Groups Commission relevant to the Convention, particularly the status of the draft law implementing the Convention. Finally, the Committee would be grateful if the Government would provide practical examples of the manner in which the peoples concerned have participated in the development of the measures referred to in the Government's report and attached Accords.

5. The Committee notes that article 173 of the Honduran Constitution provides that "the State shall preserve and stimulate the native cultures, as well as all authentic expressions of national folklore, popular art and handicrafts". Please indicate the manner in which article 173 is implemented and enforced in practice, and provide practical examples of the application of this article.

6. With regard to Article 2(2)(c), the Government states that there are no socio-economic gaps or gaps of any other nature between the indigenous and tribal peoples of Honduras and the national citizenry. The Committee requests the Government to indicate the basis for its statements in this regard, and to state whether any studies have been done comparing the socio-economic status and/or income levels of indigenous peoples with the national average in Honduras.

Guatemala, direct request 2001:

3. *Article 2.* The Committee notes the information provided by the Government on the work undertaken for the implementation of the Peace Agreements, which has resulted in the creation of a number of

joint committees, two special commissions and one on the recognition of indigenous languages and sacred places. It also notes that the indigenous peoples themselves have organized eight national permanent commissions on questions including women, indigenous law and constitutional reform for which there are corresponding mechanisms for dialogue with the Government. The Committee notes, however, that the MINUGUA report[45] referred to in the observation indicates in paragraph 88 that, while the joint committees are important mechanisms for discussion and consultation, they also have encountered problems including: (1) the representative nature of the indigenous side has been questioned as the broad and dispersed indigenous movement evolves; (2) the Government's representatives have not always had the power to take decisions; and (3) there have been budgetary limitations on their functioning, and for disseminating and consulting on their proposals. Recalling that these are important mechanisms for the implementation of the Convention and for consolidating the Peace Agreements, the Committee hopes the Government will do everything possible to improve their functioning and that it will keep the Committee informed of their progress in future reports.

On occasion, questions raised under the Article reflect serious conflicts among parts of the national population:

Direct request, Fiji, 2013:
Article 2 of the Convention. Action to protect the rights of indigenous peoples. The Committee notes that the Fijian Affairs (Amendment) Decree 2010, No. 31 of 2010, amended all written laws and state documents by deleting the word "Fijian" wherever it appears and wherever it refers to indigenous Fijians, and replaced it with the term "iTaukei". It notes that the term "iTaukei" has also been used to refer to the indigenous peoples in the Constitution adopted in September 2013. The Committee notes from the FICTU observations[46] that this change was done against the

---

45   MINUGUA was the United Nations Verification Mission in Guatemala (MINUGUA), established by the General Assembly in 1997 to verify compliance with the Peace Agreements.

46   This comment was based in large part on trade union comments made under article 23 of the ILO Constitution. The same direct request began with the following: 'The Committee notes the information provided by the Government in its report received in June 2013. It also notes the detailed observations and concerns raised by the Fiji Islands Council of

general wish of the indigenous peoples. The Government indicates that the iTaukei Land Trust Board (TLTB), formerly known as the Native Land Trust Board (NLTB), has adopted a Strategic Corporate Plan (SCP) since 2009, which continues with the plan for 2013–15. Priority strategic measures are identified, including those that are to meet the growing expectations of the indigenous landowners' communities throughout 14 Provinces under the iTaukei Administration System. The SCP is closely aligned to the Government's vision, mission and goals in the People's Charter for Change, Peace and Progress introduced in 2007. It is also linked to the Government's annual budgetary measures, especially on capital and infrastructure developments. Furthermore, the Government indicates that programmes are in place but their effects, impact and implications need to be assessed and evaluated. Trust income for landowners has increased over the years and, in 2012, $51 million was collected and $49 million was distributed. The Government reports that a survey will need to be undertaken to assess the use and the impact of these funds in the communities in relation to the development status, education, welfare and the enhancement of living standards. The TLTB has therefore identified that there is a need for financial literacy programmes and awareness and education programmes for the iTaukei. The Government indicates that all the stakeholders need to coordinate and work collaboratively together to reach out to the targeted/marginalized groups in rural communities and villages. *Keeping in mind the concerns raised by the fictu, the Committee once again requests the Government to indicate in its next report how the adoption of a new Constitution in September 2013 will facilitate the development, with the participation of and in consultation with the indigenous peoples, of actions to protect the rights of these peoples and to guarantee respect for their integrity. It also invites the Government to provide information on the impact of the programmes adopted by the TLTB, including copies of its annual reports. Please indicate how the indigenous peoples have been associated in the development of these programmes.*

Trade Unions (FICTU), dated 24 September 2013, on the application of the Convention in Fiji. The observations submitted are supported by various indigenous individuals, institutions and groups in Fiji, and several other groups. The FICTU describes policies that were implemented and laws that were adopted without proper consultation of indigenous peoples, such as a legislative amendment to remove and terminate the existence of the Great Council of Chiefs.'

In sum, the supervision of Article 2 has not so much developed the understanding of the meaning of this provision, as it has made use of it to gather (and make widely available) information on how it is implemented, and pushed governments to adopt meaningful and coordinated action to ensure that the Convention is properly applied.

CHAPTER 4

Article 6 – Consultation

The principles of consultation and participation that are based in Articles 6 and 7 of Convention No. 169 are the operationalization of the principle that indigenous and tribal peoples should be accorded greater respect and that their identities should be recognized.

These Articles are of general application throughout the Convention, but in a number of other Articles expressions such as 'with the participation of' or 'in consultation with' indigenous and tribal peoples remind the user that these principles are of particular importance.

Article 6 of Convention No. 169 provides:

> 1. In applying the provisions of this Convention, governments shall:
> (a) consult the peoples concerned, through appropriate procedures and in particular through their representative institutions, whenever consideration is being given to legislative or administrative measures which may affect them directly;
> (b) establish means by which these peoples can freely participate, to at least the same extent as other sectors of the population, at all levels of decision-making in elective institutions and administrative and other bodies responsible for policies and programmes which concern them;
> (c) establish means for the full development of these peoples' own institutions and initiatives, and in appropriate cases provide the resources necessary for this purpose.
> 2. The consultations carried out in application of this Convention shall be undertaken, in good faith and in a form appropriate to the circumstances, with the objective of achieving agreement or consent to the proposed measures.

Article 6 of Convention No. 169 is in many ways the core of the Convention, and is closely connected to Article 2 as the reason that Convention No. 107 was revised. There were related provisions in the Indigenous and Tribal Populations Convention, 1957 (No. 107).

A. Convention No. 107

Convention No. 107 was based on the concept of integration of indigenous and tribal populations into the national society. As indicated above, this concept was concentrated in Article 2 of that Convention. However, the approach of making these populations the objects of government efforts rather than participants in them was reinforced in Article 5 of the Convention, which was the closest this instrument came to the later concept of consultation:

> *Article 5*
> In applying the provisions of this Convention relating to the protection and integration of the populations concerned, governments shall –
> (*a*) seek the collaboration of these populations and of their representatives;
> (*b*) provide these populations with opportunities for the full development of their initiative;
> (*c*) stimulate by all possible means the development among these populations of civil liberties and the establishment of or participation in elective institutions.

Thus under C. 107 governments were to seek the collaboration of these populations in implementing government plans, without prior discussion of what measures should be put in place.

This concept was touched upon only indirectly in the Office's 1956 'Law and Practice' report that launched the consideration of Convention No. 107. The conclusions of the Office's examination of the measures that needed to be taken brought this up in connection with the need to 'raise the social and economic standards' of indigenous communities seen as lagging behind. As the conclusions of the Office's examination stated it, in a passage that is emblematic of the cultural arrogance that underlaid so much of the discussion at that time:

> 15. One of the key factors in any programme to raise the social and economic standards of non-integrated indigenous peoples is the process of cultural adaptation of these peoples to the ethical, legal and labour standards of modern society. It is generally admitted that if this process is to be successful, legislation and administrative methods should be adapted temporarily in one way or another to the actual conditions in which indigenous communities live in order to guarantee respect for their basic rights and to make a fair assessment of their responsibilities towards the national community. It is also admitted that in the enforcement of the law allowance should be made not only for the cultural differences

between indigenous and non-indigenous peoples but also for the degree of integration reached by the indigenous group or tribe concerned.

In some countries the idea has been gaining ground that so long as indigenous peoples continue to live in a state of tribal isolation allowance must be made, in defining their rights, for their own customary norms of behaviour; it is not enough to fit the penalties to the level of cultural development of the offenders and to strive to understand the cultural reasons that lead them to commit their offences or crimes: it is also important to respect and use the customary means by which social discipline is maintained within the tribes, provided that the interests of the nation as a whole are not thereby affected.

Co-operation with tribal leaders can be a decisive factor in the introduction of new forms of life and work into indigenous communities that are already in process of integration. Otherwise it will be difficult to appreciate the significance and social function of certain traditional cultural, religious and legal values and institutions or to grasp the complex nature of the problems that arise when these values do not fit in with those that the national authorities may look upon as a necessary accompaniment of integration. Experience in many countries demonstrates the advisability of avoiding any change in these values and institutions unless it is essential in the interests of the social and economic progress of the communities concerned and unless they can be replaced by suitable substitutes with the approval and understanding of the peoples concerned.[1]

The proposed conclusions the Office submitted to the first discussion in 1956 therefore included the following:

> 11. In carrying out programmes of integration, special attention should be paid to the desirability of securing the co-operation of genuinely representative indigenous leaders of a traditional or modern type, whose authority is exercised in accordance with the aspirations of their respective communities and with the requirements their social, economic and cultural progress.[2]

The discussion in the 1956 Session of the Conference also betrayed a deep disdain for indigenous leadership capacity and methods, though by the narrowest

---

[1] Report VIII (2), p. 153.
[2] p. 158.

of margins the responsible committee avoided expressing this attitude too clearly in its conclusions:

> 55. The Committee had a prolonged discussion of the text, which stated that in carrying out programmes of integration it would be desirable to secure the co-operation of genuinely representative leaders, of a traditional or modern type, whose authority was exercised in accordance with the aspirations of their communities and with the requirements of their progress.
> 56. The Ukrainian Government member expressed the opinion that the tribal structure was anachronistic and inconsistent with the development of indigenous populations, and moved an amendment calling for the establishment of democratic practices and elective institutions among these populations.
> 57. Other members of the Committee expressed the doubt whether the policy implied in the amendment might not be construed as representing an interference with the political structure of the countries having indigenous populations.
> 58. A revised version of the amendment was adopted, stating that in taking measures for the protection of indigenous populations governments should seek the collaboration of their representatives, should provide these populations with opportunities for the full development of their initiative and should stimulate by all possible means the development among them of democratic liberties and of elective institutions. The result of the vote on the amendment was as follows: 30 votes for, 29 against, with 2 abstentions. A record vote on the point, as amended, was then taken, resulting as follows: 40 votes for, 36 against, with 3 abstentions.[3]

The conclusion thus adopted avoided the worst prejudices expressed in the discussion, though it also inherently called for the replacement of indigenous structures by more 'modern' and democratic ones:

> 12. In taking measures for the protection of indigenous populations, governments should seek the collaboration of their representatives; they should provide these populations with opportunities for the full development of their initiative; they should stimulate by all possible means the development among them of democratic liberties and of elective institutions.[4]

---

3   Proceedings 1956, p. 741.
4   Ibid., p. 749.

In the draft Convention submitted to constituents following the first discussion this was expressed as follows:

> *Article 5*
> In applying the provisions of this Convention relating to the protection and the integration of indigenous peoples, governments shall –
> (*a*) seek the collaboration of the representatives of these peoples;
> (*b*) provide these peoples with opportunities for the full development of their initiative;
> (*c*) stimulate by all possible means the development among these peoples of democratic liberties and of elective institutions.[5]

As will be seen, the draft no longer referred to seeking collaboration only in the protection of these populations – it had added that this collaboration should also be sought in their integration.

Only three governments commented on this proposed Article in the consultation that followed:

> *Argentina:* This collaboration must be considered as indispensable.
> *United Kingdom:* See under Article 4.
> *United States:* The principles set forth are acceptable.[6]

The proposed Article that was submitted to the Conference was thus almost the same wording as in the first version, except that the reference was now to 'populations' and no longer to 'peoples':

> *Article 5*
> In applying the provisions of this Convention relating to the protection and integration of the populations concerned, governments shall –
> (*a*) seek the collaboration of the representatives of these populations;
> (*b*) provide these populations with opportunities for the full development of their initiative;
> (*c*) stimulate by all possible means the development among these populations of civil liberties and of elective institutions.[7]

---

5 Report VI (1), p. 47.
6 Report VI (2), p. 16. The United Kingdom Government had said under proposed Article 4 that 'In Articles 4 and 5 the words "relating to the protection and integration of indigenous peoples" are redundant', which the Office declined to take into account.
7 Ibid., p. 54.

The discussion in the 1957 Session of the Conference displayed some awareness that the traditional governance institutions of indigenous and tribal peoples were not necessarily inherently undesirable and ineffective, but also showed that for most of the delegates attitudes remained fundamentally disdainful:

> 44. The Employers' member of Mexico moved an amendment to delete the words "of the representatives" from clause (a). It was stated in support of the amendment that the proposed text of clause (a) was restrictive and might help to perpetuate undesirable systems of leadership among the indigenous populations. The amendment did not exclude collaboration with the representatives of these populations when advisable. Several members of the Committee pointed out that, in dealing with groups of people, governments had necessarily to contact their representatives; the effect of the amendment would be to leave a free hand to governments to circumvent the established tribal authorities, which could result in upsetting the social cohesion of the group. Article 4 of the proposed text stated that due account should be taken of the forms of social control of the populations concerned.
>
> 45. In view of these considerations, the Employers' member of Mexico revised his amendment to read: "seek the collaboration of these populations and of their representatives." The amendment, as revised, was adopted unanimously.
>
> 46. The Government member of New Zealand moved an amendment to replace, in clause (c), the words "and of elective institutions" by the words "and the establishment of or participation in elective institutions". The purpose of the amendment was to make it clear that the clause covered participation by indigenous peoples in local and national bodies as well as in those pertaining solely to their own communities. The amendment was adopted unanimously.
>
> 47. Article 5, as amended, was then adopted unanimously.[8]

The text of the new instrument thus provided:

Article 5
In applying the provisions of this Convention relating to the protection and integration of the populations concerned, governments shall –

---

[8] Proceedings 1957, p. 726.

(a) seek the collaboration of these populations and of their representatives;
(b) provide these populations with opportunities for the full development of their initiative;
(c) stimulate by all possible means the development among these populations of civil liberties and the establishment of or participation in elective institutions.

B   Convention No. 169

By the time the ILO came to consider the revision of Convention No. 107 attitudes had changed.

i   *The Meeting of Experts*

This change is reflected in the deliberations of the 1986 Meeting of Experts on the basic orientation of the Convention, closely linked to discussions of respect, self-determination and consultation. In its discussion of basic orientation, the following long extract from the report of the Meeting of Experts foreshadowed both the arguments that would emerge in drafting Convention No. 169, and the solutions that eventually would be adopted. This discussion also foretold that the ILO Conference would be unable to arrive at a formulation that would explicitly meet the demands of the indigenous representatives for their right to self-determination to be recognized:

> 45. The Governing Body had noted when it convened the present Meeting of Experts that the Convention's basic orientation was towards integration as the fundamental objective of all activities undertaken by governments in relation to indigenous and tribal populations, and that it was necessary to re-examine this orientation to take into account different views and changed circumstances. In particular, it was necessary to revise the instrument in order to take account of the existence of organisations of indigenous and tribal peoples and of their capacity to express the views and to defend the interests of the groups they represented.
>
> 46. The Meeting is unanimous in concluding that the integrationist language of Convention No. 107 is outdated, and that the application of this principle is destructive in the modern world. In 1956 and 1957, when Convention No. 107 was being discussed, it was felt that integration into the dominant national society offered the best chance for these groups to be a part of the development process of the countries in which they live.

This had, however, resulted in a number of undesirable consequences. It had become a destructive concept, in part at least because of the way it was understood by governments. In practice it had become a concept which meant the extinction of ways of life which are different from that of the dominant society. The inclusion of this idea in the text of the Convention has also impeded indigenous and tribal peoples from taking full advantage of the strong protections offered in some parts of the Convention, because of the distrust its use has created among them. In this regard, it was recalled that the Sub-Commission's Special Rapporteur had stressed in his study[9] (see paragraph 19 above) the necessity of adopting an approach which took account of the claims of indigenous populations. In his opinion, the policies of pluralism, self-sufficiency, self-management and ethno-development appeared to be those which would give indigenous populations the best possibilities and means of participating directly in the formulation and implementation of official policies.

47. It was recognised generally by the Meeting that governments feel a legitimate concern over national identity and the sovereignty of the State. This concern should not, however, be translated into policies which seek to eliminate all differences among the various cultural groups which make up most nations. This was the implication which had been given to the concept of integration by many governments.

48. Reference was made to the changes which had taken place in views on economic development. When Convention No. 107 was adopted in 1957, the process could be described as a "top-down" approach, that is one in which the national government decided what was best for all inhabitants of the country including the indigenous and tribal populations, and imposed its own concepts without discussion or consultation. This had also been the attitude of the international organisations working with governments on development projects. There had been a change in perceptions, however, as stated in the working document before the Meeting. There was an increasingly general recognition that development has to involve the persons affected at all levels of decision-making and implementation if it is to be valid. The same concepts apply to other subjects affecting indigenous and tribal peoples as well.

---

9 United Nations, Sub-Commission on Prevention of Discrimination and Protection of Minorities, in *Study of the problem of discrimination against indigenous populations,* Ch. XXI: "Conclusions" (United Nations doc. E/CN.4/Sub.2/1983/21/Add.8).

49. Definition of the concept which should be used to replace the basic orientation of integrationism gave rise to a long and complex discussion. Clearly, there must be guarantees of equality of treatment, combined with recognition of the right to be different. There should also be scope for individual choice by members of the groups concerned. The first ideas offered in attempting to define these concepts were that there should be recognition of the basic principles of increased consultation of indigenous and tribal peoples and participation by them in decision-making. It was quickly agreed by most experts, however, that these ideas by themselves were too weak to take account of the real needs. Experts and observers from non-governmental organisations, especially those representing indigenous and tribal peoples, supported by experts from workers' circles, pointed out that any such obligations could quickly be perverted – as they often had been – to mean *pro forma* consultations in which no real account was taken of the views expressed and of the true needs of the people being affected. The weight of these views was endorsed by most of the participants in the meeting.

50. The representatives of indigenous and tribal organisations who were present stated that the only concept which would respond to their needs was that of self-determination. The intention behind this was supported by most of the experts, who felt however that the use of the term posed some difficult problems. They recognised that it had been used in a number of international documents adopted both before and after Convention No. 107, including some referring directly to indigenous and tribal peoples. It was stated, however, that the term might be understood as implying a right to secede from the States within which they live and to form new independent political entities. This idea was outside the mandate of the ILO and of the present Meeting. Even if defined to exclude this notion, it implied a greater degree of decision-making power being reserved to the indigenous and tribal peoples than some experts could accept. It was also felt that the use of this term in a revised instrument would in itself prevent ratification because of fears of such implications.

51. The proponents of the idea recalled that the term had been used in a number of international instruments already, a point clarified by the Assistant Secretary-General for Human Rights of the United Nations. They stated that any use of the term should make it clear that it was to be applied only to economic, social and cultural rights, which were clearly within the ILO's mandate. There was also some discussion of using a phrase such as "internal self-determination" to indicate that it would be understood only to mean self-determination within the structure of

existing States, but no agreement could be reached on this. They thought that the fears that use of this term would prevent ratification were unfounded. During this discussion, reference was made to the following paragraphs of the Study of Discrimination against Indigenous Populations carried out for the United Nations Sub-Commission on the Prevention of Discrimination and Protection of Minorities.

> 580. Self-determination, in its many forms, must be recognised as the basic precondition for the enjoyment by indigenous peoples of their fundamental rights and the determination of their own future.
> 581. It must also be recognised that the right to self-determination exists at various levels and includes economic, social, cultural and political factors. In essence, it constitutes the exercise of free choice by indigenous peoples who must, to a large extent, create the specific content of this principle, in both its internal and external expressions, which do not necessarily include the right to secede from the State in which they live and to set themselves up as sovereign entities. This right may, in fact, be expressed in various forms of autonomy within the State, including the individual and collective right to be different and to be considered different, as recognised in the statement on Race and Racial Prejudice adopted by UNESCO in 1978.

52. It was generally agreed that it would be counter-productive to suggest including the term "self-determination" in the operative part of a revised ILO instrument. Some of the experts expressed the opinion that the ILO should not take a retrograde step in revising this instrument, by failing to take into account developments in international law and relations, and strongly favoured including the term as the guiding principle of a new Convention, but no general consensus emerged in favour of this suggestion. On the other hand, there was a large measure of consensus for a reference of some kind to this concept in the preamble of the revised instrument.

53. The Director of the Inter-American Indian Institute read out to the Meeting Resolution No. 4 of the IXth Inter-American Indian Congress (Santa Fe, New Mexico, United States, 1985), which called upon States to ensure the organised participation of these peoples in making decisions on development; to recognise the multi-ethnic and pluricultural nature of national societies; to stimulate bilingual education; and to replace integrationist concepts by a policy of respect and autonomous development based on the values, objectives and aspirations of these peoples, in order to achieve equality within diversity.

54. After considerable discussion, a group of experts and observers offered the following text as an attempt to meet the objections which had been raised while reflecting the principles included in the concept of self-determination:

Replace the fourth preambular paragraph of Convention No. 107 with:
Considering that the International Covenant on Economic, Social and Cultural Rights affirms the fundamental importance of the right to self-determination, as well as the right of all human beings to pursue their material, cultural and spiritual development in conditions of freedom and dignity;

Recognising that these rights are fundamental to the survival and future development of indigenous and tribal peoples as distinctive and viable societies;

Replace Articles 2 and 5 with:
Article 2
In co-operation with indigenous and tribal peoples, governments shall have the responsibility for developing co-ordinated and systematic action to ensure:
(*a*) that indigenous and tribal peoples are able to enjoy the full measure of human rights and fundamental freedoms without hindrance or discrimination;
(*b*) that indigenous and tribal peoples' territorial rights, economic rights, and political, social, cultural, and religious institutions are recognised and protected;
(*c*) that indigenous and tribal peoples be accorded the respect of determining for themselves the process of development as it affects their lives and institutions.

55. This proposal received substantial general support among many experts, who endorsed the ideas contained in it. They felt that, while it was clear that the present Meeting had not been convened to offer specific amendments to the text of the present Convention, the text quoted above reflected many elements of consensus among them. All of the employer experts and some government experts, expressed reservations, however.
56. Those offering the proposal wished it to be clarified that the principle of self-determination to which reference was made in the draft preambular paragraphs should be understood to mean self-determination in economic, social and cultural fields. In addition, the reference to political

institutions in the draft Article 2, paragraph (b), should be understood to refer to the political institutions of indigenous and tribal peoples themselves which were used to regulate their internal affairs. It was also stated that the intention was that draft Article 2 would create no rights in itself, but would provide basic guide-lines in the light of which the rest of the revised Convention would be interpreted.

57. Reservations were expressed by some experts concerning the concept contained in draft Article 2, paragraph (c), while others supported it strongly. The point at issue was whether indigenous and tribal groups would have the right to full control of the development process as it affected them. Those in favour of including this concept pointed to the evolution of perceptions of how the development process should be decided upon, citing an increase in recognition of the need for a more participatory process. They felt that the reason for the failure of so many of the economic development programmes was that they were imposed from above instead of emerging from the wishes of the people being directly affected. They also felt strongly that indigenous and tribal peoples should have the right under all circumstances to determine whether and how programmes of economic development would affect them.

58. Others felt strongly that national governments neither could nor would surrender the right to make decisions on economic development which often affected the entire population of the country. These experts agreed fully that indigenous and tribal peoples should have the right, reinforced by procedural mechanisms, to play an effective participatory role in the planning and implementation of development programmes affecting them, but did not agree that they should have absolute control and the right of ultimate decision. Mr. Yllanes Ramos, employer expert,[10] identified himself particularly with this position, which was also shared by a certain number of other experts.

59. Some of the participants felt that the above-mentioned draft did not go nearly far enough. They felt that it was the role of the present Meeting to suggest the highest possible standards, fully reflecting the aspirations of the indigenous and tribal peoples, rather than anticipating already at

---

10 Mr. Yllanes Ramos, an imposing employer representative from Mexico, had been the Employer Vice-Chairman on the Conference Committee that had prepared Convention No. 107 in 1956 and 1957. It was the impression of the author of this volume, who was closely involved in the adoption of C. 169, that he courageously accepted the need for a different approach, while simultaneously wishing to defend the work of the Conference from 30 years earlier.

this early stage compromises which might be made at later stages of the discussion of a revised Convention.

60. As already stated, however, all the experts felt that some statement of principles similar to that contained in the above draft should be the basic orientation of any new instrument on the rights of indigenous and tribal peoples. While there was not full agreement on every element of this statement of principles, it did reflect broad consensus among them on the kind of principles which should guide the interpretation of all other provisions of the revised Convention, subject to the reservations indicated above.[11]

Several points emerge from this discussion at the Meeting of Experts.

First, the ILO did not originate the idea of involving representatives of indigenous and tribal peoples in decisions affecting them, though it did respond to this idea as soon as was possible. Indeed, this idea was 'in the air', with the developments that had taken place at the international level. It may be recalled that when C. 107 was drafted, there were quite simply no indigenous organizations at the international level that could have been consulted.[12]

However, by the end of the 1970s there had been a number of developments that all went in this direction. The first international indigenous organization, the World Council of Indigenous Peoples, had been established in 1975. The Martinez Cobo study, which was completed in 1982, had recommendations for the ILO among others: for example, that "the International Labour Organisation should be supported in its efforts to effect a revision of Convention No. 107…so as to take into account the wishes and demands of indigenous populations". The study also states that in revising the ILO standards, "more suitable and precise substantive provisions and more practical and effective procedural principles are needed. Particularly in substantive terms, stress must be placed on ethno-development and independence or self-determination, instead of on 'integration and protection'."[13] In other words, the 'top-down' non-consulting development and rights approach that C. 107 had embodied was being repudiated from all sides, and no one yet had anything specific to put in its place. The main point is simple: C. 107 needed to be either revised or abandoned, and if revised

---

11 Report of the Meeting of Experts, reproduced in Report VI (1), pp. 107–110.

12 With the possible exception of the Nordic Sami Conference, which however acted very discreetly and at a purely Scandinavian level at this time.

13 United Nations: *Study of the problem of discrimination against indigenous populations*, by Mr. José R. Martinez Cobo, Special Rapporteur of the Sub-Commission on the Prevention of Discrimination and Protection of Minorities (Geneva; doc. E/CN.4/Sub.2/1983/21/Add.8, p. 44, paras. 336 and 337).

it had to include a very solid recognition of the right of indigenous peoples themselves to be involved in decision-making.

ii   *The 1988 Discussion*

ILO Report VI (1) that launched the revision process included the forthright statement that "One of the major developments that have taken place since the adoption of Convention No. 107 and Recommendation No. 104 in 1957 is the establishment of organisations of indigenous and tribal people to defend and promote their own interests. One of the most important reasons for revising the Convention is to incorporate the principle that such groups should have a role in making decisions which affect them."[14]

Report VI (1) developed this concept further as it examined the possible basic orientation of a revised Convention:

> The basic orientation which should replace this integrationist approach is also clear from national and international developments, and from the conclusions of the Meeting of Experts. While its formulation in an international Convention poses a difficult problem, the new orientation should encompass two basic principles:
> – respect for the cultures, ways of life and traditional institutions of these peoples; and
> – effective involvement of these peoples in decisions that affect them.[15]

The report then raised the point that would determine the direction of the discussion about the rights to be involved:

> While these principles will be explored in more detail below, it may be noted here that they raise problems as to the degree of autonomy which these groups should have. These concerns were discussed extensively by the Meeting of Experts, with contributions from the representatives of indigenous and tribal populations present. The indigenous and tribal representatives felt that the term "self-determination" best expressed their own aspirations, but added that it should not be construed so as to imply, in the context of the revision of Convention No. 107, any form of political independence from the countries in which they live. The experts themselves recognised that this term represented the aspirations of the indigenous and tribal representatives, as expressed by their organisations in a

---

14   Report VI (1), p. 13.
15   Ibid., pp. 18 and 19.

number of meetings and other forums, but felt that because of its connotations the term was inappropriate for an ILO instrument, even though it has been used in other international instruments and by other organisations. This should be kept in mind in the following parts of this section.[16]

The report went on to explore these notions in more detail as it began to consider preliminary ideas on the revised instrument:

> As noted in the introduction to this chapter and elsewhere in this report, Convention No. 107 has been found by many commentators among academic writers, other international organisations and representatives of indigenous and tribal peoples, in particular, to reflect an integrationist approach which urgently needs to be modified. The first three conclusions adopted by the Meeting of Experts convened to advise the Governing Body on this subject read as follows:
> 1. The Convention's integrationist approach is inadequate and no longer reflects current thinking.
> 2. Indigenous and tribal peoples should enjoy as much control as possible over their own economic, social and cultural development.
> 3. The right of these peoples to interact with the national society on an equal footing through their own institutions should be recognised.
>
> In the opinion of the Meeting of Experts, the integrationist approach of the Convention manifested itself in two fundamental ways. In the first place, the 1957 Convention assumed that all government programmes should, for the ultimate benefit of the groups covered by the Convention, be directed toward their integration into national society. Safeguards were provided, as in Article 2, paragraph 4: "Recourse to force or coercion as a means of promoting the integration of these populations into the national community shall be excluded."
>
> This, however, is merely a restriction on the kinds of measures to be used, and does not change the basic orientation of the instrument, best expressed in Article 2, paragraph 1:
>
>> "Governments shall have the primary responsibility for developing co-ordinated and systematic action for the protection of the populations concerned *and their progressive integration into the life of their respective countries.*"(Emphasis added)

---

16   Ibid. p. 19.

The second aspect of the integrationist approach of the Convention is an inherent assumption of the cultural inferiority of the groups covered by the instrument. This, of course, is the justification of the basic impulse towards integration. An example of this assumption is found in Article 3, paragraph 1, of Convention No. 107:

> "So long as the social, economic and cultural conditions of the populations concerned prevent them from enjoying the benefits of the general laws of the country to which they belong, special measures shall be adopted for the protection of the institutions, persons, property and labour of these populations." (Emphasis added)

A number of similar references are found in the Convention, implying a lower stage, or degree, of cultural development of the populations covered. This approach can also be characterised as "paternalistic", with benevolent as well as harmful aspects. It is benevolent in its adoption of a protective attitude toward weaker elements of society – which the Meeting of Experts insisted should be maintained, as will be indicated below. It is harmful, however, in the sense that it assumes that governments can and should take measures for the benefit of these groups regardless of their wishes, since they are presumed to be incapable of expressing a valid opinion.[17]

The Office also noted that the model of development that prevailed in the international community had evolved:

> Mention has already been made of the change of attitude toward the "top down" development model which prevailed during the early years of the United Nations system, when governments and intergovernmental organisations felt that it was necessary to centralise all development decisions, and that the wishes of those affected were at best irrelevant. It has now become evident that such an approach is simply unworkable, and that development cannot succeed unless there is a broadly based participatory approach to both planning and implementation. This does not mean that global approaches should be abandoned, but that the involvement of all those concerned, starting from the local level, greatly augments the chances of success, even when those being consulted are seen by their governments as unsophisticated in the context of the wider

---

[17] Ibid., pp. 27 and 28.

society. This is, of course, one of the philosophical bases for the decolonisation movement which began in the early 1960s.[18]

This discussion led to further deliberation on the degree of control that would be implied by greater participation in the decision-making process:

> As noted above and examined in detail in the report of the Meeting of Experts, although the indigenous and tribal representatives present voiced a preference for the concept of "self-determination" as the basic orientation of the revised instrument, the experts did not agree that this phrase should appear in its operative part (paragraphs 50 to 52 of the report of the Meeting of Experts).
>
> There was, however, some support for the idea that a reference might be made to this concept in the Preamble to the revised Convention, which will be examined at a later stage by the Conference. All of the experts agree that the principle expressed in Conclusion 2 should be incorporated: that these peoples "should enjoy *as much control as possible* over their own economic, social and cultural development".
>
> It is evident that the granting of "as much control as possible" will vary considerably among different member States and among different indigenous and tribal groups. As is the case in many other international labour Conventions, a degree of flexibility is essential in consideration of the wide variety of national situations. In analysing the question of control, the Meeting of Experts first considered whether the revised Convention should recognise the basic principles of increased consultation of indigenous and tribal peoples and their participation in decision-making (see paragraph 49 of the report). It was noted, however, that such obligations on ratifying States "could quickly be perverted – as they often had been – to mean *pro forma* consultations in which no real account was taken of the views expressed and of the true needs of the people being affected". On the other hand, granting a higher degree of decision-making power to groups within the national population could result in the establishment of a "State within a State". Reference has already been made in the first section of this chapter

---

18   Ibid., p. 29. It should be noted that the ILO itself had been one of the earliest promoters of respect for the rights of colonized peoples, in its adoption and promotion of the so-called 'Native Labour Code' in the years immediately before World War II – see, e.g., *The Quest for Social Justice, op. cit.*, xxxx. However, by the time of the adoption of C. 107 this attitude had not yet been adopted as concerned the internal colonization that the situation of indigenous and tribal peoples embodies, and that was covered by that Convention.

to cases in which governments have even incorporated the phrases "self-determination" or "autonomy" into national legislation or basic policy documents, without creating any implication of a right to secede or of political separation. In balancing these arguments, a consensus emerged which is reflected in paragraph 58 of the experts' report and in Conclusion 2:

> Indigenous and tribal peoples should have the right, reinforced by procedural mechanisms, to play an effective participatory role in the planning and implementation of development programmes affecting them...[They should not] have absolute control and the right of ultimate decision.

In examining this aspect of the report of the Meeting of Experts, participants in the Conference discussion should keep in mind that it does not reflect the highest aspirations of the indigenous and tribal peoples. It would, however, constitute a considerable advance over the assumption of cultural inferiority and the integrationist approach inherent in Convention No. 107. Issues of self-determination, and the exact definition of the meaning of this term, must be left to the highest political organs of the United Nations and cannot be debated in the ILO. In drafting the proposals in the present report, the Office has proceeded on the assumption that a revised Convention must recognise:

(a) that indigenous and tribal peoples have a right to participate in the decision-making process in the countries in which they live for all issues covered by the revised Convention and which affect them directly;

(b) that this right of participation should be an effective one, offering them an opportunity to be heard and to have an impact on the decisions taken;

(c) that in order for this right to be effective it must be backed up by appropriate procedural mechanisms to be established at the national level in accordance with national conditions; and

(d) that the implementation of this right should be adapted to the situation of the indigenous and tribal peoples concerned in order to grant them as much control as is possible in each case over their own economic, social and cultural development.

The Office considers that, if the above-mentioned principles are accepted on the basis for revising the orientation of the Convention, it will not be necessary to attempt a more precise definition.[19]

---

19 Ibid., pp. 29–31.

The questionnaire sent to the constituents for the 1988 discussion included the following questions on this point, surprisingly concise in the light of the extensive discussion that had taken place in gthe Meeting of Experts:

> 19. Do you consider that Article 5 should replaced by a provision which requires that governments should, whenever possible, undertake consultations with the peoples concerned, or with their representatives where they exist, whenever consideration is being given to legislative or administrative measures which may affect them?
> 20. Do you consider that these consultations should be carried out in such a way as to provide these peoples with an effective voice in deciding on such measures?[20]

The replies to question 19 reveal some of the complexity of this subject and the concerns of the constituents:

> Replies to this question were broadly affirmative, and while a number of specific proposals have been made for revised wording, most seek the same result. Certain governments have indicated in their replies that consultation should be a definite requirement and obligation, or that consultation arrangements should be subsidiary to the principle of greatest possible internal autonomy. Others have stated that an emphasis on consultation alone, without corresponding reference to the development of civil liberties and participation in elected institutions, might have the undesired effect of reducing the rights of the peoples concerned.
>
> A number of indigenous and other non-governmental organisations have stated in their comments that the principle of consultation is not in itself adequate. They have indicated that the emphasis should be on the capacity of these peoples to determine their own lives and actions and to give their consent with regard to the programmes and activities which may affect them. In this regard, reference may be made to the deliberations of the Meeting of Experts (see in particular paragraphs 45–60, reproduced in Appendix I of Report VI (1)).
>
> These observations raise highly complex issues of control and autonomy, among other things, with which it will prove difficult to deal in this one Article of a revised Convention. It does not appear possible to reconcile these viewpoints entirely, but it may be possible to revise Article 5 in such a way as to place more emphasis on the requirement to give

---

20 Ibid., p. 95.

indigenous and tribal peoples a voice in the decisions affecting them. The question of the degree of decision-making to be lodged with them is discussed further under question 20.

As concerns the point raised by the Government of the United States,[21] both here and elsewhere in its reply, it seems clear that the proposals so far made focus on national governments and their subdivisions, and not on the internal governmental processes of these peoples. There are, however, elements of the Proposed Conclusions which would tend towards protection of the rights of members of these peoples vis-à-vis their own governments, including Point 13 (*b*) and (*c*) and, more particularly, Point 11 of the Proposed Conclusions.[22]

The replies to the closely related Question 20 further complicated the possibilities, and raised points on the content of consultation and the concept of consent that would still resonate a quarter of a century later:

> While the majority of replies to this question were in the affirmative, doubts have been raised concerning the meaning and implications of the term "effective". While some replies have called for the use of a stronger term, such as "decisive", others have pointed to the possible ambiguities in interpretation.
>
> In this regard, it should be noted that the provision which would emerge from the Proposed Conclusions contains a general principle for the application of all Articles of the present Convention (Article 6 of Convention No. 107 and the proposals for its revision deal more specifically with development policies and programmes). The term "effective" was proposed in the questionnaire in order to convey the principle that consultations should be more than *pro forma*, and should ensure genuine involvement of and negotiation with indigenous and tribal peoples whenever consideration is given to legislative or administrative measures which may affect them.
>
> Certain indigenous organisations have proposed the term "decisive voice". It has been brought to the attention of the Office that similar

---

21 The US Government's reply was: 'No. The existing wording already requires collaboration. However, the nature of the consultations is not clear. In addition, it is not clear whether the term "governments" only refers to national governments. The revision should clearly indicate that tribal governments also have the responsibility of consulting with their members.'

22 Report VI (2), p. 30.

language has been proposed in the reports of recent international commissions concerning indigenous peoples, human resources and the environment (e.g. the 1987 Report of the United Nations World Commission on the Environment and Development and the 1987 Report of the Independent Commission on International Humanitarian Issues entitled *Indigenous peoples*). An ILO Convention should of course not promote concepts which are contrary to international law or to a consensus which may be emerging in the United Nations system or wherever else the situation of indigenous and tribal populations is being discussed. It clearly must also take close account of the express wishes of those it is intended to protect.

At the same time, a Convention must be drafted in a form which lends itself to ratification. Fears have been expressed that a specific provision requiring consent by indigenous and tribal peoples would prevent the revised Convention from being ratified, and that its application could even lead to dissolution of States.

The 1986 Meeting of Experts discussed these questions at length. While all of the experts supported the principle of control by indigenous and tribal peoples of all the measures affecting them, most of them recognised the difficulties inherent in including an unreserved obligation to this effect in a revised Convention. For these reasons the Proposed Conclusions include an amended version of questions 19 and 20 which go further than Convention No. 107 in requiring ratifying States to seek the consent of the peoples concerned, while leaving the degree of control to be exercised by these peoples and by governments to decision at the national level. This formulation is also consistent with the promotional aspects of the revised Convention, indicating a tendency toward requiring consent in appropriate fields.

Finally, the Proposed Conclusions would require governments to provide these peoples with the opportunities to develop their own institutions in accordance with their own wishes.[23]

The proposed conclusions drawn up on the basis of these two questions were combined in point 13 (with the text in italics being new or amended language compared to C. 107):

13. In applying the provisions of the revised Convention, governments should –

---

23   Ibid., pp. 30–32.

(a) seek the *consent of the peoples concerned through appropriate procedures whenever consideration is being given to legislative or administrative measures which may affect them;*
(b) *promote the participation of the said peoples in elective institutions, and in administrative bodies responsible for policies and programmes affecting them;*
(c) provide *these peoples* with opportunities for the full development of their *own institutions and* initiative.[24]

The discussion in the 1988 Conference was detailed, laying out the positions and alternatives that were before the Conference – and that would be reproduced in later discussions around the subject of indigenous and tribal peoples, inside and outside the ILO. The first part of the discussion concerned subparagraph (a), as the Conference wrestled with the idea of seeking the consent of these peoples, and how to carry out consultations. It shows that the Conference was ready to vote regularly on the different proposals, and that those who sought to strengthen the requirement were being defeated by real but narrow margins. (See point 13 above).

73. The Workers' members proposed a two-part amendment to substitute "obtain the informed consent" for "seek the consent", and to add that it should be "freely expressed through their own institutions". They considered it essential that indigenous peoples have a real influence on decision-making. The Employers' members opposed the amendment since, in their opinion, it implied a right of veto to indigenous populations over government action. The Government member of Canada supported the Employers' members' views and added that the amendment could threaten the supremacy of legislative bodies. She also felt that it might not always be possible for governments to obtain the views of every group. Several Government members supported this view. The first part of the amendment was rejected by 1,980 votes in favour, 2,880 against, with 180 abstentions. The Workers' members noted this decision with regret, as it was a crucial concern for the indigenous peoples.

74. An amendment calling for full consultation in lieu of seeking the consent was submitted by the Government member of the United States. A similar amendment proposed by the Government member of New Zealand was withdrawn in its favour. The Government member of the United States explained that it was his Government's practice to consult

---

24 Ibid., pp. 106 and 107.

with tribal governments concerning new proposals which would affect them, and that this amendment provided for greater participation on the part of indigenous populations. The Employers' members supported the amendment and withdrew a similar amendment they had tabled. The Government member of Norway proposed a subamendment to change this to "consult fully with a view to obtaining the consent". The Workers' members proposed another subamendment to make the goal of consent stronger still. The Government member of Canada opposed the subamendments, particularly since she believed their adoption would jeopardise ratification of the revised Convention, stating that the amendment submitted by the Government member of the United States already implied what was stated in the Norwegian subamendment. For her delegation, this language required not only formal consultations, but consultations in good faith through appropriate mechanisms. The Government members of Brazil, Ecuador and France further supported the United States amendment. The subamendment proposed by the Government member of Norway was supported by the Government member of Peru and by the Workers' members, who withdrew their subamendment in favour of it. The subamendment submitted by Norway was rejected by 2,034 votes in favour, 2,390 against, and 180 abstentions.

75. At the request of the Workers' members, in accordance with Article 65, paragraph 8, of the Standing Orders, a record vote was taken. The results of the vote were as follows: 2,163 votes in favour, 2,610 votes against, with 180 abstentions. The subamendment was rejected. The amendment which had been submitted by the Government member of the United States was adopted by consensus.

76. The second part of the Workers' members' amendment sought to replace "through appropriate procedures" by "freely expressed through their own representative institutions". The amendment was supported by the Employers' members. The Government member of Canada felt that the text was too restrictive and did not allow for individual consultation and she introduced a subamendment to ease the restriction. The Workers' members appreciated the intention and said they could support it if it was further subamended to emphasise the need for action where legislation was concerned. This text was adopted as subamended. The Employers' members tabled an amendment to add the word "directly", which was adopted.

77. As regards paragraph (*b*) of this Point, the Workers' members introduced an amendment to replace the proposed text by wording which would increase the emphasis on participation of indigenous and tribal peoples in decision-making. They proposed a subamendment to make the text focus on those directly affected by policies and programmes. A

number of Government members supported the amendment, though there was some debate over whether the word "freely" should be included in the text. The Employers' members proposed an amendment designed to permit participation of the people concerned in administrative and other bodies, and the Government member of Japan submitted an amendment which would provide for their participation on an equal footing with other members of the national community. Several Government members were of the opinion that this proposal accorded with the philosophy of the paragraph and supported it. The Workers' members and a number of other Government members opposed the amendment since they felt it would cause problems for governments which had adopted measures of positive discrimination in favour of their indigenous and tribal populations regarding, for instance, representation in legislative bodies. The Government member of Japan pointed out that the concerns which had been voiced were adequately protected in Point 72. The Employers' members proposed that the amendment of the Workers' members be supported as subamended by the word "directly". The Government member of Colombia opposed the addition of the word "directly" because in his opinion it was undemocratic. The Government members of Peru and Venezuela shared this view.

78. The amendment, as subamended, was adopted. The Government members of Colombia, Peru, Venezuela and Japan expressed their reservations and the Government member of Japan said he would reintroduce his amendment at the 76th Session of the Conference. A Workers' members' amendment to reorder the Proposed Conclusions under Point 13 was withdrawn. Amendments by the Government member of New Zealand and the Employers' members were superseded by the adopted text and were therefore not considered.

79. The Workers' members tabled an amendment to Point 13(c) intended to strengthen the proposed text by adding a reference to resources and changing "initiative" to "initiatives" (English text only). The Employers' members were of the opinion that the amendment made the text too vague. They pointed out that the obligation of governments extended only to the provision of an opportunity for development. The Workers' members explained that the term "resources" was used in an economic sense and excluded natural resources; it was intended to refer to the means necessary to develop their own institutions. Several governments supported the amendment which was adopted by consensus.

80. Point 13 as amended, was adopted.[25]

---

25 Proceedings 1988, pp. 32/10 and 32/11.

The conclusions adopted on this point after the discussion were included in the Committee report (recalling that at this point in the discussion, the Conference had decided to use the expression '(peoples/populations)' pending a final decision):

> 13. In applying the provisions of the revised Convention, governments should:
> (*a*) consult fully the (peoples/populations) concerned, through appropriate procedures and in particular through their representative institutions, whenever consideration is being given to legislative or administrative measures which may affect them directly;
> (*b*) establish means by which the said (peoples/populations) may freely participate at all levels of decision-making in elective institutions and administrative and other bodies responsible for policies and programmes which may affect them directly;
> (*c*) make available to these (peoples/populations) opportunities and resources for the full development of their own institutions and initiatives.[26]

iii   *The 1989 Discussion*

In Report IV (1) for the 1989 discussion, the first draft of the Convention on this point read as follows, with no proposed change in the wording except the obligatory replacement of 'should' in the conclusions by 'shall' in the proposed Convention:

> Article 6
> In applying the provisions of this Convention, governments shall:
> (*a*) consult fully the (peoples/populations) concerned, through appropriate procedures and in particular through their representative institutions, whenever consideration is being given to legislative or administrative measures which may affect them directly;
> (*b*) establish means by which these (peoples/populations) may freely participate at all levels of decision-making in elective institutions and administrative and other bodies responsible for policies and programmes which may affect them directly;
> (*c*) make available to these (peoples/populations) opportunities and resources for the full development of their own institutions and initiatives.[27]

---

26   Ibid., pp. 32 and 34.
27   Report IV (1), p. 8.

The Office introduced the second discussion in Report IV (2A) with the following comment on the terminology being used in draft Article 6, as well as in other provisions of the proposed Convention that spoke of consultation and consent:

Consent, consultation, co-operation and participation
Several questions of terminology have arisen in preparing this report. (The use of "peoples" or "populations" is dealt with under Article 1.) Rather than discuss them each time they arise, it appears sensible to deal with them only once.

During the first discussion an important conceptual decision was taken to recognise explicitly in a number of provisions that indigenous and tribal peoples should have an active role in decision-making and in planning and administering programmes affecting them. As this developed through the discussion, the formulas used were not always consistent. Several respondents have expressed concern that this inconsistency might lead to unintended differences of interpretation. One difference was that the conclusions adopted during the first discussion sometimes require consultation, and sometimes *full* consultation, with similar problems for other expressions. In addition, the terms "participation", "consultation", "co-operation" and "collaboration" are all used. The text now proposed does not include the word "full", and there is no intention thereby of lessening the degree of consultation, etc., required. In addition, the term "collaboration", where it appeared, has been changed to "co-operation".

As concerns consent, at the first discussion the Office had offered the formula "seek the consent" in two instances with the aim of indicating that governments should make a serious attempt to obtain the agreement of indigenous and tribal peoples in specified fields. This wording did not mean, as some participants stated, that the groups concerned would have a veto power; however, even this flexible language did not prove acceptable.

At the same time, several of the non-governmental organisations representing indigenous and tribal peoples have argued that it is inconsistent to speak of respect for their cultures, institutions and ways of life, while reserving the right for governments to take actions to which they are opposed. The argument that acceptance of the concept of attempting to obtain agreement would justify the creation of "a State within a State" has been invoked, as has the idea that its use would create special rights for these sectors of the national community, provoking backlash against them and constituting unacceptable reverse discrimination. The Office considers that these concerns are not justified by a requirement to attempt to obtain the agreement of the groups affected by governmental action, when it is clear that governments would retain the residual power to take the action they deem necessary if agreement cannot be reached after a sincere effort is made.

An alternative formulation has been proposed in Article 6, with a view to securing agreement at the second discussion. It should be emphasised again, as in the past, that the Convention will contain minimum standards only, and that it has been deliberately framed not to impede the development of other – and possibly higher – standards in other forums and in particular at the national level.[28]

The Office commentary on the observations of the constituents directly on the proposed Article 6 deals with the same general area, but is more focused on the text:

> The concerns of the Governments of Canada[29] and Japan[30] regarding (*b*) appear to be well-founded and are taken into account. The formula proposed is intended to be flexible enough to allow, but not require, measures such as the allocation of special seats in legislatures or reserved posts in government employment. This should overcome the objections to a similar proposal not adopted during the first discussion.
>
> The concern expressed over the term "resources" in (*c*), added during the first discussion, also appears to be well-founded. An alternative designed to overcome the objection is included.
>
> The proposal to add "constitutional" in (*a*) has not been retained, as it has always been understood by the ILO's supervisory bodies to be covered

---

28   Report IV (2A), pp. 5 and 6.
29   Canada had stated: 'Replace (*b*) by: "ensure that the said (peoples/populations) are, to the same extent as the rest of the population of the State, able to participate in decision-making in elective institutions and administrative and other bodies responsible for policies and programmes which may affect them directly". A requirement that any group freely participate in decision-making at *all* levels could affect the power of legislative bodies and the power and responsibility of governments to make decisions.' Ibid., pp. 19 and 20.
30   Japan's concern was: 'Furthermore, (*b*) should be revised to make it clear that this provision does not necessarily mean that special seats should be reserved for these (peoples/populations), but leaves the question of whether to take such measures to each country.' Ibid., p. 20.

by references to legislation. The proposals by Canada (IPWG) on (b) have not been retained as they would be contrary to the trend of the discussion.

The proposal to add "with a view to obtaining the consent of" in (a) was rejected during the first discussion. It nevertheless represents an attempt to clarify the meaning of the Convention's requirements. An additional paragraph has therefore been added, based on explanations given during the first discussion, in particular by the Government of Canada, as well as on proposals listed above, to clarify this term.[31]

The text that emerged from these exchanges was found in a new Article 6 in the draft sent to the Conference:

Article 6
1. In applying the provisions of this Convention, governments shall:
    (a) consult the peoples concerned, through appropriate procedures and in particular through their representative institutions, whenever consideration is being given to legislative or administrative measures which may affect them directly;
    (b) establish means by which these peoples may freely participate, to at least the same extent as other sectors of the population, at all levels of decision-making in elective institutions and administrative and other bodies responsible for policies and programmes which may affect them directly;
    (c) make available to these peoples opportunities for the full development of their own institutions and initiatives, and in appropriate cases provide the resources necessary for this purpose.
2. The consultations carried out in application of this Convention shall be undertaken, in good faith and in a form appropriate to the circumstances, with the objective of achieving agreement or consent to the proposed measures.[32]

The revised text that emerged from these exchanges did not differ greatly from the conclusions adopted by the Conference in 1988 in the quantum of drafting changes, but the tenor had changed considerably.

The introductory phrase had remained the same, making it clear that this Article would apply to the entire Convention, making it perhaps the central provision of the proposed new instrument.

---

[31] Ibid., pp. 20 and 21.
[32] Report IV (2B), p. 10.

Para. 1(a) had lost the reference to consulting these peoples 'fully', because the kinds of consultations to be undertaken were defined in the rest of the Article.

Para. 1(b) had acquired the important qualification 'to at least the same extent as other sectors of the population', setting up a situation in which the right to participate could be enhanced for these peoples compared to other parts of the national population – the notion of 'affirmative action' – but this kind of measure remained a decision to be taken at the national level.

Para. 1(c) had been redrafted to read better, without any real change in the meaning.

The most important change was the addition of paragraph 2 of this Article, in an attempt to require that consultations carried out under the new Convention would be real and not *pro forma*. It attempted to bridge the gap between the justified cynicism of the indigenous and other non-governmental representatives who well knew how badly the notion of consultation had been abused in practical terms, and the idealism of those who felt the concept carried its own guarantee. While the discussions that would follow would endorse this drafting, many delegates felt that it was too weak and non-specific to make much of a change. Fortunately, later events would demonstrate that this wording would become the defining strength of the new instrument, and that much of the supervision of the Convention's application over the following quarter century – by the ILO and by others – would turn on the meaning of this paragraph.

The emotional temper of the discussion of this central Article in the 1989 Conference is illustrated by the intervention of the indigenous representatives on the committee as it was opening the discussion on this part of the Convention.

> ...a representative of the World Council of Indigenous Peoples made a statement on Articles 6 to 12 of the proposed Convention. .... Rather than addressing the degree of control within the relationship between these peoples and States, the speaker believed it important to address the essence of the relationship itself. He considered that Article 6 to 12 addressed the issues surrounding the building of a new relationship with indigenous and tribal peoples as equals. To do so it was necessary to step back from the existing model of the oppressor and the oppressed which, over time, had merely dehumanised both sides. The speaker insisted that, in relation to Article 6, indigenous and tribal peoples should have the power to accept or reject actions or programmes which affected them. Anything less would constitute a denial of their integrity as peoples to control their own destiny. [33]

---

33   Proceedings 1989, pp. 25/10 and 25/11.

However, neither governments nor employers were going to accept that indigenous and tribal peoples should have entire control over what happened to them in their own hands. This was usually referred to as a 'right to veto', but could more properly be called internal autonomy even when it would not lead to secession from States.

This opposition of views was made clear at the beginning of the discussion of draft Article 6. The discussion turned around both the degree of control to be allotted to these peoples, and to serious mistrust of the concept of consultation. As concerns paragraph 1(a),

> The Workers' members submitted an amendment to paragraph *1(a)* to replace "consult" by "obtain the consent of". They felt that the draft text would require only contact rather than consent, and that this would enable government to undertake unilateral action. The Employers' members considered that the language in the draft text was in accordance with ILO use of the term "consult" which meant dialogue at least. The amendment would make the text too rigid and they did not support it. The Government member of Canada recalled that during the first discussion there had been consensus that the term "consult" meant to consult in good faith. He felt that expressing the objective of obtaining consent was unrealistic, especially in countries with many different indigenous and tribal groups. He opposed the amendment. Several other Government members also opposed the amendment. The Workers' members regretted the lack of support for the amendment from the other members of the Committee. The amendment was not adopted.[34]

Exactly the opposite sense was then proposed in the final attempt to amend this subparagraph:

> 69. The Government member of Brazil introduced the second amendment to paragraph 1 which was to replace "consult" by "hear". He noted that this term was used in the new Brazilian Constitution and felt that its use in this Article would facilitate acceptance of the Convention by Brazil and other countries without detracting from the substance of the provision. The Workers' members felt that the draft text submitted by the Office was appropriate since it required a dialogue, whereas the amendment could refer to a one sided procedure. They did not support the amendment. The Government member of Brazil stated that for his

---

34   Ibid., p. 25/11

Government "consult" meant openly finding out opinions. He withdrew the amendment.[35]

Article 6 (1)(a) was thus cleared for adoption in the form in which it was submitted to the Conference. Paragraph 1(b) was somewhat more complicated, and in addition to conceptual questions the discussion reflected the difficulty of drafting in several languages at once:

> 70. Two amendments to paragraph 1(b) were submitted by the Government member of Brazil and the Workers' members, each of which sought to amend that part of the text which referred to other sectors of the population. The Workers' members withdrew their amendment. That of the Government member of Brazil was not seconded and was not considered.
>
> 71. Two amendments to paragraph 1(b), submitted by the Government members of Ecuador and Colombia, were considered together. The Government member of Ecuador stated that he wished to make the paragraph more consistent within the framework of a law or treaty through the use of "could" rather than "may". He also proposed to replace "affect them directly" by the words "concern them". The Government member of Colombia considered that it would be discriminatory if indigenous and tribal peoples could only participate in decision-making on matters which directly affected them. He therefore supported the proposal to use the words "concern them". He also noted that he wished to use a word which was stronger than "podrán" in the Spanish text. The Workers' members strongly supported the amendments. The Employers' members supported the change of emphasis in the Spanish text but felt that the other changes were unnecessary. They noted that the Convention pointed out the equality between these peoples and other citizens of a given country, and felt that the Office text corresponded perfectly with the needs of these peoples. They did not support the amendments. The Government member of Brazil accorded with the Employers' members' point of view. The Government member of the Netherlands agreed with the idea of according the full right to participate in decision-making. He noted, however, that this had been dealt with in Article 2 and that Article 8 dealt with other relevant matters. He did not support the amendments. The Government member of Portugal supported the amendments, since she felt that there should not be any negative discrimination between

---

35   Ibid.

indigenous and tribal peoples and the rest of the population. Several other Government members (Botswana, Denmark, New Zealand, Nicaragua and USSR) supported the amendments. The Employers' members withdrew their opposition and the amendments were adopted.[36]

This description does not make it entirely clear what changes were made. The final difference from the text submitted to the Conference was, first, that 'can freely participate' replaced 'may freely participate', making this a requirement and not simply a possibility; and second that 'policies and programmes which concern them' replaced 'policies and programmes which may affect them directly'. While the differences are subtle, both changes appear to reinforce the right of participation and the range of questions that are affected.

Article 6(1)(c) then went through the same polishing process, which like earlier discussions demonstrated the abiding mistrust that both indigenous representatives and the Workers' Group on their behalf felt for the honesty of governments' intentions and conduct.

> 72. An amendment to paragraph 1(c) which was proposed by the Government member of Ecuador was not seconded and was not discussed. The Workers' members submitted a three-part amendment. They said that the use of the words "establish means for" would ensure that governments provided assistance, whereas opportunities were already available. They considered the replacement of "their" by "these peoples" to be consistent with the rest of the text and felt that the deletion of "in appropriate cases" would remove opportunities for governments to avoid co-operation. The Employers' members proposed a subamendment to delete the third part of the amendment, in order to retain flexibility in the Convention. The Workers' members did not accept this subamendment. Several Government members supported the subamendment. The Workers' members withdrew the third part of their amendment, which was then adopted as subamended. [37]

Paragraph 2 of Article 6, which had been inserted to reflect discussions in 1988, was examined closely as it was intended to set the tone for what consultations would meet the test of the Convention, and occasioned a long discussion.

---

36   Ibid.
37   Ibid.

73. An amendment to paragraph 2 submitted by the Government member of Ecuador was not seconded and was not considered. An amendment submitted by the Government member of Canada was withdrawn in favour of an amendment submitted by the Government members of Argentina and Bolivia. The Government member of Argentina said that the purpose of the amendment was to ensure effective participation of peoples in decisions which affected them, avoiding the use of the words "consent" or "agreement" which could make it difficult to ratify the Convention. The Workers' members considered that the replacement of the phrase relating to the achieving of agreement or consent would weaken the Article and opposed the amendment. Government members were evenly divided in their support for the amendment and for the draft text submitted by the Office. The Government member of Portugal, who opposed the amendment, believed that governments' concerns were fully covered in paragraph 1(a) of Article 6. The Government member of Denmark felt that sufficient flexibility in the wording was secured by the words "with the objective of" and opposed the amendment. The Employers' members considered that the extent of countries' experience with the issue had to be borne in mind and pointed out that not all countries had adequate resources to implement such requirements. They considered the text of the amendment to be realistic and supported it. The Workers' members pointed out that the purpose of any consultations was to reach an agreement, not merely to exchange information, but the amendment did not convey this meaning. The Government members of Australia, USSR and the United States supported this view. The Government member of Bolivia said that he did not wish to belittle the concept of consultation or to deprive these peoples of the opportunity of airing their opinions. The consultative system had to be applied in good faith. Before public authorities could obtain either agreement or consent, they had to consult. He did not want to see the opportunities for consultation reduced, but he felt that national legislative requirements should be taken into account. He supported the amendment. The Government members of Ecuador and India supported this view. The Government member of Argentina, in a statement clarifying the intention of the amendment, stated that the draft text submitted by the Office would give indigenous and tribal peoples opportunities to veto governments' decisions. States would have to obtain the consent of these peoples before taking decisions; such a procedure was not feasible. He realised the necessity of consulting with and involving these peoples, but felt that the draft text was too rigid and would lead to problems for ratification. The

Government member of Brazil expressed his full support for the amendment and stated that his Government would be unable to ratify the Convention with the text as it stood. The Workers' members called for a vote. The Government member of Venezuela, supporting the statement of the Government member of Argentina on the intent of the amendment, which he supported, felt that for the Convention to be universal in its application, efforts to reach an agreement should continue. The Government member of Portugal understood that the amendment addressed the fact that no part of a nation's population had the right to oppose a law after its adoption. She pointed out, however, that the situation under discussion was a prior phase of the legal process when consideration was being given to proposed measures.

Consultations were imperative at this juncture if governments were to be able to persuade people of the validity of their policies. She considered that the text did not clash with the legitimate concerns expressed by some Government members.

74. A representative of the Secretary-General stated that in drafting the text, the Office had not intended to suggest that the consultations referred to would have to result in the obtaining of agreement or consent of those being consulted, but rather to express an objective for the consultations. The Government members of Peru and the United States felt that the explanation was helpful, and considered that no right of veto would be acceptable. The Employers' members, in the light of the explanation, proposed to subamend the Office text. The Workers' members pointed out that the Office text could not be subamended at this stage[38] and repeated their call for a vote. The amendment was rejected by 750 votes in favour, 795 against, with 45 abstentions.

75. The Workers' members introduced an amendment to add words to paragraph 2 which they considered would make it more specific and not subject to misinterpretation. The Employers' members noted that the amendment overlapped part of the text in Article 33 of the proposed Convention and would also introduce new elements in the amendment (that) were alien to the goals of paragraph 2 as explained by the Office. They opposed the amendment. The Government member of the United States supported the views of the Employers' members. The amendment was not adopted.

---

[38] Note that by established procedure, subamendments from the floor can be made only to proposed amendments to the text submitted in writing to the Conference.

76. The Government member of Ecuador introduced an amendment to add a paragraph to Article 2 with the intention of making it more specific so that it would facilitate the consultative process and make it clear who was to be consulted under the terms of Article 6. The Employers' members agreed with the concept of the amendment but felt that it was already covered by the wording of paragraph 1(*a*) of the Article. They considered that the addition of administrative detail would endanger the future of the text. They did not support the amendment. The Workers' members opposed the amendment, which was not adopted.[39]

Thus paragraph 2 was not amended, and Article 6 was adopted as amended.

C. Development through Supervision

The subject of consultation, and the associated right of participation, has been the aspect of the rights of indigenous and tribal peoples that has received the most attention, both by the ILO supervisory process and outside the ILO.

The ILO's primary supervisory body, the Committee of Experts on the Application of Conventions and Recommendations, has monitored the application of this right in virtually all the ratifying countries. This section will not review the Committee's comments across all these countries individually, as most of the considerations that have emerged are reflected in a 2011 review of the situation by the Committee. In 2011 it summarized its approach to this question in a General Observation.[40]

This General Observation was prompted in part by the discussion in the 2010 Conference Committee on the Application of Conventions of the application by Peru of Convention No. 169.[41]

The Conference Committee was examining an observation on the application of the Convention in Peru which was in turn following up a discussion of this situation in 2009 in the Conference Committee. As the Committee of Experts had stated, *inter alia*:

---

39   Ibid., pp. 25/11 and 25/12.
40   Report of the Committee of Experts 2011. See on the ILO web site at www.ilo.org under NORMLEX.
41   International Labour Conference 2010, Proceedings of the Committee on the Application of Conventions, Provisional Record 16, pp. PartII/103 et seq.

The Committee shares the *grave concerns* of the Conference Committee about the incidents in Bagua in June 2009 and considers that they are related to the adoption, without consultation or participation, of decrees affecting the rights of peoples covered by the Convention to their lands and natural resources. The Committee notes that both the United Nations Special Rapporteur on the situation of human rights and fundamental freedoms of indigenous people and the United Nations Committee on the Elimination of Racial Discrimination have likewise expressed such concern at the situation of the indigenous peoples in Peru (see respectively, A/HRC/12/34/Add.8, 18 August 2009, and CERD/C/PER/CO/14-17, 31 August 2009). The Committee recalls that the Conference Committee called on the Government to make further efforts to guarantee indigenous peoples' human rights and fundamental freedoms without discrimination in accordance with its obligations under the Convention. The Committee is of the view that a prompt and impartial inquiry into the events in Bagua is essential to ensuring a climate of mutual trust and respect between the parties, a prerequisite for establishing genuine dialogue in the search for agreed solutions, as the Convention requires. ***The Committee accordingly urges the Government to take the necessary steps to have the incidents of June 2009 in Bagua effectively and impartially investigated, and to provide specific information on the matter.*** ...

The Committee also notes that several bodies have been set up whose purpose, according to the Government's report, is to establish dialogue with the indigenous peoples of the Amazonian and Andean areas. The Committee notes that, in March 2009, a Bureau for Ongoing Dialogue between the State and the Indigenous Peoples of the Amazonian Area of Peru was established and that, according to section 2 of Supreme Decree No. 002-2009-MIMBES establishing the Bureau, it "may" (*podrá*) include representatives of indigenous peoples. It also notes the Multisectoral Committee to deal with indigenous problems in the Amazonian area (Supreme Decree No. 031-2009-PCM of 19 May 2009), and observes that the minutes of the opening and first ordinary session of the Committee make no mention of indigenous representatives. It further notes the Bureau for Comprehensive Development of Andean Peoples (RS 133-2009-PCM, of 24 June 2009), the Bureau for Dialogue on the Comprehensive Development of Andean Peoples in Extreme Poverty (RS 135-2009-PCM of 26 June 2009) and the National Coordinating Group for the Development of Amazonian Peoples, which is responsible for formulating a comprehensive sustainable development plan for these peoples (Supreme Resolution No. 117-2009-PCM of 26 June 2009). With regard to the latter body, the Committee notes that it set up four working group to work on the composition of the Commission of Inquiry into the Bagua incidents, the revision of the legislative decrees, mechanisms for consultation and a national development plan for the Amazon region. The Committee likewise notes the concern expressed by the People's Ombudsperson about the status of the dialogue process established within the abovementioned Group.

The Committee has insufficient information to assess the level of participation ensured for indigenous peoples in the various bodies mentioned above. It nonetheless considers that the information supplied appears to indicate that, at least in some cases, the participation of indigenous peoples through their legitimate representatives and dialogue between the parties is not effective. The Committee also expresses *concern* that the proliferation of bodies with mandates that sometimes overlap may hamper the development of a coordinated and systematic response to the problems of protecting and ensuring the rights of indigenous peoples established in the Convention. *The Committee urges the Government to ensure full and effective participation and consultation of the indigenous peoples through their representative institutions in the preparation of the abovementioned plan of action, in accordance with Articles 2 and 6 of the Convention, so as to address in a coordinated and systematic manner outstanding problems concerning the protection of the rights of the peoples covered by the Convention, and to align law and practice with the Convention. It also asks the Government to provide information on this matter and on the work of the various bodies mentioned above, indicating how the participation of the peoples concerned and the coordination of the activities of these bodies are ensured, as well as coordination between the work of these bodies and the preparation of the plan of action. Please provide a copy of the plan of action as soon as it is finalized.*

In the discussion in that year's Conference Committee, the issues of competence and mandate examined in the introductory materials of this volume resurfaced in a way that indicated that some of the more conservative members of the Employers' group had never really accepted the very existence of the Convention. This is also a part of a much broader and on-going examination in the ILO of the Employers' Group's criticism of the Committee of Experts for over-interpreting the meaning of Conventions, which will not be examined in detail here.[42]

---

42 See, e.g., the discussion of this issue in the November 2014 Session of the ILO Governing Body, which as this volume is written is only the latest manifestation of a long discussion.

The Employers' members' spokesperson stated in the discussion of Peru's application of Convention No. 169:

> They recalled that Article 6 of the Convention was the principal clause concerning the right of consultation, and that the definition of the latter term had been extensively discussed in the deliberations preceding the Convention's adoption. From the records of these discussions, it was clear that consultation did not equate to, or require, the consent of the parties being consulted. The record of the second round of discussions preceding the Convention's adoption showed that the Employers' group believed the term "consultations" to signify "dialogue, at least", and the Office itself had stated that it did not consider the consultations referred to, to require the agreement or consent of those being consulted. In its observation, however, the Committee of Experts appeared to have interpreted the term so as to impose a more exacting requirement upon the Government beyond that envisaged by the Convention; the potential consequences of this interpretation would be discussed and examined by several of the Employer members in the course of the discussion.

This statement was followed up by statements of some members who were adamantly opposed to basic concepts in the Convention, at least in the formulation by the ILO, and by a lively rebuttal by others:

> **The Employer member of Mexico** argued that the Committee of Experts had exceeded its mandate. He explained that he had been the Employer spokesperson during the discussions that led to the adoption of Convention No. 169 and that he knew well the spirit of the provisions. It was inaccurate that consultations had to achieve agreement and it was incorrect to interpret that it was possible to require a hold on or suspension of economic activities. Article 6 of the Convention did not have, and never had, a binding nature. The Committee of Experts should not be able to change the meaning of the provisions of Conventions. He concluded by declaring that he felt that the Government was adopting a legislative package appropriate for implementation of the Convention.
> **The Worker member of the Bolivarian Republic of Venezuela** highlighted the importance of ancestral rights of indigenous peoples as native peoples. She recalled that 70 per cent of the country's population had its ancestral roots in indigenous communities. She requested that the Government acknowledge the right of Peruvian indigenous peoples to maintain their culture and traditions. She urged the Government to enact

the Bill on the right to prior consultations, end indiscriminate overexploitation of natural resources, put an end to the persecution of Andean and union leaders and guarantee the right of indigenous peoples to mandatory consultation on decisions in which they had a say.

The Employer member of Colombia stated that only five of the provisions of the Convention related to labour issues and that the other topics included were outside the ILO's competence. There were many regional and international instruments, as well as specialized organizations, to guarantee the protection of indigenous peoples. The ILO should limit itself to the field of labour. He expressed his concern that the Committee of Experts wished to introduce an injunctive measure to suspend economic activity that did not exist in the Convention. He also pointed out that there was no justification in the Convention for a need to reach agreement through consultations.

The Worker member of France responded to certain statements of the Employer members by recalling that Convention No. 169 was not the only Convention in which the ILO had addressed questions of civilization in close synergy with the United Nations. The Convention had been adopted by the Conference, and it was an international treaty that, once ratified by a member State, had to be implemented in its entirety. As regards the calling into question of the Committee of Experts' mandate and impartiality, it should be recalled that the interpretation of the text of a Convention was indispensable in order to clarify how its objective might be effectively attained. It should therefore be stressed that the Committee of Experts had not exceeded its prerogatives. The speaker emphasized that the word "consultation", as reflected in the text of the Convention, implied that consultations had to be undertaken in good faith, that is to say taking into account the views expressed. In the case under discussion, however, the Committee of Experts considered that the Government had not conformed to the objective of the Convention. He expressed the hope that the Act on Prior Consultation, referred to by the Government, would resolve the problem. However, the fact that three-quarters of the country had already been handed over for exploitation was a source of concern. The value of the territories went far beyond their market value. The discussion of this case revealed two conflicting ideologies: on the one hand, a capitalist approach, and on the other, a philosophy of sustainable development.

There was a good deal more of this discussion along the same polarized lines, and the discussion concluded with further remarks on behalf of the Employers' and Workers' Groups, and an attempt by the Office to calm the situation:

The Employer members...noted that no person or institution was infallible and that, based on the testimony and evidence presented, it would be prudent for the Committee of Experts to reconsider its conclusions with respect to the interpretation of certain provisions of the Convention that had been addressed by Employer members.

The Worker members considered that the Employer members had unjustly challenged Convention No. 169 and that their discourse on treaty interpretation could not hide the lack of any real arguments on the substance of the case. ...

The representative of the Secretary-General stated that she wished to provide some clarifications. The word "consultation" was probably found in every ILO instrument; it was the very backbone of international labour standards, since all Conventions and Recommendations included a provision on consulting with workers' and employers' organizations, or required consulting with "workers and employers" concerned or groups of persons concerned, such as persons with disabilities. However, this common, very important concept had to be construed within the overall context of the instrument in which it was placed. Consultation was an obligation irrespective of the language used, such as the expression "shall consult". Article 6 of Convention No. 169 highlighted this term more than most provisions, and to interpret it correctly, one needed to look at the Article in its entirety, and not just part of it. Paragraph 2 of Article 6 set out that consultations carried out in application of the Convention had to be taken in good faith, and in a form appropriate to the circumstances, with the objective of achieving agreement or consent. This provision did not require that consultations had to reach agreement, but meant more than merely consulting and moving on. One had to consult in good faith and with the objective of achieving consent. Both the English and the French versions of the text were clear. They did not compel agreement or consensus. The same understanding was reflected in the Committee of Experts' observation which was being discussed in this case. She further stated that, as an ILO Convention, Convention No. 169 could not be disowned; it was a revision of the Indigenous and Tribal Populations Convention, 1957 (No. 107). The ILO was the first organization with a Convention on indigenous peoples and it was the only organization with a binding instrument on indigenous peoples. These elements of clarification were provided while recognizing that this remained a sensitive and controversial issue.

The Employer members thanked the Office for the clarifications but indicated that the word "consult" had a different meaning in English than in French, where it had a stronger connotation. Leaving this distinction aside, it was clear that failure to consult should not be taken to mean that one might stop economic development. To this end, when they questioned the Committee of Experts as to the true meaning of the Convention, they were referring to its injunctive aspects.

Observers of this discussion might be justified in thinking that – broader issues of the power of the Committee of Experts to interpret Conventions aside – the discussion was triggered by what the Employers' spokesperson referred to in his concluding remarks, and what the Employer member from Colombia mentioned: that a conscientious application of the obligation to hold full consultations before undertaking development activities affecting indigenous and tribal peoples would slow down business interests with regard to exploitation of natural resources.

Following this discussion the Committee of Experts adopted a General Observation on the meaning and implications of the obligation to consult. A large part of the text reviews the drafting history, which is already examined above and is omitted, so the following extracts of the General Observation focus on the Committee's understanding of the meaning and implications of the requirement.

> In light of the above, the Committee makes this general observation in order to clarify its understanding of the concept of "consultation" in the hope that this will result in an improved application of the Convention particularly as it concerns this right. This would be a follow-up to the general observation made by this Committee in 2008...
>
> As a general matter the Committee notes that, in view of the tripartite nature of the ILO, most of its Conventions make specific provision for consultation between governments and representatives of employers and workers or their organizations and of those concerned by the issues involved on the matters covered by the Conventions. Convention No. 169 is no exception. However, the provisions relating to "consultation" in Convention No. 169 specifically address consultation with indigenous and tribal peoples. The relevant provisions of the Convention are Articles 6, 7, 15 and 17.[43]...Articles 27 and 28 also refer to consultation specifically regarding education.
>
> The presence of consultation in the abovementioned provisions signifies a comprehensive approach. These provisions on consultation were among the fundamental principles included in the revision of the

---

43   The texts of Articles 6, 7, 15 and 17 of Convention No. 169 were quoted here.

Indigenous and Tribal Populations Convention, 1957 (No. 107), as a necessary requirement to eliminate the integrationist approach of that Convention. In order to properly understand the scope of this new principle inserted in Convention No. 169, the Committee undertook an exhaustive review of the preparatory work leading up to the inclusion of this principle and right in Convention No. 169.

...

The Committee of Experts in reviewing countries' compliance with the Convention has remained true to the above understanding of the Convention. It has consistently indicated that "consultation and participation" constitute the cornerstone of Convention No. 169 on which all its provisions are based. Its general observation of 2008, published in 2009, reflected the above understanding of the relevant provisions of the Convention concerning the concept of consultation. The Committee stated:

With regard to consultation, the Committee notes two main challenges: (i) ensuring that appropriate consultations are held prior to the adoption of all legislative and administrative measures which are likely to affect indigenous and tribal peoples directly; and (ii) including provisions in legislation requiring prior consultation as part of the process of determining if concessions for the exploitation and exploration of natural resources are to be granted. The form and content of consultation procedures and mechanisms need to allow the full expression of the viewpoints of the peoples concerned, in a timely manner and based on their full understanding of the issues involved, so that they may be able to affect the outcome and a consensus could be achieved, and be undertaken in a manner that is acceptable to all parties. If these requirements are met, consultation can be an instrument of genuine dialogue, social cohesion and be instrumental in the prevention and resolution of conflict. The Committee, therefore, considers it important that governments, with the participation of indigenous and tribal peoples, as a matter of priority, establish appropriate consultation mechanisms with the representative institutions of those peoples. Periodic evaluation of the operation of the consultation mechanisms, with the participation of the peoples concerned, should be undertaken to continue to improve their effectiveness.

The Committee encourages governments to continue their efforts, with the participation of indigenous and tribal peoples, in the following areas, and to provide information in future reports on the measures taken in this regard:

- developing the measures and mechanisms envisaged in Articles 2 and 33 of the Convention;
- establishing mechanisms for participation in the formulation of development plans;
- including the requirement of prior consultation in legislation regarding the exploration and exploitation of natural resources;
- engaging in systematic consultation on the legislative and administrative measures referred to in Article 6 of the Convention; and
- establishing effective consultation mechanisms that take into account the vision of governments and indigenous and tribal peoples concerning the procedures to be followed.[44]

The Committee notes…that the above understanding of the relevant provisions of Convention No. 169 has also been endorsed by a number of tripartite committees examining representations against governments for failure to comply with the provisions of the Convention.[45]

In the case of Ecuador, the tripartite committee, in its report approved by the Governing Body in 2001, referred to the preparatory work of the Convention and stated that it considered that the "concept of consulting the indigenous communities…includes establishing a genuine dialogue between both parties characterized by communication and understanding, mutual respect, good faith and the sincere wish to reach a common accord".[46] It indicated that a simple information meeting cannot be considered as complying with the provisions of the Convention and that the consultation should occur beforehand, which implies that the communities affected should participate as early as possible in the process, including in the preparation of environmental impact studies. Taking into account the preparatory work, the tripartite committee in that case concluded that, while Article 6 did not require consensus to have been reached in the process of prior consultation, it does stipulate that the peoples involved should have the opportunity to participate freely at all levels in the formulation, implementation and evaluation of measures

---

44   See ILC, 98th Session, 2009, Report of the Committee of Experts on the Application of Conventions and Recommendations, Report III (Part 1A), pp. 672–673.

45   Four tripartite committees established by the Governing Body under article 24 of the ILO Constitution to examine representations have examined this obligation in the context of Convention No. 169: the cases of Colombia and Ecuador in 2001, Argentina in 2008 and Brazil in 2009.

46   See GB.282/14/2, paras 36–39.

and programmes that affect them directly, as from the date on which the Convention comes into force in the country.[47]

In the representation filed against Colombia under the Convention, the tripartite committee, in its report approved by the Governing Body in 2001, considered that the concept of consultation under the Convention must encompass genuine dialogue between the parties, involving communication and understanding, mutual respect and good faith and the sincere desire to reach consensus. The tripartite committee concluded that a meeting conducted merely for information purposes or meetings or consultations conducted after the granting of an environmental licence did not meet the requirements of Articles 6 and 15(2) of the Convention.[48]

In the case of the representation filed against Argentina, the tripartite committee, in its report approved by the Governing Body in 2008, pointed out that Article 6 of the Convention does not stipulate that consent must be obtained in order for the consultation to be valid, but that it does require pursuit of the objective of achieving consent, which means setting in motion a process of dialogue and genuine exchange between the parties to be carried out in good faith.[49]

Finally, in the representation filed against Brazil, the tripartite committee, in its report approved by the Governing Body in 2009, gave an extensive explanation of the consultation process provided for under Article 6 of the Convention.[50] The tripartite committee in that case recalled that consultation and participation are the cornerstone of the Convention and that such mechanisms are not merely a formal requirement, but are intended to enable indigenous peoples to participate effectively in their own development.[51] It stated that consultation must take place in accordance with procedures that are appropriate to the circumstances, through indigenous peoples' representative institutions, in good faith and with the objective of achieving agreement or consent to the proposed measures. Concerning "appropriate procedures", the tripartite committee stated that there is no single model, which should take into account national circumstances, the circumstances of the indigenous peoples concerned and the nature of the measures which are the object

---

47 Ibid., para. 36.
48 See GB.282/14/3, para. 90.
49 See GB.303/19/7, para. 81
50 See GB.304/14/7, paras 42–44.
51 Ibid., para. 44.

of the consultation process.[52] The tripartite committee also made it clear that Article 6 must be understood within the broader context of consultation and participation, particularly within the framework of Article 2(1) and Article 33, which require the development, with the participation of the peoples concerned, of coordinated and systematic action to protect their rights and guarantee their integrity,[53] and to ensure that agencies or other appropriate mechanisms exist to administer the programmes affecting the peoples concerned.[54] The tripartite committee noted that "consultation, as envisaged in the Convention, extends beyond consultation on specific cases: it means that application of the provisions of the Convention must be systematic and coordinated, and undertaken with indigenous peoples..."[55]

Taking into account all the elements indicated above, the Committee wishes thus to restate its understanding of the concept of consultation as concerns: the subject matter of consultation or participation; who should be responsible for such consultation; and the characteristics of consultation.

Concerning the subject matter, the Committee considers that consultation of indigenous and tribal peoples is specifically required in respect of the following: legislative or administrative matters which may affect them directly (Article 6(1)(a)); undertaking or permitting any programmes for the exploration or exploitation of mineral or sub-surface resources pertaining to their lands (Article 15(2)); whenever consideration is being given to their capacity to alienate their lands or otherwise transmit their rights outside their own community (Article 17(2)); and specific matters related to education (Articles 27(3) and 28(1)).

Free and informed consent of indigenous and tribal peoples is required where relocation of these peoples from lands which they occupy is considered necessary as an exceptional measure (Article 16(2)).

The participation of indigenous and tribal peoples is required in respect of the following: the development of coordinated and systematic action to protect the rights of indigenous and tribal peoples and to guarantee respect for their integrity (Article 2(1)); the adoption of policies aimed at mitigating the difficulties experienced by these peoples in

---

52   Ibid., para. 42.
53   Article 2(1).
54   Article 33(1).
55   See GB.304/14/7, para. 43.

facing new conditions of life and work (Article 5(c)); decision-making in elective institutions and administrative and other bodies responsible for policies and programmes which concern them (Article 6(1)(b)); the formulation, implementation and evaluation of plans and programmes for national and regional development which may affect them directly (Article 7(1)); the improvement of the conditions of life and work and levels of health and education (Article 7(2)); the use, management and conservation of the natural resources pertaining to their lands (Article 15(1)); and ensuring that traditional activities are strengthened and promoted (Article 23(1)).

With respect to the authority responsible for consultation, Articles 2 and 6 put that responsibility on governments. Governments are required under Article 6 to "consult the peoples concerned, through appropriate procedures..." and to "establish means by which these peoples can freely participate..."

Concerning the nature of consultation, from the review of the preparatory work concerning Convention No. 169 and from the review of the wording of the two authoritative texts of the Convention, the Committee concludes that it was the intention of the drafters of the Convention that the obligation to consult under the Convention was intended to mean that:

(1) consultations must be formal, full and exercised in good faith;[56] there must be a genuine dialogue between governments and indigenous and tribal peoples characterized by communication and understanding, mutual respect, good faith and the sincere wish to reach a common accord;

(2) appropriate procedural mechanisms have to be put in place at the national level and they have to be in a form appropriate to the circumstances;

(3) consultations have to be undertaken through indigenous and tribal peoples' representative institutions as regards legislative and administrative measures;

(4) consultations have to be undertaken with the objective of reaching agreement or consent to the proposed measures.

It is clear from the above that pro forma consultations or mere information would not meet the requirements of the Convention. At the same

---

56   See ILC, 76th Session, 1989, Report IV (2A), pp. 19–21.

time, such consultations do not imply a right to veto,[57] nor is the result of such consultations necessarily the reaching of agreement or consent.[58]

With this text the Committee of Experts, summarizing also the findings of four article 24 representations, has explained and developed the requirements of consultation in the Convention.

---

57 Ibid., para. 74.
58 Ibid.

CHAPTER 5

Article 7 of Convention No. 169 – Participation, Development and the Environment

Article 7 of Convention No. 169 reads:

> 1. The peoples concerned shall have the right to decide their own priorities for the process of development as it affects their lives, beliefs, institutions and spiritual well-being and the lands they occupy or otherwise use, and to exercise control, to the extent possible, over their own economic, social and cultural development. In addition, they shall participate in the formulation, implementation and evaluation of plans and programmes for national and regional development which may affect them directly.
> 2. The improvement of the conditions of life and work and levels of health and education of the peoples concerned, with their participation and co-operation, shall be a matter of priority in plans for the overall economic development of areas they inhabit. Special projects for development of the areas in question shall also be so designed as to promote such improvement.
> 3. Governments shall ensure that, whenever appropriate, studies are carried out, in co-operation with the peoples concerned, to assess the social, spiritual, cultural and environmental impact on them of planned development activities. The results of these studies shall be considered as fundamental criteria for the implementation of these activities.
> 4. Governments shall take measures, in co-operation with the peoples concerned, to protect and preserve the environment of the territories they inhabit.

This Article has no immediate predecessor in C. 107. It is an extension and development of the concepts contained in Article 6, and much of the background to Article 6 which is reproduced in the chapter on that Article applies equally here. The right of indigenous and tribal peoples to participation and to an active role in determining their own future and priorities is another step beyond the concept of consultation.

A   The Meeting of Experts

The first suggestion of what was to become Article 7 is found in a proposal made during the 1986 Meeting of Experts, which has already been reproduced earlier:

> 54. After considerable discussion, a group of experts and observers offered the following text as an attempt to meet the objections which had been raised while reflecting the principles included in the concept of self-determination:
> *Replace the fourth preambular paragraph of Convention No. 107 with:*
> Considering that the International Covenant on Economic, Social and Cultural Rights affirms the fundamental importance of the right to self-determination, as well as the right of all human beings to pursue their material, cultural and spiritual development in conditions of freedom and dignity;
> Recognising that these rights are fundamental to the survival and future development of indigenous and tribal peoples as distinctive and viable societies;
> *Replace Articles 2 and 5 with:*
> *Article 2*
> In co-operation with indigenous and tribal peoples, governments shall have the responsibility for developing co-ordinated and systematic action to ensure:
> (*a*) that indigenous and tribal peoples are able to enjoy the full measure of human rights and fundamental freedoms without hindrance or discrimination;
> (*b*) that indigenous and tribal peoples' territorial rights, economic rights, and political, social, cultural, and religious institutions are recognised and protected;
> (*c*) that indigenous and tribal peoples be accorded the respect of determining for themselves the process of development as it affects their lives and institutions.
> 55. This proposal received substantial general support among many experts, who endorsed the ideas contained in it. They felt that, while it was clear that the present Meeting had not been convened to offer specific amendments to the text of the present Convention, the text quoted above reflected many elements of consensus among them. All of the employer experts and some government experts, expressed reservations, however.

56. Those offering the proposal wished it to be clarified that the principle of self-determination to which reference was made in the draft preambular paragraphs should be understood to mean self-determination in economic, social and cultural fields. In addition, the reference to political institutions in the draft Article 2, paragraph (b), should be understood to refer to the political institutions of indigenous and tribal peoples themselves which were used to regulate their internal affairs. It was also stated that the intention was that draft Article 2 would create no rights in itself, but would provide basic guide-lines in the light of which the rest of the revised Convention would be interpreted.[1]

Among the conclusions adopted by the Meeting of Experts was:

2. Indigenous and tribal peoples should enjoy as much control as possible over their own economic, social and cultural development.[2]

B   The 1988 Discussion

As the Office prepared the law and practice report it evoked the approach taken to indigenous affairs in various States. In doing so it cited one of the trends it found in some States:

...bodies directly concerned with indigenous and tribal questions can be established within the legislative branch of government, or indigenous peoples guaranteed participation in development commissions examining issues which affect their interests.[3]

The report cited a number of instances at the national level in which measures had been taken to ensure indigenous participation in development planning and implementation. The report went on to examine approaches to this that might be taken in a new instrument:

In commenting on the draft of the present report, UNESCO noted that it was not wise to rely on a single policy of integrationism or non-integrationism. Some indigenous peoples prefer one approach, and some

---

1   Report of the Meeting of Experts, reproduced in Report VI (1) of 1988, pp. 109 and 110.
2   Ibid., p. 117.
3   Ibid., p. 20.

the other, while the greater part prefer integration and equality in the public domain (work, education, etc.), and non-integration in the private domain (cultural rights, religious rights, certain language rights, etc.). What is needed is a number of possible models, all of which involve the principles of equality and of participation in decisions affecting the community.[4]

The Office report then began to explore how these concepts might be reflected in a revised Convention, initially making proposals that eventually would be re-divided and placed in different parts of a new instrument:

> *Article 6*
> During the Meeting of Experts frequent mention was made of this Article, which was considered to be of fundamental importance because of the emphasis it places on the economic development of areas inhabited by these peoples. None of the participants found it to be in need of revision in itself, but it was felt that some additional reinforcement of the principle of consultation might be appropriate here.
>
> This concern might be met by making the present text of Article 6 the first paragraph of an expanded Article; a second paragraph might then provide that the peoples concerned should be involved at all stages in the formulation and implementation of development plans, and should enjoy as much control as possible over their own economic, social and cultural development. The first part of this sentence would specifically call for the application of the principle expressed in general terms under the proposed Article 2 above to the development process, while the second part would correspond to the suggestion made in Conclusion 2 of the Meeting of Experts, which was discussed earlier in this chapter under the heading "Degree of control over the decision-making process".[5]

The questionnaire sent to the ILO's constituents therefore included the following:

> 22. *Do you consider that a paragraph should be added to Article 6 providing -*
> (a) *that the peoples concerned should be involved at all stages in the formulation and implementation of plans for development of the areas which they inhabit, and*

---

4   Ibid., p. 29.
5   Ibid., p. 36.

(b) *that they should enjoy as much control as possible over their own economic, social and cultural development?*

23. Do you consider that another paragraph should be added to Article 6 providing that, whenever appropriate, social and environmental studies should be carried out before any such development activities are begun, in order to assess the possible impact of these activities on the peoples concerned?[6]

The replies to these questions began to define the concepts that would appear in C. 169, while also expressing the division of opinions among participants.

> The great majority of replies to this question were in the affirmative. Certain textual changes have been put forward either to provide for some flexibility, or to strengthen the terminology adopted. With regard to the former, it has been suggested in two replies that the words "whenever possible" or "to the extent possible" should be inserted because it may not always be possible for the peoples concerned to be involved at all stages in development plans and programmes. It has been proposed by Canada (IWG)[7] – reflecting a view strongly endorsed by other indigenous organisations – that the words "enjoy as much control as possible" should be replaced by the words "should control". This relates to the same issues discussed above, particularly under questions 10, 11, 19 and 20.
>
> The Proposed Conclusions recognise the general principle that the peoples concerned should have the right to decide their own priorities for the process of development and to exercise control over it. In order to achieve this, they should therefore be involved to the extent possible in the formulation and implementation of plans and programmes for the development of the areas which they inhabit. The inclusion of the words "to the extent possible" is not intended to be a limitation in any way of the right to be involved in the formulation and implementation of development plans and programmes, but simply to provide the necessary flexibility if involvement at all stages does not prove logistically possible.
>
> The proposal by Canada (IWG) under question 22 (*a*) reflects the difficulty of formulating concepts which accurately take account of the

---

6 Ibid., p. 95.

7 IWG was the consultative group of indigenous representatives that Canada had convened to advise it on Canadian proposals for the ILO discussions. By including the recommendations made by this group in its own report, the Government of Canada made it possible for the Office to take explicit notice of them in analyzing reactions to the proposals being made.

many kinds of living and land use patterns among these peoples. The issue is discussed under questions 33 to 46.[8]

The proposed conclusions on this point that were forwarded to the first discussion in 1988 read as follows (with the changes or additions compared to C. 107 in italics):

> 14. The improvement of the conditions of life and work and level of education of the *peoples* concerned should be given high priority in plans for the overall economic development of areas inhabited by *them*. Special projects for development of the areas in question should also be so designed as to promote such improvement.
> 15. *The peoples concerned should have the right to decide their own priorities for the process of development as it affects their lives and institutions, and to exercise control over their own economic, social and cultural development. To this end, they should be involved to the extent possible in the formulation and implementation of plans and programmes for the development of the areas which they inhabit.*
> 16. *Whenever appropriate, social and environmental studies should be carried out, in collaboration with the peoples concerned, to assess the possible impact of planned development activities on the said peoples.*[9]

The discussion of proposed conclusion 14 in the 1988 Conference discussion began the process of moving to new language:

> *Point 14*
> 82. The Workers' members submitted an amendment calling for the deletion of this Point. They said it contained old-fashioned language and was paternalistic, and that the concepts expressed were already contained in Point 6. There was considerable discussion on whether the proposed Point was valid and useful. The Government member of Bolivia stated that the Point was valid within the general objectives of promoting the development of indigenous populations. Several Government members expressed similar opinions. The Government member of India advised against overemphasising the paternalistic aspect and the Government member of the United States preferred to see a full range of

---

8 Report VI (2), pp. 34 and 35.
9 Ibid., p. 107.

opportunities for development expressed in the document. In the light of their views, the Workers' members withdrew the amendment.

83. The Government member of New Zealand proposed an amendment to replace "co-operation" by "partnership" and to provide that these measures should be a matter of the highest priority. The Workers' members introduced a subamendment to amend "partnership" to "full participation and co-operation" and supported the amendment. The Committee discussed whether the terms participation, cooperation or consultation should be used, and noted that all three had been agreed to in different contexts. The Employers' members and several Government members were opposed to the use of the term "highest" in connection with priority, and stated that a high priority was sufficient. A consensus emerged that the term "participation and co-operation" was acceptable.

84. Point 14, as amended, was adopted.[10]

For once, the report of the Conference Committee leaves gaps between the text submitted, the discussion and the conclusions – perhaps an editorial error. For instance, the text contained in Report VI (2) for point 14 contains no reference to participation and co-operation. The amended text of Point 14 that was adopted by the Committee, in spite of the gaps in the written record, was the following:

> 14. The improvement of the conditions of life and work and level of education of the (peoples/populations) concerned should with their participation and co-operation, be a matter of priority in plans for the overall economic development of areas inhabited by them. Special projects for development of the areas in question should also be so designed as to promote such improvement.[11]

The discussion of point 15 in the 1988 Conference session revealed continuing disagreement over the orientation of the revised Convention (see para. 85 of the selection below), as well as growing consensus among the majority of participants.

Point 15
85. The Government member of Bangladesh made a general statement in which he explained the system of development relating to indigenous

---

10 Proceedings 1988, p. 32/11.
11 Ibid., p. 32/24.

populations in his country, which included significant representation in parliament, various walks of life and professions. A member of the cabinet belonged to the tribal population. Tribal population had appropriate representation in the sub-district councils, district councils and municipal bodies, which were always consulted before any development project was undertaken. He pointed out that the objective of Convention No. 107 was to integrate tribal populations into the mainstream of national life so that they could benefit from economic progress. In his view, Point 15 was contrary to this objective and he had submitted an amendment calling for its deletion. However, in the light of the discussion on Point 14, he withdrew his amendment. Two amendments intended to emphasise participation and consultation but to retain the right of control of governments, were submitted by the Government member of India and the Employers' members. The amendments were considered jointly. The Government member of India said that while his Government supported the ideas of participation and consultation it had reservations about conferring the right of decision-making on any group. He felt that while the Office text for the revision had been drafted with good intentions, Point 15 was unrealistic in suggesting that these peoples be given the right to exercise control over the development process. This view was shared by the Employers' members so far as their amendment was concerned. The Government member of Brazil emphasised the need to have a Convention which would be widely ratified and supported the attempt of the Government member of India to introduce an element of flexibility. The Workers' members did not support the amendment of the Government member of India which, in their opinion, would severely weaken the influence of indigenous and tribal peoples on decision-making. This view was echoed by the Government member of Colombia.

86. The amendment submitted by the Government member of India was rejected by 315 votes in favour, 2,700 against, with 2,160 abstentions. The amendment submitted by the Employers' members was rejected by 2,430 votes in favour, 2,520 against, with 225 abstentions.

87. The Workers' members introduced an amendment to include the term territories in this Point. They withdrew that part of the amendment calling for its inclusion in Point 14 and the deletion of the word "should". The Employers' members said that the term territories was inappropriate in view of the objective of the text to allow indigenous populations to determine their own priorities. Moreover, they felt that the use of the term could cause legal difficulties and pointed out that it was included in the original Convention. Several governments expressed their opposition

to the use of the term since it had implications for national sovereignty. The amendment was adopted by 2,565 votes in favour, 2,530 against, with 180 abstentions.

88. The amendment proposed by the Government member of New Zealand to include reference to spiritual well-being was supported by the Government member of Colombia who proposed a subamendment to include the term "belief". The amendment was adopted by consensus.

89. An amendment introduced by the Government member of Canada to add the words "to the extent possible", intended to leave the text flexible enough to ensure a higher level of ratification, was adopted by 3,465 votes in favour, 3,213 against, with 189 abstentions.

90. An amendment calling for the insertion of a reference to national legal standards was submitted by the Government member of Bolivia. The Employers' members felt that the text of Point 15 already covered the matter. The Workers' members held a similar view and the amendment was not adopted.[12]

91. The Committee considered two amendments intended to safeguard participation by indigenous peoples in matters concerning them. The amendment proposed by the Government member of Peru was withdrawn in favour of that submitted by the Workers' members. The Employers' members considered that the original text was more appropriate and opposed the amendment. The Government member of Mexico stated in supporting the amendment that the involvement of these peoples in the process of development should be as broad as possible. The amendment was adopted by 3,402 votes in favour, 819 against, with 2,226 abstentions.

92. Point 15, as amended, was adopted.[13]

The outcome of these discussions was a revised point 15:

15. The (peoples/populations) concerned should have the right to decide their own priorities for the process of development as it affects their lives, beliefs, territories, institutions and spiritual well-being and to exercise control, to the extent possible, over their own economic, social and cultural development. In addition, they should be involved in the formulation

---

[12] Note that under ILO procedures, once the Employers' and Workers' members of a Conference committee agree, there is no need to pursue the question to a vote because between them they control 2/3 of the Committee's voting power.

[13] Proceedings 1988, pp. 32/11 and 32/12.

and implementation of plans and programmes for national and regional development which may affect them directly.[14]

The discussion of point 16 in the 1988 Conference was briefer than on the other two points.

Point 16
93. Five amendments had been submitted on Point 16. The Workers' members withdrew an amendment referring to the preservation of environmental integrity. They now felt this should be considered in Part III of the proposed revised instrument, and stated that they would return to it next year. A second amendment submitted by the Workers' members put greater emphasis on environmental impact studies and was intended to put an obligation on governments to carry them out; it also added the word "spiritual". A more limited amendment to the same effect, which had been proposed by the Government member of Peru, was withdrawn in favour of the former amendment. The Government member of Peru said that governments should carry out social and other studies in developing plans involving indigenous populations. The Employers' members, and the Government member of Botswana, were of the opinion that the original text was more relevant and opposed the amendment. In supporting the amendment, the Government member of India considered that the clause should start with the words "Wherever appropriate". The Government member of Japan supported this view. After several Government members had expressed their support for the Workers' members' amendment, the Employers' members withdrew their opposition and the amendment was adopted by consensus. The Government member of Japan expressed his reservations over the adoption. In view of the adoption of the Workers' members' amendment, the Government member of New Zealand withdrew a related amendment.
94. The Workers' members tabled an amendment intended to require governments to ensure that the peoples concerned had adequate resources to carry out such studies for themselves. The Employers' members and several Government members expressed their opposition since they were of the opinion that its adoption would result in the undertaking of parallel sets of studies. The Workers' members proposed a subamendment to modify the text to require governments to make adequate resources available for indigenous people to carry out studies for themselves.

---

14   Ibid., pp. 32/24 and 32/25.

The Employers' members opposed the subamendment since in their opinion it was unnecessary and would dilute the impact of the Convention. The Workers' members withdrew the subamendment, reserving the right to address the issue at the 76th Session of the Conference.
95. Point 16, as amended, was adopted.[15]

The amended version of point 16 adopted by the Conference was:

> 16. Governments should ensure that studies are carried out, in collaboration with the (peoples/populations) concerned, to assess the social, spiritual, cultural and environmental impact of planned development activities on them.[16]

C The 1989 Discussion

When these points were translated into a draft Convention for submission to the constituents pending the 1989 Session of the Conference, the Office rendered the draft on this point as follows:

> *Article 7*
> 1. The improvement of the conditions of life and work and level of education of the (peoples/populations) concerned, with their participation and co-operation, shall be a matter of priority in plans for the overall economic development of areas inhabited by them. Special projects for development of the areas in question shall also be so designed as to promote such improvement.
> 2. The (peoples/populations) concerned shall have the right to decide their own priorities for the process of development as it affects their lives, beliefs, territories, institutions and spiritual well-being and to exercise control, to the extent possible, over their own economic, social and cultural development. In addition, they shall be involved in the formulation and implementation of plans and programmes for national and regional development which may affect them directly.
> 3. Governments shall ensure that studies are carried out, in collaboration with the (peoples/populations) concerned, to assess the social, spiritual,

---

15 Ibid., p. 32/12.
16 Ibid., p. 32/25.

cultural and environmental impact of planned development activities on them.[17]

The Office commentary on the comments received on this proposed Article made it clear that a number of governments were still not entirely reconciled to the proposal that indigenous and tribal peoples should exercise any degree of control whatsoever over the development process, even when this was qualified by limitations on their ability of make final decisions. The relevant passages in the report were as follows:

> The proposals for an additional provision on protection of environmental integrity[18] would fit well in this Article on development activities. The listing of aspects of the environment has not been included. This would appear also to meet the concern expressed by Brazil (CONTAG).
>
> The observations by the Governments of India and Japan and by Brazil (CNI) appear to be based on a reading of paragraph 2 which does not correspond to the Office's understanding of that text.[19] The first sentence would establish the principle of the right to decide on their priorities, but the words "to the extent possible" qualify the right to exercise control over the development process and would not remove a government's power to decide. The proposal to delete "to the extent possible" has not been retained for this reason. In the same connection, the proposal by the Government of Norway appears to be based on the supposition that development activities would always be administered by these peoples in their areas, and thus has not been retained. The suggestion by the Government of Argentina has been included.[20]
>
> The proposal to add "whenever appropriate" in paragraph 3 has been retained. It would not be desirable to make the requirement of this paragraph absolute, for the reasons expressed.
>
> The proposal by the Government of Chile would not be inconsistent with the wording of this Article if official channels are adequate to the

---

17   Report IV (1), p. 8.
18   Proposal made by the Government, the trade unions and the Sami representatives of Norway, and by the IPWG (Indigenous Peoples Working Group) of Canada.
19   The Government of Japan said: 'paragraph 2 is not acceptable, as governments cannot surrender the right to decide priorities and to make decisions on economic development affecting the entire population.'
20   Argentina proposed adding "evaluation" after "implementation".

needs of consultation.[21] As in many other regards, however, the situation of these peoples often makes it impossible for them to have access to these official channels in practice, in which case appropriate additional consultative measures would be required. Similarly, the proposal by the Government of India[22] would unduly restrict the kinds of consultation which would be carried out and limit the flexibility of this Article.

The proposals by Canada (IPWG) for additional wording in paragraphs 1 and 2 have not been retained, since the more general terms already used would not appear to benefit from narrower definition. The proposal by the Government of Colombia on paragraph 1 would remove an inconsistency in the original.

The proposal by the Government of Canada to replace "territories" by "lands" in paragraph 2 has not been retained, independently of any decisions which may be made concerning Part II. The term "territories" is appropriate here as being more flexible and somewhat wider, without requiring in this particular context that decisions be made as to its exact meaning.

The proposal by the Government of Colombia[23] on paragraph 2 would reduce flexibility and impose a positive obligation on these communities which they may not be able to assume. Its proposal on paragraph 3 would also reduce flexibility without adding any positive protection.[24]

The proposed text of Article 7 that emerged from the consultations was the following:

Article 7
1. The improvement of the conditions of life and work and levels of health and education of the peoples concerned, with their participation and

---

21   Chile proposed that in paragraph 2, participation should be through official channels to which all citizens have access.
22   India stated that 'paragraph 2 is not acceptable, as governments cannot surrender the right to decide priorities and to make decisions on economic development affecting the entire population. Amend as follows: "Governments shall have the ultimate decision-making power for establishing priorities for the process of development. They should, however, take into account the priorities which the populations concerned may express, through democratic and representative forums in this regard, in so far as it affects directly"'
23   On paragraphs 2 and 3, Colombia proposed: 'In paragraph 2, replace "to exercise control, to the extent possible, over" by "to attain through self-management". In paragraph 3, replace "ensure that studies are carried out" by "carry out studies".'
24   Report IV (2A), pp. 22 and 23.

co-operation, shall be a matter of priority in plans for the overall economic development of areas inhabited by them. Special projects for development of the areas in question shall also be so designed as to promote such improvement.

2. The peoples concerned shall have the right to decide their own priorities for the process of development as it affects their lives, beliefs, territories, institutions and spiritual well-being and to exercise control, to the extent possible, over their own economic, social and cultural development. In addition, they shall be involved in the formulation, implementation and evaluation of plans and programmes for national and regional development which may affect them directly.

3. Governments shall ensure that, whenever appropriate, studies are carried out, in co-operation with the peoples concerned, to assess the social, spiritual, cultural and environmental impact on them of planned development activities.

4. Governments shall take measures, in co-operation with the peoples concerned, to protect and preserve the environment of the territories they inhabit.[25]

When this proposed Article was discussed by the Conference in 1989, a fairly large number of amendments were proposed, but the Article was only lightly amended. The long section on this Article in the Committee's report[26] discussing proposed amendments that were not adopted is not reproduced *in toto*, but some passages are quoted here. However, the discussions that resulted in changes to the proposed text are noted.

There were no successful proposals for amendment to paragraph 1. There were proposals to add more flexibility to this provision by the addition of "to the extent possible" which were rejected because the proposed Article 34 (which was adopted later) provided that the entire Convention had to be applied in a flexible manner taking into account the situation in each country.

As concerned the terminology in paragraph 2 referring to territories,[27] the Conference Committee noted the following decision that was taken in function of the discussions on land rights:

> Consideration of three amendments proposing to replace the word "territories" by "lands", which were submitted by the Government members of

---

25 Report IV (2B), p. 10.
26 Proceedings 1989, pp. 25/12 to 25/14.
27 The significance of these terms is explored in the chapters on land rights.

India and Canada and by the Employers' members, was deferred until Part II of the Convention had been discussed. When that Part of the Convention had been discussed, the Committee decided to replace the word "territories" in paragraph 2 by "the land they occupy or otherwise use".[28]

As concerns paragraph 3, there was a long and fairly involved discussion of whether to remove the expression "whenever appropriate", or to reinforce the obligation to carry out environmental impact studies by making the requirement mandatory for all proposed development activities. In the end, the Committee accepted an amendment to replace "appropriate" by "possible".[29]

With these small changes, Article 7 was adopted in its final form:

Article 7
1. The peoples concerned shall have the right to decide their own priorities for the process of development as it affects their lives, beliefs, institutions and spiritual well-being and the lands they occupy or otherwise use and to exercise control, to the extent possible, over their own economic, social and cultural development. In addition, they shall participate in the formulation, implementation and evaluation of plans and programmes for national and regional development which may affect them directly.
2. The improvement of the conditions of life and work and levels of health and education of the peoples concerned, with their participation and co-operation, shall be a matter of priority in plans for the overall economic development of areas they inhabit. Special projects for development of the areas in question shall also be so designed as to promote such improvement.
3. Governments shall ensure that, whenever appropriate, studies are carried out, in co-operation with the peoples concerned, to assess the social, spiritual, cultural and environmental impact on them of planned development activities. The results of these studies shall be considered as fundamental criteria for the implementation of theses activities.
4. Governments shall take measures, in co-operation with the peoples concerned, to protect and preserve the environment of the territories they inhabit.[30]

---

28   Ibid., p. 25/13.
29   Ibid.
30   Ibid., p. 25/27.

D Development through Supervision

The supervision of Article is closely tied to the supervision of Article 6, so much of what is said in the previous chapter applies here as well.

The most concise and thorough expression by the Committee of Experts on the implementation of Article 7 was a General Observation made nearly 20 years after the adoption of the Convention, in 2008. Whereas the General Observation on Article 6 quoted above focused on consultation, this comment linked Articles 6 and 7 as integral parts of the Convention:

> On the eve of the 20th anniversary of the adoption of the Convention, the Committee notes that the establishment of appropriate and effective mechanisms for the consultation and participation of indigenous and tribal peoples regarding matters that concern them is the cornerstone of the Convention, yet remains one of the main challenges in fully implementing the Convention in a number of countries. Given the enormous challenges facing indigenous and tribal peoples today, including regularization of land titles, health and education, and the increased exploitation of natural resources, the involvement of the indigenous and tribal peoples in these and other areas which affect them directly, is an essential element in ensuring equity and guaranteeing social peace through inclusion and dialogue.
>
> The Committee notes that the Convention refers to three interrelated processes: coordinated and systematic government action, participation and consultation. It notes that Articles 2 and 33 of the Convention, read together, provide that governments are under an obligation to develop, with the participation of indigenous and tribal peoples, coordinated and systematic action to protect the rights and to guarantee the integrity of these peoples. Agencies and other appropriate mechanisms are to be established to administer programmes, in cooperation with indigenous and tribal peoples, covering all stages from planning to evaluation of measures proposed in the Convention. The Committee recalls that pursuant to Article 7 of the Convention, indigenous and tribal peoples have the right to decide their own development priorities and to participate in the formulation, implementation and evaluation of plans and programmes for national and regional development which may affect them directly. Article 6 sets out the Convention's requirements regarding consultation.
>
> The Committee notes that in many countries genuine efforts have been made regarding consultation and participation with the aim of implementing the Convention. However, these efforts have not always

met the expectations and aspirations of indigenous and tribal peoples, and also fell short of complying with the requirements of the Convention. In certain cases agencies have been established with responsibility for indigenous or tribal peoples' rights, however, with little or no participation of these peoples, or with insufficient resources or influence. For example, the key decisions affecting indigenous or tribal peoples are in many cases made by ministries responsible for mining or finance, without any coordination with the agency responsible for indigenous or tribal peoples' rights. As a result, these peoples do not have a real voice in the policies likely to affect them. While the Convention does not impose a specific model of participation, it does require the existence or establishment of agencies or other appropriate mechanisms, with the means necessary for the proper fulfilment of their functions, and the effective participation of indigenous and tribal peoples. Such agencies or mechanisms are yet to be established in a number of countries that have ratified the Convention.

The Committee cannot over-emphasize the importance of ensuring the right of indigenous and tribal peoples to decide their development priorities through meaningful and effective consultation and participation of these peoples at all stages of the development process, and particularly when development models and priorities are discussed and decided. Disregard for such consultation and participation has serious repercussions for the implementation and success of specific development programmes and projects, as they are unlikely to reflect the aspirations and needs of indigenous and tribal peoples. Even where there is some degree of general participation at the national level, and ad hoc consultation on certain measures, this may not be sufficient to meet the Convention's requirements concerning participation in the formulation and implementation of development processes, for example, where the peoples concerned consider agriculture to be the priority, but are only consulted regarding mining exploitation after a development model for the region, giving priority to mining, has been developed.

With regard to consultation, the Committee notes two main challenges: (i) ensuring that appropriate consultations are held prior to the adoption of all legislative and administrative measures which are likely to affect indigenous and tribal peoples directly; and (ii) including provisions in legislation requiring prior consultation as part of the process of determining if concessions for the exploitation and exploration of natural resources are to be granted. The form and content of consultation procedures and mechanisms need to allow the full expression of the viewpoints of the peoples concerned, in a timely manner and based on their full understanding of the issues involved, so that they may be able to affect the outcome and a consensus could be achieved, and be undertaken in a manner that is acceptable to all parties. If these requirements are met, consultation can be an instrument of genuine dialogue, social cohesion and be instrumental in the prevention and resolution of conflict. The Committee, therefore, considers it important that governments, with the participation of indigenous and tribal peoples, as a matter of priority, establish appropriate consultation mechanisms with the representative institutions of those peoples. Periodic evaluation of the operation of the consultation mechanisms, with the participation of the peoples concerned, should be undertaken to continue to improve their effectiveness.

The Committee encourages governments to continue their efforts, with the participation of indigenous and tribal peoples, in the following areas, and to provide information in future reports on the measures taken in this regard:
– developing the measures and mechanisms envisaged in Articles 2 and 33 of the Convention;
– establishing mechanisms for participation in the formulation of development plans;
– including the requirement of prior consultation in legislation regarding the exploration and exploitation of natural resources;
– engaging in systematic consultation on the legislative and administrative measures referred to in Article 6 of the Convention; and
– establishing effective consultation mechanisms that take into account the vision of governments and indigenous and tribal peoples concerning the procedures to be followed.

This General Observation was of course drafted once the Committee had acquired considerable experience in exploring the different implications of this Article. The first aspect to be examined is the principle that these peoples can decide their own priorities for development and to "participate in the formulation, implementation and evaluation of plans and programmes for national and regional development which may affect them directly." (paragraph 1) The Convention sets the objective of establishing mechanisms for these purposes without laying down specific methods, so a good number of comments have requested information on what is being done, and examined the results. For instance, a direct request made to Argentina in 2004 included the following:

13. *Article 7. Development policies.* The Committee asks the Government to provide information on the manner in which indigenous communities are enabled to decide on their own priorities for development, as required by this Article. The Committee trusts that in its next report the Government will be able to give information on specific cases, indicating in particular the activities conducted under the "*Ramón Lista* Comprehensive Development Project"; the "Care for Indigenous Peoples Component" (CAPI) of the Programme of Care for Vulnerable Peoples; and the "Project for the Development of Indigenous Communities and the Protection of Biodiversity". The Government is also asked to provide information on the manner in which the indigenous communities concerned have participated in the formulation, implementation and evaluation of the activities conducted under the abovementioned projects, including activities to preserve and protect the environment.

14. The Committee again requests the Government to supply information on any progress made in the passage of the bill submitted to the Senate for the creation of the Programme of Basic Social Infrastructure for Indigenous Communities, indicating the manner in which the indigenous peoples were consulted in its preparation. The Committee would be grateful if the Government would provide a copy of the bill.

The Committee is often able to note that the governments concerned are making progress. See the following extract from an observation to Argentina nine years after the comment quoted above:

> Council for Indigenous Participation (CPI). Consultation and participation. The Government states that the Coordination Council, provided for in Act No. 23302 of 1985 concerning indigenous policy and support for aboriginal communities, is no longer functioning, and that the Council for Indigenous Participation (CPI), which is part of the INAI, has initiated the necessary steps for consultation. The Committee notes the Regulations for the operation of the CPI, which were adopted in March 2011. The CPI consists of two representatives elected by each community assembly of indigenous peoples and plays a major role in the National Programme for Identification of the Status of Indigenous Community Lands and the Commission for Analysis of the Implementation of Indigenous Community Ownership. In its most recent observations, the CTA raises questions about the functioning of the CPI. *The Committee invites the Government to continue to provide information in its next report on how the effective participation of indigenous peoples is ensured in the CPI and in the other*

institutions administering the programmes that concern them (Articles 2 and 33 of the Convention). The Committee also hopes that the report will contain further information on how it has ensured the existence of appropriate prior consultation procedures for the effective participation of indigenous peoples in decisions that are liable to affect them directly (Articles 6 and 7).

In a direct request to Colombia in 1998, the Committee had already evoked the sometimes significant gap between laws and policies and implementation:

> 8. The Committee previously noted with interest Decree No. 1386 of 1994, according to which the indigenous authorities in the resguardos have the right to decide the manner and form of the share of national revenue which corresponds to their resguardos, and that this is done through projects formulated by the indigenous communities themselves which are presented to the local municipal authorities for consideration and approval. The Committee again requests the Government to provide information in its next report on the practical application of this Decree, including the number of communities which have availed themselves of this opportunity and the modalities for cooperation between the municipal authorities, CONAPI and other state entities providing assistance to indigenous communities.

As concerns the establishment of "plans for the overall economic development of areas they inhabit" and "(s)pecial projects for development of the areas in question...designed as to promote... (the) improvement of the conditions of life and work and levels of health and education of the peoples concerned, with their participation and co-operation" (paragraph 2), a number of comments by the Committee of Experts have evoked the requirement. Most often the Committee has asked for information, as in the following direct request to Honduras in 1999:

> 9. Article 7. The Committee notes with interest the information supplied by the Government regarding the Accords it has signed with the peoples concerned, undertaking to grant lands and provide agricultural technical assistance, construct and improve housing, clean up the environment, improve existing systems of health and education, and strengthen the security of the indigenous communities. Please provide particulars of measures taken for the development of the regions in question, indicating the status of their implementation following Hurricane Mitch, as well as

the manner in which the participation of the peoples concerned in the formulation, implementation and evaluation of these measures is ensured.

It also takes note of plans that have been made – sometimes in significant detail, as in the following – and asks for progress reports. See the direct request made to Ecuador in 2002:

> 11. *Article 7.* The Committee notes that the action proposed under the Operational Action Plan, 1999–2003, includes the multiplication and strengthening of autonomous political and administrative units (action 1.1), the recognition of the political competence of the various forms of organization of indigenous nationalities (action 2.1), the formulation of a basic law on indigenous peoples and nationalities (action 2.4), the proposal to formulate a law on indigenous areas with a view to ensuring that indigenous nationalities and peoples benefit from the space required to ensure their own existence (action 3.1), and the enactment of laws protecting indigenous areas (action 3.2). Noting that the implementation of these measures would contribute significantly to the exercise of the right to decide their own priorities for the process of development, as required by the Convention, the Committee requests the Government to provide information on the implementation and results of the Plan of Action with regard to the above points.

And again, in a 2008 Observation to Colombia:

> *Article 7. Development plans.* The Committee notes that according to the report, the National Development Plan "Estado Comunitario: Desarollo para Todos" 2006–10, approved by Act No. 1151 of 24 July 2007 sets as one of its objectives a policy which accommodates, among other things, the formulation of specific programmes relating to ethnic groups and intercultural relations, for which strategies will be developed for the benefit of all ethnic groups (the indigenous, Afro-Colombian, Raizales and Roma or Gypsy peoples). The Committee also notes that the National Department for Planning (NDP), has promoted the elaboration and establishment of strategies to develop national public policies in social, economic and environmental fields with a view to fostering equality and combating discrimination, through a legal instrument called CONPES (document of the National Council on Economic and Social Policy). The Committee notes that CONPES 2007 "State Policy for the Colombian Pacific Area" seeks renewed advancement of the Afro-Colombian people by integrating the

Pacific region into national and international development as part of a strategic programme for economic and social revival. The Committee notes that according to the report, the highest concentration of Afro-Colombian peoples is in the Pacific region (Chocó, Valle del Cauca, Cauca and Nariño) and reminds the Government that according to *Article 7(1)* of the Convention "the peoples concerned...shall participate in the formulation, implementation and evaluation of plans and programmes for national and regional development which may affect them directly." *The Committee accordingly asks the Government to ensure such participation for the peoples covered by the Convention that inhabit the area covered by conpes 2007 and to provide information on this matter, and requests it to include all the peoples covered by the Convention in the relevant plans in order to enable them to participate fully in building the model for development which may affect them directly.*

The Committee of Experts has paid a great deal of attention to *paragraph 3*, which for the first time in an international instrument required environmental and social impact studies. See the following direct request to Bolivia from 2005:

> 10. *Impact studies.* The Committee notes that no impact study has been undertaken on investments in productive and other types of infrastructure in indigenous areas and indigenous municipal districts. There is a significant void in this respect, as the processes of reviewing the TCOs are relatively recent and the DMIs have not achieved any real administrative or economic decentralization. The Committee would be grateful if the Government would keep it informed on the progress achieved and the difficulties encountered in this respect. With regard to the forestry and hydrocarbon management plans, the Committee notes the information supplied by the Government and refers to its observation of 2005.

The Committee is often critical of the approach taken in this regard, as in the direct request to Costa Rica in 2003:

> 7. *Article 7 (environmental conservation).* The Committee notes the information contained in the report on the work of the Office of the Ombudsman (2000–01) denouncing the Boruca hydroelectric project. It also notes the establishment of "biological corridors" in indigenous lands. The Committee requests the Government to provide detailed information on the consultations held with the participation of the representatives of the communities affected to evaluate the impact of these projects,

including information on the characteristics of the "biological corridors". The Committee also notes the Government's indication that environmental impact studies are not kept. The Committee would be grateful if the Government would take the necessary measures for the conservation of these studies.

The Committee made it clear in the following direct request to Paraguay in 2003 that the requirement covers all development projects, whether government or privately run:

> 9. *Article 7, paragraph 4.* The Committee notes that, according to the report, the protection of the environment is carried out through the Environmental Superintendance and the Environmental Directorate of the Ministry of Agriculture and Livestock. It adds that in the case of projects undertaken by public institutions, the corresponding studies are usually undertaken, and that with regard to private projects, the INDI is not aware that such studies are carried out in areas inhabited by indigenous communities. The Committee recalls that, in the same way as the requirement of consultation, the principle of participation is a fundamental precept of the Convention. As such, occasional participation, the carrying out of studies only in certain cases for State projects, and the failure to undertake them when the projects are private, does not give full effect to this Article of the Convention. The Committee hopes that the Government will make the necessary efforts, in consultation with the peoples concerned, to give effect to this Article in practice and that it will supply detailed information on the law and practice in this respect, on the measures which have been adopted or are envisaged and on the progress achieved.

As concerns the protection of the environment required by *paragraph 4*, there are many comments that refer to it directly or less directly. One of the clearest statements of the Committee's concern, here involving also the search for coherence among international supervisory systems, is found in an extract from a 2011 observation to Guatemala:

> The Committee also notes that the Inter-American Commission on Human Rights (IACHR), in Decision No. MC 260/07 of 20 May 2010, imposed protective measures with regard to this issue and requested the State of Guatemala to suspend mining operations connected with the Marlin I project and other activities connected with the licence awarded to

Goldcorp/Montana Exploradora de Guatemala SA and to take effective measures to prevent environmental pollution pending the adoption of a decision by the IACHR concerning the substance of the petition linked to the application for protective measures.

These extracts from comments by the Committee of Experts make it clear that Article 7 has been a useful tool not only for monitoring performance, but also for stimulating governments to take measures they probably would not have taken but for the ratification of the Convention and the supervision carried out under it.

CHAPTER 6

Articles 13 to 19 of Convention No. 169 – Land Rights

The complexity and interrelated nature of the land rights provisions has led to their being treated in a single chapter. At times it is difficult to separate the threads that led to the adoption of specific provisions. These provisions in C. 169 are the following.

Article 13
1. In applying the provisions of this Part of the Convention governments shall respect the special importance for the cultures and spiritual values of the peoples concerned of their relationship with the lands or territories, or both as applicable, which they occupy or otherwise use, and in particular the collective aspects of this relationship.
2. The use of the term lands in Articles 15 and 16 shall include the concept of territories, which covers the total environment of the areas which the peoples concerned occupy or otherwise use.

Article 14
1. The rights of ownership and possession of the peoples concerned over the lands which they traditionally occupy shall be recognised. In addition, measures shall be taken in appropriate cases to safeguard the right of the peoples concerned to use lands not exclusively occupied by them, but to which they have traditionally had access for their subsistence and traditional activities. Particular attention shall be paid to the situation of nomadic peoples and shifting cultivators in this respect.
2. Governments shall take steps as necessary to identify the lands which the peoples concerned traditionally occupy, and to guarantee effective protection of their rights of ownership and possession.
3. Adequate procedures shall be established within the national legal system to resolve land claims by the peoples concerned.

Article 15
1. The rights of the peoples concerned to the natural resources pertaining to their lands shall be specially safeguarded. These rights include the right of these peoples to participate in the use, management and conservation of these resources.

2. In cases in which the State retains the ownership of mineral or subsurface resources or rights to other resources pertaining to lands, governments shall establish or maintain procedures through which they shall consult these peoples, with a view to ascertaining whether and to what degree their interests would be prejudiced, before undertaking or permitting any programmes for the exploration or exploitation of such resources pertaining to their lands. The peoples concerned shall wherever possible participate in the benefits of such activities, and shall receive fair compensation for any damages which they may sustain as a result of such activities.

Article 16

1. Subject to the following paragraphs of this Article, the peoples concerned shall not be removed from the lands which they occupy.

2. Where the relocation of these peoples is considered necessary as an exceptional measure, such relocation shall take place only with their free and informed consent. Where their consent cannot be obtained, such relocation shall take place only following appropriate procedures established by national laws and regulations, including public inquiries where appropriate, which provide the opportunity for effective representation of the peoples concerned.

3. Whenever possible, these peoples shall have the right to return to their traditional lands, as soon as the grounds for relocation cease to exist.

4. When such return is not possible, as determined by agreement or, in the absence of such agreement, through appropriate procedures, these peoples shall be provided in all possible cases with lands of quality and legal status at least equal to that of the lands previously occupied by them, suitable to provide for their present needs and future development. Where the peoples concerned express a preference for compensation in money or in kind, they shall be so compensated under appropriate guarantees.

5. Persons thus relocated shall be fully compensated for any resulting loss or injury.

Article 17

1. Procedures established by the peoples concerned for the transmission of land rights among members of these peoples shall be respected.

2. The peoples concerned shall be consulted whenever consideration is being given to their capacity to alienate their lands or otherwise transmit their rights outside their own community.

3. Persons not belonging to these peoples shall be prevented from taking advantage of their customs or of lack of understanding of the laws on the

part of their members to secure the ownership, possession or use of land belonging to them.

Article 18

Adequate penalties shall be established by law for unauthorised intrusion upon, or use of, the lands of the peoples concerned, and governments shall take measures to prevent such offences.

Article 19

National agrarian programmes shall secure to the peoples concerned treatment equivalent to that accorded to other sectors of the population with regard to:

(a) the provision of more land for these peoples when they have not the area necessary for providing the essentials of a normal existence, or for any possible increase in their numbers;

(b) the provision of the means required to promote the development of the lands which these peoples already possess.

A   Introduction

The land rights articles of Convention No. 169 are long and complex. In addition, the way in which agreement was reached on the final version of them was less transparent than for every other provision of the Convention, so it is not always possible to trace their development word by word at the very final stage. Nevertheless, the origins of all the concepts are clear, even if the exact steps by which conclusions were reached are sometimes lost in back-room smog.

When the revision of Convention No. 107 was mooted, it had become urgent to update that instrument on land rights among other subjects. As the Office noted in introducing this subject in the 1986 Meeting of Experts, the situation at the national level had changed since C. 107 was adopted 30 years earlier:

> Considerable attention had been given to land rights in several countries, and action had been taken to delimit land and to return some or all of the land which these groups had lost, as well as to create mechanisms that would ensure progress in this respect. However, in a great many cases, the situation had considerably worsened. Indigenous and tribal peoples faced constant pressure on the land they occupied; procedures were in most cases inadequate to deal with complaints on situations not provided for in national legislation, as many of these groups did not hold title to their land. Demographic and other internal change in many countries also

exerted pressure on formerly isolated populations who then found themselves regarded as obstacles to national development. Relocation programmes in frontier areas for reasons of national security had also affected them. A large number of countries were implementing large-scale projects to develop their infrastructure, often with international assistance, and this also resulted in the displacement of such populations from their lands, as did mining operations. They were losing their land rapidly without possibility of adequate recourse. At the same time, new development strategies were being implemented by increasing numbers of international organisations and governments which called for a greater degree of participation by the persons affected rather than the hierarchical approach implicit in Convention No. 107.[1]

It was recognized from the beginning that this subject would be difficult to deal with. As was stated in the first report produced by the Office for the 1988 and 1989 discussions (the 'Law and Practice Report'):

> The issue of land rights is bound to prove particularly complex when attempting to define international standards. First, there are great differences in national systems of land ownership and tenure, and ownership and control of natural and environmental resources under and around the land. Second, it must be remembered that there is a fundamental difference between the relationship which many indigenous peoples have with the land, and the attitude of other sectors of many national populations who view land as an alienable and productive commodity. As the United Nations Special Rapporteur on indigenous populations has written on this issue, from the perspective of indigenous peoples, "The whole range of emotional, cultural, spiritual and religious considerations is present where the relationship with the land is concerned... The land forms part of their existence."[2]

B   Before the Standards

It has long been a truism that land rights are vital for the survival of indigenous and tribal peoples. An example of the ILO's awareness of this can be found in

---

1 Report of the Meeting of Experts, reproduced in Report VI (1), p. 102.
2 Report VI (1), p. 44.

the report of the Second Session of the Committee of Experts on Indigenous Labour, which was held in Geneva from 15 to 26 March 1954.[3]

Land Tenure.
The Committee emphasised the importance of the land question for forest-dwelling indigenous peoples and requested the Governing Body of the I.L.O. to urge the governments concerned to study this problem with particular care. It suggested that any legislation or regulations on this subject should be based upon certain principles designed to ensure that the title of indigenous forest dwellers to the land they occupy is recognised and its possession defined and guaranteed. Indigenous forest dwellers should be provided with more land if they have not the area necessary for the subsistence and any possible future development of the tribe. Leasing should be prohibited, save exceptionally as defined by law, and a ban placed upon mortgaging. Indigenous forest dwellers should be made secure in a fair share of profits arising from development of underground wealth within their land and receipt of reasonable rents for any land which they may lease. Ownership of land should be secured to tribes which move periodically owing to seasonal, climatic or economic conditions but generally remain on their traditional tribal territory. Steps should also be taken to ensure that rights over land are transferred in conformity with the usage of the respective indigenous forest-dwelling tribes. The removal of indigenous forest dwellers without their freely given consent from their habitual territory should be prohibited and the specific reservation of lands for occupation by indigenous forest dwellers should not be permitted to develop into a permanent system of segregation.

The Committee repeated the request it had made at its First Session that the Governing Body should examine the possibility of including in the agenda of the next session of the Committee of Experts on Indigenous Labour a consideration of the general problems involved in the various socio-economic and juridical conditions under which indigenous peoples work the land.

Here we find some principles that are very far-reaching for their time, and that would not all find their way into the standards until 1989 – for instance the deletion of listed reasons to justify removal of indigenous populations from their

---

[3] The following is the summary reproduced in Report VIII (1), the first preparatory report for the adoption of Convention No. 107.

lands without their freely given consent, and the desirability of indigenous and tribal peoples sharing in the benefits of resource exploitation on their lands.

As already indicated the work of the Committee of Experts on Indigenous Labour was one of the influences on the decision to adopt the Indigenous and Tribal Populations Convention in 1957.

C   Convention No. 107 – Introduction

The land rights provisions of Convention No. 107 were shorter and simpler than those the Conference would adopt for Convention No. 169, though far-reaching in their way.

Article 11
The right of ownership, collective or individual, of the members of the populations concerned over the lands which these populations traditionally occupy shall be recognised.

Article 12
1. The populations concerned shall not be removed without their free consent from their habitual territories except in accordance with national laws and regulations for reasons relating to national security, or in the interest of national economic development or of the health of the said populations.

2. When in such cases removal of these populations is necessary as an exceptional measure, they shall be provided with lands of quality at least equal to that of the lands previously occupied by them, suitable to provide for their present needs and future development. In cases where chances of alternative employment exist and where the populations concerned prefer to have compensation in money or in kind, they shall be so compensated under appropriate guarantees.

3. Persons thus removed shall be fully compensated for any resulting loss or injury.

Article 13
1. Procedures for the transmission of rights of ownership and use of land which are established by the customs of the populations concerned shall be respected, within the framework of national laws and regulations, in so far as they satisfy the needs of these populations and do not hinder their economic and social development.

2. Arrangements shall be made to prevent persons who are not members of the populations concerned from taking advantage of these customs or

of lack of understanding of the laws on the part of the members of these populations to secure the ownership or use of the lands belonging to such members.

Article 14

National agrarian programmes shall secure to the populations concerned treatment equivalent to that accorded to other sections of the national community with regard to –

(a) the provision of more land for these populations when they have not the area necessary for providing the essentials of a normal existence, or for any possible increase in their numbers;

(b) the provision of the means required to promote the development of the lands which these populations already possess.

As the Office outlined the principles that should underlie the new standards, the vital importance of land rights was stressed. For instance, Report VIII (1) included the following:

> In the remaining pages of this section an attempt will be made to outline briefly the type of action which in various parts of the world appears to be necessary if the existence of indigenous communities as economic and social entities is to be assured.[4]

The report also included the following passage which, while it supported the integrationist approach of the proposed Convention, also left a margin of manoeuvre:

> In recent years the view has been gaining ground that the most appropriate way of promoting the economic resurgence of indigenous communities would be to turn them into modern co-operative units. In 1940 the First Inter-American Indian Congress adopted a resolution urging the American States concerned to consider the advisability of enacting the relevant legislation for the transformation of Indian *comunidades* "into agricultural and stock-raising co-operatives, or into agricultural societies which, under the technical supervision of the State, could be incorporated into the general economy of the country". With rare exceptions, however, and despite the efforts made, this type of action has not yet made much headway in a number of countries. It would appear that the main reason for this situation resides in the fact that insufficient attention has so far been given

---

4   Report VIII (1), p. 67.

to the need to adapt the modern methods of co-operative production to the traditional forms of communal use of land and working implements and to the traditional systems of mutual service and aid among indigenous peoples.

From the conditions described at the beginning of this chapter it is obvious that in general indigenous communities are not likely to succeed in developing their lands for more productive purposes and in freeing themselves from indebtedness, if they are not provided with adequate financial and technical aid. As will be seen in the following chapter, in a number of countries special schemes of assistance, including subsidies, co-operative credit and low-cost loans, are already operating for the benefit of certain sections of the indigenous farming population, and their positive results clearly indicate the advisability of making them extendible to larger sections of this population.

Experience has shown also that the successful execution of an over-all land policy in indigenous areas is basically dependent on the existence of adequate machinery for the protection of land rights, the co-ordination of governmental action in the field of economic development, and the control of the juridical and socio-economic conditions under which indigenous tenant labourers work the land.

It is apparent that any programme undertaken to assist the indigenous farming population must be broadly conceived. In many cases action may consist in the first place in the removal of handicaps rather than in the provision of assistance. Any legislative or other measures which will remove the disabilities under which indigenous communities find themselves in relation to the land will provide a chance of development of an indigenous spirit of enterprise. It must be recognised, however, that the development of these communities will proceed more rapidly where forces external to their traditional environment are acting to facilitate the integration of their members into a market economy. In this respect the problem of the indigenous community and the land takes its place as part of the wider problem of national economic development. It must be emphasised, however, that a basic condition for the success of this larger development is the elimination of certain semi-feudal forms of land tenure and tenancy which in most indigenous areas constitute a major obstacle to economic and social progress.[5]

---

5   Ibid., pp. 70 and 71.

The questionnaire sent to the constituents in Report VIII (1) in 1956 contained the following on land questions:

v. Land

23. *Do you consider that indigenous peoples should be granted property rights, either collective or individual, as the case may be, over the lands they traditionally occupy?*

24. *Do you consider that there is a need to secure ownership of tribal land to semi-nomadic forest-dwelling and desert tribes which, though they periodically move for seasonal, climatic or economic reasons, habitually return to the same starting point and generally remain there?*

25. *Do you consider that there is a need to establish zones of nomadism in which these tribes should have an undisturbed right to graze their herds and flocks?*

26. (a) *Do you consider that, except for reasons of national security or in the interest of national economic development, as prescribed by law, indigenous peoples should not be removed without their freely given consent from their habitual territories?*

(b) *Do you consider that when, in these exceptional circumstances, such removal is necessary, the indigenous peoples affected should be provided with other lands suitable for their existence and future development?*

(c) *Do you consider that when, in these exceptional circumstances, such removal is necessary the indigenous peoples affected should be fully compensated for any loss resulting from such removal?*

27. *Do you consider that care should be taken to prevent the reservation of lands for indigenous groups from developing into a system of permanent segregation and that such reservation should be conceived as an element in a policy of gradual integration of these groups into the national community?*

28. (a) *Do you consider that, save in exceptional circumstances defined by law, the leasing of lands owned by indigenous peoples to persons or bodies not belonging to the indigenous tribe or group concerned should be prohibited or restricted?*

(b) *Do you consider that, in the exceptional circumstances mentioned above, arrangements should be made whereby indigenous peoples will receive reasonable rents for any land they may lease and will have a fair share in the profits arising from the development of underground wealth within the land leased:*

29. *Do you consider that indigenous peoples should be assured of a land reserve adequate for the needs of shifting cultivation so long as no other satisfactory system can be introduced?*

30. Do you consider that the mortgaging of lands owned by indigenous peoples to persons or bodies not belonging to the indigenous tribe or group concerned should be prohibited or restricted?

31. Do you consider that the transmission of rights concerning the ownership and use of land established by the customs of the indigenous tribe or group should be respected as long as these customs satisfy the needs of the tribe or group and do not represent an obstacle to economic and social development?

32. Do you consider that, in order to promote the social and economic development of indigenous communities, national agrarian reform programmes should provide for the granting of more land to indigenous peoples who have not the area necessary for their subsistence or for any possible future development of the tribe or the group?

33. Bo you consider that the development of indigenous agricultural and stock-raising communities should be facilitated by adapting modern methods of co-operative production, supply and marketing to the traditional forms of communal ownership and use of land and working implements among indigenous peoples and to their traditional systems of mutual service and aid?

34. Do you consider that subsidies, co-operative credit, low-cost loans and technical aid should be extended to indigenous farmers so that they may free themselves from indebtedness and may develop their lands?

35. Do you consider that legal and administrative measures are necessary for the control of the various tenancy arrangements prevailing in areas inhabited by indigenous peoples?[6]

In a very unusual procedure, that affected the land rights provisions even more than the rest of the instruments, after the draft conclusions were submitted to discussion in the Conference in 1956 the Conference asked the Secretariat to divide consideration of these questions and the responses to them, into a discussion of a draft Convention that would include the most fundamental provisions, and a draft Recommendation that would explore these concepts in more detail. This led to the adoption of both Convention No. 107 and of its accompanying Recommendation No. 104 in 1957. This volume will concentrate on those questions and discussions that found their way into the Convention. It will then review how these provisions evolved into the corresponding provisions of Convention No. 169.

---

6   Ibid., pp. 177 to 179.

D   From C. 107 to C. 169

1   *Article 13 of Convention No. 169: Lands and Territories and the Spiritual Relationship*

Although Article 13 precedes the other land rights provisions of Convention No. 169, it actually emerged from the discussions on what was to become Articles 14 and 15. It had no precedent in Convention No. 107, and was adopted to resolve problems over the use of the terms 'land' and 'territories' in 1988 and 1989. It is nevertheless presented first here because it comes before those articles in the text, and sets up the way in which they must be understood.

It is difficult to separate the consideration of the eventual Articles 13, 14 and 15 of C. 169, as they went through various permutations *en route* to adoption. In addition, the Office (see the procedural discussions under Article 14 of Convention No. 169), the constituents and the participants in the 1989 session of the Conference took account of the extensive discussions in 1988 which were not reported in detail in the report of the 1988 Session of the Conference. Nevertheless, the emergence of the concepts is reasonably clear.

The influence of the indigenous participants in the discussion, supported by the Workers' members and by some governments, is particularly evident in the eventual Article 13 and in the ways in the terms 'lands' and 'territories' were used. As quoted above, the Office had suggested that 'It appears that the issues raised during the Conference discussion might be resolved if the word "lands" were used in connection with the establishment of legal rights, while "territories" could be used when describing a physical space, when discussing the environment as a whole or when discussing the relationship of these peoples to the territories they occupy.' The Office had pointed out that both terms were used in C. 107 and had given rise to no difficulties of interpretation, and in fact the word 'territories' is used once in the land rights section of that Convention in referring to the possibility of removing indigenous and tribal populations from their 'habitual territories'. However, no particular significance had been attached to the implications of this term either in the adoption of C. 107 or in the supervisory work of the Committee of Experts since then. The possible meaning of 'lands' as being used in connection with legal rights, and 'territories' in a much wider sense, had only emerged in the (unreported) 1988 discussion.

In discussing the whole of the land rights section, the Office pointed out in Report IV (1) for the 1989 Session that the question of lands and territories had been discussed.

> *Lands/territories.* A discussion was held in the working party on this issue which is not fully reflected in the Committee's report but which may

assist in clarifying the issues raised. Two basic positions became apparent. First, the indigenous and tribal representatives, supported by the Workers' members and some governments, felt that the word "lands" is too restrictive and does not express the relationship between these peoples and the territories they occupy. Nor, on a purely practical level, does the word "lands" cover elements such as sea ice for the northern peoples, which are parts of their territories but are not land. It also does not reflect other elements which are inherent in their concept of territory, such as the flora and fauna, waters and the environment as a whole. On the other hand, a number of governments and the Employers' members pointed out that some internal legal systems are based on the concept of lands and not territories, at least where the acquisition of enforceable rights is concerned. Furthermore, the word "territories" is used in many national legal texts only to refer to the national territory as a whole, and its use in this context might raise problems in connection with national sovereignty.

While this issue remains to be explored fully at the 76th Session of the Conference, the Office points out that both terms were already used in Part II of Convention No. 107 and that no problems have arisen in interpreting them since 1957. It appears that the issues raised during the Conference discussion might be resolved if the word "lands" were used in connection with the establishment of legal rights, while "territories" could be used when describing a physical space, when discussing the environment as a whole or when discussing the relationship of these peoples to the territories they occupy.[7]

Spiritual relationship. The discussion of the concepts of lands and territories is closely linked to the idea that indigenous and tribal peoples have a special spiritual relationship with the lands they occupy. While this is by no means universal in fact it is often the case, and it was decided to propose to take account of it in the proposed instrument. As was said in Report IV (2A):

> Several respondents have made similar proposals for the inclusion of a new Article at the beginning of this Part. As this proposal also received considerable support during the first discussion, such a provision (Article 13 in the new text) has been included, providing a useful introductory basis for considering the complex issue of land rights in the subsequent Articles of this Part. Furthermore, this may help to establish the principle

---

7 Report VI (1), pp. 4 and 5.

that, because of the special relationship between their lands and cultures, in certain matters the peoples concerned should indeed be accorded treatment different from that accorded to other sectors of the national population.[8]

On the basis of these considerations, the Office included the following proposal in the draft Convention submitted to the 1989 discussion in the Conference:

Article 13
In applying the provisions of this Part of the Convention governments shall have due regard to the special importance for the cultures of the peoples concerned of their relationship with the lands and territories they occupy, and in particular the collective aspects of this relationship.

When the Conference Committee came to consider the parts of the proposed Convention on land rights, 101 amendments were submitted on the proposed draft, and the entire text of this part was submitted to a Working Party, as had been done already in 1988.[9]

In this session of the Conference Committee, as in 1988, indigenous representatives were given the possibility to make statements on the entire section concerning land rights, as the Committee began its discussions on this part of the draft. Several of these statements referred to the general questions of the concept of 'territory', and may reveal some of the passionate nature of the indigenous representatives' statements on this subject, in spite of the inevitable toning down of the emotions as international officials reflected them in the texts. Among them,

> The representative of the Nordic Sami Council... Firstly, he recalled that the indigenous and tribal peoples' own concepts of their rights to land were not reflected in national legal systems. He referred to the legal systems in Nordic countries in this regard and said that the indigenous and state concepts could not be fairly resolved unless the States took steps to harmonise them. The speaker also expressed satisfaction that the collective aspects of land rights had been accepted and were reflected in Article 13, and hoped that they would also be reflected in other Articles. In this

---

[8] Report IV (2A), p. 33.
[9] Proceedings 1989, p. 25/16. This is explored more thoroughly as concerns the adoption of Article 14 below.

regard, the use of the term "territories" was the only appropriate means of spelling out that the relevant provision was dealing with a collective group having certain rights which were held collectively.[10]

A representative of the Co-ordinator for Indigenous Peoples' Rights, speaking on behalf of the Inuit Circumpolar Conference and the National Indian Youth Council, stated that, like self-determination, the assertion of indigenous land and territorial rights presented a challenge to State assertions of supremacy, and considered that it would be similarly resisted in the Committee. He added, however, that indigenous and tribal peoples had been encouraged by the movement towards principles based on concern for the human condition of these peoples. The extent to which the revised Convention would accelerate this process would depend on its ability to reach beyond notions of absolute sovereignty, particularly in addressing land and territorial rights. The speaker stressed that for these peoples, land and territory were central to life. Land was the core of the collective body of the people, upon which its survival depended, not simply a material possession. He stated that the discriminatory tendencies which had diminished the status of land holdings in colonial times persisted. The question of lands was therefore one of restoring rights previously denied, not of granting or creating new rights. For this reason, the Convention must reflect the historical nature of indigenous lands and territorial entitlements in order that rights extended to lands which peoples have used or occupied. The speaker referred to the collective nature of indigenous land and territorial rights, which should be a premise for their development. He stressed the importance of using the term "territory" in the Convention in order to capture the essential nature of indigenous and tribal peoples' relationships with the Earth, which was fundamental to their survival as distinct peoples, and to their social and cultural integrity. He stated that objections to the use of the term "territory" demonstrated the same misunderstanding of international law that appeared when objections to the use of the term "peoples" were put forward.[11]

A representative of the Co-ordinator for Indigenous Peoples' Rights rejected what he perceived as an attempt by the Committee to cut indigenous and tribal peoples off from their fundamental human rights. He stated that representatives of the indigenous non-governmental

---

10   Ibid., para. 108.
11   Ibid., para. 109.

organisations and other nongovernmental organisations which supported them had walked out following the decision on the use of the term "peoples" in the Convention. He considered also that the Committee's decision on Article 6.2, in failing to requires these peoples' consent before adopting measures which affected them, undercut the foundation of mutual respect of peoples that was necessary for the revised Convention to be meaningful to them. As far as land rights were concerned, he felt that the Committee to be meaningful to them. (sic) As far as land rights were concerned, he felt that the Committee was moving away from the minimum rights necessary for the survival of indigenous and tribal peoples. He maintained that the Committee, in its revision of Convention No. 107 – a revision that was not sought by these peoples – was acting to preserve the power of governments over these peoples and their territories.[12]

As the Committee began to consider the report of the Working Party, it was obvious that emotions ran nearly as high among delegates as among the indigenous observers.

112. The Working Party held four sittings. Its Chairman reported to the Committee that the key issues identified concerned the use of the term "land and territories"; the form and extent of land rights to be recognised; surface and sub-surface resources; and the question of removal or relocation of indigenous peoples from areas inhabited by them.
...
114. Central to the discussion was the use of the term "territories", the deletion of which had been proposed in several amendments. In discussing Article 13, the Workers' members stated that this term was the only appropriate one to describe the special relationship which indigenous peoples collectively attach to specific geographic areas. Article 13 enshrined respect for cultural and spiritual values of indigenous peoples, with no implications for ownership or national sovereignty. The Employers' members and some of the Government members stressed that the unqualified use of the term "territories" anywhere in the Convention would give rise to serious, if not insurmountable, legal and constitutional problems in many countries which could jeopardise the prospects for ratification. Several proposals were made to find a formulation which would meet these concerns. The Employers' members and the

---

12   Ibid., para. 111.

Government members felt that retention of "territories" would be acceptable if "or" were to replace "and". The Workers' members then suggested for Article 13 the words "lands or territories, or both as applicable". The Working Party agreed to this. There was also discussion of the terms "lands", but the Working Party did not pursue this.

115. Following further discussion on Article 13, the Working Party recommended the adoption of the following text:

In applying the provisions of this Part of the Convention, governments shall respect the special importance for the cultures and spiritual values of the peoples concerned of their relationship with the lands or territories, or both as applicable, which they occupy or otherwise use, and in particular the collective aspects of this relationship.[13]

The objections to the term 'territories' arose from the fact that in a number of countries the word was used exclusively to refer to the national territory, and thus was considered to touch on the identity of the nation. As was stated at one point by a Government representative:

135. The Government member of Venezuela recalled that the main problem in Part II of the Convention was the use of the term "territories", which in his country referred exclusively to the national territory over which the State exercised jurisdiction and had sovereignty according to the national Constitution.[14]

Thus, to extend rights of ownership, possession and use over 'territories' for one part of the population was deeply felt to compromise the notion of the nation itself. This contrasted with the feeling among indigenous participants and their supporters that this is not at all what they meant by the same term, which was a much broader vision of the whole environment and not only of the land itself.

At this point in the discussions, the Chair noted that there was a lack of consensus around the land rights provisions, even though some parts of the text had already been adopted on the basis of the Working Party's proposals. He proposed to go away and return with a new package text, after allowing time for all concerned to express their positions and after carrying out various consultations.

---

13   Ibid., p. 25/17.
14   Ibid., p. 25/19.

122. The Chairman noted that, despite the advances which had been made by the Working Party, the Committee was still some way from adopting by consensus a text on the important and delicate issue of land. In order to avoid the adoption by numerous votes of a text that was unlikely to be lucid and could well be contradictory, as well as jeopardising adoption of the Convention and its subsequent ratification, he made the following suggestion concerning consideration of Part II of the proposed Convention. On the basis of the Working Party's report, which proposed texts for Articles 13 and 17(2), as well as agreed solutions for Articles 17(1) and (3), 18 and 19, he would consult with governments and the Employers' and Workers' groups with a view to formulating and submitting to the Committee for its consideration a new complete text for Part II. Prior to these consultations, he invited Committee members to address the critical aspects of the land issue.[15]

There ensued a long exchange of views, which is reproduced in the report. It covered the entire section, and the aspects referring to Articles 14 to 19 will be dealt with below, but among the proposals submitted was a second paragraph to Article 13.

There was no separate discussion of Article 13, or any of the Articles in this section (with the exception of Article 17(2), examined below). The Chair's submission of this proposed new text was referred to as follows:

143. Following his consultations with Government members and with the Employers' and Workers' groups concerning Part II of the draft Convention, the Chairman indicated that he would propose that the Committee consider a "package" text dealing with Articles 13 to 19, with the exception of Article 17(2) which would be considered separately. Articles 13 to 16 had been amended in the light of the Working Party's deliberations (for Article 13) and in the light of his discussions. Articles 17(1), 17(3), 18 and 19 in the package were the draft Office texts, in accordance with the Working Party's recommendations. He suggested that the package of Articles would constitute a basis to reach a firm understanding in order to finalise the task the Committee had been given by the Conference. He felt that in view of the agreements which had been reached concerning the issues dealt with in Part II of the draft Convention, only amendments to Article 17(2) should be considered. The Chairman then put the consolidated text for Part II of the draft Convention, with the

---

15   Ibid, p. 25/18.

exception of Article 17(2), before the Committee. This approach received general support, though a number of members expressed reservations on various aspects of these texts.[16]

The Chair returned with a new text. It added a second paragraph to Article 13. As adopted, it read:

> 2. The use of the term *lands* in Articles 15 and 16 shall include the concept of territories, which covers the total environment of the areas which the peoples concerned occupy or otherwise use.

There was no recorded discussion of the terms of the new complete text before adoption, except for general agreement with the method and some other general considerations. As reported:

> 147. The Chairman sought the agreement of the Committee on the adoption of the package of Articles in Part II of the draft revised Convention. The texts were adopted by consensus.
> 148. Articles 13, 14, 15 and 16, as amended, were adopted. Articles 17(1), 17(3), 18 and 19 were adopted without change.[17]

It was clear from the discussion that followed, however, that the package was adopted not because everyone liked it but in order to achieve consensus. Certainly Article 13 is not a model of clarity. After the decision to adopt it, a number of delegations expressed their reservations on the package of land rights provisions in spite of accepting the text. As concerns Article 13, two of these statements are reproduced here:

> 150. The Government member of Canada thanked all the members of the Committee for their efforts towards achieving a consensus text which would be widely acceptable. Her delegation accepted Articles 15, 16, 17(1), 17(3), 18 and 19. Other elements of the text, however, raised major concerns. ... A second concern of her delegation had to do with Article 13(2). The definition of the term "land" in that Article, for the purposes of Articles 15 and 16, was vague in its reference to "the concept of territories which covers the total environment of the areas which they occupy or otherwise use". She questioned the meaning of "total environment" and

---

16   Ibid., pp. 25/20 and 25/21.
17   Ibid., p. 25/21.

expressed a preference for the formulation proposed by the Working Party for Article 13, which referred to "lands, or territories, or both, as applicable". Her delegation regretted that, because of her Government's serious and valid concerns, it could not join in a consensus applicable to all elements of the package deal. It would not, however, stand in the way of consensus.[18]

151. The Government member of India recalled his earlier statements that the concept of territories did not apply to the tribal situation in his country and had suggested using the word "areas". Any use of the term "territories"' without a qualification would not be acceptable. He had also supported using "lands or territories, or both, as applicable". He felt that paragraph 2 of Article 13 which defined the use of "land" in Articles 15 and 16 lacked the flexibility of paragraph 1, since it still included the term "territories". It was also ambiguous and did not lead to clear interpretation. He reiterated that in India "territories" had political connotations and meant only the territories of the nation. He expressed his Government's reservations on Article 13.[19]

2 Article 14 of Convention No. 169: Rights of Ownership and Possession
a Article 11 of C. 107

Article 11 of C. 107 is the basic land rights provision in that Convention. The origin of Article 11 lies in the analysis of problems connected with land, outlined in the law and practice report. An extract of a long and complex analysis follows, and foreshadowed a number of the points that would be discussed not only in adopting Convention No. 107 but also later in the adoption of Convention No. 169:

> There would appear to be a growing recognition of the principle that indigenous peoples should be granted property rights, whether collective or individual, over the lands they occupy. However, in order to achieve this objective, it is necessary to define clearly the true areas of these lands. Since in legal terminology "vacant land" is often construed to mean "all land other than tribal land", the definition of "tribal land" becomes crucial. It will be equitable only if it is determined with due regard to customary law and if, in addition to cultivated land, it includes also uncultivated land which will cover the needs of coming generations, as

---

18 Ibid., pp. 25/20 and 25/21.
19 Ibid., p. 25/21.

well as land which at present may not be cultivated but which, in the course of shifting cultivation, may be put into use subsequently. Such a broad interpretation appears to be necessary since, in a number of areas, the indigenous land system continues to recognise only usufructuary rights and does not recognise the existence of vacant or ownerless land. Land which is not kept under cultivation or land which belonged to families which have died out or have migrated, automatically goes back to the land reserve of the group. Special problems arise in the case of semi-nomadic forest-dwelling and desert tribes which, owing to economic, climatic and other conditions, move periodically from one place to another but return regularly to their starting point and generally remain in their traditional territories. With particular reference to these tribes, the Committee of Experts on Indigenous Labour has stated that a rational solution of the land problem could be achieved only by recognising rights to "those lands with which indigenous groups have established a relationship of ecological dependence during the course of a long adjustment process". On the other hand, the need for guaranteeing these tribes an undisturbed right to graze their flocks in the areas of their nomadic movements should not be overlooked. While there may sometimes be compelling reasons for a shift of population in the interest of national security, economic development or health, there has been a growing recognition of the principle that indigenous peoples should not be removed from their habitual territories without their freely given consent. Care should be taken, however, to draw the line between measures that merely preserve a status quo, which may be undesirable, and those designed to promote the integration of indigenous communities into the national life of their countries.

It is, of course, important that the genuine indigenous occupants should not lose their land to speculators and absentees, but it is equally important to prevent the reservation of land for occupation by indigenous groups from developing into a system which encourages segregation. Such a system may not only maintain these groups in a permanent state of social and economic inferiority but also render impossible their fruitful collaboration with the other sections of the population for the economic and social development of the national community as a whole.

In a number of countries arrangements have been made whereby, save in exceptional circumstances defined by law, the leasing of lands owned by indigenous peoples to persons or bodies not belonging to the tribe or group concerned are prohibited or restricted. It is perhaps too much to expect that all such land will remain indefinitely untouched by non-indigenous enterprise.

Nor would this necessarily be desirable, since economic development in any country may require changes in land use which can often be carried out effectively only when such enterprise comes in to work the land or exploit its mineral resources. However, when indigenous land is leased out to nonindigenous interests, it is essential to ensure that the indigenous owners will receive reasonable rents as well as a fair share in the profits which derive from the development of underground wealth within the land leased. A notable example of the wealth that may be derived by indigenous peoples from mineral leases is illustrated by the situation of the Osage Indians of Oklahoma (United States), where revenue in excess of $250 million has been obtained from oil leases and royalties over a period of about 40 years. Another example is that of the Bakhtiaris in Iran who, with the oil royalties derived from the leasing of tribal land, have been steadily improving their standard of living.

In order to prevent alienation of indigenous land, the policy has been gaining ground in a number of countries that the mortgaging of the land to persons or bodies not belonging to the tribe or group should be prohibited or restricted. While there can be no doubt as to the intrinsic wisdom of such a policy, attention must be drawn, however, to the fact that it is not likely to yield positive results if it is not accompanied by the extension of agricultural credit facilities to indigenous farmers that will enable them to secure the necessary capital for developing their holdings economically.[20]

The concerns raised surfaced in question 23 of the questionnaire in Report VIII (1) of 1956, which read as follows:

23. Do you consider that indigenous peoples should be granted property rights, either collective or individual, as the case may be, over the lands they traditionally occupy?[21]

The Office's analysis of the replies received noted that "Of the 16 governments which replied to this question, 14 replied in the affirmative (two by

---

20   Report VIII (1), pp. 67 to 69.
21   Ibid., p. 177.

implication)."[22] The Office concluded that "In the light of these considerations the wording of the corresponding point in the proposed Conclusions is based on the text of the question, and in the English version the word "recognise" has been substituted for the word "grant". (*Point 21.*)" Point 21 in the proposed conclusions thus read:

> The property rights, either collective or individual, as the case may be, of indigenous peoples over the lands they traditionally occupy should be recognised.[23]

The importance of this change in wording can hardly be stressed too strongly, even though there is no record of any discussion of it in the exchanges that resulted in C. 107. It constituted an acknowledgement that the rights of indigenous and tribal populations to the lands they occupied already existed, and that the existence of the rights did not depend on government action. What was required was a recognition of the rights, but the existence of these rights was not in question. (This characterization would be carried over into Convention No. 169.)

In the 1956 discussion the proposed conclusion was not changed. It had been renumbered to be point 17, and the discussion in the Committee was reported as follows:

> 77. Point 17 of the text under consideration stated that the collective or individual property rights of indigenous peoples on the lands they traditionally occupied should be recognised. The Government member of Ecuador moved an amendment with the object of limiting the application of this point to lands in the public domain. After a detailed discussion, in which the situation of indigenous peoples dispossessed of their traditional lands through conquest or colonisation was discussed, the amendment was rejected, the necessary quorum not having been reached (3 votes for, 30 against, with 35 abstentions).
>
> 78. Point 17 of the text under consideration was then adopted by 64 votes to 0, with 7 abstentions.[24]

When the Office circulated the first report for the second (1957) discussion for comments by the constituents, it included the following proposed text of

---

22   Report VIII (2), p. 118.
23   Ibid., p. 159.
24   Proceedings 1956, p. 743.

Article 11, which was the same as the conclusions adopted in the 1956 Conference (except to replace 'should' by 'shall'):

> The property rights, collective or individual, of indigenous peoples over the lands they traditionally occupy shall be recognised.[25]

The final Office report for the 1957 Conference included governments' observations on each proposed Article, the Office's analysis, and the Office's proposals for the draft Convention. Some general observations made on the land rights part of the proposed Convention, and the Office's comments on them, are important to note:

> The comments of the United Kingdom Government provide the occasion to point out that Part II of the proposed Convention does not in any way relate to the establishment of land reservations for the populations concerned. On the contrary, the fundamental purpose of this part is to ensure that these populations will be treated on an equal footing with the remainder of the national community, firstly as regards the full recognition of their property rights, which are often based on immemorial occupation of the land, and, secondly, as regards their right to obtain, under national agrarian programmes, additional land as well as the means required to develop the land.
>
> The provisions of this part – as well as of the entire text – are aimed at meeting the actual and concrete needs of the populations concerned. This explains, among other things, why Article 11 provides for the recognition of ownership rights, both collective and individual, without expressing a preference for either system. It is clear that some tribal populations having reached a sufficient degree of cultural integration can derive benefit from the individual ownership of land; nevertheless, long experience has shown how the premature application of such a system to tribal land can result in the dispossession of the non-integrated peoples who by reason of their ignorance are more easily exploited than others individually. In these circumstances it would seem desirable that Article 11 should not express a preference for either one of the two systems and that each government should be free to recognise the right of ownership in the form most likely to serve the interests of the persons whom it is sought to protect. The need for reconciling the form in which this right is recognised with the interests of third parties claiming to have acquired more or less

---

25 Report VI (1), p. 48.

recent rights on land traditionally occupied by the populations concerned is a problem which governments would have to examine carefully in each individual case.[26]

There were only a few observations specifically on Article 11, followed by the Office's analysis:

> *Argentina:* The concrete cases in which such recognition of property rights would be practicable should be specified.
> *United Kingdom:* Since "property" has a special significance in this context, it is suggested that the word should be deleted since it is assumed that the provisions of Article 11 are not intended to be restrictive in this sense.
> *United States:* In principle the Government has no objection.
>
> In regard to the observation of the Government of Argentina, it must be pointed out that the purpose of Article 11 is to lay down a general principle, the need for which is brought out in the analysis of the general observations made on Part II, and that it will be for each government to specify the cases in which the principle should apply. As concerns the suggestion of the United Kingdom Government, it has seemed appropriate to replace the word "property" by "ownership". This change, furthermore, enables this Article to be brought more into line with Article 13, in which the word "ownership" has been used from the outset.[27]

The proposed Convention submitted to the Conference included the following text, which amended the previous version by referring to 'ownership', and made some other minor drafting changes which appear to have no significance:

> The right of ownership, collective or individual, of the members of the populations concerned over the lands which these populations traditionally occupy shall be recognised.[28]

The discussion of Article 11 in the 1957 Conference resulted in no changes. There were proposed amendments to the text, but they were not adopted. The brief discussion is reproduced *in toto* here:

---

26   Report VI (2), pp. 20 and 21.
27   Ibid., p. 21.
28   Ibid., p. 58.

57. The Employers' member of Mexico moved an amendment to redraft Article 11 as follows: "Member States, taking into account conditions characteristic of each country and in accordance with their legislation, shall recognise for the exclusive benefit of the members of the populations concerned the right of ownership, collective and/or individual, of these populations, over the lands which they traditionally occupy." A majority of the Committee felt that the points proposed were covered adequately elsewhere in the text. The amendment was rejected by 10 votes to 32, with 3 abstentions.

58. The Employers' member of Peru moved an amendment to insert the words "by virtue of just title" to qualify the term "lands which these populations traditionally occupy". The amendment was opposed on the grounds that the rights mentioned in the text related to occupation over very long periods of time and that the concept of just title, in the case of indigenous populations, would greatly weaken the principle. The amendment was rejected by 13 votes to 34, with 2 abstentions.

59. Article 11 was then adopted by 33 votes to 0, with 16 abstentions.

Article 11 was thus adopted in the form proposed to the Conference in 1957.

b   Adoption of Article 14 of Convention No. 169

In the Meeting of Experts in September 1986 the Experts felt that Convention No. 107 should be revised, though there was considerable discussion on the ways in which it should be revised. This concerned the land rights provisions among others.

As concerns the basic provision on land rights in Article 11 of Convention No. 107, the Report of the Meeting of Experts included the following passage:

> 61. As stated in the working document, the continued possession of the lands they occupy is essential to the cultural and even physical survival of indigenous and tribal peoples. These groups are facing unprecedented pressure on their lands, largely as a result of the fact that many of them do not hold title to the lands they occupy in a form recognised by the national societies, combined with increased development activities and population movements into their territories by non-indigenous or non-tribal persons and organisations.
>
> 62. While many experts felt that Articles 11, 13 and 14 of the Convention offer significant protection in several respects, it was widely felt that they needed to be adapted to take account of these pressures as well as to

reflect more closely the special nature of the relationship between indigenous and tribal peoples and the lands they occupy. On Article 11 in particular, the feeling was expressed by experts on several occasions that the strong fundamental guarantee in this Article should not be attenuated.[29]

The Meeting of Experts felt that the basic protection in Article 11 of C. 107 should not be weakened, though they also felt that some additional considerations should perhaps be examined. The first Office report to examine revision – the 'Law and Practice report' – stated as follows:

> While views were expressed in the Meeting of Experts to the effect that indigenous peoples have generally expressed a preference for collective forms of ownership, individual forms of ownership are also widespread, in particular among certain tribal peoples covered by this Convention. The present wording of this Article should therefore be retained. However, a new paragraph might be added, providing that governments should take steps, where this has not already been done, to determine the lands which the peoples concerned traditionally occupy, and to guarantee effective protection of the right of ownership.[30]

The Law and Practice report contained the following passages on this provision (somewhat mixed with considerations relating to other provisions):

> All issues concerning the protection of indigenous and tribal lands are related closely to the right of ownership. Where there are firm provisions concerning the effective ownership and control of lands and resources by these peoples, there is less danger that ownership rights may be curtailed owing to conflicting national priorities. It has been noted that the relevant Articles of Convention No. 107, while recognising the right of these peoples to own the land they occupy, do not provide for any administrative measures to render that right of ownership effective. Furthermore, Article 11, while recognising the right of ownership over lands, makes no mention of other resources which pertain to these territories, and the control of which may be necessary for the continuation of the traditional lifestyle of these peoples, or alternatively for their economic development under conditions which will not destroy their cultures. A further

---

29 Quoted in Report VI (1), Appendix I, p. 110.
30 Report VI (1), p. 71.

criticism which has been made of this part of the Convention, both at the Meeting of Experts and elsewhere, is that Articles 12 and 13 place too many limitations on the effective exercise of ownership, thereby facilitating the appropriation of indigenous and tribal lands or the removal of these peoples from their traditional lands, without providing for adequate safeguards and procedures when conflicts of interest arise.

It is therefore suggested that some amendments be made to Articles 11 to 14 of Convention No. 107, in the light of national developments and of problems noted in the application of the Convention. The amendments suggested here have two basic purposes (in addition to revising the Convention's integrationist approach, as suggested for Articles considered in the previous chapter). As indicated above, it appears that land questions must be re-examined substantively, more so than the other Articles of the Convention. Thus, the first reason for reviewing these Articles is to modify or strengthen them to take account of the needs of these peoples, in the light of developments since 1957. The second reason is perhaps even more important than any modifications concerning substantive land rights. The suggestions made below would above all provide for procedures reflecting the basic approach of promoting consultations with representatives of the peoples affected, and their participation in taking all decisions which affect them.

Article 11

While views were expressed in the Meeting of Experts to the effect that indigenous peoples have generally expressed a preference for collective forms of ownership, individual forms of ownership are also widespread, in particular among certain tribal peoples covered by this Convention. The present wording of this Article should therefore be retained. However, a new paragraph might be added, providing that governments should take steps, where this has not already been done, to determine the lands which the peoples concerned traditionally occupy, and to guarantee effective protection of the right of ownership.[31]

The questionnaire therefore included the following points:

33. *Subject to question 34 below, do you consider that Article 11 should remain unchanged?*

34. *Do you consider that a paragraph should be added to Article 11 providing that governments should take steps, where this has not already been*

---

31 Report VI (1), p. 71.

> *done, to determine the lands which the peoples concerned traditionally occupy, and to guarantee effective protection of their right of ownership?*[32]

The observations received on these two questions raised complex issues, and began the evolution of this provision. On Question 33, the Office's analysis of replies and proposals was as follows:

> The clear majority of replies to this question were affirmative. However, a number of complex issues have been raised, both in the responses to this specific question and in the more general observations concerning land rights. These issues include, among other things: whether the notion of "land" should be extended to "territory" for the purposes of Article 11; whether this Article should cover the notions of "possession" and "use" of land, as well as the notion of "ownership" itself; whether the use of the term "traditionally" might be deleted; whether the rights of land ownership should accrue to the peoples as a group, rather than to their members; whether a preference might be expressed for collective rather than individual forms of land ownership; and whether specific reference might be made to the concept of "inalienable" land ownership.
>
> It should be noted that both terms "lands" and "territories" are used in the present Convention. While the term used in Article 11 is "lands", Article 12 refers to "habitual territories". Where the question of ownership is concerned, it would seem preferable to retain the term "lands" in Article 11 because – in spite of the preference expressed by indigenous representatives at the Meeting of Experts – not all of the peoples concerned can be said to occupy or possess "territories" in the sense in which this term is generally used in international law. For several centuries many of the groups concerned have farmed small land areas and plots, either individually or in communal holdings and communities, whereas others have enjoyed the possession and occupation of contiguous and undivided land areas more easily referred to as "territories". Thus the use of the term "territories" for the purposes of Article 11 might raise complex issues with regard to the peoples covered by this instrument.
>
> The importance of the concepts of possession and use has been raised both in government replies, and by participants at the Meeting of Experts. In view of the fact that certain of the peoples concerned may indeed

---

32   Report VI (1), p. 96.

attach more importance to these concepts than to the legal notion of ownership, it would indeed seem appropriate also to refer to possession and use in this provision. It may be noted here that the Committee of Experts, in supervising the implementation of Convention No. 107, has recognised the importance of these concepts.

Two governments have suggested that consideration be given to deleting the term "traditionally" from Article 11. This term cannot realistically be taken to imply that these peoples should have recognised rights of ownership over all the lands traditionally occupied by them at all previous stages of their history (although procedures may be established to deal with land claims made on the basis of immemorial possession – see below). The Committee of Experts has taken the view that the use of the term "traditionally" refers to the manner of, and criteria for, land occupation, rather than giving rise to a detailed inquiry into past history, though it is also consistent with claims for restitution. In this light it would appear preferable to retain the term "traditionally" in a revised instrument.

With regard to the forms of land ownership, it would appear that one purpose of this Article is to recognise that the peoples concerned have a right of land ownership, possession and use, in accordance with their own customs and traditions, even though these may be different from those prevailing for other members of national society. The Government of Colombia has suggested that Article 11 be complemented by a phrase indicating that the property rights of indigenous and tribal peoples should be recognised and respected in the same manner as those of other citizens. This would, however, appear to require that these peoples adapt to the prevailing national system rather than that the national system recognise their right to ownership and possession of these lands, which is what the present instrument requires and which appears to reflect the prevailing opinion.

One respondent has suggested that provision be made for inalienability in this Article. In this regard, it may be noted that the indigenous and tribal representatives present at the Meeting of Experts unanimously concluded that these lands should be inalienable and that this is consistent with other available information on the wishes of these peoples. However, as this issue concerns the transmission of rights of ownership, it would be dealt with more appropriately under Article 13.[33]

---

33   This discussion was eventually reflected in Article 17 of Convention No. 169.

In view of the opinions expressed, and of the doubts raised as to the use of the word "ownership" alone, the Proposed Conclusions add a reference to possession. If this amendment were to be accepted, there would appear to be no need to retain the words "collective or individual" in the first paragraph of a revised Article 11. No preference would be expressed, and it could be left to the peoples concerned to determine their own preferential form of land holding and ownership.[34]

Points 28 and 29 of the proposed conclusions for the first discussion were worded as follows. The words which would differ from C. 107 were indicated in italics.

> 27. The rights of ownership *and possession* of the *peoples* concerned over the lands which *they* traditionally occupy should be recognised.
> 28. *Governments should take steps as necessary to identify the lands which the peoples concerned traditionally use and occupy, and to guarantee effective protection of their rights of ownership and possession.*[35]

One significant change was made by the Office from C. 107 for which no explanation emerges from the materials: the substitution of 'rights' for 'right'. Although it clearly is merited for grammatical reasons as there are two rights recognized, no record exists of this ever having been discussed by anyone in the proceedings that followed, but the use of the plural has proven important in future supervisory and advisory work on C. 169, as denoting that there are options between ownership and possession, and that they are not necessarily the same right.

In addition, the references to individual ownership and to the members of the populations concerned, disappeared. Whatever rights existed, they were henceforth recognized as belonging to the peoples, leaving open the interpretation that this could vary from case to case between individual and collective rights. This was reinforced by the eventual addition of a reference to collective rights in the second paragraph of Article 13.

The discussion of land rights in 1988 encountered too many problems to be resolved during that session. As the Committee's report stated:

> 125. The Committee had 77 amendments before it on the section concerning land, and it decided to refer the entire section to a Working Party.

---

34 Report VI (2), pp. 48 and 49.
35 Ibid., p. 108.

The Working Party held three sessions and reported to the Committee that since there were deeply divided views on several aspects of this issue, it was unable to reach a consensus in the time available. The Committee agreed to the Working Party's suggestion that it postpone the detailed examination of the Proposed Conclusions in Part III of Report VI (2) and of the amendments submitted to it. The Committee also agreed with the recommendation of the Working Party that the Employers' and Workers' members and the Government members of the Committee should, if they wished, make general statements on the whole section, and that these statements together with the Proposed Conclusion in Report VI (2), should be used as the basis for discussion at the 76th Session of the Conference.[36]

The procedure to be followed for the second discussion on these points was outlined by the Chair of the Committee:

126 The Chairman pointed out that in accordance with the Standing Orders of the Conference, the Office must use the text which emanated from the Committee for the next consultation with Governments, Employers and Workers. He advised that when addressing the section on land, the Office would use the text of the Proposed Conclusions in Report VI (2). When comments were received, the Office would thus prepare the final draft of the revised Convention on the basis of the general statements on land made in the Committee, the amendments which had been submitted and the elements of agreement which were attained in the Working Party.[37]

Paragraphs 127 to 136 of the Conference Committee report reproduced statements on the entire land rights section by representatives of the Inuit Circumpolar Conference (speaking on behalf of NGOs attending the Session), the Employers' and Workers' members of the Committee, and 19 Government members. These were intended to be taken into account as the Office prepared the second round of reports to be submitted to the 1989 Session.

As indicated above, the discussion that took place in 1988 was not reported in detail in the Conference Committee's report, but some elements did emerge. Concern was expressed from the beginning of the process that the revised instrument should preserve the rights acquired already in C. 107, and that indigenous and tribal peoples' rights should be respected. As the discussion began,

---

36 Proceedings 1988, p. 32/15.
37 Ibid.

> The Workers' members suggested that the major concerns of governments and employers in relation to the recognition of land rights should be identified and addressed with a view to developing a better notion of the scope and nature of claims procedures. They felt that indigenous peoples should not have to accept any form of land rights less than the highest form of ownership or tenure accorded to others in the country.[38]
>
> (The Employers' members) considered it important to include specific references to the need to protect property ownership and the use of traditionally-occupied land (a term they preferred to "territories") in national legislation, and agreed that it was necessary to create adequate procedures to deal with land claims.[39]

The discussion in the plenary sitting of the 1988 Conference when the Committee's report was submitted to it signalled some of the discussion that had taken place in the Committee, and foreshadowed some of the concerns that would be made more concrete the following year. The following statement, by the US employer representative – herself a member of the Cherokee people working in the field of enterprise creation in indigenous communities – would be taken up more concretely in what was to come, especially the move from individual ownership in the 1957 Convention towards a recognition of collective rights in C. 169.

> The existing Convention, adopted in 1957, made certain assumptions: first, it defined and ensured the individual indigenous person's right to own land; and second, it recognised that the practice of displacing indigenous peoples or dispersing them from the lands and territories they occupied should not go unchecked.
>
> In the 30 years since the Convention's adoption, it became apparent that the limited focus on individual ownership failed to provide for the intrinsic and fundamental collectiveness of indigenous societies. It also became an incontestable fact that indigenous land rights were violated and threatened, owing to the absences of procedures for protecting and guaranteeing those rights. At a minimum, next year's work must ensure and safeguard indigenous peoples' use of the territories they traditionally occupy, and recognise that the right of possession should equal that of ownership. Provisions regarding land in this revised Convention must give greater recognition to means other than ownership for the effective control. The rights of indigenous peoples should be broadened to a territorial concept which would encompass flora, fauna as well as natural

---

38　Ibid., p. 32/16.
39　Ibid.

resources, such as coastal fishing and sub-surface mineral resources. The flourishing of indigenous peoples, the strengthening and development – let alone the very survival – of their societies, economies, cultures and lifestyles depends upon adequate land and resource bases. Human rights is the counterpart of economic freedom, and only when the two are united, like two sides of a coin, do they acquire meaning and currency.[40]

In Report IV (1) for the 1989 Session, the Office followed the procedure outlined by the Chair in the 1988 discussion, and circulated the same text on land rights it had circulated in Report VI (2) for the 1988 session, but converted the text (as is usual) from the form of proposed conclusions to that of a draft Convention (and using the '(peoples/populations)' formulation throughout the draft at this stage):

Article 13
1. The rights of ownership and possession of the (peoples/populations) concerned over the lands which they traditionally occupy shall be recognised.
2. Governments shall take steps as necessary to identify the lands which the (peoples/populations) concerned traditionally use and occupy, and to guarantee effective protection of their rights of ownership and possession.[41]

It added the following additional paragraphs of discussion:

> The text of the proposed Convention is taken directly from the Proposed Conclusions contained in Report VI (2) submitted to the 75th Session of the Conference. Following its referral to a working party and a general discussion in the Conference Committee, this subject was set aside for more detailed consideration at the 76th Session. The text of the proposed Convention thus does not reflect either the agreements which were reached on similar language in respect of other parts of the Conclusions, or the elements of agreement which appeared to emerge during the working party's discussions. Governments and other respondents may therefore wish to take the following considerations into account in preparing their comments.
>
> Lands/territories. (This is reproduced under the section on Article 13 of Convention No. 169, *supra.*)

---

40   Proceedings 1988, pp. 36/21 and 36/22.
41   Ibid., p. 9.

> *Ownership, possession or use.* Some consensus appeared to be emerging to use this expression uniformly instead of more limited expressions such as "rights of ownership and possession" (Article 13 of the proposed Convention).[42]

There were a number of observations by constituents on this draft Article, which has various aspects.

As concerns the rights that should be recognized, Canada and Norway made the following proposal, based on an amendment proposed but not dealt with during the 1988 discussion:

> Replace paragraph 1 by: "The rights of possession, use or ownership of the (peoples/populations) concerned over the lands which they traditionally occupy shall be (i) recognised; or (ii) equitably addressed through procedures established in accordance with Article 19."[43]

The Office declined to take this suggestion into account in the new draft:

> As concerns the use of the terms "ownership", "possession" and "use", the Governments of Canada and Norway have made identical proposals based on a proposal submitted during the first discussion. In view of other observations received, the Office considers that to assimilate the term "use" to ownership and possession would weaken the revised Convention by comparison with Convention No. 107, which recognises the right to ownership; it has therefore dealt with this question separately.[44]

Very little was said in the constituents' observations about the need to identify the lands concerned, which thus seems to have met with general agreement. The one reference in the Office's observations to constituents' replies is the following:

> Some respondents have suggested that the present Article should refer to Article 19 concerning the resolving of land claims. The Office has proposed to incorporate that Article in the present one (Article 14 in the new text) in recognition of the close links between the identification of the

---

42   Report VI (1), pp. 4 and 5.
43   Report IV (2A), p. 34.
44   Ibid., p. 36. The term 'use' did eventually appear in Convention No. 169, as concerned multiple use of lands.

relevant lands and the resolving of claims. It appeared appropriate to retain the existing wording for maximum flexibility.[45]

i   *Multiple Use and Nomads*

In the meantime, further amendments were being made to this Article by the Office on the subject of multiple use and nomadic peoples, which were included in this Article with very little discussion. There had been some background on this in 1956 and 1957. The 1956 questionnaire that led to the adoption of C. 107 included the following questions:

> 24. Do you consider that there is a need to secure ownership of tribal land to semi-nomadic forest-dwelling and desert tribes which, though they periodically move for seasonal, climatic or economic reasons, habitually return to the same starting point and generally remain there?
> 25. Do you consider that there is a need to establish zones of nomadism in which these tribes should have an undisturbed right to graze their herds and flocks?[46]

This was not retained for Convention No. 107, but was included in a different form in the Indigenous and Tribal Populations Recommendation, 1957 (No. 104), adopted alongside the Convention. Paragraph 3 (1) of that instrument provides:

> The populations concerned should be assured of a land reserve adequate for the needs of shifting cultivation so long as no better system of cultivation can be introduced.

This subject was not picked up by the Office in its initial proposals for the revised Convention, as it had not appeared in C. 107 which was the basis for the revision process. Report VI (1) of 1988 did contain the following, but this was not reflected in the draft conclusions:

> ...the Programme of Action adopted at the FAO's World Conference on Agrarian Reform and Rural Development in 1979 recommended new approaches to agrarian reform, and urged governments to protect the rights of nomadic populations, and to preserve and adapt or create

---

45   Ibid.
46   Report VIII (1), pp. 177 and 178.

systems of broad-based community control and management of land and water rights in accordance with development needs.[47]

The next time a reference to this subject appears in the preparatory materials for C. 169 is in the final report submitted to the 1989 Conference discussion; this suggests that the subject had been raised in the Working Group that met during the 1988 Conference although it was not included in the report of the Conference discussion. The Government of Sweden included the following in its comments on the first draft of the Convention:

> Nomadic tribes who require extensive areas of land for their cattle herding are unlikely to be covered by the Article as worded here. A provision should be added concerning rights of users. The report makes it clear that there was a certain degree of unanimity during the first year's discussions in this connection.[48]

Thus, although no direct proposal had emerged in the previous discussion, the Office included a provision in the draft Convention submitted to the Conference, apparently taking the Swedish comment as the basis. As it stated in the final report for the 1989 discussion:

> Different views have been expressed concerning users' rights, and such concerns were raised earlier also by the Food and Agriculture Organisation of the United Nations with special reference to nomadic peoples. Recommendation No. 104, which supplements Convention No. 107, contains provisions dealing with land-use rights for nomads and shifting cultivators. An additional paragraph has therefore been inserted to distinguish between the right of use and the rights of ownership and possession. The term "preferential use" has not been retained, as the concept would in this context be contrary to the objective sought.[49]

The draft Convention submitted to the Conference therefore included the following, appearing for the first time as Article 14, paragraph 3:

> Where appropriate, measures shall be taken to safeguard the right of the peoples concerned to use lands not exclusively occupied by them, but to

---

47 Report VI (1), p. 69.
48 Report IV (2A), p. 35.
49 Ibid., p. 36.

which they have traditionally had access for their subsistence activities. Particular attention shall be paid to the situation of nomadic peoples and shifting cultivators in this respect.[50]

There was no further explicit discussion of this draft provision in the 1989 Conference session. In the Chairman's redraft during that Session, he included it as part of paragraph 1 of Article 14, and it was adopted in that form.

ii   *Adequate Procedures to Resolve Land Claims*

No provision to this effect was included in C. 107. The 1986 Meeting of Experts did, however, consider the question of restitution of lost territories, a related but not identical question:

> 81. In addition to providing for the security of lands currently occupied by indigenous and tribal peoples, a number of experts and observers stressed the importance of restitution to these peoples of lands of which they had been dispossessed. In some countries they had rights, which were not given the respect they deserved, based on treaty rights, on grants or on immemorial possession, but these lands had been taken from them over the centuries. They now occupied lands which were greatly reduced from their earlier holdings, and which in many cases was insufficient to provide for their present needs and future development. One expert described in some detail that the principle of restitution had been recognised in the constitutions or legislation in several Latin American countries, and stated that it should be included in the revised Convention. There were practical problems with its full implementation, but the principle was an important one. In some such cases, the right to restitution was accorded in relation to lands lost over a certain number of years previous to the adoption of legislation in this connection.[51]

The question of restitution of lands lost by indigenous and tribal peoples received considerable attention in the Office's first report, at that stage arising in the context of agrarian reform programmes. As this report stated:

> Where their lands have been fragmented over hundreds of years, their major demand may be for the restitution of sufficient ancestral land to provide them with a cohesive territory over which they may exercise management and control in accordance with their own traditions.

---

50   Report IV (2B), p. 14.
51   Report of the Meeting of Experts, Appendix I, Report VI(1), p. 114.

It is thus necessary to distinguish between the provision of adequate lands as a measure of good policy, and the restitution of land in recognition of some form of obligation. The question of restitution is immensely complex. In its most extreme variant, restitution on the basis of historical claims to indigenous land would require a drastic revision of national systems of property ownership. But the principle of restitution on the basis of need and entitlement has been included in the declarations of indigenous peoples' organisations, in the recommendations of the United Nations Special Rapporteur on Indigenous Populations, and in the legislation of a number of States.

The Special Rapporteur recommended that indigenous lands should be returned under agrarian reform programmes. He stated that restoration of the indigenous land base under agrarian reforms which would return ownership of the land to indigenous peoples without purchase or taxation, is crucial, and that it is also essential that indigenous lands be contiguous in order to preserve the unity of the people. He stated that priority must be given to the return of land seized from indigenous communities, and that governments should be encouraged to appoint commissions of inquiry to establish how lands can be obtained for the indigenous communities that need them, and how land rights can best be granted and protected once they have been restored to those indigenous peoples who have been deprived of them.

A number of experts and observers at the ILO Meeting of Experts also stressed the importance of restitution, noting that rights based on treaties, grants or immemorial possession were not given the respect they deserved. It was noted that indigenous and tribal peoples occupied lands which were greatly reduced from their earlier holdings, and which in many cases were insufficient to provide for their current needs and future development. The Meeting was also informed that the principle of restitution had been recognised in the constitutions or legislation of several Latin American countries. In some cases, the right to restitution was accorded in relation to lands lost during a specified period preceding the adoption of the pertinent legislation. Although it was acknowledged that there were practical problems in fully implementing such a right, there was support for the inclusion of this principle in the revised Convention.[52]

The Office therefore proposed at this stage to add the question of land claims to the consideration of provision of adequate land for the development and

---

52   Report VI (1), pp. 69 and 70.

maintenance of indigenous peoples, which was dealt with in Article 14 of Convention No. 107 (and eventually in Article 19 of Convention No. 169). Question 46 in the report circulated to the constituents read as follows:

> *Do you consider that a paragraph should be added to Article 14 providing that adequate procedures should be established within the national legal system to resolve land claims by the peoples concerned?*[53]

The replies to this question were largely positive, and the Office included the following in its second report:

> The large majority of affirmative replies indicates general agreement that a provision of this kind should be included in a revised Convention. However, there have been certain proposals for partial rewording. First, under both this and other questions, certain replies have indicated that particular reference should be made to treaty rights and obligations. Second, it has been pointed out that administrative as well as legislative measures are required to deal with land claims. Third, it has been proposed by the Government of Canada that this provision should specify more clearly the lands to which claims may be made. The suggestion has also been made that this provision is of sufficient importance to merit a separate Article.
>
> It would indeed appear appropriate to make specific reference to treaty claims in this provision, and this view is reflected in the Proposed Conclusions. While it is true that administrative measures as well as legislative measures are required to deal with land claims, it is the view of the Office that specific reference to administrative measures would be superfluous. This would appear already to be implied in the existing language. The Office also considers that it would be inappropriate to define in too much detail the lands to which this provision applies, as the current legal status of the lands to which claims may be made will vary greatly from country to country. It is therefore proposed to leave the text as formulated in this question, except for the inclusion of a reference to treaty claims and obligations.
>
> The question of whether this provision should be a separate Article can be considered at a later stage.[54]

Point 40 of the proposed conclusions thus stated as follows:

---

53 Report VI (1), p. 97.
54 Report VI (2), pp. 63 and 64.

> 40. *Adequate procedures should be established within the national legal system to resolve land claims by the peoples concerned, including claims arising under treaties.*[55]

The kind of discussions held on land rights in the 1988 Session of the Conference has already been dealt with above, and no identifiable discussion on this point appears in the Committee's report. The general discussions that took place before these draft provisions were sent to the Working Party are reproduced, however. During the general discussion the following appears in the report of the responsible committee to the plenary of the Conference:

> The Government member of Canada felt that the revised Convention should reflect the different types of land rights which exist; there should not be any revival of claims to traditionally occupied lands which had been the subject of treaties or other arrangements; and the Convention should provide means for dealing with the fact that governments were not always able to recognise all claims for a variety of reasons.[56]
>
> The Workers' members suggested that the major concerns of governments and employers in relation to the recognition of land rights should be identified and addressed with a view to developing a better notion of the scope and nature of claims procedures.[57]
>
> The Employers' members...agreed that it was necessary to create adequate procedures to deal with land claims.[58]

The Committee duly included in its report the following conclusion:

> 39. Adequate procedures should be established within the national legal system to resolve land claims by the (peoples/populations) concerned, including claims arising under treaties.[59]

When the Office circulated the first draft of the proposed Convention for comment it did not include any further discussion of this point, but did translate this conclusion into a draft Article 19:

---

55   Ibid., p. 109.
56   Proceedings 1988, p. 32/3.
57   Ibid., p. 32/16.
58   Ibid.
59   Ibid., p. 32/26.

Adequate procedures shall be established within the national legal system to resolve land claims by the (peoples/populations) concerned, including claims arising under treaties.[60]

A number of observations were made on this draft Article, but the Office analysis said simply, and in its entirety: 'The text of this Article has been incorporated in Article 14.'[61] It therefore appeared in the report submitted to the second discussion as Article 14, paragraph 4, without change:

Adequate procedures shall be established within the national legal system to resolve land claims by the peoples concerned, including claims arising under treaties.[62]

The Committee's report in 1989 – though it did not report in detail the discussions on land rights – did contain some indications as to how the constituents viewed the draft of Article 14(4). For instance:

The Government member of Canada agreed with the objective of the Convention to oblige governments to deal fairly with indigenous claims to traditional lands. Legally settled claims, however, should not be reopened. The provisions dealing with the obligation to recognise rights in traditionally occupied land should therefore be more closely linked with the provisions obliging governments to provide for the settlement of disputes over land claims.[63]

The Article proposed to the 1989 Conference – which now had become draft Article 14 after the inclusion of the first version of the new Article 13 discussed above – read as follows:

Article 14
1. The rights of ownership and possession of the peoples concerned over the lands which they traditionally occupy shall be recognised.
2. Governments shall take steps as necessary to identify the lands which the peoples concerned traditionally occupy, and to guarantee effective protection of their rights of ownership and possession.

---

[60] Report IV (1), p. 11.
[61] Report IV (2A), p. 51.
[62] Report IV (2B), p. 14.
[63] Proceedings 1989, p. 25/4.

3. Where appropriate, measures shall be taken to safeguard the right of the peoples concerned to use lands not exclusively occupied by them, but to which they have traditionally had access for their subsistence activities. Particular attention shall be paid to the situation of nomadic peoples and shifting cultivators in this respect.

4. Adequate procedures shall be established within the national legal system to resolve land claims by the peoples concerned, including claims arising under treaties.

When the Conference met in 1989, as already indicated it had to deal with the lack of agreement in 1988 on land rights. It once again constituted a Working Party to attempt to find solutions. This was not entirely successful at that level, however, because some of the draft Articles submitted to it did not find a consensus in the Working Party. In reporting the outcome of its discussions, the Working Party indicated:

> 116. During consideration of Article 14, views diverged as to the use of the terms "ownership", "possession" and "use". The Government members stressed that the addition of the word "use" would help to expand the scope of the rights conferred by this Article. They also argued that for practical reasons the forms of legal recognition of these rights had to be rendered sufficiently flexible to reflect the varying national constitutional and legal circumstances. The Workers' members, however, suggested that this carried the risk of reducing the effect of the obligation incorporated in the Article, and the consequence would be a lesser protection than that provided in Convention No. 107. The Working Party was unable to reach agreement.[64]

In the draft submitted by the Chairman to deal with the many views being expressed on land rights, this formula was included in paragraph 1 of Article 14 along with the rights of ownership and possession:

> 1. The rights of ownership and possession of the peoples concerned over the lands which they traditionally occupy shall be recognised. In addition, measures shall be taken in appropriate cases to safeguard the right of the peoples concerned to use lands not exclusively occupied by them, but to which they have traditionally had access for their subsistence and traditional activities. Particular attention shall be paid to the situation of nomadic peoples and shifting cultivators in this respect.

---

64   Proceedings 1989, p. 25/17.

No further discussion arose in the consideration of the proposed Convention in the plenary session in 1989, and we are left with the bare fact of its adoption, stimulated by the FAO and a late-stage comment by Sweden, picked up by the Office, and accepted as a good idea by the Conference.

iii   *Adoption of Article 14 as a Whole*

In view of the lack of agreement in the Committee on this Article – along with many of the rest of the land rights provisions – the Chairman then proposed to withdraw for consultations and to return with a proposed text for this provision among others. Once this procedure had been agreed, further statements were made for the Chairman to take into account, which consisted of the following as concerns the kinds of rights to be recognized:

> 124. The Government member of Norway referred to an amendment submitted by several Government members to include the word "use" in Article 14. He explained that the intention had been to extend the rights that should be protected, not to weaken the paragraph.
>
> 125. The Employers' members noted that they had difficulties with Article 14(1) and felt that it should be more flexible. They would accept the inclusion of "use" in the provision. ...
>
> 126. The Government member of Canada recalled the three main concerns he had expressed during the general discussion. ... His delegation had problems with Article 14 as it was drafted and recognised that the inclusion of "use" could cause problems for some countries. He proposed "ownership or possession". ...
>
> 130. The Government member of India...considered that more flexibility should be provided in the text of Article 14(1) so that different situations would be covered. ...
>
> 131. The Government member of Brazil noted that from the outset his delegation had stressed that the Convention should be as universal as possible. ... She preferred the use of "lands" in Article 13 and, in Article 14, favoured rights of possession and use of land by these peoples in view of the State's ownership of indigenous land. ...
>
> 132. The Government member of the USSR recalled that his delegation had submitted an amendment to Article 14(1) in accordance with national legislation concerning the possession of land by virtue of property and use. Thus the three terms "ownership, possession and use" would be required in order to be in accordance with national legislation. ...

133. The Government member of Japan noted the differences of legal systems between countries as far as lands, territories and resources were concerned. He also noted the differences of the relationship with lands and resources between indigenous and tribal peoples. For this reason, the text of Articles 14 to 16 should be more flexible and give due regard to the different conditions. ...

134. The Workers' members had the feeling that the revision of the Convention was leading to a worse position for indigenous and tribal peoples than obtained in Convention No. 107. If the proposed text weakened the draft Office text they would have great difficulty in supporting it. They...noted with interest the views put forward by the Government members of Canada and Norway regarding "use", which they felt could be a basis for consensus on Article 14. ...

138. The Government member of New Zealand interpreted Article 14(1) as requiring governments which ratify this Convention to recognise the rights of indigenous peoples to ownership and possession of the lands which they have occupied over time by right of tradition and which they currently occupy and accepted the text. ...

140. The Government member of Colombia...agreed with other speakers on the need to discuss the word "use", but felt that the inclusion of the words "or use" in Article 14(1) would weaken it. ...

141. The Government member of Portugal...supported the concept of ownership, possession and use of land and territories but noted that one could not be substituted for the other.

142. A representative of the Workers' members expressed understanding of the difficulty of achieving a universally applicable Convention. While there was recognition of the diversity of indigenous and tribal peoples, she said there was a failure to understand that they shared among themselves concepts of life and relationships with land and nature. What differed were the national legal systems. She considered that international law should set standards to be attained, even if this would involve changing national legislation. She stressed the fundamental relationship between these peoples and the land and noted the relationship with lands and territories which was mentioned in Article 13. She emphasised that these peoples required ownership of land on which they lived, which was the basis for their existence. Failure to use the term territories would be a retrograde step. She urged the Committee to recognise the indigenous and tribal peoples' right to the ownership, possession and use of lands and territories.... She stated that the text of the revised Convention could not be weaker than that of Convention No. 107,

particularly as far as land was concerned, if the credibility governments needed to obtain with indigenous and tribal peoples was to be achieved and maintained.[65]

As concerns draft paragraph 3, there is one recorded reference to this subject in the Committee's report for the 1989 session, as the whole land rights part of the proposed Convention was dealt with in the Working Party, as signalled above. Once the consolidated text was submitted to the Committee, the Government representative of Colombia made the only mention of it:

> 140. The Government member of Colombia...considered that the right of these peoples to use lands and territories they temporarily occupied should be clearly stated in Article 14(3).[66]

It does not appear that this representative actually understood what this provision meant when he made this comment, as the draft provision referred to multiple use rather than temporary use.

The Chairman undertook consultations with the various parts of the Committee membership, and returned with a proposed 'package deal' that included what became the final text of Article 14. A number of delegations took the floor to support the compromise, but expressed their reservations on some aspects of it, including the subjects discussed in this section. Relevant portions of their statements are reproduced here:

> 144. The Government member of Brazil congratulated all those involved in reaching a consensus on the package of Articles and expressed his full awareness of the fact that there had been very difficult negotiations. He noted that major concessions had been made and that the resulting wording showed the force of the Committee's determination. Although some points were not ideal from his delegation's point of view, he was prepared to accept them as drafted as far as Articles 13, 15, 16, 17(1), 17(3), 18 and 19 were concerned. He stressed, however, that the solution which had been found with regard to ownership in Article 14 would create insurmountable problems for Brazil and would practically remove the possibility of his country ratifying the Convention. ...[67]
>
> 145. The Government member of the United States expressed appreciation for the deep commitment and effort expended in achieving

---

65 Ibid., pp. 25/18 to 25/20.
66 Ibid., p. 25/20.
67 Brazil did later ratify Convention No. 169.

consensus on the Articles concerned in the face of deeply divergent points of view. His Government accepted the Articles as proposed. He noted, however, that lack of clarity made many parts very difficult to interpret, and he felt that this could pose a problem for governments concerning adoption of the Convention. He considered that many of the clauses which were apparently intended to strengthen the rights of indigenous peoples could in fact be taken to weaken those rights. He also felt that there could be a number of unintended consequences in the revised Convention, particularly as far as Article 14 was concerned. He believed that the use of "ownership and possession" rather than the more flexible "ownership or possession" could make it impossible for governments to ratify the revised Convention. He noted that "ownership and possession" should not be interpreted to support policies like "Allotment" (1877) and "Termination" (1953) which have had a decidedly negative effect on Indians. Both the tribes and Congress have rejected these policies.

150. The Government member of Canada thanked all the members of the Committee for their efforts towards achieving a consensus text which would be widely acceptable. Her delegation accepted Articles 15, 16, 17(1), 17(3), 18 and 19. Other elements of the text, however, raised major concerns. As far as Article 14 was concerned, she noted that in Canada individual rights of ownership of land were available to everyone. Regarding Articles 14(1) and (2), which dealt with collective land rights, she stated that the phrase "rights of ownership and possession" did not accommodate the cases of countries such as her own where indigenous rights in land could be other than those of ownership. While indigenous groups in Canada sometimes had complete rights of ownership to their land, in most instances, such as Indian reserve lands, the rights were in the form of extensive rights of use, possession and occupation. Domestic courts had interpreted the aboriginal rights in land as being those of traditional rights of use and occupation. She pointed out that in many cases Indians had expressed a preference for the retention of these rights and had consequently chosen not to avail themselves of collective rights of ownership. She stated that use of the term "rights of ownership and possession" implied a requirement that indigenous land rights must always be those of both ownership and possession and that this would not be compatible with the Canadian situation.

...

154. The Government member of the USSR stated that he was able to support the consolidated text. However, he expressed the reservations of his

Government on Article 14(1) because his country's Constitution gave the State exclusive right of property on lands. This paragraph might considerably reduce the likelihood of ratification.[68]

Some of the uncertainties of meaning may have been attenuated by an explanation provided by the Secretariat on the way in which one of the terms had been interpreted under C. 107:

> 163. The Government member of the United States sought a clarification from the Office on the term "ownership" as used in Convention No. 107. A representative of the Secretary-General said that the problem of dealing with the meaning of "ownership" in Convention No. 107 had often arisen in the Committee of Experts on the Application of Conventions and Recommendations, which had recognised on a number of occasions that the exact contents of the concept of ownership varied in different countries and under different legal systems. The Committee of Experts had concluded that it was difficult to say precisely that what was called "ownership" in one country had exactly the same implications in another country. The Committee of Experts had also concluded on a number of occasions that firm, permanent and assured possession did not constitute a violation of the requirement of ownership in Convention No. 107, which was considered to be among the ILO's "promotional" Conventions in many respects. This concept had been considered to be a good interim measure until full conformity with Convention No. 107 had been achieved. While the Committee of Experts had not found an exact equivalence between "possession" and "ownership", it had not found the firm assurance of possession and use to be in violation of the requirement for "ownership".[69]

In spite of the passion and the disagreements surrounding this discussion, it does not appear that it has had any effect on the way the ILO supervisory bodies have understood the rights of indigenous and tribal peoples that are recognized under C. 169. This would require a separate examination, but ILO supervision has concluded that any arrangement that gives these peoples guaranteed access to and possession of their lands falls within the meaning of the Convention.

---

68 Proceedings 1989, pp. 25/21 and 25/22.
69 Proceedings 1989, p. 25/23.

3   Article 15 of Convention No. 169: Natural Resources

If the articles on land rights acquisition and conservation were difficult, the adoption of Article 15 aroused even more intense emotions.

Article 15 of C. 169 reads as follows:

> 1. The rights of the peoples concerned to the natural resources pertaining to their lands shall be specially safeguarded. These rights include the right of these peoples to participate in the use, management and conservation of these resources.
>
> 2. In cases in which the State retains the ownership of mineral or subsurface resources or rights to other resources pertaining to lands, governments shall establish or maintain procedures through which they shall consult these peoples, with a view to ascertaining whether and to what degree their interests would be prejudiced, before undertaking or permitting any programmes for the exploration or exploitation of such resources pertaining to their lands. The peoples concerned shall wherever possible participate in the benefits of such activities, and shall receive fair compensation for any damages which they may sustain as a result of such activities.

Convention No. 107 contained no such provisions, though Recommendation No. 104 provided as follows:

> 4. Members of the populations concerned should receive the same treatment as other members of the national population in relation to the ownership of underground wealth or to preference rights in the development of such wealth.

The subject was discussed in some detail in the 1986 Meeting of Experts, which had a lively exchange on it. As the Meeting's report stated:

> 73. There was a significant amount of discussion on whether the rights of indigenous and tribal peoples to the subsoil and other natural resources pertaining to their lands should be recognised in a revised Convention. It was noted that their own traditions included these concepts, but in many countries the owners of land did not have rights to the subsoil and other resources. These rights were instead retained by the State. It was pointed out that this resulted with increasing frequency in the State according to non-indigenous and non-tribal entities the right of exploration and exploitation of subsoil resources in traditional indigenous or tribal territories,

involving effective dispossession and damage to the land itself and disruption of their way of life.

74. Many experts pointed to the practical problems that would ensue if a revised Convention extended to subsoil resources the rights contained in the present Article 11. The Meeting therefore examined other ways of accommodating these different views and needs. One expert explained how recent legislation and practice relating to one area of his country had recognised the right of the indigenous peoples to exercise a right of veto over mineral ventures within their lands, even though the State retained rights to the subsoil, and to share in the profits once exploitation was begun. There were various procedures provided for to negotiate the conditions under which exploitation could take place and to obtain the consent of the indigenous people, but the government retained the right of decision. The observer from the Inter-American Indian Institute described recent negotiations between the government and indigenous groups in one Latin American country concerning indigenous participation in mineral profits, which might provide an important precedent. One expert stressed the need for social and environmental impact studies preceding development activities, and for information on proposed projects to be made publicly available.

75. Several experts and other participants referred to the need to recognise the rights of indigenous and tribal peoples to water and for special measures in this regard. Whereas many participants felt that the land rights of indigenous and tribal peoples should include rights over water resources within their traditional territories, different opinions were expressed concerning the issue of coastal waters. One expert stated in this regard that no State could concede rights over coastal economic zones and the continental shelf.[70]

While the Meeting of Experts arrived at no firm conclusions in this regard, it did draw the attention of the Governing Body to the discussion. It set the discussion in the context of the principle that 'indigenous and tribal peoples should enjoy "as much control as possible" over their own economic, social and cultural development.'[71] As the Office reported the Meeting of Experts, it stated that:

> There was also much discussion as to whether a revised Convention should recognise the rights of indigenous and tribal peoples to the

---

70 Report of the Meeting of Experts, from Report VI (1), pp. 112 and 113.
71 Report VI (1), p. 45.

subsoil and other natural resources pertaining to their lands. While several experts pointed to the practical problems which would ensue if a revised Convention were to extend the ownership rights contained in Convention No. 107 to the subsoil and other natural resources, there was general agreement in the meeting that procedures should be established to negotiate the conditions under which the exploitation of these resources might take place, and to obtain the consent of the indigenous and tribal peoples concerned.[72]

The report took note of growing demands in this respect by indigenous and tribal peoples themselves. For instance, it stated that they

> ...have increasingly been demanding the right to control all aspects of the resources pertaining to the lands they occupy. For example, a draft declaration of principles drawn up in 1985 by the Inuit Circumpolar Conference, the Four Directions Council, the International Indian Treaty Council and other indigenous organisations and submitted to the United Nations Working Group on Indigenous Populations, stated that indigenous nations and peoples are entitled to the permanent control and enjoyment of their aboriginal ancestral-historical territories. This includes surface and subsurface rights, inland and coastal waters, renewable and non-renewable resources, and the economies based on these resources.[73]

The report laid down some markers for how the Office proposed that this difficult question should be handled:

> An international convention cannot provide detailed guide-lines on the precise conditions in which all activities relating to the exploitation of natural resources may or may not take place on the lands of indigenous and tribal peoples; rather, it should provide a general framework for dealing with these questions. (It should be noted, however, that such detailed guide-lines have been included in the recommendations of the United Nations Special Rapporteur on Indigenous Populations.)[74]

As the Office discussed further the measures that might be taken in the new Convention, it made certain points rather strongly:

---

72 Ibid., pp. 45 and 46.
73 Ibid.
74 Ibid.

> Clearly, the insertion in a revised Convention of rights which would require radical changes in national legal systems, if the Convention were ratified, would be counterproductive. Whatever provision is adopted on this subject should therefore establish the general principle that these peoples should have certain rights, while providing also for special measures for their protection where there may be difficulty in the immediate recognition of these rights.
>
> A new provision might therefore provide that the right of ownership over lands, provided for already in Article 11 of Convention No. 107, should extend to natural resources, including flora and fauna, waters, ice and mineral and other subsoil resources pertaining to the lands traditionally occupied by the peoples concerned. Taking account of objections which are likely to be raised, a second paragraph might provide that, where under the national legal system, land ownership does not carry with it the ownership of mineral and other subsoil resources pertaining to the land, special measures should be taken to protect the peoples concerned in relation to the exploitation of such resources. It would of course be understood that, in accordance with other suggestions made in this connection, the adoption of such special measures would follow consultations with representatives of these peoples.[75]

The questionnaire sent to the constituents in this report therefore contained the following two points:

> *35. Do you consider that the right of ownership over lands already provided for in Article 11 should extend to natural resources, including fauna and flora, waters, ice and mineral and other subsoil resources, pertaining to the lands traditionally occupied by the peoples concerned?*
>
> *36. Do you consider that where, under the national legal system, land ownership does not carry with it the ownership of mineral and other subsoil resources pertaining to the land, special measures should be taken to protect these peoples in relation to the control and exploitation of such resources?*[76]

As might be imagined from the profound questions raised in the Meeting of Experts and evoked in the Office report, governments reacted strongly to these questions. The Office's analysis of the replies to question 35 was the following:

---

75   Ibid., p. 72.
76   Ibid., p. 96.

> There was a marginally greater number of affirmative than negative replies to this question. However, a number of governments raised very strong objections to the inclusion of a provision of this nature in a revised instrument, generally stating that it would be incompatible with domestic legislation which gives the State exclusive rights over subsoil and natural resources. In this regard one government has drawn a distinction between natural resources on the one hand, and subsoil and mineral resources on the other, stating that it would be possible to provide for ownership over the former, but not the latter, in a revised instrument.
>
> In view of the widespread concerns expressed by governments, it would not appear possible to include a provision on the basis of question 35. Nevertheless, in view of the absolute majority of affirmative replies to this and the following question, it would seem appropriate that a revised instrument provide for special measures in this area (see under question 36).[77]

The replies to question 36 were much more positive, leading to the Office proposals that figured in the second report. The analysis of replies is reproduced in some detail to give a flavour of the reasoning used:

> The large majority of replies to this question were affirmative. As noted above, a distinction has been drawn in certain cases between control over surface natural resources, including flora and fauna and waters, and mineral and subsoil resources. For example, the Government of Canada has indicated that in that country most indigenous populations have the use and benefit of fauna and flora on lands which they legally occupy, but that access to such natural resources as mineral and other subsoil resources generally depends on the provisions of specific treaties, negotiated settlements and legislation. At the same time, whereas land ownership in Canada does not always carry with it the ownership of mineral and other subsoil resources, minerals can only be developed with indigenous consent. The Government of Australia has described the diverse state laws within its federal system. In that country ownership of land extends to certain minerals pertaining to the land in the state of New South Wales, but is otherwise vested in the Crown. In the Northern Territory Commonwealth land rights legislation provides for compensation at the mining stage, linked to the value of minerals. The Government

---

77 Report VI (2), pp. 51 and 52.

of Nigeria notes that, although the State generally has exclusive rights to subsoil and natural resources, a percentage of the profit is given to the peoples affected. The Government of Mexico considers that in the first place it should be arranged that the peoples concerned carry out the exploitation of their subsoil resources. Meanwhile one workers' organisation considers that indigenous societies must have full control over mineral extraction and the right to share equitably in the proceeds from any extraction to which they have given consent, and that in no circumstances should such extraction take place without the informed consent of the peoples concerned expressed through their own institutions. Similar views have been expressed by indigenous peoples' organisations in Australia, and in a number of their meetings and declarations.

There are thus diverging views with regard to the extent of indigenous control, in particular where the extraction of mineral resources is involved. However, there would seem to be a wide measure of agreement, firstly that the peoples concerned should be enabled to control wildlife and other resources which pertain to their traditional lands, and which are fundamental to the continuation of their traditional lifestyles; and secondly, that the consent of the peoples concerned should always be sought before mineral development takes place on their lands, and fair compensation paid for such activities. It would be inappropriate to specify the manner in which such consent should be sought at the national level, and the exact procedures to be undertaken before any mineral activity on their lands commences in individual countries. Nevertheless, in view of the evident dangers that these activities may hold for the preservation of indigenous and tribal lands, it would seem important that a revised instrument establish the general principle that the consent of these peoples be sought, through appropriate procedures, before any such activities be undertaken. In the light of these considerations, the Proposed Conclusions contain two separate paragraphs on this point. The first provides for measures to safeguard the rights of these peoples to surface resources without reference to ownership. The second deals with exploration for or exploitation of mineral and other subsoil resources.[78]

The draft conclusions proposed to the Conference for its first discussion on the basis of this analysis were:

---

78   Ibid., pp. 53 and 54.

> 29. Special measures should be taken to safeguard the control of the peoples concerned over natural resources pertaining to their traditional territories, including flora and fauna, waters and sea ice, and other surface resources.
> 30. Governments should seek the consent of the peoples concerned, through appropriate mechanisms, before undertaking or permitting any programmes for the exploration or exploitation of mineral and other subsoil resources pertaining to their traditional territories. Fair compensation should be provided for any such activities undertaken within the territories of the said peoples.[79]

The way in which the discussion relating to land rights was handled in the 1988 Session of the Conference has already been detailed above. Once this question emerged from the Conference Committee Working Party without results, the Committee decided to defer further consideration to another round of consultation and to the 1989 discussion. The Committee's report included several statements relating to resource rights to move the discussion along.

> A representative of the Inuit Circumpolar Conference, speaking for the accredited non-governmental organisations, made a statement on indigenous lands and resources. The speaker reiterated that guaranteed access and rights to an adequate land and resource base were crucial to the survival and growth of indigenous peoples. She stressed that if the revised Convention was to be a useful instrument, the fundamental territorial and resource rights of indigenous peoples must be respected by it, and that without adequate land and resource provisions the Convention would not provide a meaningful framework for the world's indigenous and tribal peoples.[80]
>
> So far as subsoil resources were concerned, the Workers' members argued that it was essential that there existed provision for far greater control by indigenous peoples, particularly a requirement that their informed consent be obtained. They felt it important that the question of subsoil exploitation be separated from issues relating to removal or relocation.[81]
>
> The Employers' members...felt exclusive rights to territories or resources could not be attributed to one sector of the population. They

---

79   Ibid., p. 108.
80   Proceedings 1988, p. 32/15.
81   Ibid., p. 32/16.

recalled that the rights to subsoil resources were held by the State in most countries, while only a few recognised private ownership of these resources. Since it was difficult to make absolute statements on this important issue, they favoured the adoption of a position which would not interfere with the rights of States, but which would call for consultation with indigenous and tribal peoples concerning resource development, and the protection of their living conditions as far as possible.[82]

The Committee therefore forwarded unchanged conclusions to the plenary for further consideration. These were in turn adopted without change, and the Office used them as the basis for the draft Convention circulated in Report IV (1) for the 1989 discussion. Once converted into Convention language, this provision read as follows (recalling that the term '(peoples/populations)' was being used at this stage):

> 1. Special measures shall be taken to safeguard the control of the (peoples/populations) concerned over natural resources pertaining to their traditional territories, including flora and fauna, waters and sea ice, and other surface resources.
> 2. Governments shall seek the consent of the (peoples/populations) concerned, through appropriate mechanisms, before undertaking or permitting any programmes for the exploration or exploitation of mineral and other subsoil resources pertaining to their traditional territories. Fair compensation shall be provided for any such activities undertaken within the territories of the said (peoples/populations).[83]

The Office commentary on the constituents' replies reveals that a very complex set of concerns was expressed, and that the Office made a number of proposals to respond to them:

> The replies indicate a general consensus regarding the substance of paragraph 1, to the effect that these peoples should have rights over the natural resources pertaining to the areas they occupy, though reservations have been expressed by some respondents over elements of existing wording. The Government of India considered that it was unacceptable to extend the right of ownership to natural resources; however, as all other governments appear to accept that rights to lands include rights to

---

82   Ibid.
83   Report IV (1), p. 10.

surface resources at least, the provision has been maintained. Some respondents have proposed that the rights of these peoples over both surface and subsurface resources should be the same, but in view of the general acceptance of the approach whereby different rights apply to the different categories of resources, the differentiation has been retained. Others consider that the provision should refer to "rights" rather than "control", and this has been taken into account in the proposed text. Account has also been taken of the proposal by the Government of Colombia to include a reference to participation in the management and conservation of these resources.

The term "traditional territories" has occasioned some reservations. The Office has therefore proposed the phrase "their lands and territories", intended to indicate that the areas to which the present Article applies are the same as those to which these peoples have rights under the preceding Article. As concerns the observation by the Government of Japan, this Article appears to be worded sufficiently flexibly that no such qualifying phrase is called for.

Paragraph 2 has elicited widely differing views regarding the use of the term "seek the consent" and the principles of consent and consultation. Some governments and most workers' organisations, as well as the representative organisations of indigenous and tribal peoples, consider that this provision should require that consent be obtained in relation to mineral and other subsurface resources. Others appear to consider, in spite of the explanations given, that the phrase "seek the consent" used in the original proposal would in itself require that consent be obtained. It must be clear from the first discussion that this phrase is not acceptable to a sufficiently large proportion of the membership that it cannot be put forward again. The Office has, however, proposed alternative wording intended to convey that an attempt should be made in good faith to obtain the consent of the peoples concerned before undertaking activities of this kind in their territories, without indicating that they should have a veto power over government decisions.

The proposal to differentiate between the levels of agreement required before authorising exploration and exploitation has merit; but such a differentiation would be permitted on the national level by the existing text.

The proposed text does not reflect the suggestions that the term "fair compensation" be defined, as this appears to be a subject which would have to be approached in a different way in each country and in each situation, in accordance with the rules and procedures laid down at the national level. The proposals that references to water and energy resources should be made in paragraph 2 have not been retained, as these resources are of a different character from the mineral and other subsurface resources which this provision was designed to cover. It would appear that the concerns that these proposals reflect can be handled at the national level without explicit mention in the Convention – as in the case of Brazil, to which reference is made – and that the problems which might occur could be considered by the supervisory bodies under several provisions of the revised Convention. The proposed text reflects the suggestion that the peoples concerned should have the right to participate in the benefits of exploitation of the resources pertaining to their lands.[84]

The resulting language proposed to the 1989 Conference, now contained in draft Article 15, was the following:

1. The rights of the peoples concerned to the surface resources pertaining to their lands and territories, including flora and fauna, waters and sea-ice, shall be specially safeguarded. These rights include the right of these peoples to participate in the management and conservation of these resources.
2. Governments shall establish or maintain procedures, in accordance with Article 6 of this Convention, through which they shall seek to obtain the agreement of these peoples before undertaking or permitting any programmes for the exploration or exploitation of mineral and other subsurface resources pertaining to their lands and territories. The peoples concerned shall wherever possible participate in the benefits of such activities, and shall receive fair compensation for any such activities undertaken within their territories.[85]

At the second Conference discussion, the question of resources was referred to a Working Party along with the rest of the land rights provisions, but some indications of the forces acting on the Committee appear in the comments of the delegates. In the general statements at the beginning of the discussion, for instance,

The Employers' members pointed to the diverse meanings of the concept of "territory" at the national level, and stressed that national legislation with regard to ownership of resources including waters, flora, fauna,

---

[84] Report IV (2A), pp. 40 and 41.
[85] Report IV (2B), p. 14.

sub-surface resources and sea ice had to be respected. In this context, the use of the term "lands and territories" would lead to controversy, and careful analysis of this issue was therefore required which, above all, respected national legislation.[86]

For the Workers' members of the Committee,

> Special attention needed to be given to the rights of indigenous and tribal peoples to the lands which they occupy or to which they have a legitimate claim, including sub-surface and other resources which are part of the lands and territories. When exploration and exploitation of natural resources were being considered, these peoples must have the maximum possible influence on decision-making and priority in the benefits of such exploitation.[87]

Representatives of the indigenous non-governmental organizations also hoped to set the tone with their own comments. Among them,

> 21. The representative of the International Organization of Indigenous Resource Development...took exception to the concept that the scope of the Convention should remain within existing national legislation, and pointed out that existing legislation had not protected these peoples, who remained the poorest of the poor. ... The representative recognised that while all States endorsed the concept of cultural rights, support for social and economic rights faded away when land and resources were concerned; the theft of lands and resources had been instrumental in causing the present situation of indigenous peoples. He emphasised the need for the protection and respect of the traditional economies of these peoples, including the use of their natural resources as a means of sustaining a viable economic base.[88]

When the Working Party returned to the Committee and reported that its members had not arrived at solutions on several points, the question of 'surface and sub-surface resources' was among them.[89] The Chairman proposed formulating a new text on the basis of consultations, but gave an opportunity

---

86 Proceedings 1989, p. 25/4.
87 Ibid.
88 Ibid., pp. 25/5 and 25/6.
89 Ibid., p. 25/17.

to the Committee's members to express their views first. As concerned draft Article 15, the Employers' members 'were awaiting the opinions of governments since many States would find it difficult to implement the draft Office text in the light of their national legislation. They considered that the text of Article 15(2) in the draft before the Committee would violate the States' ownership of sub-surface resources.'[90] Several Government members (Argentina, Bolivia, India, Japan, USSR, *et al.*) expressed serious reservations about the proposed draft for Article 15 because they felt it would assign ownership of natural resources to indigenous and tribal peoples in spite of the fact that this was reserved by national law to State ownership. The Government members of Australia and USSR floated suggestions that would later be partially taken into account in finding a solution:

> The Government member of Australia noted that while the ownership of sub-surface resources was largely vested in the constituent states and territories of Australia, legislation existed which gave indigenous and tribal peoples a major say in resource development. In the Northern Territory, where the Commonwealth owned the resources, these peoples had the right of veto over exploitation. He was at a loss to see why a requirement that these peoples should be consulted in respect of resource development which would have a large social impact would violate the principle of state ownership.[91]
>
> The Government member of the USSR recalled that...the State had exclusive right of ownership of natural resources. Before any exploitation commenced, however, the consent of all those living in the territory was required.[92]

The Workers' members intervened just before the Chairman took the land rights provisions for consultation and produced a new draft. On this point:

> A representative of the Workers' members expressed understanding of the difficulty of achieving a universally applicable Convention. ... She considered that international law should set standards to be attained, even if this would involve changing national legislation. .... She noted that some countries were concerned that too many rights were being granted to these peoples and that the revised Convention would give

---

90   Ibid., p. 25/18.
91   Ibid., p. 25/19.
92   Ibid.

them too much power. The traditional rights of indigenous peoples to lands should be recognised, as well as the rights of those who were currently acquiring land. The issue of resource rights was vital to these peoples' development. They did not wish to remain dependent on States but rather to be able to ensure their own survival. She had difficulty in understanding the extreme position taken by the Employers' members in the Working Party concerning the ownership of resources, and wondered whether they were afraid of economic development being impeded.[93]

Having undertaken consultations, the Chairman returned with a proposed text. The Chair's proposals were adopted without further discussion.

The Chairman sought the agreement of the Committee on the adoption of the package of Articles in Part II of the draft revised Convention. The texts were adopted by consensus.[94]

Once these provisions were adopted a number of Government representatives expressed reservations along the same lines as earlier, to do with the idea that resources remained the property of the State and that rights to them could not be compromised. It should be noted that subsequently several of the countries that expressed strong reservations at the adoption stage (Argentina, Peru and others) later ratified the Convention, apparently having understood that Article 15 did not compromise State ownership of resource rights but rather assigned a role to indigenous and tribal peoples in how these resources are managed.

Article 15 of C. 169 therefore reads as follows:

1. The rights of the peoples concerned to the natural resources pertaining to their lands shall be specially safeguarded. These rights include the right of these peoples to participate in the use, management and conservation of these resources.
2. In cases in which the State retains the ownership of mineral or subsurface resources or rights to other resources pertaining to lands, governments shall establish or maintain procedures through which they shall consult these peoples, with a view to ascertaining whether and to what degree their interests would be prejudiced, before undertaking or permitting any programmes for the exploration or exploitation of such resources

---

93 Ibid., p. 25/20.
94 Ibid., p. 25/21.

pertaining to their lands. The peoples concerned shall wherever possible participate in the benefits of such activities, and shall receive fair compensation for any damages which they may sustain as a result of such activities.

A look at the changes made in paragraph 1 from the version submitted to the Conference for the second discussion will be productive.

- First, in paragraph 1 the word 'control', which awoke the fears of a number of governments, was replaced by the concept of the 'rights...to the natural resources pertaining to their lands'.
- These rights are to be 'specially safeguarded', a concept broader than the 'special measures' referred to in the draft, which attenuated the fears expressed by some governments over special measures singling out a part of the national population for special treatment.
- The reference to 'traditional territories' was replaced by 'their lands', with its implied reference to the areas already referred to in Article 14, removing the temptation to reinterpretation between the two Articles.
- The enumeration of the resources to which the previous draft referred was replaced by the much broader reference to all natural resources, and is therefore inclusive of all such resources rather than risking limitation only to those enumerated.

The changes to paragraph 2 are just as extensive – while simpler they are also broader and more inclusive.

- The reference of this paragraph to cases in which 'the State retains the ownership of mineral or sub-surface resources or rights to other resources pertaining to lands' refers to a more limited number of cases than the broadly inclusive rights of the State assumed in the earlier version, while allowing for national differences on the resources over which the State concerned would retain control.
- It requires procedures to consult these peoples to ascertain whether programmes of exploration or exploitation would prejudice their interests. This 'impact statement' is broader than only an *environmental* impact assessment (which in any case was by this time provided for in Article 7), though this is included – it encompasses also an examination of the potential social impact.
- This may appear to be less stringent than the requirement in the earlier draft to seek their consent, but in fact it is probably broader. First, seeking the consent of these peoples to measures which will affect them directly is

already provided for in the general requirement in Article 6 of the Convention, and clearly applies here. Second, with no antecedents the Conference inserted a requirement for impact assessments, which appears nowhere in earlier drafts, significantly broadening the requirements of this Article.
- Finally, while the previous draft referred simply to 'fair compensation', the final draft requires that these peoples 'shall wherever possible participate in the benefits of such activities, and shall receive fair compensation for any damages which they may sustain as a result of such activities.' It therefore raises the possibility of profit-sharing rather than mere one-time compensation. Also the benefits referred to may go well beyond financial compensation, and may extend to such things as jobs and skills training, access to roads and schools, and other benefits.

4 Article 16 of Convention No. 169: Removal from Their Lands

Article 16 of C. 169 reads as follows:

> 1. Subject to the following paragraphs of this Article, the peoples concerned shall not be removed from the lands which they occupy.
> 2. Where the relocation of these peoples is considered necessary as an exceptional measure, such relocation shall take place only with their free and informed consent. Where their consent cannot be obtained, such relocation shall take place only following appropriate procedures established by national laws and regulations, including public inquiries where appropriate, which provide the opportunity for effective representation of the peoples concerned.
> 3. Whenever possible, these peoples shall have the right to return to their traditional lands, as soon as the grounds for relocation cease to exist.
> 4. When such return is not possible, as determined by agreement or, in the absence of such agreement, through appropriate procedures, these peoples shall be provided in all possible cases with lands of quality and legal status at least equal to that of the lands previously occupied by them, suitable to provide for their present needs and future development. Where the peoples concerned express a preference for compensation in money or in kind, they shall be so compensated under appropriate guarantees.
> 5. Persons thus relocated shall be fully compensated for any resulting loss or injury.

This was derived from Article 12 of C. 107:

> 1. The populations concerned shall not be removed without their free consent from their habitual territories except in accordance with national laws and regulations for reasons relating to national security, or in the interest of national economic development or of the health of the said populations.
> 2. When in such cases removal of these populations is necessary as an exceptional measure, they shall be provided with lands of quality at least equal to that of the lands previously occupied by them, suitable to provide for their present needs and future development. In cases where chances of alternative employment exist and where the populations concerned prefer to have compensation in money or in kind, they shall be so compensated under appropriate guarantees.
> 3. Persons thus removed shall be fully compensated for any resulting loss or injury.

a   Article 12 of Convention No. 107

In reviewing the work of the Committee of Experts on Indigenous Labour in the first report prepared for the adoption of Convention No. 107, the Office noted that the Committee had said:

> The removal of indigenous forest dwellers without their freely given consent from their habitual territory should be prohibited and the specific reservation of lands for occupation by indigenous forest dwellers should not be permitted to develop into a permanent system of segregation.[95]

The questionnaire for the 1956 discussion therefore included question 26, without further discussion (noting that at the same time it broadened the reference beyond forest dwellers):

> 26. (a) *Do you consider that, except for reasons of national security or in the interest of national economic development, as prescribed by law, indigenous peoples should not be removed without their freely given consent from their habitual territories?*

---

95   Report VIII (1), p. 16.

(b) *Do you consider that when, in these exceptional circumstances, such removal is necessary, the indigenous peoples affected should be provided with other lands suitable for their existence and future development?*
(c) *Do you consider that when, in these exceptional circumstances, such removal is necessary the indigenous peoples affected should be fully compensated for any loss resulting from suck removal?*[96]

The Office's analysis of the replies received was as follows:

Of the 16 governments which replied to this question, 14 answered in the affirmative. The Government of Belgium makes the following reservation with regard to clause (c): if the removal of indigenous peoples to another territory has been found essential in the interests of the peoples themselves (e.g. transfer from unhealthy areas), no compensation should be granted, though this should not rule out the grant of generous assistance and acts of liberality. The Governments of Colombia and Ecuador state that the population transfers to which the question refers have never occurred in their respective countries; the second of these Governments adds that it agrees with the principles embodied in clauses (b) and (c). The Government of Brazil considers that the authorities responsible for a transfer should be liable to penal sanctions if it leads to oecological maladjustment that is apt to give rise to greater penury, and that in the case of indigenous peoples who have left their habitual territories either spontaneously or as a consequence of official action the State should be under an obligation to grant new land as compensation for land lost, and in this last case to grant also some compensation for the loss of other property that cannot be moved.

The Belgian Government's suggestion with regard to clause (c) of the question seems to be made with an eye to the exceptional case of the removal of indigenous peoples for their own benefit and without loss or economic injury to them. Even admitting the possibility that such a case may arise in practice, it has not seemed advisable to include the Belgian Government's suggestion in the corresponding point of the proposed Conclusions since if that were done a general rule would be laid down which might lead to a weakening of the principle of due compensation for the economic injury that might result in most cases of such removal, even if the removals were intended to serve objectives that would be advantageous in other respects. On the other hand the principle

---

96   Ibid., p. 178.

advocated by this Government would naturally apply in practice if a population transfer were in no way economically detrimental to the people who were moved.

With regard to the observation made by the Brazilian Government, it would seem impossible to include in an instrument a clause relating to the penal liability of authorities which find themselves faced with the need to decide on a population transfer in the exceptional circumstances mentioned in clause (*a*) (reasons of national security or national economic development). As regards the suggestion that the State should accept an obligation to grant new land and compensation for property that could not be moved to tribes displaced from their habitual territories, it may be pointed out that clauses (*b*) and (*c*) of the question would seem to cover this position when the removal is organised for one of the reasons mentioned in clause (*a*). On the other hand the extent of the State's obligation in the case of "spontaneous" movements of indigenous peoples, even if they were due, for example, to the impoverishment of the soil or to natural disasters, would depend on various special factors.

In view of these considerations it has seemed particularly advisable to draft the corresponding point of the Conclusions on the basis of the text of the question, on account of the flexibility which this would make possible when it came to applying the point in practice. (*Point 24.*)[97]

Thus most of the comments made were deemed by the Office to be without particular relevance to the point being made. The draft conclusions forwarded to the Conference were listed as point 24:

24. (1) Indigenous peoples should not be removed without their free consent from their habitual territories except for reasons, determined by national laws and regulations, relating to national security or the interest of national economic development.

(2) When, in such exceptional cases, removal is necessary, the indigenous peoples affected should be provided with other lands of at least equal quality suitable to provide for their present needs and future development.

(3) The indigenous peoples affected should be fully compensated for any loss or injury resulting from such removal.[98]

---

[97] Report VIII (2), pp. 120 and 121.
[98] Ibid., p. 160.

When the Conference began to consider the proposed conclusions, as indicated above it decided to restructure them to present the most important points in a Convention, and more detailed points in a draft Recommendation. The numbering of the land rights points in the Conference discussion is therefore not the same as in Report VIII (2), and the point on removal of indigenous and tribal populations became Point 20. The discussion of this point in 1956 was relatively brief:

> 79. The Committee then proceeded to discuss point 18 of the text under consideration. Paragraph (1) of this point contained the principle that indigenous peoples should not be removed without their free consent from their habitual territories, except under certain determined conditions. Paragraph (2) stated that in cases where such removal was necessary other lands of at least equal quality should be provided for the peoples concerned. Paragraph (3) stated that compensation should be given for any loss or damage resulting from such removal. Paragraph (2) was the object of one amendment moved by the Portuguese Government member which was subsequently sub-amended by the Indian Workers' member in order to add the words "In cases where chances of alternative employment exist, and where the people concerned prefer to have compensation in money or in kind, they should be so compensated".
> 80. Point 20, thus amended, was adopted by 71 votes to 0, with 6 abstentions.[99]

The conclusions on this point were reformulated by the Office as a draft Convention, and were submitted to the membership for comments as draft Article 12:

> *Article 12*
> 1. Indigenous populations shall not be removed without their free consent from their habitual territories except in accordance with national laws and regulations for reasons relating to national security or in the interest of national economic development.
> 2. When in such exceptional cases removal is necessary, the indigenous peoples affected shall be provided with lands of quality at least equal to that of the lands previously occupied by them, suitable to provide for

---

99 Proceedings 1956, p. 743.

their present needs and future development. In cases where chances of alternative employment exist and where the peoples concerned prefer to have compensation in money or in kind, they shall be so compensated under appropriate guarantees.
3. The indigenous peoples affected shall be fully compensated for any loss or injury resulting from such removal.[100]

On the basis of the few observations received, the Office made the following brief analysis:

The suggestion of the United Kingdom Government that health should be included among the grounds for the removal of peoples as provided for in paragraph 1 of the Article seems appropriate, and the proposed text has been amended accordingly. On the other hand, it would seem that the inclusion of the words "wherever possible" in paragraph 2 would weaken the protection afforded by the proposed text.[101]

The revised proposed Article 12 sent to the Conference for the second discussion was the following:

Article 12
1. The populations concerned shall not be removed without their free consent from their habitual territories except in accordance with national laws and regulations for reasons relating to national security, or in the interest of national economic development or of the health of the said populations.
2. When in such cases removal of these populations is necessary as an exceptional measure, they shall be provided with lands of quality at least equal to that of the lands previously occupied by them, suitable to provide for their present needs and future development. In cases where chances of alternative employment exist and where the populations concerned prefer to have compensation in money or in kind, they shall be so compensated under appropriate guarantees.
3. Persons affected by such removal shall be fully compensated for any resulting loss or injury.[102]

---

100   Report VI (1), pp. 48 and 49.
101   Report VI (2), p. 22.
102   Ibid., p. 58.

The very brief examination in the 1957 Session of the Conference that resulted in the final text was as follows:

> 60. Article 12 was adopted, without discussion, by 34 votes to 0, with 12 abstentions.

b   Adoption of Article 16 of Convention No. 169

The 1986 Meeting of Experts reported that it had discussed this question in some detail:

> 76. Another part of the discussion concerned Article 12 of Convention No. 107. This Article provides that the "populations concerned shall not be removed without their free consent from their habitual territories", but then goes on to provide a number of exceptions whereby governments can remove them even without their consent, subject to certain conditions. This Article has been subjected to increasing criticism by many organisations of indigenous and tribal peoples and others working for their benefit. Their position, expressed again in the present Meeting, is that as it is worded the Article provides no effective restrictions on the right of States to remove these groups whenever they may wish to do so. It was stated that increasing numbers of removals were being imposed, usually in order to allow economic development projects to be carried out in these territories, as well as for national security reasons.
>
> 77. Some experts and observers argued that to recognise the principle that indigenous and tribal peoples had full control over their territories would not constitute a real barrier to constructive and well-considered development. In order to protect their interests, these peoples had to be accorded a real degree of power, but they would not stand in the way of all development. Most experts recognised the need for these peoples to have an effective voice in the decisions affecting them, as has been reflected elsewhere in this report, but they could not recommend including in a revised Convention a power equal to that enjoyed by States. There was, however, a substantial measure of agreement that the revised Convention should include the requirement that the removal of indigenous and tribal peoples from the lands or territories which they have traditionally occupied should not be undertaken except with the informed consent of these peoples, or after an examination of whether the removals are necessary for overriding reasons of national interest,

decided upon after procedures designed to ensure full involvement in the decision-making process by the groups affected. If such removals did prove necessary after carrying out such procedures, these groups should receive compensation, including lands at least equal in extent, quality and legal status to that which they had lost, which allowed the continuation of their traditional lifestyles and which were suitable to provide for their present needs and future development, in addition to the other forms of compensation provided for in Article 12 of Convention No. 107.

78. In this connection, several experts and a number of observers stated that any removals which were carried out should only take place in emergency situations and should be of a temporary nature. It was stated these peoples should have a residual right to these territories, which would revert to them after the circumstances occasioning the removal had ended.[103]

The Conclusions adopted by the Meeting included the following:

6. The authority of States to appropriate indigenous or tribal lands, or to remove these peoples from their lands, should be limited to exceptional circumstances, and should take place only with their informed consent. If this consent cannot be obtained, such authority should be exercised only after appropriate procedures designed to meet the exceptional circumstances for such taking and which guarantee to these peoples the opportunity to be effectively represented.

7. In cases where the appropriation or removals referred to in the previous paragraph proves necessary after these procedures, these groups should receive compensation including lands of at least equal extent, quality and legal status which allow the continuation of their traditional lifestyles and which are suitable to provide for their present needs and future development.[104]

These two paragraphs were accompanied by the note that 'The employer experts expressed their reservations on these two points.'

In its review of developments leading up to consideration of revision, the Office noted that this point was in urgent need of attention:

---

103 Report of the Meeting of Experts, in Report VI (1), p. 113.
104 Ibid., p. 117.

In the three decades since Convention No. 107 was adopted, the conflict between the needs of indigenous and tribal peoples and government development policies and programmes has often been a serious problem. In recent years the Office has received much information concerning the actual or threatened removal of indigenous and tribal peoples whose traditional lands have been selected as the site for hydroelectric or mineral extraction projects. For the most part, available information indicates that there has been little or no meaningful prior consultation with the indigenous and tribal peoples concerned, and more often than not, no attempt is made to soften the impact of these projects on vulnerable groups.[105]

In the Law and Practice Report the Office examined the application of Article 12 of C. 107 and developments since its adoption:

This Article has elicited widespread criticism, on the grounds that its wording tolerates dispossession whenever a government wishes to put these lands to alternative use.

It has been suggested that a new instrument should include the principle that removals be of a *temporary* nature, wherever possible. In this regard, the United Nations Sub-Commission study on indigenous populations recommends that whenever the removal of populations is necessary for an exhaustively justified reason, the indigenous populations involved should be moved to areas that resemble their ancestral lands as closely as possible with fauna and flora of the same type. The suffering of these populations should be reduced to an absolute minimum and any losses compensated. Unless natural phenomena make it impossible, their return to their ancestral lands should always be an essential part of any plan.

...The Meeting concluded unanimously that the authority of States to appropriate indigenous or tribal lands, or to remove these peoples from their lands, should be limited to exceptional circumstances, and should take place only with the informed consent of these peoples. If this consent cannot be obtained, such authority should be exercised only after appropriate procedures designed to meet the exceptional circumstances for such appropriation or removal and which guarantee to these peoples the opportunity to be effectively represented.

---

105   Ibid., p. 45.

Actual or threatened removals continue to occur in disturbing numbers throughout the world. Broadly speaking, such removals appear to fall into three categories. First, there are cases where large-scale hydro-electric and other construction or mineral extraction projects have either flooded indigenous and tribal lands, or wrought such damage to their traditional environment as to make it impossible for them to preserve their traditional lifestyles. Second, there have been "internal colonisation" or transmigration programmes, under which governments have promoted or sponsored the settlement of indigenous and tribal lands, leading at times to the effective dispossession of these groups from their traditional territories. Third, there have been conflicts which have led governments to evacuate these peoples from their traditional territories, sometimes on a temporary basis; in other cases, the conflict itself has compelled the peoples concerned to flee their lands.

In recent years a considerable number of major hydroelectric and dam construction projects have led to the appropriation of large areas of indigenous and tribal lands, and the displacement of these peoples from their traditional territories.[106]

The problems and solutions outlined above bear out the conclusions of the Meeting of Experts to which reference was made at the beginning of this section. That appropriation should take place only in exceptional circumstances and with the consent of these peoples is already stipulated in Article 12 of Convention No. 107 and will be questioned by no one. The Meeting of Experts recognised that it was impossible to define for all cases of appropriation exactly what conditions should apply; it therefore added that in exceptional circumstances States should order removals without consent only after defining appropriate procedures which guarantee that these peoples will be effectively represented. This recommendation would not appear to be controversial.[107]

Finally, in examining how individual Articles of C. 107 should be revised, the Office suggested the following:

The Meeting of Experts strongly endorsed the need to revise this Article in order to limit the circumstances in which removals from indigenous and tribal lands may occur, and to provide for adequate safeguards against potential removals. It has been noted that safeguards do exist in

---

106   Ibid., pp. 62 and 63.
107   Ibid., p. 67.

certain countries, to the extent that parliamentary or other public inquiries are required before the appropriation of any indigenous or tribal lands may occur. A revised Article might first establish the general principle that the peoples concerned should not be removed from their habitual territories without their free consent. The list of situations in which removals can take place might be deleted from the first paragraph of this Article. The revised Article might go on to provide that, in cases where removal is necessary as an exceptional measure, and where the free consent of these peoples cannot be obtained, no such removal should take place except following adequate procedures, including public inquiries, which provide the opportunity for effective representation of the peoples concerned. Examples were given above of cases in which such procedures have been established.

During the Meeting of Experts concern was expressed that the second paragraph of Article 12 of Convention No. 107 does not provide that these peoples have the right of ownership over new lands provided to them in compensation for lands from which they have been removed. Thus, this paragraph might be amended by adding that lands with which they are provided as compensation should, in addition to the present requirement, also have a legal status at least equal to that of the lands previously occupied by them. No amendments are needed to the second sentence of paragraph 2 of this Article, or to paragraph 3, concerning other forms of compensation in cases of removals.[108]

After this extensive discussion of the problems and possible solutions, the Office put the following questions to the constituents:

> *37. Do you consider that paragraph 1 of Article 12 should be amended by deleting all the words after "habitual territories", taking into account the next question?*
> *38. Do you consider that in cases where the removal of these peoples is necessary as an exceptional measure, and where the free consent of these peoples cannot be obtained, no such removals should take place except following adequate procedures including public inquiries, which provide the opportunity for effective representation of the peoples concerned?*
> *39. Do you consider that paragraph 2 of Article 12 should remain unchanged, except for the addition of a requirement that lands provided*

---

108 Ibid., pp. 72 and 73.

in compensation should be of legal status at least equal to that of the lands previously occupied by them?

40. Do you consider that paragraph 3 of Article 12 should remain unchanged?[109]

The replies to these questions were complex, and the Office's reactions to the replies were conspicuously assertive. The Office had in mind a reasoning that covered all the parts of former Article 12 as a whole, and insisted on putting this forward.

As concerned question 37, the Office stated:

> While the majority of replies to this question were affirmative, a number of reservations have been expressed. Two replies indicated that the reference to national security should be retained in some form, while others stated that the phrase "except in accordance with national laws and regulations" should be retained. For example, the Governments of the Ukrainian SSR and the USSR consider that this phrase should be retained because it defines clearly those exceptional cases where the removal of the peoples concerned may take place.
>
> The proposed revision of Article 12 should be seen as a whole. The concept in Report VI (1) was that the first paragraph would include the statement of principle that indigenous and tribal peoples should not be removed from their habitual territories without their free consent. The rest of the revised Article (see under question 38) would specify the procedures which should be followed if this consent could not be obtained, but would not specify any reasons which would justify their removal without following these procedures. The suggestion that the words "except in accordance with national laws and regulations" be retained would also be covered by the procedural steps required.
>
> It should also be pointed out that omitting the reference to national security, or other exceptional reasons, would by no means prohibit removals for these motives. They would quite simply be subject to the procedures contemplated in subsequent paragraphs. This principle is reflected in the Proposed Conclusions.[110]

---

109 Ibid., p. 96.
110 Report VI (2), pp. 54 and 55.

The replies to question 38 were more positive, and the Office took the occasion to propose a refinement of the approach to the questions raised in the replies:

> The majority of replies to this question were in the affirmative. The Government of Colombia considers that the text as drafted in this question is insufficiently clear, and that the provision should rather establish that any removal of indigenous peoples for whatever reason should take place with the consultation and agreement of their representatives. The Government of the United States suggests that the term "effective representation" requires clarification.
>
> With regard to the first of these observations, the Office considers that this provision might be given a more positive content. It might provide that, where the removal of these peoples is considered necessary as an exceptional measure, such removals should take place only with their free and informed consent, moving to this provision an element contained in paragraph 1 of Article 12 of Convention No. 107. The next sentence might provide for the procedures to be followed in the cases where this consent cannot be obtained. The exact nature of such procedures would have to be determined at the national level. Nevertheless, for purposes of clarification, the revised Convention could provide that these procedures should be established by national laws or regulations, which provide the opportunity for effective representation of the peoples concerned. The term "effective representation" means that the peoples concerned should have a real and meaningful opportunity to participate in making the decision, which would appear to cover the point made by the Government of Colombia. It appears worth while to require special procedures for removals, rather than leaving them to the general consultation mechanism, in view of the particular importance they may play. The Proposed Conclusions in this regard are based on the language of the conclusions reached by the Meeting of Experts, which includes the reference to public inquiries.[111]

The reactions to question 39 also occasioned the insertion of an additional concept, on the quality and status of replacement lands:

> A substantial majority of replies to this question were in the affirmative, though some proposals have been made for small modifications. One

---

111 Ibid., p. 56.

proposal is that reference be made to the right of ownership over the lands provided as compensation. Another is for the rewording of the relevant passage to read: "...they shall, wherever possible, be provided with lands of quality and legal status at least equal", etc. Yet another is for the insertion of the words "and size" after the words "lands of quality".

The notion of equal legal status appears useful, in that the peoples concerned should have the same rights over their new lands as over the lands from which they may be removed. As indicated under question 33, this may not always include ownership, and ownership may not always be desirable. A reference to size would seem too precise and limiting, in that it may prove logistically impossible to provide alternative lands of identical dimensions. The Government of Canada has proposed the insertion of the words "wherever possible", to reflect the fact that it may not always be possible to provide land of equal quality and legal status. However, when an identical suggestion was made at the time of adoption of the original Convention No. 107, the prevailing view then was that the inclusion of the words "wherever possible" would weaken the protection afforded by the proposed text. This view would seem to be equally valid today. The suggestion by the Government of Bolivia merits attention, but would appear covered by the idea of "at least equal", which does not necessarily mean identical. In view of the generally positive response, the Proposed Conclusions are based on the text put forward in this question.[112]

Finally, as concerns question 40, the Office noted: "The vast majority of replies to this question were affirmative. It is therefore proposed that this paragraph be left unchanged."[113]

On the basis of these exchanges, the Office offered the following proposed conclusions (with as usual the parts in italics reflecting what would be changes from the language of C. 107):

> 31. *Subject to Points 32, 33 and 34 below, the peoples* concerned should not be removed from their habitual territories.
> 32. *Where the removal of the said peoples is considered* necessary as an exceptional measure, *such removals should take place only with their free and informed consent. Where their consent cannot be obtained, such removals should take place only following appropriate procedures established by*

---

112 Ibid., pp. 56 and 57.
113 Ibid., p. 58.

> *national laws and regulations, including public inquiries, which provide the opportunity for effective representation of the peoples concerned.*
>
> 33. *In such exceptional cases of removal, these peoples* should be provided with lands of quality *and legal status* at least equal to that of the lands previously occupied by them, suitable to provide for their present needs and future development. In cases where chances of alternative employment exist, and where the *peoples* concerned prefer to have compensation in money or in kind, they should be so compensated under appropriate guarantees.
>
> 34. Persons thus removed should be fully compensated for any resulting loss or injury.[114]

At the Conference, as for the rest of the Articles on land rights, there were discussions in a Working Group but no amendments were made to the proposed conclusions (see above). The small number of references to removal and relocation in the general discussion around the land rights provisions made it fairly clear that a consensus was emerging toward making removal from their lands more difficult, but that it would have to be cemented in the final version of the instrument. The few references to these questions made in the discussion are reproduced below:

> A representative of the Inuit Circumpolar Conference, speaking for the accredited non-governmental organisations, made a statement on indigenous lands and resources. ... She underlined the importance of including the concept of indigenous control and consent in the Convention, and stressed that involuntary removal from land was repugnant and contrary to the objectives of the revised Convention.[115]
>
> The Workers' members...felt it important that the question of subsoil exploitation be separated from issues relating to removal or relocation.[116]
>
> The Employers' members supported the Proposed Conclusions in so far as they contemplated the removal of peoples concerned from their habitual territories only in exceptional circumstances.[117]
>
> The issue of expropriation of lands was raised by several speakers. The Government member of Canada stated that it was one of the principal

---

114   Ibid., p. 108.
115   Proceedings, 1988, p. 35/15.
116   Ibid., p. 35/16.
117   Ibid.

themes of the section on land, and the Convention should ensure that indigenous populations could only be removed from their lands in exceptional circumstances, and only then in accordance with procedures which allowed for adequate compensation. The Government members of Australia and Norway emphasised the need for a provision which would deal with the expropriation of land of indigenous peoples which did not involve their actual removal.[118]

When the Office circulated the first draft of the proposed Convention in Report IV (1) for the 1989 discussion, this provision – now Article 15 – read as follows, based precisely on the conclusions:

> 1. Subject to the following paragraphs of this Article, the (peoples/populations) concerned shall not be removed from their habitual territories.
> 2. Where the removal of the said (peoples/populations) is considered necessary as an exceptional measure, such removals shall take place only with their free and informed consent. Where their consent cannot be obtained, such removal shall take place only following appropriate procedures established by national laws and regulations, including public inquiries, which provide the opportunity for effective representation of the (peoples/populations) concerned.
> 3. In such exceptional cases of removal, these (peoples/populations) shall be provided with lands of quality and legal status at least equal to that of the lands previously occupied by them, suitable to provide for their present needs and future development. In cases where chances of alternative employment exist, and where the (peoples/populations) concerned prefer to have compensation in money or in kind, they shall be so compensated under appropriate guarantees.
> 4. Persons thus removed shall be fully compensated for any resulting loss or injury.[119]

The Office commentary on the observations received is rather long, but reveals very little in the way of changes from the previous version. The most important change, which receives very little attention in the text, is the addition of a 'right to return' to their lands once the reasons for relocation have ended.

---

118   Ibid.
119   Report IV (1), p. 10.

In order to respond to the concern expressed by the Governments of Canada and the United States in relation to the term "habitual territories", and to provide consistency between the various provisions of this Part, the term has been replaced by the term "lands and territories".

Some respondents consider that paragraph 2 should specify more clearly those exceptional circumstances under which the peoples concerned may be removed or that it should limit the possibility to emergency situations. This proposal would prove both unduly limiting if other imperative reasons should exist, and unduly permissive by giving explicit authorisation to removal in specified circumstances (an argument often invoked in criticising Article 12 of Convention No. 107).

Various concerns have been expressed concerning public inquiries (paragraph 2). The concern expressed by the Government of India appears to be covered by the existing wording.[120] The Office has nevertheless included the words "where appropriate" as indeed such public inquiries may not prove necessary or possible in all cases. The Government of the United States considers that the use of the term "effective representation" needs clarification. The term "effective representation" is taken from the conclusions of the 1986 Meeting of Experts, and implies that the procedures should ensure full involvement in the decision-making process for the peoples concerned. Further detail would limit the flexibility of this paragraph and risk excluding valid consultative procedures in some countries. No change is suggested.

A number of respondents consider that this Article should provide explicitly that removals should be temporary wherever possible, and that the peoples concerned should have the right to return to their lands or territories once the grounds for such removal have ceased to exist. A new paragraph to this effect is inserted. It would not appear necessary to provide more explicitly for a differentiation between expropriation and temporary removal.

Several respondents consider that paragraph 3 should include a specific reference to the size as well as to the quality and legal status of replacement lands; but there are also proposals to include the qualifying phrase "wherever possible", as it may not always prove possible to meet

---

120 The Government of India had stated: 'As it may not always be possible to undertake removals "only with their free and informed consent", the words "as far as possible" should be inserted in paragraph 2 after "place"; the word "only" after "place" should be deleted. As it may not always be possible to hold public inquiries, add "if considered necessary" after "inquiries".' Report IV (2A), p. 43.

these conditions. The Government of the United States considers furthermore that the term "legal status" requires clarification. Proposals of this nature were considered at length during the 1986 Meeting of Experts. In its conclusions, this meeting in fact proposed the terms "at least equal extent, quality and legal status", though reservations were expressed by the employer experts on this point. However, the Office subsequently dropped the reference to size, quantity or extent, precisely because it might prove logistically impossible to provide alternative lands of identical dimensions. When an identical suggestion was made at the time of drafting Convention No. 107 in 1956, the prevailing view was that the inclusion of the words "wherever possible" would weaken the protection afforded by the proposed text. This view would seem to be equally valid today. On this point the Office has therefore retained the substance of the text as previously drafted. The term "legal status" implies that the peoples concerned should have rights over their new lands which are at least equal to the rights they enjoyed over the lands from which they may be removed.

The proposal of the Government of Mexico on paragraph 3 has not been taken up, as the principle would seem to be implicit in the existing provision.[121] The Government of Canada has proposed the deletion of the words "In cases where chances of alternative employment exist", on the grounds that this might link the issue of compensation to the availability of alternative employment opportunities. Brazil (CUT) has proposed, conversely, that any reference to compensation apart from land should be deleted from the text. The Office has retained the Canadian proposal, but feels it would be unwise to remove any reference to alternative forms of compensation.

As concerns the proposals by the Government of Japan for paragraph 4, the Office considers that the principle of full compensation for any resulting loss or injury is indeed appropriate, and has not taken up these proposals. The Office considers that the responsibility covered by the proposal by the Government of Mexico is implicit in the concept of full compensation.

Thus amended, Article 15 appears as Article 16 of the new text.[122]

---

[121] The Government of Mexico proposed: 'In paragraph 3, after "future development" add "so that they may preserve their ethnic integrity in accordance with their culture".' Ibid.

[122] Ibid., pp. 44 and 45.

The resulting language submitted to the 1989 Conference for the second discussion was the following draft Article 16:

> 1. Subject to the following paragraphs of this Article, the peoples concerned shall not be removed from the lands and territories which they occupy.
> 2. Where the removal of these peoples is considered necessary as an exceptional measure, such removals shall take place only with their free and informed consent. Where their consent cannot be obtained, such removal shall take place only following appropriate procedures established by national laws and regulations, including public inquiries where appropriate, which provide the opportunity for effective representation of the peoples concerned.
> 3. In such exceptional cases of removal, these peoples shall be provided with lands of quality and legal status at least equal to that of the lands previously occupied by them, suitable to provide for their present needs and future development. Where the peoples concerned express a preference for compensation in money or in kind, they shall be so compensated under appropriate guarantees.
> 4. Whenever possible, these peoples shall have the right to return to their traditional lands and territories, as soon as the grounds for removal cease to exist.
> 5. Persons thus removed shall be fully compensated for any resulting loss or injury.[123]

At the 1989 Session of the Conference, as explored above, the section on land rights was referred to a Working Party, whose discussions are not reported in detail except as reflected in the discussions in the full Committee. When the Working Party reported back to the Committee, it indicated:

> The Working Party held four sittings. Its Chairman reported to the Committee that the key issues identified concerned the use of the term "land and territories"; the form and extent of land rights to be recognised; surface and sub-surface resources; and the question of removal or relocation of indigenous peoples from areas inhabited by them.[124]

---

123 Report IV (2B), pp. 14 and 16.
124 Proceedings 1989, p. 25/17.

The only explicit mention of the Working Party's discussion of Article 16 is that it was grouped with Articles 14 and 15: "It was decided that Articles 14, 15 and 16 should be referred back to the Committee."[125] However, the Committee was unable to come to agreement on them in its open discussion, and the Chairman undertook to submit a revised text of several provisions, including Article 16, after consultations.

The Committee was offered the possibility of making remarks on these provisions before the Chairman undertook his consultations. The principal comments made on Article 16 included the following:

> The Employers' members (stated that) Article 16 was basically an administrative issue for governments. The principle of compensation, as well as the possibility of the return of lands, should be included. They noted that if indemnification was provided, the option to return lands would be removed.[126]
>
> The Government member of Canada...agreed with the basic intent of Article 16.[127]
>
> The Government member of Argentina...considered that Article 16(3) would be very difficult to adapt to national legislation.[128]
>
> The Government member of India...felt that Article 16 should emphasise a comprehensive rehabilitation package for displaced peoples. Although admirable, the concept of "land for land" would not work where land was scarce.[129]
>
> The Government member of Ecuador...expressed a preference for "resettlement and relocation" rather than "removal" and felt that compensation should cover damage caused by the relinquishment of lands.[130]
>
> A representative of the Workers' members...urged the Committee to recognise the indigenous and tribal peoples' right to the ownership, possession and use of lands and territories, and to protect these peoples against exploitation under Article 16, rather than allowing governments to prescribe under what exceptional circumstances compensation would be paid for removal from land.[131]

---

125 Ibid., p. 25/18.
126 Ibid.
127 Ibid.
128 Ibid., p. 25/19.
129 Ibid.
130 Ibid., p. 25/20.
131 Ibid.

Following consultations, the Chairman returned to the Committee with the following statement:

> Following his consultations with Government members and with the Employers' and Workers' groups concerning Part II of the draft Convention, the Chairman indicated that he would propose that the Committee consider a "package" text dealing with Articles 13 to 19, with the exception of Article 17(2) which would be considered separately. Articles 13 to 16 had been amended in the light of the Working Party's deliberations (for Article 13) and in the light of his discussions.[132]

Without further discussion, "Articles 13, 14, 15 and 16, as amended, were adopted."[133]

The provision as adopted by the Committee reads as follows:

> *Article 16*
>
> 1. Subject to the following paragraphs of this Article, the peoples concerned shall not be removed from the lands which they occupy.
>
> 2. Where the relocation of these peoples is considered necessary, as an exceptional measure, such relocation shall take place only with their free and informed consent. Where their consent cannot be obtained, such relocation shall take place only following appropriate procedures established by national laws and regulations, including public inquiries where appropriate, which provide the opportunity for effective representation of the peoples concerned.
>
> 3. Whenever possible, these peoples shall have the right to return to their traditional lands, as soon as the grounds for relocation cease to exist.
>
> 4. When such return is not possible, as determined by agreement or, in the absence of such agreement, through appropriate procedures, these peoples shall be provided in all possible cases with lands of quality and legal status at least equal to that of the lands previously occupied by them, suitable to provide for their present needs and future development. Where the peoples concerned express a preference for compensation in money or in kind, they shall be so compensated under appropriate guarantees.

---

132   Ibid.
133   Ibid., p. 25/21.

5. Persons thus relocated shall be fully compensated for any resulting loss or injury.

The differences between this version and the one submitted to the Conference were small but important. Paragraph 1 added 'and territories' after 'lands'. In paragraph 2 the word 'relocation' replaced 'removal' in two places compared to the previous version, thus implying that these peoples should be moved to other lands and territories rather than simply being expelled. The new 'right to return' provision had been added as paragraph 3.

The most extensive amendment was made to paragraph 4 (paragraph 3 in the earlier version) which maintained the focus on the primacy of return whenever possible, making a decision that return was not possible subject to agreement or appropriate procedures.

Paragraph 5 followed the example set in paragraph 2 by replacing 'removed' by 'relocated'.

5   Article 17 of Convention No. 169: Transmission of Rights

Article 17 of C. 169 reads as follows:

> **Article 17**
> 1. Procedures established by the peoples concerned for the transmission of land rights among members of these peoples shall be respected.
> 2. The peoples concerned shall be consulted whenever consideration is being given to their capacity to alienate their lands or otherwise transmit their rights outside their own community.
> 3. Persons not belonging to these peoples shall be prevented from taking advantage of their customs or of lack of understanding of the laws on the part of their members to secure the ownership, possession or use of land belonging to them.

a   Adoption of Article 13 of Convention No. 107

The comparable Article in C. 107 was Article 13:

> 1. Procedures for the transmission of rights of ownership and use of land which are established by the customs of the populations concerned shall be respected, within the framework of national laws and regulations, in so far as they satisfy the needs of these populations and do not hinder their economic and social development.

2. Arrangements shall be made to prevent persons who are not members of the populations concerned from taking advantage of these customs or of lack of understanding of the laws on the part of the members of these populations to secure the ownership or use of the lands belonging to such members.

As the Office examined the problems affecting indigenous communities for the Conference discussion on Convention No. 107, it concentrated in part on the loss or transfer of rights to lands. Among the considerations put forward by the Office were the following:

> In a number of countries arrangements have been made whereby, save in exceptional circumstances defined by law, the leasing of lands owned by indigenous peoples to persons or bodies not belonging to the tribe or group concerned are prohibited or restricted. It is perhaps too much to expect that all such land will remain indefinitely untouched by non-indigenous enterprise. Nor would this necessarily be desirable, since economic development in any country may require changes in land use which can often be carried out effectively only when such enterprise comes in to work the land or exploit its mineral resources. However, when indigenous land is leased out to nonindigenous interests, it is essential to ensure that the indigenous owners will receive reasonable rents as well as a fair share in the profits which derive from the development of underground wealth within the land leased. A notable example of the wealth that may be derived by indigenous peoples from mineral leases is illustrated by the situation of the Osage Indians of Oklahoma (United States), where revenue in excess of $250 million has been obtained from oil leases and royalties over a period of about 40 years. Another example is that of the Bakhtiaris in Iran who, with the oil royalties derived from the leasing of tribal land, have been steadily improving their standard of living.
>
> In order to prevent alienation of indigenous land, the policy has been gaining ground in a number of countries that the mortgaging of the land to persons or bodies not belonging to the tribe or group should be prohibited or restricted. While there can be no doubt as to the intrinsic wisdom of such a policy, attention must be drawn, however, to the fact that it is not likely to yield positive results if it is not accompanied by the extension of agricultural credit facilities to indigenous farmers that will enable them to secure the necessary capital for developing their holdings economically.

...

In indigenous communities where certain traditional customs of allocating and using land are still in practice, these customs should be respected unless profound changes are taking place in community organisation and economic development. Such customs may sometimes include shifting cultivation or the movement of the whole community from one harvest site to another, made necessary by unbalanced land holdings. As long as the people keep their land under cultivation, measures should be taken to preserve these practices.

Steps should also be taken to ensure that rights over land are transferred in conformity with the customary usages and rules of the respective indigenous tribes or groups. On the other hand, when these usages and rules obstruct economic development they should be reformed with the aid of educational measures. Although the importance of the ethnic aspect of the problem is sometimes overemphasised, it is nevertheless true that inheritance rules, established by religious tribal law, may contribute to the minute subdivision of indigenous land and lead to the economic stagnation of agriculture. It is equally true that social and religious customs associated with indigenous land tenure systems – for instance, the burying of the dead in the fields and the belief that land is owned by long-dead ancestors, or that it must be preserved for the spirits – may tie the tribal peoples to specific areas and inhibit the development of natural resources. It is therefore necessary to find appropriate psychological and anthropological techniques whereby these customs can be, if not gradually eliminated, at least adapted to the economic and social needs of the communities concerned. Experience has shown that this can be done provided that adequate educational measures are applied and agricultural training is given. The reconciling of the interests of the indigenous peoples with the requirements of national economic and social development lies at the bottom of any constructive land policy in indigenous areas. Tribal customs should be protected but this does not mean that they must be conserved at any price, since they may constitute obstacles to the improvement of the living conditions of the indigenous peoples themselves if they prevent the introduction of progressive methods of agriculture. On the other hand economic planning and legal measures should provide the necessary protection for indigenous communities during the period of transition.

It seems obvious that the legal protection of land rights, while essential, must be accompanied by measures designed to promote the economic development of indigenous lands. Attention must be drawn in this respect to the overcrowded state of certain indigenous areas which, owing to the population increase, loss or depletion of land, etc., are unable to provide a bare subsistence. In various countries, these areas are receiving special consideration in the planning of national agrarian reform programmes. The same applies to areas where holdings are not large enough to include land of varying fertility and topography, thus leading to uneconomic use, or where family holdings are not balanced as between different types of land.

In recent years the view has been gaining ground that the most appropriate way of promoting the economic resurgence of indigenous communities would be to turn them into modern co-operative units. In 1940 the First Inter-American Indian Congress adopted a resolution urging the American States concerned to consider the advisability of enacting the relevant legislation for the transformation of Indian *comunidades* into agricultural and stock-raising co- operatives, or into agricultural societies which, under the technical supervision of the State, could be incorporated into the general economy of the country. With rare exceptions, however, and despite the efforts made, this type of action has not yet made much headway in a number of countries. It would appear that the main reason for this situation resides in the fact that insufficient attention has so far been given to the need to adapt the modern methods of co-operative production to the traditional forms of communal use of land and working implements and to the traditional systems of mutual service and aid among indigenous peoples.[134]

These passages were both protective and severely assimilationist, in the spirit of the 1950s and the agrarian reform wave of the time. The conclusions drawn by the Office on the problems confronting indigenous and tribal populations included the following that encompassed a number of the questions that would be codified in the Convention:

6. The link between indigenous peoples and the land on which they live and from which they derive their livelihood constitutes an important factor in any plan to promote the welfare of these peoples. Two aspects of this problem must be distinguished. The first relates to the need to recognise the right of indigenous peoples over their traditional territories which have, in various regions, passed into the hands of

---

134   Report VIII (1), pp. 68 to 70.

non-indigenous persons in the form of grants or as a result of occupation of so-called "free land". The second aspect concerns indigenous communities whose rights to the land have been affected by the impact of a technologically more advanced society resulting in some cases in the introduction of various systems of tenancy and peonage, which are characterised in some areas by the obligation to render unpaid personal services. The chief problems arising in various regions out of the social, economic and juridical conditions under which indigenous peoples work the land would appear to be the following: (*a*) the lack on the part of settled farming communities of collective or individual title deeds to the land they occupy; (*b*) the insecure possession by seminomadic tribes of their usual territories or of the use of the land to which they periodically move; (*c*) the disproportion between the available arable land and the natural growth of the population; (*d*) the alienation of tribal land to persons or bodies outside the indigenous community by lease or mortgage; (*e*) the lack or inadequacy of farm credit and marketing facilities, and of technical aid, which makes it difficult for indigenous communities to free themselves from the burden of indebtedness caused by excessive interest rates, and to develop their resources economically; and (*f*) the absence or inadequate enforcement of legal and administrative measures designed to control the abuses of certain forms of land tenancy and share-cropping, and to prevent the custom of exacting personal services for the benefit of landowners and local authorities.[135]

The questionnaire sent to the constituents in 1956 therefore included the following:

> *30. Do you consider that the mortgaging of lands owned by indigenous peoples to persons or bodies not belonging to the indigenous tribe or group concerned should be prohibited or restricted?*
> *31. Do you consider that the transmission of rights concerning the ownership and use of land established by the customs of the indigenous tribe or group should be respected as long as these customs satisfy the needs of the tribe or group and do not represent an obstacle to economic and social development?*[136]

---

[135] Ibid., pp. 167 and 168.
[136] Ibid., p. 178.

The replies of governments and the Office's analysis were discussed in the second report:

Question 30
Of the 16 governments which replied to this question, 13 replied in the affirmative. Three of them came out in favour of prohibition and two in favour of restriction; the others expressed no preference for either of these alternatives. The Belgian Government considers that the mortgaging to which the question refers should be subject to regulation and whenever possible restricted to bodies that are licensed by the State. The Government of New Zealand takes the view that mortgages should be allowed only under the strict control of the national body responsible for protecting the interests of the indigenous people. In the opinion of the Government of Honduras it would be better to give advice to indigenous communities in order to safeguard them from the hazards involved in such an operation for persons or groups of a relatively low cultural level. The Government of Ecuador considers that absolute prohibition would not be possible unless other assistance measures were taken as substitutes for the method of securing loans by mortgages; it considers, moreover, that there should be restriction only in the case of communal land. The Governments of India and Iran emphasise the need to promote the development of co-operative credit societies for the benefit of tribal peoples.

With regard to the second observation of the Government of Ecuador, it has to be recognised that in the case of land under individual ownership belonging to indigenous people who have already become integrated there would be no justification for a restriction or prohibition of mortgaging, and that the conditions in respect of such land should be the same as those for obtaining mortgage loans on individually owned land in general. It should be pointed out, however, that in certain parts of the world there are individual indigenous agriculturists who have not yet become integrated in the national community and who, owing to their economic and cultural isolation, their ignorance of the official language, or their ignorance or lack of understanding of the laws and the relevant administrative procedures, are liable to be defrauded in mortgage dealings with private non-indigenous persons or bodies.

In view of the fact that the proposed instrument would be intended to protect the interests of all non-integrated indigenous people it would seem wise not to confine the scope of the measure in question exclusively to land under collective ownership. The observations of the

Governments of India and Iran would seem to be met by question 34 and by clause (*g*) of question 96.

In the light of the foregoing considerations and in view of the fact that the majority of the governments which replied to this question appear to prefer the principle of simple restriction, the drafting of the corresponding point of the proposed Conclusions has been based on this principle. (*Point 29.*)

Question 31

Of the 16 governments which replied to this question, 13 replied in the affirmative, but with reservations in some cases. The Government of Egypt is opposed to the principle involved in the question and declares that the transmission of ownership rights should be governed by national legislation and regulations. The Government of Honduras expresses a similar view.

In the opinion of the Governments of Ecuador and Iran tribal customs should be respected in so far as they are compatible with national legislation. On the other hand, the Government of New Zealand considers that even when these customs represent an obstacle to progress they should not be removed arbitrarily but should be made the subject of an educational programme designed to show the need for changes and to win the acceptance of the indigenous people concerned. The Government of Brazil considers that tribal customs should be respected as regards use within the tribe and not for the purpose of alienation.

The reservation expressed by the Government of Brazil is apparently intended to protect tribal lands from alienation to persons or groups not belonging to the tribe, and from this point of view it is of considerable assistance in eliminating possible ambiguity. The same may be said of the reservations made by the Governments of Ecuador and Iran with regard to the compatibility of these customs with national legislation. Since most of the governments have come out in favour of the principle involved in the question the wording of the corresponding point of the proposed Conclusions is based on the text of the question and takes into consideration the observations of the Governments of Brazil, Ecuador and Iran. (*Point 30.*)[137]

The related points of the proposed conclusions were therefore as follows:

29. The mortgaging of lands owned by indigenous peoples to persons or bodies not belonging to the indigenous group concerned should be restricted.

---

137   Report VIII (2), pp. 125 and 126.

> 30. Procedures for the transmission of rights concerning the ownership and use of land which are established by the customs of the indigenous group should be respected, within the framework of national laws and regulations, so long as they satisfy the needs of the group and provided they do not hinder its economic and social development. At the same time, arrangements should be made to prevent non-indigenous persons from taking advantage of these customs to secure for themselves the ownership or use of the lands of indigenous peoples.[138]

In the 1956 discussion in the Conference, only point 30 of the above was retained for discussion leading to the adoption of a Convention (the rest being transferred to discussion for inclusion in the Recommendation), and it was renumbered as point 19. The discussion in the Conference was the following:

> 81. The Committee then considered point 19 of the text under consideration, which stated that customary procedures among indigenous peoples for the transmission of rights of ownership or use of land should be respected under certain specified conditions, and that arrangements should be made to prevent non-indigenous persons from availing themselves of such procedures for their own benefit.
> 82. An amendment moved by the Workers' members, as sub-amended by the New Zealand Government member, had the effect of adding the words "or of lack of understanding of the law on the part of the indigenous people concerned".
> 83. Point 19 of the text under consideration, thus amended, was then adopted by 65 votes to 0, with 6 abstentions.[139]

This conclusion was numbered 21:

> 21. Procedures for the transmission of rights concerning the ownership and use of land which are established by the customs of the indigenous group should be respected, within the framework of national laws and regulations, so long as they satisfy the needs of the group and provided they do not hinder its economic and social development. At the same time, arrangements should be made to prevent nonindigenous persons from taking advantage of these customs or of lack of understanding of

---

138   Ibid., pp. 160 and 161.
139   Proceedings 1956, p. 743.

the laws on the part of the indigenous people concerned, to secure the ownership or use of the lands of indigenous peoples.[140]

This was in turn converted into Article 13 of the draft Convention, and circulated to the membership for comments:

> *Article 13*
> Procedures for the transmission of rights concerning the ownership and use of land which are established by the customs of the indigenous groups shall be respected, within the framework of national laws and regulations, in so far as they satisfy the needs of the groups and do not hinder their economic and social development. At the same time arrangements shall be made to prevent non-indigenous persons from taking advantage of these customs or of lack of understanding of the laws on the part of the indigenous peoples concerned to secure the ownership or use of the lands of those peoples.

No observations were received on this draft Article and it was submitted to the second discussion in 1957 in the same form. In the Conference there was once again no discussion, and the Committee adopted this Article unchanged:

> 60. Articles 13 and 14 were each adopted, without discussion, by 34 votes to 0, with 15 abstentions.[141]

In the process of finalizing the draft, Article 13 was divided into two paragraphs, with a few drafting changes that are not discussed in the Conference reports:

> 1. Procedures for the transmission of rights of ownership and use of land which are established by the customs of the populations concerned shall be respected, within the framework of national laws and regulations, in so far as they satisfy the needs of these populations and do not hinder their economic and social development.
> 2. Arrangements shall be made to prevent persons who are not members of the populations concerned from taking advantage of these customs or of lack of understanding of the laws on the part of the members of these populations to secure the ownership or use of the lands belonging to such members.

---

140   Ibid., p. 749.
141   Proceedings 1957, p. 727.

One of the changes made was to amend the references to 'peoples' to 'populations', as was done throughout, and the other is to add language referring to 'members of these populations' which refers more directly to individual rights than to collective land holding.

b   Adoption of Article 17 of Convention No. 169

The presentation of this subject in the Law and Practice Report of 1988 emphasized the two different problems covered in Article 13 of C. 107:

> Article 13 of Convention No. 107 contains two paragraphs which cover substantially different issues. The first one provides for the recognition of customary procedures concerning land ownership and use, while the second calls for measures against potential abuses by outsiders who seek to secure the ownership or use of these lands.
>
> During the Meeting of Experts, emphasis was laid on the importance of recognising the traditional institutions and procedures of indigenous and tribal peoples for transmitting rights to their lands, although it was also recalled that all land rights had to be exercised within the framework of national legislation. This apparent contradiction need not lead to the kind of conflict between competing systems that some of the experts feared.
>
> Earlier in this chapter it was seen that the legislation of a number of countries, particularly in Latin America, has in recent years reaffirmed the right of indigenous communities to the ownership and control of their communal lands. However, in certain cases the legislation provides for the extinction of this right, and even for the dissolution of the indigenous communities themselves when indigenous peoples have abandoned their communities and thus relinquished their rights, or where the lands under communal ownership are exploited individually by most or all of the members of the community concerned. Complex issues can also arise in the context of agrarian reform and colonisation programmes. For instance, while codified national law may recognise rights to land primarily on the basis of actual use and occupation, traditional or customary law often provides for the rights of shifting cultivators or nomadic groups to lands which are used on an intermittent basis. Colonisation programmes which are conducted without due regard to traditional forms of ownership and control are likely to lead to land disputes caused by conflicting concepts of ownership. During the ILO Meeting of Experts, a number of experts pointed to the need for studies on the relationship between customary laws and the positive law of the countries in which

indigenous and tribal peoples live. These studies are of particular importance with regard to concepts of ownership and inheritance laws.

With regard to Article 13, paragraph 2, of Convention No. 107, the Meeting of Experts stressed the need for effective protection against dispossession by persons or bodies not belonging to the peoples concerned. In many countries there are no prescribed sanctions for trespass on indigenous and tribal lands, though some general provisions may exist. ...

In recent years a number of international non-governmental human rights organisations as well as indigenous peoples' organisations have drawn attention to the widespread encroachments, often accompanied by coercion or violence, on indigenous and tribal lands. Stronger provisions may therefore be advisable, in order to provide for more effective protection against such encroachments.[142]

When the report went on to examine what amendments might be needed to Article 13 in the context of the revision, it suggested as follows:

The first paragraph of this Article concerns procedures for the transmission of rights of ownership and use of land. As reported above, the indigenous and tribal representatives present at the Meeting of Experts unanimously considered that their lands should be inalienable, and indeed, legislation enacted in recent years in several countries has provided for inalienable forms of indigenous or tribal land ownership, or placed other restrictions on the transfer of these lands. Yet an absolute prohibition on the transfer of rights of ownership and use of land may not always be appropriate or acceptable to the indigenous and tribal peoples concerned. Thus, although there is a clear and pressing need for protection, it may not be possible to reach agreement on a general requirement of inalienability in the revised Convention. It is however suggested that, in accordance with the general approach of respect for these peoples' customs, the final phrase of paragraph 1 of this Article beginning with "in so far", be deleted; thus, the paragraph would still require that the traditional procedures for the transmission of rights of ownership and use of land of the peoples concerned be respected, within the framework of national laws and regulations. In order to take account of cases in which additional protection is needed, this paragraph might also provide that any decision regarding the capacity to transmit rights of ownership and use of land should be taken in consultation with the peoples concerned.

---

142 Report VI (1), pp. 67 and 68.

No changes are required to paragraph 2 of Article 13. However, it has been suggested that a revised Convention should specify that penalties should be imposed in the event of harmful trespass on the traditional lands of these peoples. While the proposed revision of Article 11 would require States to guarantee effective protection of these lands, it is not without merit to suggest that a further requirement in Article 13 concerning sanctions in the event of harmful trespass would reinforce this general principle. To this end, an additional paragraph in this Article might provide that any unauthorised intrusion upon, or use of, the lands of the peoples concerned by persons not belonging to these peoples should be considered an offence, and that appropriate penalties should be established by law.[143]

While the revised Article would eventually take the shape suggested by the Office in the first report, there was considerable drama at the final stage of discussion, as will be seen below. The Office put the following questions to the constituents in this first report:

> *41. Do you consider that paragraph 1 of Article 13 should be amended by deleting all the words after "regulations"?*
> *42. Do you consider that paragraph 1 of Article 13 should be supplemented by providing that any decision regarding the capacity of these people to transmit rights of ownership and use of land should be taken in consultation with the peoples concerned?*
> *43. Do you consider that paragraph 2 of Article 13 should remain unchanged?*
> *44. Do you consider that a paragraph should be added to Article 13 providing that any unauthorised intrusion upon, or use of, the lands of the peoples concerned by persons not belonging to these peoples should be considered as an offence, and that appropriate penalties for such offences should be established by law?*[144]

The Office commented on the replies to question 41:

> The great majority of replies to this question were affirmative. The concept of possession has been added in the Proposed Conclusions, in line with the formulation adopted above.[145]

---

143   Ibid., p. 73.
144   Ibid., pp. 96 and 97.
145   Report VI (2), p. 59.

The responses to question 42 were more complex. In this case the Office resisted a strongly phrased position of the indigenous representatives, transmitted by the Canadian Labor Congress, and this set up a difficult decision by the Conference Committee at the final discussion in 1989:

> The great majority of replies to this question were affirmative. The Government of Canada has proposed a reference to the concept of possession. The Canadian Labour Congress considers that any decision regarding this capacity to transmit ownership rights should be determined by the peoples concerned, and that land should be inalienable beyond transmission among the indigenous peoples themselves. Similar views have been expressed by indigenous organisations. Concern has also been expressed that the meaning of this provision is unclear.
>
> In view of these observations, the Office feels it would be useful to provide further clarifications. At the Meeting of Experts, as noted earlier, all the indigenous and tribal representatives present expressed their view that their lands should be inalienable. Furthermore, as noted in Report VI(1), legislation has been enacted in a number of countries in recent years providing for restrictions on the alienation, mortgaging or other encumbrance of indigenous lands. Laws have thus been adopted in a number of countries, providing special procedures for the transmission of rights of ownership and use of land for the peoples concerned. While the view has been expressed that these lands should be inalienable, it would appear preferable – and more consistent with the agreed basic orientation for a revised instrument – that the decision regarding the capacity of the said peoples to alienate their lands or otherwise transmit rights of ownership and use should be taken with the consent of these peoples themselves. There are, indeed, cases in which the peoples concerned may wish to transmit such rights outside the group.
>
> These considerations are reflected in the Proposed Conclusions.[146]

On question 43, the answers were less complex:

> The large majority of replies to this question were affirmative. However, the opinion has also been expressed that this provision should be stronger. In view of the serious consequences of the abuses contemplated by this provision, a somewhat stronger version is suggested (Point 37).[147]

---

146 Ibid., p. 60.
147 Ibid., p. 61.

Question 44 had proposed a new provision, which was mostly received positively:

> In view of the very large majority of affirmative replies to this question, a provision to this effect has been included in the Proposed Conclusions. While the suggestion has been made that the words "or groups" be added after the word "persons", it would seem that the word "persons" is sufficient to cover any number of intruders on the lands of the peoples concerned. The addition of a reference to recourse procedures appears useful, in allowing these peoples to take appropriate measures to compel the expulsion of intruders. Finally, the point made by Canada (IBC) appears valid.[148]

The point made by Canada (IBC) referred to above was: "Such a provision should also recognise that unauthorised intrusion or use could also be undertaken by persons belonging to the indigenous people."[149]

The conclusions proposed by the Office were as follows (with new or amended language compared to C. 107 appearing in italics):

> 35. Procedures for the transmission of rights of ownership, *possession* and use of land which are established by the customs of the *peoples* concerned should be respected, within the framework of national laws and regulations.
> 36. *The consent of the peoples concerned should be sought when considering the adoption of national laws or regulations concerning the capacity of the said peoples to alienate their land or otherwise transmit rights of ownership, possession and use of their land.*
> 37. Persons who are not members of these *peoples should be prevented* from taking advantage of the customs referred to in Point 35 or of lack of understanding of the laws on the part of the members of these *peoples* to secure the ownership, *possession* or use of land belonging to *them*.
> 38. *Unauthorised intrusion upon, or use of, the lands of the peoples concerned should be considered as an offence, and appropriate penalties for such offences and other appropriate recourse procedures should be established by law.*[150]

---

148   Ibid.
149   Ibid.
150   Ibid., pp. 108 and 109.

The way the lands rights provisions were discussed in the two sessions of the Conference has been indicated above. Statements that referred to these subjects reveal how the delegates were thinking about them as they were referred to the Working Party and after the Working Party reported on its discussions to the Committee; and the fact that nothing particular was mentioned specifically on these points in 1988 emphasizes how thinking was centred at this stage on the basic notion of assured land rights and the quality of those rights. The conclusions adopted in 1988 were those submitted to the Conference, and the Office translated them into Convention language in Report IV (1) for the 1989 discussion.

The draft circulated to the constituents for the 1989 discussion was as follows:

> **Article 16**
> 1. Procedures for the transmission of rights of ownership, possession and use of land which are established by the customs of the (peoples/populations) concerned shall be respected, within the framework of national laws and regulations.
> 2. The consent of the (peoples/populations) concerned shall be sought when considering the adoption of national laws or regulations concerning the capacity of the said (peoples/populations) to alienate their land or otherwise transmit rights of ownership, possession and use of their land.
> 3. Persons who are not members of these (peoples/populations) shall be prevented from taking advantage of the customs referred to in paragraph 1 of this Article or of lack of understanding of the laws on the part of the members of these (peoples/populations) to secure the ownership, possession or use of land belonging to them.[151]

A number of comments were made on this draft, some proposing extensive redrafting and others reviving proposals made and not taken up earlier. The Office's commentary on these suggestions indicates the suggestions made and the direction taken. The Office here is attempting to maintain internal coherence and was resisting some strongly held views expressed by some participants in the discussion:

> The proposals that this Article be revised simply to recognise the procedures established by these people for the transmission of land

---

151   Report IV (1), pp. 10 and 11.

rights are not likely to be accepted by the Conference. However, if the applicability of paragraph 1 were limited to transmission of such rights among members these peoples – that is, to internal distribution of such rights among themselves – as has been suggested, this might be acceptable. It would also eliminate the need for the phrase "within the framework of national laws and regulations". The reservations expressed on the use of the terms "ownership", "possession" and "use" are taken into account by making reference simply to the land rights of these peoples.

Paragraph 2 therefore should refer to the transmission of land rights beyond these communities. Objections have again been raised to the inclusion of a requirement that consent be sought, and several respondents have proposed that these lands simply be made inalienable. The latter view was strongly expressed at the 1986 Meeting of Experts, and indigenous and tribal representatives have repeatedly stated that they share this view. Convention No. 107 makes no direct reference to inalienability, but the accompanying Recommendation (No. 104) contains two provisions recommending restrictions on indirect leasing or mortgaging of the lands of these communities. Moreover, legislation along these lines has been adopted in several countries in recent years. Yet problems remain. First, in spite of a certain movement in this direction, no clear trend can be discerned in national legislation. In addition, there may well be cases in which the peoples concerned wish – or may decide in the future – to alienate part or all of their lands outside the community. To adopt provisions simply prohibiting alienation would restrict the options of these communities to an unacceptable degree. It would also go contrary to every other provision of the proposals for revising this instrument by putting restrictions on the capacity of these peoples to take action which they might wish to take after full and mature consideration. In view of this clear conflict of objectives, the Office has adapted its original proposal to take account of the discussions.

Paragraph 3 has been slightly amended in view of the comments made and of the changes to paragraph 1.

Thus amended, Article 16 appears as Article 17 of the new text.[152]

The draft submitted to the second discussion in 1989 was the following:

---

152   Report IV (2A), pp. 47 and 48.

ART. 13 TO 19 NO. 169 – LAND RIGHTS 317

Article 17
1. Procedures established by the peoples concerned for the transmission of land rights among members of these peoples shall be respected.
2. The peoples concerned shall be consulted whenever consideration is being given to their capacity to alienate their lands or otherwise transmit their rights outside their own community.
3. Persons who are not members of these peoples shall be prevented from taking advantage of their customs or of lack of understanding of the laws on the part of their members to secure the ownership, possession or use of land belonging to them.[153]

As it had in 1988, the responsible Committee in the Conference referred the part of the text on land rights to a Working Party. The Committee report states as follows concerning the Working Party's report to it in relation to Article 17:

> 118. Following clarification by the Office, consensus was reached on retaining the text of Article 17, paragraph 1, as set out in Report IV (2B), on the understanding that all amendments to this paragraph would be withdrawn. The Government and Employers' members preferred the Office text of Article 17, paragraph 2, and regarded it as a realistic proposal which would bring about an improvement for indigenous and tribal peoples. They regarded the Workers' members' proposed amendment as being too restrictive. They also felt that governments had a role to play in preventing alienation of land in circumstances which would in the end be prejudicial to the interests of the peoples concerned. The Workers' members considered that the Office text did not really address itself to the issue of inalienability, which was a fundamental concern of these peoples. They proposed a text for paragraph 2 which had been submitted in the Working Party and which read as follows:
>
>> The lands and territories of the peoples concerned shall ordinarily be recognised as inalienable. Alienation of lands and territories shall only be possible under procedural arrangements established in consultation with the representative institutions of the peoples concerned.
>
> The Government and Employers' members continued to support the Office text. In the circumstances, the Working Party decided that this

---
153 Report IV (2B), p. 16.

paragraph should be referred to the Committee for decision between the Office text and the Workers' proposal.

119. The Working Party agreed to a proposal by the Workers' members to accept the Office text of Articles 17 (1) and (3), 18 and 19 on the understanding that all amendments would be withdrawn.[154]

As already indicated for other provisions on land rights, at this point the Chairman decided to consult various members of the Committee and return with a proposal on the entire section.

122. The Chairman noted that, despite the advances which had been made by the Working Party, the Committee was still some way from adopting by consensus a text on the important and delicate issue of land. In order to avoid the adoption by numerous votes of a text that was unlikely to be lucid and could well be contradictory, as well as jeopardising adoption of the Convention and its subsequent ratification, he made the following suggestion concerning consideration of Part II of the proposed Convention. On the basis of the Working Party's report, which proposed texts for Articles 13 and 17(2), as well as agreed solutions for Articles 17(1) and (3), 18 and 19, he would consult with governments and the Employers' and Workers' groups with a view to formulating and submitting to the Committee for its consideration a new complete text for Part II. Prior to these consultations, he invited Committee members to address the critical aspects of the land issue.

123. All the speakers fully supported the proposal as to how to proceed. Many of them considered that the Office text, for the most part, particularly Articles 17 to 19, was to be preferred.[155]

The consultations yielded consensus except for paragraph 2 of Article 17.

143. Following his consultations with Government members and with the Employers' and Workers' groups concerning Part II of the draft Convention, the Chairman indicated that he would propose that the Committee consider a "package" text dealing with Articles 13 to 19, with the exception of Article 17(2) which would be considered separately. Articles 13 to 16 had been amended in the light of the Working Party's

---

154 Proceedings 1989, p. 25/18.
155 Ibid.

deliberations (for Article 13) and in the light of his discussions. Articles 17(1), 17(3), 18 and 19 in the package were the draft Office texts, in accordance with the Working Party's recommendations. He suggested that the package of Articles would constitute a basis to reach a firm understanding in order to finalise the task the Committee had been given by the Conference. He felt that in view of the agreements which had been reached concerning the issues dealt with in Part II of the draft Convention, only amendments to Article 17(2) should be considered. The Chairman then put the consolidated text for Part II of the draft Convention, with the exception of Article 17(2), before the Committee. This approach received general support, though a number of members expressed reservations on various aspects of these texts.[156]

Thus the proposed texts that had been submitted to the Conference for paragraphs 1 and 3 of Article 17 were accepted and adopted. As concerns paragraph 2, the outstanding issue was the Workers' members' staunch support for the position of the NGO indigenous representatives who were arguing for strict inalienability of land, which had also been discussed in 1956 and 1957, contrasting to the position of those who felt that this was actually against the general approach of allowing indigenous and tribal peoples in consultation with governments to decide on the best course in each national situation, and ultimately not in the interest of indigenous and tribal peoples. The usual subfusc language of the Committee's report nevertheless allows the high emotion of this final dramatic discussion of the Conference to peek through, and it is therefore reproduced *in extenso*:

> 158. As concerned Article 17, paragraph 2, the Committee began by considering the amended version put forward by the Workers' members in the Working Party. The Employers' members proposed to subamend the text proposed by the Workers' members by deleting the word "territories". The Workers' members opposed the subamendment. During the ensuing discussion, support for both the amendment and the subamendment was expressed. The Government member of Argentina, in supporting the subamendment, recalled that in the Working Party, he had supported the Workers' members' proposal, subject to the removal of "territories". He felt that the inclusion of the term "territories", which was not covered by the definition in Article 13(2), might cause confusion in the context of this Article. This was because only land which was possessed could be

---

156   Ibid., pp. 25/20 and 25/21.

sold, and this could not be the meaning of the word "territories" according to the preceding discussions. The Government member of India noted that Article 17(2) derived its force from Article 14(1), since the right to alienate land could arise only from ownership. He recalled his previously expressed reservations regarding the use of "territories" and supported the subamendment. The Government member of Venezuela supported the statements of the Government delegates of Argentina and India. The Government member of Peru wondered why the Workers' members insisted on using a term which caused consistent and considerable problems for many governments. He suggested that this was a terminological difficulty and not a conceptual one and that they should therefore look for a different word from "territories" which, without causing difficulties to States, could include the legitimate interests of the indigenous communities. Several other Government members supported the subamendment. The Government member of Portugal recalled her previous support for the inclusion of "territories" and opposed the subamendment. She stated that, in Portugal, the condition of inalienability was not restricted to property which was owned. The subamendment was opposed by several other Government members. The subamendment was rejected in a vote by show of hands, by 2,016 votes in favour, 2,139 against, with 210 abstentions. At the request of the Employers' members, a record vote was taken, and the subamendment was rejected by 2,016 votes in favour, 2,100 against, with 252 abstentions.

159. The Employers' members, as a result of the foregoing discussion, felt that the amendment to Article 17(2) proposed by the Workers' members contained many difficulties for many countries. They expressed support for the draft Office text. The amendment was rejected in a vote by show of hands, by 2,142 in favour, 2,142 against, with 84 abstentions. Under article 65(10) of the Standing Orders of the Conference, the amendment was not adopted. At the request of the Workers' members a record vote was taken, and the subamendment was rejected by 2,184 votes in favour, 2,184 against, with no abstentions. Under article 65(10) of the Standing Orders, the amendment was not adopted.[157]

Some explanation may help the reader to understand how dramatic this episode was. As concerns paragraph 158 above, the Workers' members in the Working Party had attempted to add a reference to territories, so that the passage would have referred to the alienation of lands and territories. In the first

---

157 Ibid., pp. 25/22 and 25/23.

vote[158] taken during the Conference session – in itself an event in a consensus-seeking process – the Workers' addition of 'territories' was retained. This however referred only to the amendment of the proposed paragraph, without yet having adopted the paragraph itself.

Paragraph 159 of the report indicates that paragraph 2 of Article 17 as amended was not adopted, so that the original text before the Conference was retained. This happened in a singularly dramatic fashion, with a first vote by show of hands resulting in an absolute tie, which was a remarkable event given the ILO's voting procedures. A tie meant that the proposed amended text was not adopted. The Workers' members then called for a record vote, increasing the tension by another notch. The author of this commentary, who was responsible for conducting the vote, recalls that all sides sent out to the rest of the Conference to ensure that as many possible of their members returned from bars, toilets and other meeting rooms to take part. The record vote confirmed the results of the show of hands, again by a tie but with a different number of votes on each side and this time with no abstentions. Anyone with experience of ILO voting procedures would have stated beforehand that two tie votes with different total numbers of votes was both mathematically and politically so improbable as to approach impossibility. Thus, as the report indicates phlegmatically, "Article 17(2) was adopted without change."[159]

Following the controversy over the proposed insertion of 'territories' in Article 17(2), some relief was found in requesting a clarification of the terminology from the Office. The following was the result:

> 162. The Workers' members and the Government member of Colombia sought from the Office information on the meaning of "lands" in relation to existing ILO instruments. A representative of the Secretary-General stated that the term "lands" was used in Convention No. 107 but was not defined therein. He recalled that when Convention No. 107 and its accompanying Recommendation No. 104 were adopted in 1957 there was one sentence in the relevant Conference Committee's report concerning

---

[158] The ILO voting process can be confusing. The totals do not mean that there were more than 4,000 participants. In ILO committees the voting strength of each of the three constituents is equalized so that workers, employers and governments each have one-third the voting strength. This requires the assignment of different voting values to each member of each group, sometime inflating the number of votes enormously. To take the simplest example, if there are 10 Government members, 4 employers and 5 workers on a committee, each government has 2 votes, each employer 5 votes and each worker 4 votes, so that each group has 20 votes.

[159] Ibid., p. 25/23.

Recommendation No. 104 which appeared to be relevant. In the *Record of Proceedings* (p. 732) of the 40th Session of the International Labour Conference, it was stated, inter alia, that "The Committee agreed that the term 'land' as used in this Part was generic and should be understood to include rivers, lakes and forests." The speaker noted that this referred specifically to the Recommendation, not the Convention, and indicated that the Committee of Experts on the Application of Conventions and Recommendations had never had the occasion to interpret the meaning of "lands" as used in Convention No. 107.[160]

It is worth reporting that at this dramatic stage of its work the Committee was approaching the end of its allotted time, and that all parties were so physically and emotionally exhausted that the rest of the proposed Convention after the land rights Articles was not discussed further and was simply adopted, as it had been pretty well fully discussed at the 1988 session and in the written exchanges.[161] Before going on to other subjects, however, the history of Articles 18 and 19 has to be covered.

6   *Article 18 of Convention No. 169: Penalties for Unauthorized Intrusion*

Article 18 of Convention No. 169 reads as follows:

> Adequate penalties shall be established by law for unauthorised intrusion upon, or use of, the lands of the peoples concerned, and governments shall take measures to prevent such offences.

There was no comparable provision in Convention No. 107, though this concept is closely related to the principle that indigenous and tribal peoples should not be dispossessed from their lands. In its initial evaluation of how Convention No. 107 might be revised, the Office commented:

> No changes are required to paragraph 2 of Article 13. However, it has been suggested that a revised Convention should specify that penalties should be imposed in the event of harmful trespass on the traditional lands of these peoples. While the proposed revision of Article 11 would require States to guarantee effective protection of these lands, it is not without merit to suggest that a further requirement in Article 13 concerning

---

160   Ibid. The author of this commentary was, in fact, the 'representative of the Secretary-General' who provided this information. The intention of the explanation was to soften the resentment on all sides that had resulted from the votes on Article 17(2).

161   Ibid.

sanctions in the event of harmful trespass would reinforce this general principle. To this end, an additional paragraph in this Article might provide that any unauthorised intrusion upon, or use of, the lands of the peoples concerned by persons not belonging to these peoples should be considered an offence, and that appropriate penalties should be established by law.[162]

There is no clear line of argument in either the report of the Meeting of Experts or in the Office Report that led to this conclusion, and it therefore appears to have been an extrapolation by the Office from the wider discussion on removal and restitution. It is distinguishable from removal of these peoples from their lands for development purposes, for instance, in that it appears to be more oriented toward private action of intrusion or invasion – for instance the establishment of unauthorized settlement in reserved lands, or intrusion for resource exploration. This might be termed 'constructive removal'. The questionnaire forwarded to the constituents therefore put the question:

> 44. Do you consider that a paragraph should be added to Article 13 providing that any unauthorised intrusion upon, or use of, the lands of the peoples concerned by persons not belonging to these peoples should be considered as an offence, and that appropriate penalties for such offences should be established by law?[163]

The Office analyzed the replies received as follows:

> In view of the very large majority of affirmative replies to this question, a provision to this effect has been included in the Proposed Conclusions. While the suggestion has been made that the words "or groups" be added after the word "persons", it would seem that the word "persons" is sufficient to cover any number of intruders on the lands of the peoples concerned. The addition of a reference to recourse procedures appears useful, in allowing these peoples to take appropriate measures to compel the expulsion of intruders. Finally, the point made by Canada (IBC) appears valid.[164]

---

162 Report VI (1), p. 73.
163 Ibid., p. 97.
164 Report VI (2), p. 61. The point made by the IBC (International Business Council of Canada) was: 'Such a provision should also recognise that unauthorised intrusion or use could also be undertaken by persons belonging to the indigenous people.'

The proposed conclusions thus included the following:

> 38. *Unauthorised intrusion upon, or use of, the lands of the peoples concerned should be considered as an offence, and appropriate penalties for such offences and other appropriate recourse procedures should be established by law.*[165]

The process by which the land rights questions were discussed in the 1988 Conference session has been described above. There was in fact no explicit reference reported to this particular conclusion, and it was adopted by the Conference in 1988 exactly as it appears above (except that '(peoples/populations)' was inserted in place of 'peoples').[166] It then appeared in the draft Convention in Report IV (1) for the 1989 discussion, again unchanged except for being rewritten in Convention form, and having been placed as a standalone Article 17 for reasons not explained:

> Unauthorised intrusion upon, or use of, the lands of the (peoples/populations) concerned shall be considered an offence. Adequate penalties for such offences and appropriate recourse procedures shall be established by law.[167]

The Office commentary on the observations made on Article 17 indicates that considerable contemplation of the so far undiscussed provision had taken place:

> The adjective "unauthorised" applies to the term "use" as well as to the term "intrusion", and has therefore been retained.[168]
>
> Some worker respondents propose an additional clause, to the effect that the peoples concerned shall have the right to initiate legal proceedings on their own behalf. This important right appears to be covered already by the third paragraph of Article 8.

---

165   Ibid., p. 109.
166   Proceedings 1988, p. 35/25.
167   Report IV (1), p. 11.
168   The Brazilian CUT (Trade Union Confederation) had proposed, 'Delete the word "unauthorised", which could imply that intrusion does not constitute an offence when it is authorised.'

ART. 13 TO 19 NO. 169 – LAND RIGHTS   325

>The Government of Japan proposes a qualifying clause, according the peoples concerned rights no greater than those accorded to other citizens in the event of intrusion. The Office considers that special protection is warranted, in view of the very serious abuses affecting indigenous and tribal peoples in particular. The concern expressed by the Government of Canada has been taken into account, while retaining the overall substance of the Article.[169] An obligation on governments to prevent unauthorised intrusions – such as incursions by settlers or prospectors – has been added to clarify the intention of this provision.
>
>Thus amended, Article 17 appears as Article 18 in the new text.[170]

Draft Article 18 appeared in the text submitted to the second discussion in the Conference as follows:

>Adequate penalties shall be established by law for unauthorised intrusion upon, or use of, the lands of the peoples concerned, and governments shall take measures to prevent such offences.[171]

It will be seen that the first sentence of the previous draft had been incorporated into the new draft, and a positive duty for governments to prevent intrusions had been added.

The Article was adopted in this wording, without further discussion or amendment,

7   *Article 19 of Convention No. 169: National Agrarian Programmes*

This Article reads as follows:

>National agrarian programmes shall secure to the peoples concerned treatment equivalent to that accorded to other sectors of the population with regard to:
>(a) the provision of more land for these peoples when they have not the area necessary for providing the essentials of a normal existence, or for any possible increase in their numbers;

---

169   The Government of Canada had proposed a redrafted Article with the comment: 'This would meet the intent of the Article while more flexibly applying to different national legal systems which may not provide for specific criminal offences.'
170   Report IV (2A), pp. 48 and 49.
171   Report IV (2B), p. 16.

(b) the provision of the means required to promote the development of the lands which these peoples already possess.

Article 19 of Convention No. 169 corresponds exactly to Article 14 of Convention No. 107, allowing for the changes of vocabulary that came with the new Convention.

a   Adoption of Article 14 of Convention No. 107

Article 14 of Convention No. 107 reads as follows:

> National agrarian programmes shall secure to the populations concerned treatment equivalent to that accorded to other sections of the national community with regard to –
> (*a*) the provision of more land for these populations when they have not the area necessary for providing the essentials of a normal existence, or for any possible increase in their numbers;
> (*b*) the provision of the means required to promote the development of the lands which these populations already possess.

The reason this provision was included in Convention No. 107 was based on the analysis of the drastic reduction in lands available to indigenous and tribal peoples around the world. A brief extract from the long Office report on this problem indicated:

> In different countries of the world, particularly in Latin America and Asia, a considerable proportion of the indigenous communities that have survived is to be found in remote and infertile mountain areas which yield only a bare subsistence. In many districts the neighbouring estates have monopolised water and wood supplies and have obtained control of important rights of way so that the members of the indigenous communities have to work on the estates to gain access to these supplies and rights. Frequently, the land belonging to an indigenous community is broken up into numerous isolated parcels separated by wide stretches belonging to the estates. In various parts of the world the shortage of arable land has resulted in an atomisation of property rights by the continuous subdivision of family holdings through inheritance. It has been reported that in some areas this subdivision has reached such proportions that land is no longer divided into plots but into furrows.[172]

---

172   Report VIII (1), pp. 64 and 65.

Among the conclusions drawn by the Office from its detailed survey of the living and working conditions of indigenous and tribal peoples was the following:

> The link between indigenous peoples and the land on which they live and from which they derive their livelihood constitutes an important factor in any plan to promote the welfare of these peoples. Two aspects of this problem must be distinguished. The first relates to the need to recognise the right of indigenous peoples over their traditional territories which have, in various regions, passed into the hands of non-indigenous persons in the form of grants or as a result of occupation of so-called "free land". The second aspect concerns indigenous communities whose rights to the land have been affected by the impact of a technologically more advanced society resulting in some cases in the introduction of various systems of tenancy and peonage, which are characterised in some areas by the obligation to render unpaid personal services. The chief problems arising in various regions out of the social, economic and juridical conditions under which indigenous peoples work the land would appear to be the following: (*a*) the lack on the part of settled farming communities of collective or individual title deeds to the land they occupy; (*b*) the insecure possession by seminomadic tribes of their usual territories or of the use of the land to which they periodically move; (*c*) the disproportion between the available arable land and the natural growth of the population; (*d*) the alienation of tribal land to persons or bodies outside the indigenous community by lease or mortgage; (*e*) the lack or inadequacy of farm credit and marketing facilities, and of technical aid, which makes it difficult for indigenous communities to free themselves from the burden of indebtedness caused by excessive interest rates, and to develop their resources economically; and (*f*) the absence or inadequate enforcement of legal and administrative measures designed to control the abuses of certain forms of land tenancy and share-cropping, and to prevent the custom of exacting personal services for the benefit of landowners and local authorities.[173]

The following passage was therefore included in the questionnaire sent to the constituents with a view to a first discussion:

---

173 Ibid., pp. 167 and 168.

32. Do you consider that, in order to promote the social and economic development of indigenous communities, national agrarian reform programmes should provide for the granting of more land to indigenous peoples who have not the area necessary for their subsistence or for any possible future development of the tribe or the group?[174]

The replies to this question opened up a line of inquiry that would eventually result in Article 14.

Fourteen of the 16 governments which replied to this question gave an affirmative answer. The Government of Brazil considers that the granting of land to indigenous communities which need it should be a first priority under national agrarian reform programmes and that recognition should be given to the rights of the indigenous people as the traditional occupiers of the area, rather than to their current ability to participate in the implementation of some production plan. The Government of India declares that the granting of land to which the question refers should be carried out as far as practicable. The Government of Belgium expresses a similar opinion and adds that such a grant should be subject to the granting of compensation to the previous owner. The Government of New Zealand points out that agriculture is not the only suitable form of employment for indigenous people and that these people should be encouraged to enter all the trades and professions for which they may be qualified. The observation of the Government of Brazil is undoubtedly based on a broad approach to the notion of protection in this respect. Nevertheless, owing to the diversity of conditions in various countries, it does not seem appropriate to embody this suggestion in a general rule. The point made by the Government of New Zealand would seem to be covered in other parts of the questionnaire, especially those relating to vocational training, handicrafts and rural industries. The reply of the Government of Belgium does not affect the principle of the question but seems to refer to compensation for the previous owners in case the proposed grant is made by expropriating land under private ownership. It does not seem that this reservation either could be included in the wording of a general rule. In view of the foregoing

---

174 Ibid., p. 178.

considerations the corresponding point of the proposed Conclusions has been based on the wording of the question. (*Point 31.*)[175]

Point 31 of the proposed conclusions read as follows:

> 31. In order to promote the social and economic development of indigenous groups, national agrarian reform programmes should apply to these groups in the same way as to other interested sections of the population with regard to –
> (*a*) the granting of more land to such indigenous groups when they have not the area necessary for their subsistence or for any possible increase of the groups;
> (*b*) the granting of means to promote the development of the lands which these groups already possess.[176]

The discussion in 1956 included no specific reference to this conclusion, and resulted in the adoption of conclusion 22, which was worded exactly like point 31 above, except for the deletion of 'reform' in the second line.[177] This in turn resulted in proposed Article 14 in the first report prepared for the 1957 discussion:

> National agrarian programmes shall secure to indigenous groups treatment equivalent to that accorded to other sections of the national community with regard to –
> (*a*) the granting of more land to such groups when, they have not the area necessary for the subsistence or any possible increase of the groups;
> (*b*) the granting of the means required to promote the development of the lands which these groups already possess.[178]

The Office's analysis of the governments' comments on this proposal figured in the final report submitted to the Conference for the 1957 discussion:

> The new text as suggested by the United Kingdom Government eliminates not only the wording but the substance of subparagraph (*b*) without giving the reason for this alteration. The Government may wish at the

---

175 Report VIII (2), pp. 126 and 127.
176 Ibid., p. 161.
177 Proceedings 1956, p. 749.
178 Report VI (1), p. 49.

Conference to give clarification which will make it possible to ascertain whether or not such a deletion is called for.

In regard to the same Government's observation concerning the use of the word "granting", it has seemed appropriate to substitute the word "provision". This change does not affect the text in other languages. The suggestion of the Government of the U.S.S.R. appears to some extent to introduce a needed clarification in the proposed text, which has therefore been altered.[179] On the other hand, it does not seem indispensable to refer explicitly to workers and their families in this Article, in view of the fact that the concept of indigenous groups covers indigenous workers and their families.[180]

The resulting proposed Article 14 thus read as follows:

National agrarian programmes shall secure to the populations concerned treatment equivalent to that accorded to other sections of the national community with regard to –
(*a*) the provision of more land for these populations when they have not the area necessary for providing the essentials of a normal existence, or for any possible increase in their numbers;
(*b*) the provision of the means required to promote the development of the lands which these populations already possess.[181]

At the 1957 Session of the Conference, the following appears in the Committee's report:

61. Articles 13 and 14 were each adopted, without discussion, by 34 votes to 0, with 15 abstentions.[182]

b   Adoption of Article 19 of Convention No. 169
When the revision of Convention No. 107 was being discussed there was very little discussion of Article 14 of that instrument. There is no record of the

---

179   The USSR proposed amending as follows: 'In subparagraph (*a*) the words "necessary for the subsistence" should be replaced by the words "necessary for fulfilling the essential conditions of a normal existence and for improving the position of workers and their families*"*. Report VI (2), p. 23.
180   Ibid.
181   Ibid., pp. 58 and 60.
182   Proceedings 1957, p. 727.

Meeting of Experts having discussed it, and the Office's analysis of the possible amendments was as follows:

> There would seem to be no need to revise the present wording of this Article. However, as noted earlier, complex issues have arisen with regard to claims made by indigenous and tribal peoples for restitution of their traditional lands, on the basis of ancient title, treaty rights or immemorial possession. With increasing frequency, these peoples have been demanding that national agrarian programmes should provide them with lands in accordance with these claims. In a number of countries machinery has already been established to deal with such claims. While a Convention applicable to a wide variety of national situations should not prescribe the exact manner in which such claims should be handled, a new provision might establish the principle that governments should, in fact, deal with such claims. A new paragraph in Article 14 might provide that adequate machinery should be established within the national legal system to resolve land claims by the peoples concerned.[183]

The questionnaire therefore included the following:

> 45. Subject to question 46, do you consider that Article 14 should remain unchanged?
> 46. Do you consider that a paragraph should be added to Article 14 providing that adequate procedures should be established within the national legal system to resolve land claims by the peoples concerned?[184]

The resulting proposed conclusions read as follows:

> 39. National agrarian programmes should secure to the *peoples* concerned treatment equivalent to that accorded to other sections of the national community with regard to –
> (a) the provision of more land for these *peoples* when they have not the area necessary for providing the essentials of a normal existence, or for any possible increase in their numbers;
> (b) the provision of the means required to promote the development of the lands which these *peoples* already possess.

---

[183] Report VI (1), p. 74.
[184] Ibid., p. 97.

> 40. Adequate procedures should be established within the national legal system to resolve land claims by the peoples concerned, including claims arising under treaties.[185]

As we have seen above the question of land claims and restitution of lands (proposed conclusion 40) was eventually moved elsewhere, leaving little room for changes here.

The way that the land rights provisions were discussed in the 1988 and 1989 Sessions of the Conference has been indicated above. The draft conclusions on this point referred to above were not mentioned in the 1988 discussion, and the Office thus translated them into the language of a Convention and circulated them to the constituents for comments before the 1989 discussion. The language circulated (now designated Article 18) was the following:

> National agrarian programmes shall secure to the (peoples/populations) concerned treatment equivalent to that accorded to other sections of the national community with regard to:
> (a) the provision of more land for these (peoples/populations) when they have not the area necessary for providing the essentials of a normal existence, or for any possible increase in their numbers;
> (b) the provision of the means required to promote the development of the lands which these (peoples/populations) already possess.[186]

There were several comments on this proposed text, which were analyzed as follows in the Office's final report:

> The understandings expressed by the Governments of Canada and the United States both appear to be correct. The intent of this Article was to provide for non-discriminatory rather than preferential treatment, and to allow indigenous and tribal peoples to benefit from general programmes of agrarian reform. Provision is, however, made for the special needs of these peoples to be taken into account.
>
> Australia (ACTU) and Canada (IPWG) have proposed amendments intended to consolidate the land rights of these peoples and to mandate that development should take place in accordance with their own aspirations. Both these concerns appear to be covered elsewhere in the revised text, and there appears to be no pressing need to duplicate these

---

185   Report VI (2), p. 109.
186   Report IV (1), p. 11.

provisions. Following minor drafting changes, Article 18 appears as Article 19 in the new text.[187]

The revised proposed provision read as follows:

> National agrarian programmes shall secure to the peoples concerned treatment equivalent to that accorded to other sectors of the population with regard to:
> (a) the provision of more land for these peoples when they have not the area necessary for providing the essentials of a normal existence, or for any possible increase in their numbers;
> (b) the provision of the means required to promote the development of the lands which these peoples already possess.[188]

The one minor change referred to was to replace 'sections of the national community' with 'sectors of the population'.

As recounted earlier, this was among the Articles that were not further discussed in the 1989 Conference, and the above text was adopted.

E   Development of the Land Rights Provisions through Supervision

Given the fundamental importance of land rights to the situation of indigenous and tribal peoples, it is not surprising that the ILO supervisory bodies have spent considerable attention on examining how they are applied.

No attempt will be made here to detail specific national situations, except as they may be revealed by the comments cited. What is found below may well reflect a situation at a particular time that later became better or worse – the researcher will have to track these situations through NORMLEX on the ILO web site.

1   *Information Gathering*

In the early comments after the Convention came into force, and in the Committee of Experts' first comments to a government after it has ratified the Convention, the first focus has nearly always been on asking what the land rights situation of indigenous and tribal peoples in the country is. For instance,

---

[187] Report IV (2A), p. 50.
[188] Report IV (2B), pp. 16 and 18.

the first comment made by the Committee after the Convention entered into force was made to Norway in a 1993 direct request:

> 14. Article 14. The Committee notes that the Government holds title to most of the traditional lands of the Sami to which the Sami have a right of usufruct. The Committee also notes in this regard that there are judicial decisions enforcing Sami prescriptive rights based on long-established use.

In a number of cases the Committee has been able to refer to reports received under Convention No. 107 if it was ratified first.

2 Consultation over Land Rights

The large majority of the comments made by both the Committee of Experts and by Governing Body committees to consider representations are either focussed directly on consultation, or involve consultation. There is naturally a large overlap with the chapter above on consultation (Article 6 of the Convention), but more pointed and detailed comments have been made under the land rights articles.

For instance one of the earliest comments on the application of Convention No. 169 was addressed to Bolivia in a 1994 direct request:

> 22. The Committee notes that the extractive activities of settlers, forestry workers, etc., have threatened the traditional activities of the indigenous communities living within these areas, e.g. hunting, fishing and gathering. Please indicate any procedural mechanisms in place, or contemplated, to facilitate consultation with indigenous communities, and their participation in the benefits of any extractive activities on their lands including the modalities for the payment of compensation for any damages sustained as a result; as well as any mechanisms to mitigate the negative effects of such activities on these communities.

A direct request addressed to Peru in 1998 went more deeply into the consultation requirements:

> 14. The Committee recalls that the Convention provides that governments shall take steps as necessary to guarantee effective protection of the rights of ownership and possession of these peoples and that adequate procedures must be established to resolve land claims by these peoples.

15. Article 15. The Committee recalls that the provisions of this Article have to be read in conjunction with Articles 6 and 7 respecting the effective consultation of the peoples concerned so that they can participate actively in decisions which concern them. Furthermore, it is necessary to consider the social, spiritual, cultural and environmental impact of any activities undertaken and to guarantee that the peoples concerned can participate effectively in decisions which may concern them.

The lack of consultation over land rights has come up repeatedly in the Committee of Experts' comments and in representations under article 24 of the ILO Constitution. The Committee has had occasion sometimes to evoke very serious abuses of indigenous land rights. See, for example another comment by the Committee, in an observation to Bolivia in 2002, following up a representation on Convention No. 169:

2. The allegations made by the COB[189] referred principally to the administrative decisions of the National Forestry Superintendency granting 27 forestry concessions for a duration of 40 years, which can be renewed, and which overlap with six traditional indigenous territories, without any prior consultation. These areas are undergoing a process of review in order to determine the rights of third parties in their respect.

3. The tripartite committee concluded that, in view of the fact that the review of claimed land, of expropriations and of concessions for the exploitation of resources may directly affect the viability and interests of the indigenous peoples concerned, *Article 15 of the Convention* should be read in conjunction with *Articles 6 and 7*, and by ratifying the Convention, governments undertake to ensure that the indigenous communities concerned are consulted promptly and adequately on the extent and implications of exploration and exploitation activities, whether these are mining, oil or forestry activities.

4. It added that, as the lands for which the forestry concessions overlap have not yet been designated as community-held lands, it had not received any evidence indicating that such consultations, whether under *Article 6(a)* or *Article 15, paragraph 2*, of the Convention, had been carried out or whether provision had been made for the peoples concerned to participate wherever possible in the benefits of such activities.

6. The Committee hopes that the Government will...indicate in particular: (1) the measures adopted or envisaged to resolve the situations which gave rise to the representation, taking into account the need to establish an

---

189 Bolivian Central of Workers.

effective mechanism for prior consultation with the peoples concerned, as required by *Articles 6 and 15* of the Convention, before undertaking any programme of exploration or exploitation of the resources pertaining to their land; (2) the progress achieved in practice with regard to the consultations held with the peoples located in the area in which the 27 forestry concessions overlap with the community-held lands, including information on the participation of these peoples in the use, management and conservation of these resources and in the benefits of forestry activities, as well as the granting to them of fair compensation for any damages which they may sustain as a result of the exploration and exploitation in the area;

Another kind of problem was mentioned in a direct request to Argentina, also in 2002, referring once again to information received from a trade union:

> *Articles 6, 7 and 15.* The CTA alleges the absence of consultations with indigenous peoples through representative institutions in general, and particularly with regard to the exploration and exploitation of natural resources. According to these allegations, the State decides on the persons or institutions which are representative, and not the indigenous communities themselves.

The situation of the indigenous peoples of Guatemala has been a matter of concern for many years. The following extract from a 2005 observation to Guatemala refers to a complaint to the ILO, as well as to a United Nations peace-keeping mission to the country that interacted strongly with an ILO presence on the ground. This comment highlights among other things the interaction among the various Articles of Convention No. 169 requiring consultations. The situation reflects a deep-seated antipathy on the part of national authorities in some countries to allowing indigenous peoples to participate in governance at any level:

> 7. The Committee notes that, according to UNSITRAGUA,[190] the Government recently granted a permit for mining prospection and exploitation in the departments of San Marcos and Izábal to Montana Exploradora S.A., a subsidiary of the Canadian mining company Glamis Gold. UNSITRAGUA indicates that the area involved contains two of Guatemala's main lakes – Atitlan and Izábal – where there are eco-tourism resorts. Mining operations, which would require 250,000 litres of water per hour, would place the potable water supply under serious risk of pollution. Furthermore, despite opposition to the mining activities by

---

190 The Union of Guatemalan Workers (UNSITRAGUA).

the population of Sololá and San Marcos, in an act of intimidation the Government allowed the company's equipment to be brought in under the escort of 1,300 members of the police and the army. This operation began on 11 January 2005. The local population staged public protests and blocked the road. According to UNSITRAGUA, the Government stated that the people were armed, although no weapons were seized. However, one villager died and many others were injured.

8. UNSITRAGUA emphasizes that the death is the consequence of a mining policy imposed – without prior consultation – on the premise that corporate interests rank higher than social interests and respect for the land, culture, beliefs and opinions of the indigenous peoples of Guatemala and even their lives. *The Committee asks the Government to provide information on what occurred, indicating whether the persons responsible have been identified, tried and punished.*

12. The Committee recalls that the Convention lays down certain requirements to ensure that the exploration and exploitation of natural resources comply with the Convention. It draws the Government's attention to the fact that these requirements were not fulfilled in the case of the permit referred to by UNSITRAGUA.

13. The impact study carried out by the company is no substitute for the consultations required by *Article 15, paragraph 2*. This provision stipulates that "governments shall establish or maintain procedures through which they shall consult these peoples, with a view to ascertaining whether and to what degree their interests would be prejudiced, before undertaking or permitting any programmes for the exploration or exploitation of such resources pertaining to their lands". As the Committee has pointed out in other similar cases, responsibility for consultation lies with the Government, not the company. Furthermore, in establishing or maintaining procedures, governments must take into account the procedural requirements laid down in *Article 6* of the Convention and the provisions of *Article 7* of the Convention, according to which "Governments shall ensure that, whenever appropriate, studies are carried out, in cooperation with the peoples concerned, to assess the social, spiritual, cultural and environmental impact on them of planned development activities. The results of these studies shall be considered as fundamental criteria for the implementation of these activities."

And on a number of occasions the limitations of the procedures in place, even when governments have made some efforts, emerge all too clearly from the Experts' comments. See the following extract of an observation to Peru in 2008:

The Committee notes from the Government's report that the Government has made some effort with regard to consultation and participation; however, it is concerned that from the communications, drawn up with full participation of the indigenous peoples, and the report from the Office of the People's Ombudsperson that these efforts appear to be isolated and sporadic and at times not in line with the Convention (for example, information meetings being held rather than consultations). There is a lack of participation and consultation for tackling the numerous disputes connected with the exploitation of resources in lands traditionally occupied by indigenous peoples. The Committee expresses its concern regarding the communications received and the lack of comments on them from the Government. *The Committee urges the Government to adopt the necessary measures, with the participation and consultation of the indigenous peoples, to ensure (1) the participation and consultation of the indigenous peoples in a coordinated and systematic manner in the light of Articles 2, 6, 7, 15 and 33 of the Convention; (2) the identification of urgent situations connected with the exploitation of natural resources which endanger the persons, institutions, property, work, culture and environment of the peoples concerned and the prompt application of special measures necessary to safeguard them. The Committee requests the Government to supply information in this respect, together with its comments on the communications received.*

Many more examples of violations of the rights to consultation and participation could be provided, and the reader is referred to the ILO web site for further cases. What is apparent from a reading of these comments in an historical sequence is that the repeated requests for information on consultations on land rights has resulted in a heightened awareness of the need for consultations and participation over land rights, *inter alia*.

3 *Invasions of Indigenous Territory*

A number of the comments of the Committee of Experts document invasions of indigenous territory, either by those deliberately seeking out these lands for resource exploitation or by landless people desperately seeking somewhere to settle. In 1996 the Committee made a direct request to Paraguay that covered both cases:

10. The Committee recalls that in an earlier report on Convention No. 107, the Government stated that during 1991 there was a pronounced increase in the "invasions by landless peasants" of indigenous lands and that illegal settlers in Naranjito, Torreskue and Ka'ajovai have been ordered by

the courts to leave the area. The Committee asks the Government to supply information on these judicial decisions and the effect given to them, including any measures taken by the Institute of Rural Welfare to restore the lands of the "Fortuna" community who lost the title to their lands to the Industrial Paraguayan SA company due to an administrative error made by the Institute. The Committee once again requests the Government to provide information on the development of this situation.

4 *Demarcation of Territories*

In application of the Article 14 (2) requirement 'to identify the lands which the peoples concerned traditionally occupy', the Committee of Experts regularly tracks such procedures. This often results from confusion over the lands concerned that has gone on for many years, as evoked in the following extract of a direct request to Paraguay in 1994:

> ...the Committee notes that some settlers' lands are included within the resguardos, and that some indigenous communities have had their traditional lands allocated to other resguardos. It also notes that some resguardos include property which earlier title holders may still claim under existing legislative provisions. The Committee requests the Government to provide information on any procedures which may have been adopted or are envisaged to resolve conflicts in land claims within the ongoing process of land demarcation in the country.

Often the problem is not simply identifying the lands, but also the other part of Article 14(2): 'to guarantee effective protection of their rights of ownership and possession', as in Brazil (direct request 2005):

> 13. *Land.* The Committee notes that the criteria for identifying and establishing borders for indigenous lands are set forth in Decree No. 1775/96 and Ordinance No. 14/MJ of 1996 and that the work of establishing borders is carried out in accordance with the Handbook of Technical Standards for Demarcating Indigenous Lands. It notes that, at present, more than 70 per cent of indigenous lands recognized in Brazil have been demarcated and approved. It also notes that of the lands demarcated or in the process of approval, 90 per cent are located in the "Legal Amazon". Please indicate how *Article 14, paragraph 3,* of the Convention is applied with regard to procedures for resolving land claims by the peoples

concerned. The Committee notes that the problem is not one of demarcation and approval, but of how to respect in practice the integrity of demarcated and approved indigenous lands: as noted in the Committee's comments under Convention No. 107, there are problems linked to the presence of private owners, timber and agricultural and stock-raising enterprises setting up on indigenous lands. The Committee would be grateful if the Government would indicate, out of the total area of land demarcated and approved, the area of the land which is free of dispute and in which indigenous peoples can live in peace, and the percentage of land in which there is dispute and in which, despite regularization, it is still not possible to ensure that the peoples concerned are able peacefully to exercise their rights over the land. Please also indicate the strategy for resolving these problems, as stipulated in the Convention.

5   Natural Resources

As seen above, the question of natural resources and the rights of indigenous and tribal peoples in connection with them, was the source of great complexity in adopting the Convention, as it has been in its implementation. This is particularly true in exploring the limits between State ownership of mineral and other resource rights, and the rights of these people to participation in the use and management. See the following from an observation to Mexico in 2004:

> 10. *Lands, and territories and natural resources.* Section 2(A)(VI) of the reform provides that the Constitution recognizes and guarantees the right of indigenous peoples and communities to "have access (...) to the use and preferential exploitation of the natural resources in the areas inhabited and occupied by communities except for those which are strategic areas" under the terms of the Constitution. Strategic areas are defined in article 27 of the Constitution. In this respect, the Government states in its report that "the reform considers that, in supplementing the use and exploitation of the natural resources in their lands and territories, these are understood as the whole of the habitat used and occupied by indigenous communities, except those for which direct control is exercised by the nation and which are enshrined in article 27 of the Constitution". The legislation in many countries provides that rights over subsurface resources remain the property of the State. In *Article 15, paragraph 2*, of the Convention, in which this legal principle is recognized, the obligation of States is set forth to consult indigenous peoples who may be

affected before permitting activities for the exploration or exploitation of subsurface resources located in indigenous territories. This means that the Convention contains specific provisions on the territories traditionally occupied by indigenous peoples which are the property of the State, but does not exclude them from the scope of the Convention. Indeed, *Article 15, paragraph 2*, of the Convention was drawn up precisely for cases in which the State retains ownership of mineral or subsurface resources.

6   *The Involvement of Religious Institutions*

There are several Latin American countries where religious institutions have long had a special role related to indigenous peoples, which have even extended to their having had a right to title over indigenous lands. While this system has attenuated in recent years, it still exists to some degree. See the following extract of a 1996 direct request to Paraguay:

> 9. Articles 13 to 18. The Committee notes the information detailing the Government's efforts to transfer property titles to indigenous communities. In this respect, the Government reports that gradually the missionary bodies are handing over definitive property titles to the indigenous communities. The Committee recalls that this practice has been under way for a number of years. It requests the Government to provide more details on how these land transfers are carried out, whether the indigenous communities are required to pay compensation and which indigenous communities have benefited from these measures. Please provide information in the next report in regard to future developments, including the activities of religious missions in this context, whether other non-governmental bodies have pursued such practices in the country and details of the different forms of land tenure prevailing in areas inhabited by indigenous peoples.

This is only a small selection of the much larger quantum of supervisory comments by the ILO Committee of Experts. They cover many subjects, and all the countries that have ratified Convention No. 169.

It should be kept in mind also that the Committee of Experts has been supervising the application of Convention No. 107 for many years, and information on land rights in Bangladesh, India and Pakistan in particular can be searched for in NORMLEX under this Convention.

Appendices

APPENDIX I

Indigenous and Tribal Peoples Convention, 1989 (No. 169)

The General Conference of the International Labour Organisation,

Having been convened at Geneva by the Governing Body of the International Labour Office, and having met in its 76th Session on 7 June 1989, and

Noting the international standards contained in the Indigenous and Tribal Populations Convention and Recommendation, 1957, and

Recalling the terms of the Universal Declaration of Human Rights, the International Covenant on Economic, Social and Cultural Rights, the International Covenant on Civil and Political Rights, and the many international instruments on the prevention of discrimination, and

Considering that the developments which have taken place in international law since 1957, as well as developments in the situation of indigenous and tribal peoples in all regions of the world, have made it appropriate to adopt new international standards on the subject with a view to removing the assimilationist orientation of the earlier standards, and

Recognising the aspirations of these peoples to exercise control over their own institutions, ways of life and economic development and to maintain and develop their identities, languages and religions, within the framework of the States in which they live, and

Noting that in many parts of the world these peoples are unable to enjoy their fundamental human rights to the same degree as the rest of the population of the States within which they live, and that their laws, values, customs and perspectives have often been eroded, and

Calling attention to the distinctive contributions of indigenous and tribal peoples to the cultural diversity and social and ecological harmony of humankind and to international co-operation and understanding, and

Noting that the following provisions have been framed with the co-operation of the United Nations, the Food and Agriculture Organisation of the United Nations, the United Nations Educational, Scientific and Cultural Organisation and the World Health Organisation, as well as of the Inter-American Indian Institute, at appropriate levels and in their respective fields, and that it is proposed to continue this co-operation in promoting and securing the application of these provisions, and

Having decided upon the adoption of certain proposals with regard to the partial revision of the Indigenous and Tribal Populations Convention, 1957 (No. 107), which is the fourth item on the agenda of the session, and

Having determined that these proposals shall take the form of an international Convention revising the Indigenous and Tribal Populations Convention, 1957;

adopts this twenty-seventh day of June of the year one thousand nine hundred and eighty-nine the following Convention, which may be cited as the Indigenous and Tribal Peoples Convention, 1989;

Part 1. General Policy

Article 1

1. This Convention applies to:

   (a) tribal peoples in independent countries whose social, cultural and economic conditions distinguish them from other sections of the national community, and whose status is regulated wholly or partially by their own customs or traditions or by special laws or regulations;

   (b) peoples in independent countries who are regarded as indigenous on account of their descent from the populations which inhabited the country, or a geographical region to which the country belongs, at the time of conquest or colonisation or the establishment of present state boundaries and who, irrespective of their legal status, retain some or all of their own social, economic, cultural and political institutions.

2. Self-identification as indigenous or tribal shall be regarded as a fundamental criterion for determining the groups to which the provisions of this Convention apply.

3. The use of the term *peoples* in this Convention shall not be construed as having any implications as regards the rights which may attach to the term under international law.

Article 2

1. Governments shall have the responsibility for developing, with the participation of the peoples concerned, co-ordinated and systematic action to protect the rights of these peoples and to guarantee respect for their integrity.

2. Such action shall include measures for:

   (a) ensuring that members of these peoples benefit on an equal footing from the rights and opportunities which national laws and regulations grant to other members of the population;

   (b) promoting the full realisation of the social, economic and cultural rights of these peoples with respect for their social and cultural identity, their customs and traditions and their institutions;

(c) assisting the members of the peoples concerned to eliminate socio-economic gaps that may exist between indigenous and other members of the national community, in a manner compatible with their aspirations and ways of life.

Article 3

1. Indigenous and tribal peoples shall enjoy the full measure of human rights and fundamental freedoms without hindrance or discrimination. The provisions of the Convention shall be applied without discrimination to male and female members of these peoples.

2. No form of force or coercion shall be used in violation of the human rights and fundamental freedoms of the peoples concerned, including the rights contained in this Convention.

Article 4

1. Special measures shall be adopted as appropriate for safeguarding the persons, institutions, property, labour, cultures and environment of the peoples concerned.

2. Such special measures shall not be contrary to the freely-expressed wishes of the peoples concerned.

3. Enjoyment of the general rights of citizenship, without discrimination, shall not be prejudiced in any way by such special measures.

Article 5

In applying the provisions of this Convention:

(a) the social, cultural, religious and spiritual values and practices of these peoples shall be recognised and protected, and due account shall be taken of the nature of the problems which face them both as groups and as individuals;

(b) the integrity of the values, practices and institutions of these peoples shall be respected;

(c) policies aimed at mitigating the difficulties experienced by these peoples in facing new conditions of life and work shall be adopted, with the participation and co-operation of the peoples affected.

Article 6

1. In applying the provisions of this Convention, governments shall:

(a) consult the peoples concerned, through appropriate procedures and in particular through their representative institutions, whenever consideration is being given to legislative or administrative measures which may affect them directly;

(b) establish means by which these peoples can freely participate, to at least the same extent as other sectors of the population, at all levels of decision-making in elective institutions and administrative and other bodies responsible for policies and programmes which concern them;

(c) establish means for the full development of these peoples' own institutions and initiatives, and in appropriate cases provide the resources necessary for this purpose.

2. The consultations carried out in application of this Convention shall be undertaken, in good faith and in a form appropriate to the circumstances, with the objective of achieving agreement or consent to the proposed measures.

Article 7

1. The peoples concerned shall have the right to decide their own priorities for the process of development as it affects their lives, beliefs, institutions and spiritual well-being and the lands they occupy or otherwise use, and to exercise control, to the extent possible, over their own economic, social and cultural development. In addition, they shall participate in the formulation, implementation and evaluation of plans and programmes for national and regional development which may affect them directly.

2. The improvement of the conditions of life and work and levels of health and education of the peoples concerned, with their participation and co-operation, shall be a matter of priority in plans for the overall economic development of areas they inhabit. Special projects for development of the areas in question shall also be so designed as to promote such improvement.

3. Governments shall ensure that, whenever appropriate, studies are carried out, in co-operation with the peoples concerned, to assess the social, spiritual, cultural and environmental impact on them of planned development activities. The results of these studies shall be considered as fundamental criteria for the implementation of these activities.

4. Governments shall take measures, in co-operation with the peoples concerned, to protect and preserve the environment of the territories they inhabit.

Article 8

1. In applying national laws and regulations to the peoples concerned, due regard shall be had to their customs or customary laws.

2. These peoples shall have the right to retain their own customs and institutions, where these are not incompatible with fundamental rights defined by the national legal system and with internationally recognised human rights. Procedures shall be established, whenever necessary, to resolve conflicts which may arise in the application of this principle.

3. The application of paragraphs 1 and 2 of this Article shall not prevent members of these peoples from exercising the rights granted to all citizens and from assuming the corresponding duties.

Article 9

1. To the extent compatible with the national legal system and internationally recognised human rights, the methods customarily practised by the peoples concerned for dealing with offences committed by their members shall be respected.

2. The customs of these peoples in regard to penal matters shall be taken into consideration by the authorities and courts dealing with such cases.

Article 10

1. In imposing penalties laid down by general law on members of these peoples account shall be taken of their economic, social and cultural characteristics.

2. Preference shall be given to methods of punishment other than confinement in prison.

Article 11

The exaction from members of the peoples concerned of compulsory personal services in any form, whether paid or unpaid, shall be prohibited and punishable by law, except in cases prescribed by law for all citizens.

Article 12

The peoples concerned shall be safeguarded against the abuse of their rights and shall be able to take legal proceedings, either individually or through their representative bodies, for the effective protection of these rights. Measures shall be taken to ensure that members of these peoples can understand and be understood in legal proceedings, where necessary through the provision of interpretation or by other effective means.

Part II. Land

Article 13

1. In applying the provisions of this Part of the Convention governments shall respect the special importance for the cultures and spiritual values of the peoples concerned of their relationship with the lands or territories, or both as applicable, which they occupy or otherwise use, and in particular the collective aspects of this relationship.

2. The use of the term *lands* in Articles 15 and 16 shall include the concept of territories, which covers the total environment of the areas which the peoples concerned occupy or otherwise use.

Article 14

1. The rights of ownership and possession of the peoples concerned over the lands which they traditionally occupy shall be recognised. In addition, measures shall be

taken in appropriate cases to safeguard the right of the peoples concerned to use lands not exclusively occupied by them, but to which they have traditionally had access for their subsistence and traditional activities. Particular attention shall be paid to the situation of nomadic peoples and shifting cultivators in this respect.

2. Governments shall take steps as necessary to identify the lands which the peoples concerned traditionally occupy, and to guarantee effective protection of their rights of ownership and possession.

3. Adequate procedures shall be established within the national legal system to resolve land claims by the peoples concerned.

Article 15

1. The rights of the peoples concerned to the natural resources pertaining to their lands shall be specially safeguarded. These rights include the right of these peoples to participate in the use, management and conservation of these resources.

2. In cases in which the State retains the ownership of mineral or sub-surface resources or rights to other resources pertaining to lands, governments shall establish or maintain procedures through which they shall consult these peoples, with a view to ascertaining whether and to what degree their interests would be prejudiced, before undertaking or permitting any programmes for the exploration or exploitation of such resources pertaining to their lands. The peoples concerned shall wherever possible participate in the benefits of such activities, and shall receive fair compensation for any damages which they may sustain as a result of such activities.

Article 16

1. Subject to the following paragraphs of this Article, the peoples concerned shall not be removed from the lands which they occupy.

2. Where the relocation of these peoples is considered necessary as an exceptional measure, such relocation shall take place only with their free and informed consent. Where their consent cannot be obtained, such relocation shall take place only following appropriate procedures established by national laws and regulations, including public inquiries where appropriate, which provide the opportunity for effective representation of the peoples concerned.

3. Whenever possible, these peoples shall have the right to return to their traditional lands, as soon as the grounds for relocation cease to exist.

4. When such return is not possible, as determined by agreement or, in the absence of such agreement, through appropriate procedures, these peoples shall be provided in all possible cases with lands of quality and legal status at least equal to that of the lands previously occupied by them, suitable to provide for their present needs and future development. Where the peoples concerned express a preference for compensation in money or in kind, they shall be so compensated under appropriate guarantees.

5. Persons thus relocated shall be fully compensated for any resulting loss or injury.

Article 17
1. Procedures established by the peoples concerned for the transmission of land rights among members of these peoples shall be respected.
2. The peoples concerned shall be consulted whenever consideration is being given to their capacity to alienate their lands or otherwise transmit their rights outside their own community.
3. Persons not belonging to these peoples shall be prevented from taking advantage of their customs or of lack of understanding of the laws on the part of their members to secure the ownership, possession or use of land belonging to them.

Article 18
Adequate penalties shall be established by law for unauthorised intrusion upon, or use of, the lands of the peoples concerned, and governments shall take measures to prevent such offences.

Article 19
National agrarian programmes shall secure to the peoples concerned treatment equivalent to that accorded to other sectors of the population with regard to:
(a) the provision of more land for these peoples when they have not the area necessary for providing the essentials of a normal existence, or for any possible increase in their numbers;
(b) the provision of the means required to promote the development of the lands which these peoples already possess.

Part III. Recruitment and Conditions of Employment

Article 20
1. Governments shall, within the framework of national laws and regulations, and in co-operation with the peoples concerned, adopt special measures to ensure the effective protection with regard to recruitment and conditions of employment of workers belonging to these peoples, to the extent that they are not effectively protected by laws applicable to workers in general.
2. Governments shall do everything possible to prevent any discrimination between workers belonging to the peoples concerned and other workers, in particular as regards:
   (a) admission to employment, including skilled employment, as well as measures for promotion and advancement;

(b) equal remuneration for work of equal value;

(c) medical and social assistance, occupational safety and health, all social security benefits and any other occupationally related benefits, and housing;

(d) the right of association and freedom for all lawful trade union activities, and the right to conclude collective agreements with employers or employers' organisations.

3. The measures taken shall include measures to ensure:

(a) that workers belonging to the peoples concerned, including seasonal, casual and migrant workers in agricultural and other employment, as well as those employed by labour contractors, enjoy the protection afforded by national law and practice to other such workers in the same sectors, and that they are fully informed of their rights under labour legislation and of the means of redress available to them;

(b) that workers belonging to these peoples are not subjected to working conditions hazardous to their health, in particular through exposure to pesticides or other toxic substances;

(c) that workers belonging to these peoples are not subjected to coercive recruitment systems, including bonded labour and other forms of debt servitude;

(d) that workers belonging to these peoples enjoy equal opportunities and equal treatment in employment for men and women, and protection from sexual harassment.

4. Particular attention shall be paid to the establishment of adequate labour inspection services in areas where workers belonging to the peoples concerned undertake wage employment, in order to ensure compliance with the provisions of this Part of this Convention.

Part IV. Vocational Training, Handicrafts and Rural Industries

Article 21

Members of the peoples concerned shall enjoy opportunities at least equal to those of other citizens in respect of vocational training measures.

Article 22

1. Measures shall be taken to promote the voluntary participation of members of the peoples concerned in vocational training programmes of general application.

2. Whenever existing programmes of vocational training of general application do not meet the special needs of the peoples concerned, governments shall, with the participation of these peoples, ensure the provision of special training programmes and facilities.

3. Any special training programmes shall be based on the economic environment, social and cultural conditions and practical needs of the peoples concerned. Any studies made in this connection shall be carried out in co-operation with these peoples, who shall be consulted on the organisation and operation of such programmes. Where feasible, these peoples shall progressively assume responsibility for the organisation and operation of such special training programmes, if they so decide.

Article 23
1. Handicrafts, rural and community-based industries, and subsistence economy and traditional activities of the peoples concerned, such as hunting, fishing, trapping and gathering, shall be recognised as important factors in the maintenance of their cultures and in their economic self-reliance and development. Governments shall, with the participation of these people and whenever appropriate, ensure that these activities are strengthened and promoted.
2. Upon the request of the peoples concerned, appropriate technical and financial assistance shall be provided wherever possible, taking into account the traditional technologies and cultural characteristics of these peoples, as well as the importance of sustainable and equitable development.

Part v. Social Security and Health

Article 24
Social security schemes shall be extended progressively to cover the peoples concerned, and applied without discrimination against them.

Article 25
1. Governments shall ensure that adequate health services are made available to the peoples concerned, or shall provide them with resources to allow them to design and deliver such services under their own responsibility and control, so that they may enjoy the highest attainable standard of physical and mental health.
2. Health services shall, to the extent possible, be community-based. These services shall be planned and administered in co-operation with the peoples concerned and take into account their economic, geographic, social and cultural conditions as well as their traditional preventive care, healing practices and medicines.
3. The health care system shall give preference to the training and employment of local community health workers, and focus on primary health care while maintaining strong links with other levels of health care services.
4. The provision of such health services shall be co-ordinated with other social, economic and cultural measures in the country.

Part VI. Education and Means of Communication

Article 26
Measures shall be taken to ensure that members of the peoples concerned have the opportunity to acquire education at all levels on at least an equal footing with the rest of the national community.

Article 27
1. Education programmes and services for the peoples concerned shall be developed and implemented in co-operation with them to address their special needs, and shall incorporate their histories, their knowledge and technologies, their value systems and their further social, economic and cultural aspirations.
2. The competent authority shall ensure the training of members of these peoples and their involvement in the formulation and implementation of education programmes, with a view to the progressive transfer of responsibility for the conduct of these programmes to these peoples as appropriate.
3. In addition, governments shall recognise the right of these peoples to establish their own educational institutions and facilities, provided that such institutions meet minimum standards established by the competent authority in consultation with these peoples. Appropriate resources shall be provided for this purpose.

Article 28
1. Children belonging to the peoples concerned shall, wherever practicable, be taught to read and write in their own indigenous language or in the language most commonly used by the group to which they belong. When this is not practicable, the competent authorities shall undertake consultations with these peoples with a view to the adoption of measures to achieve this objective.
2. Adequate measures shall be taken to ensure that these peoples have the opportunity to attain fluency in the national language or in one of the official languages of the country.
3. Measures shall be taken to preserve and promote the development and practice of the indigenous languages of the peoples concerned.

Article 29
The imparting of general knowledge and skills that will help children belonging to the peoples concerned to participate fully and on an equal footing in their own community and in the national community shall be an aim of education for these peoples.

Article 30

1. Governments shall adopt measures appropriate to the traditions and cultures of the peoples concerned, to make known to them their rights and duties, especially in regard to labour, economic opportunities, education and health matters, social welfare and their rights deriving from this Convention.

2. If necessary, this shall be done by means of written translations and through the use of mass communications in the languages of these peoples.

Article 31

Educational measures shall be taken among all sections of the national community, and particularly among those that are in most direct contact with the peoples concerned, with the object of eliminating prejudices that they may harbour in respect of these peoples. To this end, efforts shall be made to ensure that history textbooks and other educational materials provide a fair, accurate and informative portrayal of the societies and cultures of these peoples.

Part VII. Contacts and Co-operation Across Borders

Article 32

Governments shall take appropriate measures, including by means of international agreements, to facilitate contacts and co-operation between indigenous and tribal peoples across borders, including activities in the economic, social, cultural, spiritual and environmental fields.

Part VIII. Administration

Article 33

1. The governmental authority responsible for the matters covered in this Convention shall ensure that agencies or other appropriate mechanisms exist to administer the programmes affecting the peoples concerned, and shall ensure that they have the means necessary for the proper fulfilment of the functions assigned to them.

2. These programmes shall include:

   (a) the planning, co-ordination, execution and evaluation, in co-operation with the peoples concerned, of the measures provided for in this Convention;

   (b) the proposing of legislative and other measures to the competent authorities and supervision of the application of the measures taken, in co-operation with the peoples concerned.

Part IX. General Provisions

Article 34
The nature and scope of the measures to be taken to give effect to this Convention shall be determined in a flexible manner, having regard to the conditions characteristic of each country.

Article 35
The application of the provisions of this Convention shall not adversely affect rights and benefits of the peoples concerned pursuant to other Conventions and Recommendations, international instruments, treaties, or national laws, awards, custom or agreements.

Part X. Final Provisions

Article 36
This Convention revises the Indigenous and Tribal Populations Convention, 1957.

Article 37
The formal ratifications of this Convention shall be communicated to the Director-General of the International Labour Office for registration.

Article 38
1. This Convention shall be binding only upon those Members of the International Labour Organisation whose ratifications have been registered with the Director-General.
2. It shall come into force twelve months after the date on which the ratifications of two Members have been registered with the Director-General.
3. Thereafter, this Convention shall come into force for any Member twelve months after the date on which its ratification has been registered.

Article 39
1. A Member which has ratified this Convention may denounce it after the expiration of ten years from the date on which the Convention first comes into force, by an act communicated to the Director-General of the International Labour Office for registration. Such denunciation shall not take effect until one year after the date on which it is registered.

2. Each Member which has ratified this Convention and which does not, within the year following the expiration of the period of ten years mentioned in the preceding paragraph, exercise the right of denunciation provided for in this Article, will be bound for another period of ten years and, thereafter, may denounce this Convention at the expiration of each period of ten years under the terms provided for in this Article.

Article 40

1. The Director-General of the International Labour Office shall notify all Members of the International Labour Organisation of the registration of all ratifications and denunciations communicated to him by the Members of the Organisation.

2. When notifying the Members of the Organisation of the registration of the second ratification communicated to him, the Director-General shall draw the attention of the Members of the Organisation to the date upon which the Convention will come into force.

Article 41

The Director-General of the International Labour Office shall communicate to the Secretary-General of the United Nations for registration in accordance with Article 102 of the Charter of the United Nations full particulars of all ratifications and acts of denunciation registered by him in accordance with the provisions of the preceding Articles.

Article 42

At such times as it may consider necessary the Governing Body of the International Labour Office shall present to the General Conference a report on the working of this Convention and shall examine the desirability of placing on the agenda of the Conference the question of its revision in whole or in part.

Article 43

1. Should the Conference adopt a new Convention revising this Convention in whole or in part, then, unless the new Convention otherwise provides

    (a) the ratification by a Member of the new revising Convention shall ipso jure involve the immediate denunciation of this Convention, notwithstanding the provisions of Article 39 above, if and when the new revising Convention shall have come into force;

    (b) as from the date when the new revising Convention comes into force this Convention shall cease to be open to ratification by the Members.

2. This Convention shall in any case remain in force in its actual form and content for those Members which have ratified it but have not ratified the revising Convention.

Article 44

The English and French versions of the text of this Convention are equally authoritative.

APPENDIX II

Indigenous and Tribal Populations Convention, 1957 (No. 107)

The General Conference of the International Labour Organisation,

Having been convened at Geneva by the Governing Body of the International Labour Office, and having met in its Fortieth Session on 5 June 1957, and

Having decided upon the adoption of certain proposals with regard to the protection and integration of indigenous and other tribal and semi-tribal populations in independent countries, which is the sixth item on the agenda of the session, and

Having determined that these proposals shall take the form of an international Convention, and

Considering that the Declaration of Philadelphia affirms that all human beings have the right to pursue both their material well-being and their spiritual development in conditions of freedom and dignity, of economic security and equal opportunity, and

Considering that there exist in various independent countries indigenous and other tribal and semi-tribal populations which are not yet integrated into the national community and whose social, economic or cultural situation hinders them from benefiting fully from the rights and advantages enjoyed by other elements of the population, and

Considering it desirable both for humanitarian reasons and in the interest of the countries concerned to promote continued action to improve the living and working conditions of these populations by simultaneous action in respect of all the factors which have hitherto prevented them from sharing fully in the progress of the national community of which they form part, and

Considering that the adoption of general international standards on the subject will facilitate action to assure the protection of the populations concerned, their progressive integration into their respective national communities, and the improvement of their living and working conditions, and

Noting that these standards have been framed with the co-operation of the United Nations, the Food and Agriculture Organisation of the United Nations, the United Nations Educational, Scientific and Cultural Organisation and the World Health Organisation, at appropriate levels and in their respective fields, and that it is proposed to seek their continuing co-operation in promoting and securing the application of these standards,

adopts this twenty-sixth day of June of the year one thousand nine hundred and fifty-seven the following Convention, which may be cited as the Indigenous and Tribal Populations Convention, 1957:

Part I. General Policy

Article 1

1. This Convention applies to:

(a) members of tribal or semi-tribal populations in independent countries whose social and economic conditions are at a less advanced stage than the stage reached by the other sections of the national community, and whose status is regulated wholly or partially by their own customs or traditions or by special laws or regulations;

(b) members of tribal or semi-tribal populations in independent countries which are regarded as indigenous on account of their descent from the populations which inhabited the country, or a geographical region to which the country belongs, at the time of conquest or colonisation and which, irrespective of their legal status, live more in conformity with the social, economic and cultural institutions of that time than with the institutions of the nation to which they belong.

2. For the purposes of this Convention, the term *semi-tribal* includes groups and persons who, although they are in the process of losing their tribal characteristics, are not yet integrated into the national community.

3. The indigenous and other tribal or semi-tribal populations mentioned in paragraphs 1 and 2 of this Article are referred to hereinafter as "the populations concerned".

Article 2

1. Governments shall have the primary responsibility for developing co-ordinated and systematic action for the protection of the populations concerned and their progressive integration into the life of their respective countries.

2. Such action shall include measures for:

(a) enabling the said populations to benefit on an equal footing from the rights and opportunities which national laws or regulations grant to the other elements of the population;

(b) promoting the social, economic and cultural development of these populations and raising their standard of living;

(c) creating possibilities of national integration to the exclusion of measures tending towards the artificial assimilation of these populations.
3. The primary objective of all such action shall be the fostering of individual dignity, and the advancement of individual usefulness and initiative.
4. Recourse to force or coercion as a means of promoting the integration of these populations into the national community shall be excluded.

Article 3
1. So long as the social, economic and cultural conditions of the populations concerned prevent them from enjoying the benefits of the general laws of the country to which they belong, special measures shall be adopted for the protection of the institutions, persons, property and labour of these populations.
2. Care shall be taken to ensure that such special measures of protection:
   (a) are not used as a means of creating or prolonging a state of segregation; and
   (b) will be continued only so long as there is need for special protection and only to the extent that such protection is necessary.
3. Enjoyment of the general rights of citizenship, without discrimination, shall not be prejudiced in any way by such special measures of protection.

Article 4
In applying the provisions of this Convention relating to the integration of the populations concerned:

(a) due account shall be taken of the cultural and religious values and of the forms of social control existing among these populations, and of the nature of the problems which face them both as groups and as individuals when they undergo social and economic change;
(b) the danger involved in disrupting the values and institutions of the said populations unless they can be replaced by appropriate substitutes which the groups concerned are willing to accept shall be recognised;
(c) policies aimed at mitigating the difficulties experienced by these populations in adjusting themselves to new conditions of life and work shall be adopted.

Article 5
In applying the provisions of this Convention relating to the protection and integration of the populations concerned, governments shall:

(a) seek the collaboration of these populations and of their representatives;
(b) provide these populations with opportunities for the full development of their initiative;

(c) stimulate by all possible means the development among these populations of civil liberties and the establishment of or participation in elective institutions.

Article 6

The improvement of the conditions of life and work and level of education of the populations concerned shall be given high priority in plans for the over-all economic development of areas inhabited by these populations. Special projects for economic development of the areas in question shall also be so designed as to promote such improvement.

Article 7

1. In defining the rights and duties of the populations concerned regard shall be had to their customary laws.
2. These populations shall be allowed to retain their own customs and institutions where these are not incompatible with the national legal system or the objectives of integration programmes.
3. The application of the preceding paragraphs of this Article shall not prevent members of these populations from exercising, according to their individual capacity, the rights granted to all citizens and from assuming the corresponding duties.

Article 8

To the extent consistent with the interests of the national community and with the national legal system:

(a) the methods of social control practised by the populations concerned shall be used as far as possible for dealing with crimes or offences committed by members of these populations;
(b) where use of such methods of social control is not feasible, the customs of these populations in regard to penal matters shall be borne in mind by the authorities and courts dealing with such cases.

Article 9

Except in cases prescribed by law for all citizens the exaction from the members of the populations concerned of compulsory personal services in any form, whether paid or unpaid, shall be prohibited and punishable by law.

Article 10

1. Persons belonging to the populations concerned shall be specially safeguarded against the improper application of preventive detention and shall be able to take legal proceedings for the effective protection of their fundamental rights.
2. In imposing penalties laid down by general law on members of these populations account shall be taken of the degree of cultural development of the populations concerned.
3. Preference shall be given to methods of rehabilitation rather than confinement in prison.

Part II. Land

Article 11

The right of ownership, collective or individual, of the members of the populations concerned over the lands which these populations traditionally occupy shall be recognised.

Article 12

1. The populations concerned shall not be removed without their free consent from their habitual territories except in accordance with national laws and regulations for reasons relating to national security, or in the interest of national economic development or of the health of the said populations.
2. When in such cases removal of these populations is necessary as an exceptional measure, they shall be provided with lands of quality at least equal to that of the lands previously occupied by them, suitable to provide for their present needs and future development. In cases where chances of alternative employment exist and where the populations concerned prefer to have compensation in money or in kind, they shall be so compensated under appropriate guarantees.
3. Persons thus removed shall be fully compensated for any resulting loss or injury.

Article 13

1. Procedures for the transmission of rights of ownership and use of land which are established by the customs of the populations concerned shall be respected, within the framework of national laws and regulations, in so far as they satisfy the needs of these populations and do not hinder their economic and social development.

2. Arrangements shall be made to prevent persons who are not members of the populations concerned from taking advantage of these customs or of lack of understanding of the laws on the part of the members of these populations to secure the ownership or use of the lands belonging to such members.

Article 14

National agrarian programmes shall secure to the populations concerned treatment equivalent to that accorded to other sections of the national community with regard to:

(a) the provision of more land for these populations when they have not the area necessary for providing the essentials of a normal existence, or for any possible increase in their numbers;

(b) the provision of the means required to promote the development of the lands which these populations already possess.

Part III. Recruitment and Conditions of Employment

Article 15

1. Each Member shall, within the framework of national laws and regulations, adopt special measures to ensure the effective protection with regard to recruitment and conditions of employment of workers belonging to the populations concerned so long as they are not in a position to enjoy the protection granted by law to workers in general.

2. Each Member shall do everything possible to prevent all discrimination between workers belonging to the populations concerned and other workers, in particular as regards:

(a) admission to employment, including skilled employment;

(b) equal remuneration for work of equal value;

(c) medical and social assistance, the prevention of employment injuries, workmen's compensation, industrial hygiene and housing;

(d) the right of association and freedom for all lawful trade union activities, and the right to conclude collective agreements with employers or employers' organisations.

Part IV. Vocational Training, Handicrafts and Rural Industries

Article 16

Persons belonging to the populations concerned shall enjoy the same opportunities as other citizens in respect of vocational training facilities.

Article 17

1. Whenever programmes of vocational training of general application do not meet the special needs of persons belonging to the populations concerned governments shall provide special training facilities for such persons.
2. These special training facilities shall be based on a careful study of the economic environment, stage of cultural development and practical needs of the various occupational groups among the said populations; they shall, in particular enable the persons concerned to receive the training necessary for occupations for which these populations have traditionally shown aptitude.
3. These special training facilities shall be provided only so long as the stage of cultural development of the populations concerned requires them; with the advance of the process of integration they shall be replaced by the facilities provided for other citizens.

Article 18

1. Handicrafts and rural industries shall be encouraged as factors in the economic development of the populations concerned in a manner which will enable these populations to raise their standard of living and adjust themselves to modern methods of production and marketing.
2. Handicrafts and rural industries shall be developed in a manner which preserves the cultural heritage of these populations and improves their artistic values and particular modes of cultural expression.

Part v. Social Security and Health

Article 19

Existing social security schemes shall be extended progressively, where practicable, to cover:

(a) wage earners belonging to the populations concerned;
(b) other persons belonging to these populations.

Article 20

1. Governments shall assume the responsibility for providing adequate health services for the populations concerned.
2. The organisation of such services shall be based on systematic studies of the social, economic and cultural conditions of the populations concerned.
3. The development of such services shall be co-ordinated with general measures of social, economic and cultural development.

Part VI. Education and Means of Communication

Article 21
Measures shall be taken to ensure that members of the populations concerned have the opportunity to acquire education at all levels on an equal footing with the rest of the national community.

Article 22
1. Education programmes for the populations concerned shall be adapted, as regards methods and techniques, to the stage these populations have reached in the process of social, economic and cultural integration into the national community.
2. The formulation of such programmes shall normally be preceded by ethnological surveys.

Article 23
1. Children belonging to the populations concerned shall be taught to read and write in their mother tongue or, where this is not practicable, in the language most commonly used by the group to which they belong.
2. Provision shall be made for a progressive transition from the mother tongue or the vernacular language to the national language or to one of the official languages of the country.
3. Appropriate measures shall, as far as possible, be taken to preserve the mother tongue or the vernacular language.

Article 24
The imparting of general knowledge and skills that will help children to become integrated into the national community shall be an aim of primary education for the populations concerned.

Article 25
Educational measures shall be taken among other sections of the national community and particularly among those that are in most direct contact with the populations concerned with the object of eliminating prejudices that they may harbour in respect of these populations.

Article 26
1. Governments shall adopt measures, appropriate to the social and cultural characteristics of the populations concerned, to make known to them their rights and duties, especially in regard to labour and social welfare.
2. If necessary this shall be done by means of written translations and through the use of media of mass communication in the languages of these populations.

Part VII. Administration

Article 27

1. The governmental authority responsible for the matters covered in this Convention shall create or develop agencies to administer the programmes involved.
2. These programmes shall include:
    (a) planning, co-ordination and execution of appropriate measures for the social, economic and cultural development of the populations concerned;
    (b) proposing of legislative and other measures to the competent authorities;
    (c) supervision of the application of these measures.

Part VIII. General Provisions

Article 28

The nature and the scope of the measures to be taken to give effect to this Convention shall be determined in a flexible manner, having regard to the conditions characteristic of each country.

Article 29

The application of the provisions of this Convention shall not affect benefits conferred on the populations concerned in pursuance of other Conventions and Recommendations.

Article 30

The formal ratifications of this Convention shall be communicated to the Director-General of the International Labour Office for registration.

Article 31

1. This Convention shall be binding only upon those Members of the International Labour Organisation whose ratifications have been registered with the Director-General.
2. It shall come into force twelve months after the date on which the ratifications of two Members have been registered with the Director-General.
3. Thereafter, this Convention shall come into force for any Member twelve months after the date on which its ratifications has been registered.

Article 32

1. A Member which has ratified this Convention may denounce it after the expiration of ten years from the date on which the Convention first comes into force, by an act communicated to the Director-General of the International Labour Office for

registration. Such denunciation shall not take effect until one year after the date on which it is registered.

2. Each Member which has ratified this Convention and which does not, within the year following the expiration of the period of ten years mentioned in the preceding paragraph, exercise the right of denunciation provided for in this Article, will be bound for another period of ten years and, thereafter, may denounce this Convention at the expiration of each period of ten years under the terms provided for in this Article.

Article 33

1. The Director-General of the International Labour Office shall notify all Members of the International Labour Organisation of the registration of all ratifications and denunciations communicated to him by the Members of the Organisation.

2. When notifying the Members of the Organisation of the registration of the second ratification communicated to him, the Director-General shall draw the attention of the Members of the Organisation to the date upon which the Convention will come into force.

Article 34

The Director-General of the International Labour Office shall communicate to the Secretary-General of the United Nations for registration in accordance with Article 102 of the Charter of the United Nations full particulars of all ratifications and acts of denunciation registered by him in accordance with the provisions of the preceding Articles.

Article 35

At such times as it may consider necessary the Governing Body of the International Labour Office shall present to the General Conference a report on the working of this Convention and shall examine the desirability of placing on the agenda of the Conference the question of its revision in whole or in part.

Article 36

1. Should the Conference adopt a new Convention revising this Convention in whole or in part, then, unless the new Convention otherwise provides:

(a) the ratification by a Member of the new revising Convention shall ipso jure involve the immediate denunciation of this Convention, notwithstanding the provisions of Article 32 above, if and when the new revising Convention shall have come into force;

(b) as from the date when the new revising Convention comes into force this Convention shall cease to be open to ratification by the Members.

2. This Convention shall in any case remain in force in its actual form and content for those Members which have ratified it but have not ratified the revising Convention.

Article 37

The English and French versions of the text of this Convention are equally authoritative.

APPENDIX III

How the ILO Adopts Standards

As this is a different process from that of other international organizations, it is worth detailing it.

General Description

The ILO is the most prolific standard-setting organisation at the international level. It was established for the purpose of setting standards in 1919,[1] when it was founded together with the League of Nations, and from that time has steadily adopted Conventions and Recommendations on a regular basis. Over the nearly 100 years of its existence, the ILO has adopted 189 Conventions, 6 Protocols and 203 Recommendations, as of 2014. It has also taken measures to consolidate these standards, and to keep the corpus up to date.

Because of the volume of standard setting carried out by the ILO, elaborate rules and procedures are in place, and there are numerous decisions of ILO bodies about how to proceed. A schematic of the procedure is attached.

The ILO's tripartite structure is determinant for the way it sets standards. Members of the Organization are States, as for other intergovernmental organizations; but unlike other organisations the delegations to the annual Conference and to other ILO bodies consist of mixed governmental and non-governmental delegations who are selected by each country from among the 'most representative' employers' and workers' organizations. The ILO's employers' and workers' delegates have 25% each of the voting power in the Conference.

Another characteristic is that the adoption of standards by the ILO is faster than in other organizations, and takes place according to a fixed schedule. From the time a decision is taken in the Governing Body to put a subject on the Conference agenda, a new instrument is normally adopted in 43 months; indeed, it is possible to know from the beginning the date – and practically the hour – at which a new instrument will be adopted.

One of the most important features of the ILO standard-setting system is that a large degree of consensus is reached before a new instrument is put on the agenda. Where this does not happen – for instance, when the Governing Body thinks it has

---

1 The preamble to the ILO Constitution makes it clear that it was necessary to regulate conditions of work to prevent social injustice, and the adoption and supervision of Conventions and Recommendations are referred to extensively throughout the text.

more of a consensus than it in fact has, or when a decision is reached over the objections of one of the parties – then the process is much more difficult and has been known to fail.

Though a degree of consensus is necessary at all stages, there may also be strongly-held divergent views among the different forces among ILO constituents. The ILO Conference is prepared to vote to take decisions, and on occasion a two-week discussion may involve dozens of votes on hundreds of proposed amendments. The ILO does not have to wait for consensus to emerge before a provision can be adopted.

ILO Conventions may not be ratified with reservations – a fundamental difference from other international conventions. Consequently, the International Labour Conference carefully considers whether flexibility clauses should be included, allowing choices to be made within carefully defined limits.

The ILO has evolved different kinds of standards for different purposes, some of which are binding once ratified and have immediately executable obligations, and some with more promotional aspects.

Finally, the role of the ILO staff is very important. The International Labour Office (the permanent secretariat) in most cases makes the proposals from among which the political bodies choose standard-setting subjects. This is based on technical analysis of gaps in the body of standards, on needs to address issues in a changing legal context, and often on years of work before proposals are made. During the process, the staff sets out the questions that are to be examined, analyses the position of the constituents, prepares drafts, and proposes and negotiates solutions. Decisions, of course, remain firmly in the hands of the constituents.

Detailed Description

ILO standards are adopted by the International Labour Conference, which meets annually (in May/June), and from time to time in special session for maritime affairs. There is almost always at least one standard-setting item on the agenda, though the pace has been somewhat slower in recent years than previously.

Inclusion of a subject on the agenda of the Conference. It is usually the Governing Body[2] that sets the Conference agenda (ILO Constitution, art. 14(1)). The Conference itself can also decide to include a question on the agenda of its next session (art. 16(3)). Subjects are normally chosen from proposals by the Office, but may also come from proposals by member States and employers' and workers'

---

2 The Governing Body of the International Labour Office is composed of 56 members, half of which are governments, with 14 worker and 14 employer members, elected for three-year terms by the International Labour Conference.

organisations, regional conferences, technical meetings, or by any public international organisation.

Another way ideas can arise for standard-setting is from the work of the ILO supervisory bodies. Each year the Committee of Experts on the Application of Conventions and Recommendations – the ILO's principal supervisory body – carries out a General Survey on one or several instruments. Though much longer (book length) these surveys have some of the attributes of the "General comments" adopted by UN treaty bodies, in consolidating and restating the Committee's understanding of the meaning of Conventions and Recommendations. They also examine obstacles to ratification and the situation generally in non-ratifying States. In addition to all this, General Surveys in recent years have examined whether the instruments they cover are fully up to date, and on occasion have recommended changes.

The Governing Body normally discusses the proposed Conference agenda at two sessions, in November each year and in March of the following year, the definitive decision being taken at the March session. The Office submits to the Governing Body a preliminary report on each of the subjects being submitted at the first discussion, and then a shorter list based on discussions for the March session, so that it may select one or more of them for the Conference agenda.[3] The agenda adopted is for the Conference session two years later, in order to be able to comply with the delays laid down in the Standing Orders of the Conference for the preparatory work for standards.

The Governing Body may submit a subject for discussion by a preparatory technical conference before taking a decision on its inclusion on the agenda of the Conference (article 14(2), Constitution). When maritime Conventions are being considered, the maritime sessions of the Conference are preceded by the Joint Maritime Commission, and by a tripartite meeting on the proposed standards.

Implications of tripartism. The ILO is the only international organisation in which governments do not have all the votes. Its particular (and uniquely privileged[4]) NGOs are national and international workers' and employers' organisations. Each government is obliged to send to the Conference 4 delegates – 2 governmental and one each

---

3 If a government objects to the decision, the Conference itself decides on its agenda by a two-thirds majority vote (art. 16(1) and (2), Constitution). This is more a theoretical possibility than an actual practice.

4 Workers' and employers' organisations are empowered under the ILO Constitution to file complaints, to submit reports on the application of ratified and unratified Conventions, and to be consulted in various ways, beyond the rights accorded to NGOs in other intergovernmental organisations; but other NGOs have fewer rights than in the ILO than in the UN.

to represent employers' and workers' organisations.[5] The voting structure provides that the non-governmental delegations have 50% of the voting capacity in the Conference – and at the committee level where the detailed negotiations go on, workers, employers and governments each have one-third of the voting rights.

Kinds of instruments adopted. The Constitution provides for the adoption of Conventions and Recommendations, which are what is usually meant when referring to international labour standards. *Conventions* are drafted as treaties, and may be ratified, creating binding obligations. Conventions may on occasion be supplemented by *Protocols* that amend or supplement the original instrument. *Recommendations* are what the name suggests, and are drafted as guidance. They may be adopted independently of Conventions, but often are adopted together with them, in which case the Recommendation supplements the Convention and adds additional provisions to help understand or add to the ideas in the Conventions.

Other standard-setting options include *Declarations*, which have been adopted on several occasions. The Declaration of Philadelphia was adopted in 1944 to update the objectives of the Constitution as World War II drew to a close, and was incorporated into the Constitution in 1946. The Tripartite Declaration of Principles concerning Multinational Enterprises and Social Policy was adopted in 1976 and updated in 2000 and 2006. In 1998 the Conference adopted the very important Declaration of Fundamental Principles and Rights at Work, complemented 10 years later in 2008 by the Declaration on Social Justice for a Fair Globalization. Both the latter instruments launched promotional follow-up procedures, compared with the more binding supervisory procedures that apply to Conventions and Recommendations.

Finally, the ILO adopts codes of practice, which are usually drafted by technical meetings and endorsed by the Governing Body. A recent example is the ILO code of practice on HIV/AIDS and the world of work, later endorsed by the UN General Assembly, and then supplemented in 2009 by a Recommendation on the same subject.

Double discussion procedure. The Conference usually adopts Conventions and Recommendations after discussing the subject at two successive sessions of the Conference. This procedure, which is laid down in the Standing Orders of the Conference, follows a very precise schedule, under which the Conference has before it four preparatory reports.

The first report is prepared by the Office immediately after the March session of the Governing Body at which the Conference agenda is fixed. It consists of a comparative

---

5   Delegations are often much larger, with all three parts of the delegation bringing "advisers", but only 4 delegates have voting rights in the ILC plenary. The annual Conference assembling the 185 ILO member States often counts more than 4,000 participants.

study of the existing law and practice on the subject at the national and international levels, and concludes with a questionnaire on the points that might be included in the text(s) to be adopted. This report must be communicated to governments so as to reach them not less than 12 months before the opening of the session at which the question is to be discussed. Governments then have 4 months to send their replies, after consultation with the representative organisations of employers and workers in their countries. A specific question in the questionnaire always refers to difficulties that might be encountered in each country in applying the proposed standards, so that flexibility clauses may be included (this technique is examined below).

On the basis of the replies received, the Office prepares a second report containing an analysis of replies and proposed conclusions for the Conference. This report is sent to governments so as to arrive at least four months before the Conference.

During the first session, the subject is discussed in a tripartite committee of the Conference with the objective of adopting conclusions. Government, employer and worker delegations normally send to such discussions representatives who know the specific subject, and are able to negotiate among themselves without referring back to national capitals. In the committee sessions, governments, and the employers' and workers' groups, each have one-third of the voting power. Where employers and workers do not agree on a particular provision, this leaves decisions in the hands of governments; but where workers and employers agree, or are able to negotiate an agreed approach, governments are at a real disadvantage because they can never achieve either the degree of unanimity or the number of votes the non-governmental delegates can.

The discussion takes place on the basis of the proposals the Office puts before the committee after the first two rounds of written consultations. Delegates support these proposals or offer amendments to them, and often there are several hundred amendments before a committee. It votes on any that cannot be resolved by discussion and consensus, and at the end of the first discussion (which in practical terms is about 7 working days), the committee presents its conclusions to the plenary of the Conference for adoption. The Conference decides at the same time to include the question for a second discussion on the agenda of its next session. The Conference may also request the Governing Body to include the question on the agenda of the next Conference.

Within two months of the end of the Conference session, the Office is required to send to governments a third report, which contains a draft Convention and/or Recommendation prepared by the Office on the basis of the first discussion. These drafts include proposals by the Office to resolve drafting difficulties or inconsistencies arising from Conference discussions, and may even include reversion to earlier suggestions or a proposal to adopt a different approach. Governments have three months to propose amendments or make observations, after consulting the employers' and workers' organisations in their countries. On the basis of the replies received, the Office prepares the fourth report, containing the amended text of the draft Convention and/or Recommendation, and sends it to governments at least three months before the session of the Conference at which the second discussion will take place.

Discussions in the second session again take place on the same basis in a technical committee of the Conference, and the text it adopts is then examined by the Conference in plenary session.

In plenary the voting power reverts to 50% for governments, and 25% each for workers and employers. Once the text has been approved in plenary, it is referred to the Drafting Committee of the Conference for a final check (including ensuring that the English and French versions are identical as they are the official languages, and also checking the Spanish). The text is then resubmitted to the Conference for final approval, for which it is necessary to obtain two-thirds of the votes cast by the members present (art. 19(2), Constitution). If this majority cannot be obtained, the Conference may decide to send a draft Convention back to the Drafting Committee to transform it into a Recommendation (though this has never in fact occurred).

Single discussion procedure. The Standing Orders of the Governing Body stipulate that in cases of special urgency or where other special circumstances exist, it may be decided by a majority of three-fifths of the votes cast that a question should be submitted to the Conference for a single discussion.[6] In this case the Office prepares a "brief" law and practice report, together with a questionnaire. The procedure then follows the course already described until the first discussion is reached, which will in this case be the only discussion for the adoption of the instrument(s). A variant before this discussion takes place is when the subject has already been discussed previously by a preparatory technical conference, in which case the Office may (if the Governing Body has so decided) simplify the procedure and submit only one report to the Conference – sent to governments four months earlier – prepared on the basis of the preparatory technical conference.

Revision of Conventions and Recommendations, and Protocols. The ILO is the only international organisation that revises the instruments it adopts. It has done so regularly since the earliest days of the Organization, when it began in the mid-1930s to revise the first minimum age Conventions to increase the age at which young people could enter the workforce. This has become increasingly more necessary as the body of standards continues to grow. Some instruments also need to be changed to reflect more modern conceptions of, for instance, the role of women in society (a prohibition on night work for women is no longer considered a protective measure, but is now seen as discrimination), or to reflect technological advances in work processes. In the case dealt with in this volume Convention No. 107 was revised to reflect more modern conceptions than were prevalent at the time of its adoption.

---

6 Standing Orders of the International Labour Conference, art. 34(7).

Revision may take place either under the special procedure provided for this purpose, or by using the normal double discussion procedure.

Effect of revision. It was decided already in 1928 that the adoption of a Convention that revises an earlier one would not result in the derogation of the older instrument.[7] A Convention might involve reciprocal obligations between States, and it is not possible to replace these automatically when the new Convention came into force. Instead, when a revised Convention is adopted, it closes the earlier instrument to further ratifications as soon as the revised Convention enters into force. Ratification of the revised Convention entails an automatic denunciation of the earlier ratification – i.e., a replacement ratification. This is the case for Convention No. 169 in relation to Convention No. 107.

Protocols. This device – used for the first time in 1982 for the Plantations Convention, 1958 (No. 110), and later for the Night Work (Women) Convention (Revised), 1949 (No. 89), and in 2014 for the Forced Labour Convention, 1030 (No. 29)[8] – is itself considered to be a kind of Convention, and therefore to be covered by the relevant provisions of the Constitution. It must be adopted by the Conference and approved by a two-thirds majority, and it is subject to the obligation of submission to the competent authorities (see below). This device was introduced for purely practical reasons, as it avoids having two different Conventions on the same subject and offers options to States with immediately visible results. In such cases both the Convention alone, and the Convention plus its protocol, normally remain open to ratification. The ratification of the Protocol modifies the obligation undertaken when ratifying the original Convention.

Flexibility of standards. Because ILO Conventions cannot be ratified with reservations,[9] they are often adopted with flexibility clauses that allow ratifying States to make choices within specified limits. Flexibility is important if international standards are to be incorporated into national law. The ILO Constitution provides in art. 19(3) that in drawing up instruments the Conference "shall have due regard to those countries in which climatic conditions, the imperfect development of industrial organization or other special circumstances make the industrial conditions substantially different and shall suggest the modifications, if any, which it considers may be required to meet the case of such countries." It is therefore important for governments and employers' and workers' organisations to point out, both in commenting on the

---

7 A Constitutional amendment that would allow derogation of out-of-date instruments is awaiting a sufficient number of ratifications to enter into force.

8 In all the device has been used 6 times.

9 It has been ILO practice since the beginning that ILO Conventions are not subject to ratification with reservations because they are negotiated in a tripartite setting and not simply by inter-State processes.

preparatory reports and in the discussions in the Conference, any special situations that should be taken into account through flexibility clauses.

Conventions and Recommendations as minimum standards. One of the major influences on the way they are drafted is that ILO standards are *minimum* standards, intended to establish a platform from which national law may evolve, and to promote the improvement of law and practice at the national level. They are based both on national law and practice, and on a need to improve that law and practice. They should be attainable by most nations, even when the standards they set are below the level of the most advanced nations.

However, they may never be used as a pretext for reducing protections already guaranteed for workers. This is stated clearly in the ILO Constitution, in art. 19(8): "In no case shall the adoption of any Convention or Recommendation by the Conference, or the ratification of any Convention by any Member, be deemed to affect any law, award, custom or agreement which ensures more favourable conditions to the workers concerned than those provided for in the Convention or Recommendation."

This provision entails three implicit consequences. First, while the conditions established by law may be reduced to the level of a ratified Convention by a unilateral decision of the government, such a reduction is not an automatic consequence of ratification. In other words, the Constitution does not oblige governments to maintain working conditions higher than those explicitly provided for in a Convention.[10]

Second, the constitutional provision is applicable to national standards which exceed the requirements of a Convention but which are not inconsistent with it. Therefore, the more favourable nature of a national provision or practice cannot be invoked if this infringes a ratified Convention.[11]

Third, a ratified Convention puts a lower limit on the degree to which conditions may be reduced, if a government should decide to lower them.

Consultation of the most representative organisations. It has been noted above that under the procedure established for the preparation of a Convention or a Recommendation, governments are asked to consult the most representative organisations of employers and workers when they reply to the questionnaire in the first report, and when they send their observations on the third report containing the draft text of the Convention or Recommendation. This procedure, incorporated by the Conference into its Standing Orders in 1987, follows the line already established since 1971 on the basis of the resolution adopted in that year on the strengthening of tripartism in all the ILO's activities.

The consultation procedure is based on an invitation made to governments and is not obligatory. The situation is different, however, if a country has ratified the Tripartite

---

10   *OB*, Vol. XVII, 1932, No. 1; and *OB*, Vol. XXIII, 1938, No. 1.
11   *OB*, Vol. LV, 1972, Nos. 2, 3 and 4, paras. 82 and 83.

Consultation (International Labour Standards) Convention, 1976 (No. 144), which provides that the most representative organisations of employers and workers must be consulted on governments' replies to questionnaires on items on the agenda of the Conference and on governments' comments on proposed texts to be discussed by the Conference (Art. 5(a)). This Convention has now received 138 ratifications, and is thus binding on the majority of member States.

HOW THE ILO ADOPTS STANDARDS

Adoption of Conventions and Recommendations

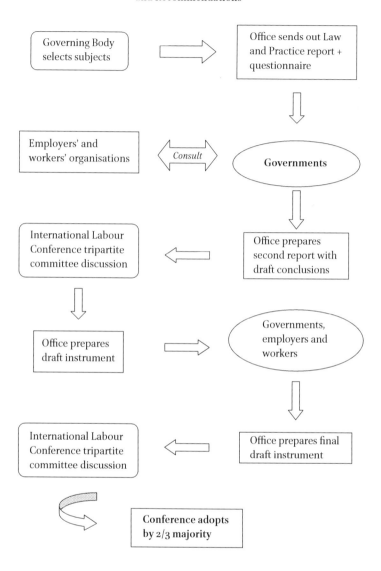

APPENDIX IV

Major Documents Consulted and Citation in this Volume

All the materials cited here are on line on the ILO web site – www.ilo.org.

The ILO normally adopts Conventions and Recommendations by the 'double discussion method', i.e., after written consultations with the constituents, the subject is discussed at two successive sessions of the International Labour Conference, and on the second occasion the new standards are adopted. This was the method used in both 1956/1957 (Convention No. 107) and in 1988/1989 (Convention No. 169).

1. *Reports by the International Labour Office.*

After a subject is placed on the Conference agenda by the Governing Body, the Office prepares a 'law and practice report' which summarizes the reasons the subject is before the Conference, and action taken so far by the ILO and at the national level. This report contains a questionnaire on the points the constituents would like to see in the new standards.

See Reports VIII (1) of 1956 and VI (1) of 1988.

A second report then summarizes the replies of the constituents, and proposes draft conclusions for the first discussion.

See Reports VIII (2) of 1956 and VI (2) of 1988.

The third report summarizes the discussion and conclusions of the first Conference discussion, and proposes draft standards for comment by the constituents.

See Reports V (1) of 1957 and IV (1) of 1989.

The final report prepared by the Office analyses the replies of the constituents and submits a revised draft of the standards.

See Report VI (2) of 1957 and Report IV (2A and 2B) of 1989.[1]

The first and second discussions in the Conference are reported in the Proceedings of the Conference for the relevant year. First is the report of the Committee concerned, followed by a verbatim transcript of the discussion in plenary session.

---

[1] In 1957 the analysis of replies and the draft instruments were included in the same volume of the final report to the Conference – Report VI (2). By 1989 the practice had changed, and this report was by now issued in two parts – Report IV (2A) contains the analysis of replies, and Report IV (2B) contains the draft instrument for Conference discussion.

1. *Preparation of Convention No. 107*

Report VIII (1), International Labour Conference, 39th Session (1956): *Living and Working Conditions of Indigenous Populations in Independent Countries* (Geneva, 1956)

Report VIII (2), International Labour Conference, 39th Session (1956): *Living and Working Conditions of Indigenous Populations in Independent Countries* (Geneva, 1956)

Report VI (1), International Labour Conference, 40th Session (1957): *Protection and Integration of Indigenous and other Tribal and Semi-Tribal populations in Independent Countries* (Geneva, 1957)

Report VI (2), International Labour Conference, 40th Session (1957): *Protection and Integration of Indigenous and other Tribal and Semi-Tribal populations in Independent Countries* (Geneva, 1957)

Record of Proceedings, International Labour Conference, 39th Session, Geneva, 1956

– Appendix XI : Report of the Committee on Living and working conditions of indigenous populations in independent countries, pp. 736–751
– Report of the Committee on Indigenous Populations: Submission and discussion, pp. 530–536, and 539–546

Record of Proceedings, International Labour Conference, 40th Session, Geneva, 1957

– Appendix IX : Report of the Committee on Protection and Integration of Indigenous and Other Tribal and Semi-Tribal Populations in Independent Countries, pp. 722–740
– Report of the Committee on Indigenous Populations: Submission and discussion, pp. 400–409, and 412–417

2. *Preparation of Convention No. 169*

Report VI (1), International Labour Conference, 75th Session (1988), *Partial revision of the Indigenous and Tribal Populations Convention, 1957 (No. 107)* (Geneva, 1988). (In an Appendix this report included extracts of the Report of the Meeting of Experts that took place in 1986.)

Report VI (2), International Labour Conference, 75th Session (1988), *Partial revision of the Indigenous and Tribal Populations Convention, 1957 (No. 107)* (Geneva, 1988)

Report IV (1), International Labour Conference, 76th Session 1989, *Partial revision of the Indigenous and Tribal Populations Convention, 1957 (No. 107)*

Report IV (2A), International Labour Conference, 76th Session 1989, *Partial revision of the Indigenous and Tribal Populations Convention, 1957 (No. 107)*

Report IV (2B), International Labour Conference, 76th Session 1989, *Partial revision of the Indigenous and Tribal Populations Convention, 1957 (No. 107)*

Record of Proceedings, International Labour Conference, 75th Session, Geneva, 1988

- Report of the Committee on Convention No. 107: pp. 32/1 to 32/28
- Report of the Committee on Convention No. 107: Submission and discussion, pp. 36/1 to 36/3, and 36/17 to 36/24

Record of Proceedings, International Labour Conference, 76th Session, Geneva, 1989

- Report of the Committee on Convention No. 107, pp. 25/1 to 25/32
- Report of the Committee on Convention No. 107: Submission and discussion, pp. 31/1 to 31/17

APPENDIX V

Interpretation of Convention No. 169

While the formal interpretation of ILO Conventions is reserved to the International Court of Justice, from time to time Governments ask the Office for a written indication of how it believes a Convention should be applied. These are informally designated as interpretations, and are published as a 'Memorandum of the International Labour Office' and circulated to the ILO's constituents.

There has been one such interpretation of Convention No. 169, requested by Switzerland on the instrument's coverage, and published in 2001. The text follows:

> ILC: Interpretation of a decision concerning Convention No. 169, Indigenous and Tribal Peoples, 1989 – Switzerland. Published: 2001

Memorandum by the International Labour Office

1. In a letter dated 20 December 2000, the Director of the Federal Department of Economic Affairs (SECO) sought the Office's official and formal opinion on the scope of certain provisions of the Indigenous and Tribal Peoples Convention, 1989 (No. 169), with a view to clarifying a number of questions that had arisen in examining options for ratification of the Convention.

2. Subject to the customary reservation that the Constitution of the International Labour Organization confers no special competence upon the ILO to interpret the Conventions, the Office must limit itself to providing governments that so request with information enabling them to assess the appropriate scope of any given provision of a Convention, while taking into account any relevant elements that may have emerged from the ILO's preparatory work and the comments of its supervisory bodies. It is primarily up to the governments concerned to judge whether or not their national law and practice are or can be compatible with the standards laid down in the international labour Convention in question, subject – in the event of the latter's ratification – to the procedures established by the International Labour Organization for the review of reports relating to the application of ratified Conventions at international level.

3. The first two questions raised by the Federal Department concern the field of application of the Convention:

– Question 1: Could travellers, such as those of Jenish, Roma or Gypsy origin, be covered by Convention No. 169 (knowing that there has been only scant discussion of

the matter, but considering the conditions laid down in Article 1 (paragraphs 1(a) and 2 in particular)?
- Question 2: Could there be any legal justification for preventing travellers from being covered by Convention No. 169?

4. The Convention's field of application is defined in Article 1, which distinguishes tribal peoples from peoples regarded as indigenous, with the reservation under paragraph 3 that the term 'peoples' 'shall not be construed as having any implications as regards the rights which may attach to the term under international law'.

5. Paragraphs 1 and 2 of Article 1 read as follows:

   1. This Convention applies to:
      (a)   tribal peoples in independent countries whose social, cultural and economic conditions distinguish them from other sections of the national community, and whose status is regulated wholly or partially by their own customs or traditions or by special laws or regulations;
      (b)   peoples in independent countries who are regarded as indigenous on account of their descent from the populations which inhabited the country, or a geographical region to which the country belongs, at the time of conquest or colonisation or the establishment of present state boundaries and who, irrespective of their legal status, retain some or all of their own social, economic, cultural and political institutions.
   2. Self-identification as indigenous or tribal shall be regarded as a fundamental criterion for determining the groups to which the provisions of this Convention apply.

6. In the case at issue, the criteria relating to indigenous peoples, as specified in paragraph 1(b) of the said Article, are not relevant; indeed, the questions that arise pertain to travellers in a State that has neither been conquered nor colonized, and whose boundaries have not been modified.

7. The criteria relating to tribal peoples covered by paragraph 1(a) are the social, cultural and economic conditions that distinguish such peoples from other sections of the national community, on the one hand, and the specific customs or traditions or the special legislation that wholly or partially regulate their status, on the other. Moreover, paragraph 2 of the said Article introduces 'a fundamental criterion for determining the groups to which the provisions of this Convention apply', namely that of self-identification – in this particular instance that of self-identification as a tribal group. Self-identification as tribal is the prerogative of the members of the community in question, who regard themselves as a 'people', whereas determining the groups to which the provisions of the Convention apply should fall within the purview of the ratifying member States.

8. The question as to whether such a people in particular (i.e. travellers) meets the criteria set out in Article 1 of Convention No. 169, and is hence covered by its

provisions, is an issue of fact that lies within the competence of the State ratifying the Convention.

9. Pursuant to the principle according to which treaties must be applied in good faith, a Member that ratifies this Convention should apply the provisions thereof to any people fulfilling the criteria under Article 1, paragraph 1(a), from the moment that self-identification as tribal has been established. The wording of the Article is clear: 'This Convention applies to: (a) tribal peoples; (b) peoples in independent countries who are regarded as indigenous (on condition, obviously, that such peoples meet the stipulated criteria. The texts of the relevant provisions are self-explanatory. The following details, drawn from the preparatory work on the Convention, may nevertheless throw some useful light on the issue.

10. The Meeting of Experts on the Revision of the Indigenous and Tribal Populations Convention, 1957 (No. 107), convened by the ILO Governing Body in 1986, noted that the Convention should be 'applicable also to nomadic populations in desert and other regions. All of these groups share certain characteristics such as being relatively isolated and less economically developed than the rest of the national community. This wide degree of coverage should not be modified, although it does make it more difficult to adopt language which is sufficiently flexible to cover all these situations'.[1]

11. In presenting the report on the partial revision of Convention No. 107,[2] the Office noted, in regard to the future instrument, that:

It must include clear statements on the basic rights of these peoples. It must also take into account that there are indigenous and tribal peoples in almost every country. Their situations are similar enough to make it possible to formulate certain fundamental rights which apply to all these peoples, wherever they are found. They should all have the right to retain their cultures and to manage their own affairs, and the countries where they live should respect these rights. The extent to which these needs exist in every State, and the manner in which these rights should be respected in every case, is not for an ILO Convention to determine in any global manner; instead, it should establish the basic principle of respect for these rights, and require ratifying countries to take the measures necessary to decide at the national level, in consultation with those affected, how they should be implemented.

- Question 3: May a State ratifying Convention No. 169 exclude a group of individuals from its coverage? What would be the legal status of such a declaration?
- Question 4: May a State ratifying Convention No. 169 exclude one or several of the obligations stipulated under the Convention?

12. The general structure of the Convention does not provide for any mechanism allowing a member State that ratifies the instrument to exclude one or several indigenous or

---

[1] Report of the Meeting of Experts, GB.234/5/4, para. 33.
[2] Report VI (1), International Labour Conference, 75th Session (1988), Partial revision of the Indigenous and Tribal Populations Convention, 1957 (No. 107) (Geneva, 1988), p. 90.

tribal peoples from its coverage; it conversely provides for the inclusion of peoples fulfilling the criteria set out in Article 1.[3] In this connection, a declaration that was to exclude a priori one or several peoples meeting the criteria under Article 1 would constitute a reservation not admissible under general ILO practice. Consequently, any exclusion would prevent registration of the ratification instrument containing a declaration to that effect.

13. It must therefore be concluded from the above that no provision of the Convention would allow exclusion of travellers from its coverage if they meet the objective criteria stipulated under Article 1, paragraph 1(a), of the Convention and if they fulfil the basic criterion of self-identification as a tribal people.

— Question 5: Has the definition of tribal peoples by a State ratifying Convention No. 169 ever been challenged by the supervisory bodies?

14. The issue has not been raised so far in the context of Convention No. 169. That being said, the comments put forward by the Committee of Experts on the question of the definition of a tribal population in the framework of the Indigenous and Tribal Populations Convention, 1957 (No. 107), would be relevant in the case of Convention No. 169, which constitutes a revision of Convention No. 107 and contains similar provisions. The definitions adopted by the ratifying countries have hitherto been endorsed by the Committee of Experts, although on several occasions the Committee has discussed the matter with the countries concerned. For example, in the context of Convention No. 107, Egypt does not consider the Bedouin as tribal populations, whereas the Syrian Arab Republic regards them as such. For many years now, the Committee has been engaged in dialogue with Iraq on the issue of the peoples of the southern marshlands, whom Iraq does not regard as a tribal population covered by Convention No. 107. More recently, the Committee took note of a declaration by the Angolan Government (in the context of Convention No. 107), according to which, for the purposes of applying the Convention, there are no indigenous populations on Angolan territory.

— Question 6: Could a State that has not included a group fulfilling the criteria under Article 1 of Convention No. 169 be compelled to recognize such a group as being covered by the Convention, following a representation (article 24 of the ILO Constitution) or a complaint (article 26)?

15. The Office cannot predetermine what position the Governing Body would adopt in regard to the recommendations of a tripartite committee charged with examining, pursuant to article 24 of the Constitution, application of the Convention in this respect or that adopted by a commission of inquiry appointed pursuant to article 26. On the

---

3   The Swedish Government's proposal that a flexibility clause be included to allow exclusion of certain provisions of the Convention was not retained (International Labour Conference, 76th Session, Geneva, 1989, Report IV(2A), p. 4).

assumption that the subject-matter of the representation or the complaint was to establish whether a given group fulfilled the criteria under Article 1 of the Convention, the Member in question would have to draw the consequences of a recommendation confirming the above and take appropriate action, subject, in the event of a complaint, to the provisions of article 29, paragraph 2, of the ILO Constitution.

- Question 7: Could a lack of interest or will on the part of the members of a minority group (or its representatives) to be covered by a Convention, either during the preparatory work on the Convention or at a later stage, have an impact on their stance vis-à-vis the instrument in question?
- Question 8: If the members of a minority group, or its representatives, have stated that they do not consider themselves to be either concerned or covered by Convention No. 169, is it possible for them to change their position?

16. As regards the consequences of a people or its representatives showing no interest in the Convention at a given moment, for example at the time of its adoption, it must be recalled that the Convention sets no time limit for the expression of self-identification. Similarly, failure on the part of a people or its representatives to demonstrate any interest at a given moment (be it the time of adoption of the instrument) has no legal implications for the future. Lack of interest in the Convention on the part of a group that meets the aforementioned objective criteria is a question of fact which implies – for as long as lack of interest persists – that the ratifying Member concerned would be under no obligation to apply the Convention's provisions to such a group. The group in question may aim to obtain another status, without its choice being exclusive and precluding subsequent expression of self-identification as a tribal people within the meaning of Article 1, paragraph 2, of the Convention.

- Question 9: May a tribal people consider that the participation of children in its traditional activities, such as street trading and peddling, forms part of its traditional work and is hence necessary to the children's training and education? Could this lead to a conflict of standards for a member State having ratified Conventions Nos. 169 and 138? To what extent would Convention No. 169, as *lex specialis*, take precedence over Convention No. 138?

17. Article 8, paragraph 2, of Convention No. 169 reads as follows:

2. These peoples shall have the right to retain their own customs and institutions, where these are not incompatible with fundamental rights defined by the national legal system and with internationally recognised human rights. Procedures shall be established, whenever necessary, to resolve conflicts which may arise in the application of this principle.

18. The participation of children in traditional activities such as street trading and peddling must be consistent with the above provision, which refers inter alia to internationally recognized human rights. Specifically regarding the Minimum Age Convention, 1973 (No. 138), the International Labour Conference, in adopting in 1998 the ILO

Declaration on Fundamental Principles and Rights at Work, has included this instrument among the fundamental ILO Conventions.[4]

19. The measures of protection relative to child labour set forth in Convention No. 138 should apply to traditional activities. Hence, in the case of a Member having ratified Convention No. 169, account must be taken of the provision in Article 8, paragraph 2, thereof, which stipulates that procedures shall be established 'to resolve conflicts which may arise in the application of this principle'. Convention No. 138, in its Articles 7 and 8 in particular, allows, under certain conditions, exceptions to the prohibition of employment or work laid down in its Article 2. Such exceptions might meet the needs of travellers in terms of their traditional activities. This is a question of fact that lies within the competence of the Member ratifying the Convention, subject to the supervisory bodies' views on the matter.

– Question 10: If travellers were to be covered by the field of application of Convention No. 169, would a State party to Convention No. 169 be under the obligation to place at their disposal land for transit purposes or certain sites traditionally used as temporary stopping places, since such sites are considered necessary to the traditional way of life of travellers?

20. Article 14, paragraph 1, of the Convention stipulates in particular that 'measures shall be taken in appropriate cases to safeguard the right of the peoples concerned to use lands not exclusively occupied by them, but to which they have traditionally had access for their subsistence and traditional activities. Particular attention shall be paid to the situation of nomadic peoples and shifting cultivators in this respect'.

21. It should be noted that Article 14, paragraph 3, of the Convention provides for the establishment of adequate procedures to resolve land claims by the peoples concerned.

22 The Convention does not specify the nature or scope of the measures to be taken in order to meet the obligation laid down in the aforementioned provisions. While the principle of the obligation is clearly established – namely to safeguard the right of the peoples concerned to use lands not exclusively occupied by them for their traditional activities, with special attention to the situation of nomadic peoples – the modalities of implementation are left up to each Member, subject to compliance with the procedural obligations under the Convention, in particular consultation of the peoples involved. In this connection, Article 34 stipulates that the nature and scope of such measures 'shall be determined in a flexible manner, having regard to the conditions characteristic of each country'. Leeway in terms of implementation does not, however, release a Member party to the Convention from its obligation under Article 14.

– Question 11: May a State ratify an ILO Convention that is not directly or indirectly relevant to it?

---

4 Convention No. 138 was ratified by Switzerland on 18 August 1999.

23. Pursuant to the Convention's final provisions, formal ratifications of the instrument are to be communicated to the Director-General for registration. The role of the depository is to ascertain that a ratification instrument meets a number of formal conditions. If such is the case, the depository is duty bound to register the ratification in accordance with the said provisions.

- Question 12: May a State that declares not to have any tribal population on its territory, and for which Convention No. 169 is hence not relevant, ratify the Convention with the sole aim of using it as an instrument of foreign policy, in particular in order to avail itself of the procedures for making a representation or a complaint (article 26 of the ILO Constitution) against another State having ratified this Convention? Would a ratification of this nature and recourse to such procedures be consistent with the principle of good faith, as defined in the Vienna Convention on the Law of Treaties?

24. Registration of an instrument of ratification of an international convention containing a statement to the effect that the sole aim of ratification was to resort to the complaints procedures might give rise to difficulties. As indicated above, a Member that ratifies a Convention accepts the obligations stemming therefrom, without being entitled to make any reservation or to exclude any provision unless exclusion is permitted under the Convention itself. The expression 'sole aim' – in this instance the lodging of a complaint – might be construed as excluding other obligations under the Convention and therefore hamper the ratification registration process. In any event, if a Member were to declare that it had no indigenous or tribal population on its territory, its statement would be subject to examination by the supervisory bodies and might be challenged on the basis of the procedures provided for under articles 24 and 26 of the ILO Constitution.

25. The question as to whether a Member that were to avail itself of the complaint procedures in the hypothetical case described in Question 12 would be complying with the principle of application in good faith of ratified treaties, as defined in the Vienna Convention on the Law of Treaties, is not a matter of interpretation of the Convention but of the ILO Constitution, on which the Office can offer no response.

Index

Adoption of Convention No. 107   17
Adoption of standards   Appendix III, 370
Andean Indian Programme   15, 18, 26
Article 1 of Convention No. 107 – coverage   45
   Conclusions adopted 1956   53
   Conference discussion 1956   51
   Conference discussion 1957   56
   Draft Convention 1957   55
   Indigenous Peoples   45
   Indigenous and tribal terminology   46
   Law and Practice report 1956   45
   Proposed conclusions 1956   51
   Questionnaire 1956   47
   Replies and analysis 1956   48
Article 1 of Convention No. 169 –
   Coverage   43, 57
   Conclusions adopted 1988   76
   Conference discussion 1988   69
   Conference discussion 1989   76
      First draft Convention   77
      Final draft Convention   80
      Adoption with understanding   85
   Cultural inferiority   63
   Development through supervision   89
      Identifying those covered   89, 91
      Establishment of legal identity   90
      Self-identification   99
   Indigenous and tribal   43, 45, 59, 63
   Interpretation requested by
      Switzerland   90, Appendix III
   Law and Practice report 1988   61
   Meeting of Experts 1986   57
   Peoples or populations   57, 61, 66, 68, 77, 80
   Proposed conclusions 1988   68
   Replies and analysis 1988   66
   Replies and analysis 1989   77
   Qualifying clause   79
   Questionnaire 1988   65
   Tribal and semi-tribal   60
Article 2 of Convention No. 107 – basic orientation   107
   Conclusions adopted 1956   113
   Conclusions proposed 1956   110
   Conference discussion 1956   111
   Conference Discussion 1957   115

Draft Convention 1957   115
Questionnaire 1956   109
Article 2 of Convention No. 169 – basic orientation and principles   107
   Convention No. 107 antecedents   107
   Change in orientation   117
   Conclusions proposed 1988   127
   Conference discussion 1988   127
   Conference discussion 1989   135
   Development through supervision   137
      Administrative arrangements   138
      Co-ordinated management   140
      Functioning of arrangements   143
      Related to Article 33   149
   Final draft Convention 1989   135
   First draft of Convention 1989   133
   Integrationist language outdated   118
   Meeting of Experts 1986   118
   Questionnaire 1988   122
   Replies   and analysis 1988   123
Article 6 of Convention No. 169 –
   Consultation   148
   Convention No. 107 antecedents   149
      Article 5 – collaboration   149
      Conference discussion 1956   151
      Conference discussion 1957   153
      Cultural arrogance   149
      First draft Convention 1957   152
      Proposed conclusions 1956   150
   Convention No. 169   154
      Conference discussion 1988   161, 169
      Conference discussion 1989   177
      Indigenous peoples' reactions   176
      Meeting of Experts   154
      Final draft Convention 1989   175
      First draft Convention 1989   172
      Proposed conclusions 1988   169
      Questionnaire 1988   166
      Replies and analysis 1989   174
      Right to a veto   177
      Terminology 1989   173
      Paragraph 2   179
   Development through supervision   182
      General observation 2011   182, 188
      Nature of consultations   193
      Conference Committee   184

INDEX 391

Employers' Group understanding   185
Workers' Group understanding   186
Article 7 of Convention No. 169 –
 Participation   195
 Conclusions adopted 1988   201
 Conference discussion 1988   200
 Conference discussion 1989   208
 Development through supervision   210
  General observation 2008   210
 Final draft of Convention 1989   207
 First draft of Convention 1989   205
 Law and Practice report   197
 Meeting of Experts   196
 Proposed conclusions 1988   200
 Questionnaire 1988   198
 Replies and analysis 1989   206
Article 34 of Convention No. 169   208
Articles 11 to 14 of Convention No. 107 – Land rights   224
 Law and Practice report   225
 Questionnaire 1956   226
 Government comments 1957   241
 Office commentary 1957   241
Article 11 of Convention No. 107   237
 Origin   237
 Conference discussion 1956   240
 Conference discussion 1957   241
 First draft Convention   241
 Final draft Convention   242
 Proposed conclusion 1956   240
 Questionnaire 1956   239
Article 12 of Convention No. 107   281
 Adoption 1957   286
 Committee of Experts on Indigenous Labour   281
 Conference discussion 1956   284
 Final draft Convention 1957   285
 First draft Convention 1957   284
 Proposed conclusions 1956   283
 Questionnaire 1956   281
 Replies and analysis 1956   282
Article 13 of Convention No. 107   301
 Conference discussion 1956   308
 Draft Convention 1957   309
 Law and Practice report 1956   302
 Questionnaire 1956   305
 Proposed conclusions 1956   307
 Replies and analysis 1956   306
Articles 13 to 19 of Convention No. 169 – Land rights   219

Background   223
Chairman's consolidated text   235
Development through supervision   334
 Consultation   334
 Demarcation of territories   339
 Information gathering   334
 Invasions of indigenous territory   338
 Involvement of religious institutions   341
 Natural resources   340
Meeting of Experts   219
Territory   231
Working Party in the Conference   231, 233
Article 13 of Convention No. 169   229
 Development   229
 Reservations expressed   236
 Submission to 1989 Conference   231
 Second paragraph added   236
Article 14 of Convention No. 107   326
 Conference discussion 1956   329
 First draft Convention 1957   329
 Final draft Convention 1957   330
 Law and Practice report 1956   326
 Proposed conclusions 1956   329
 Questionnaire 1956   328
 Replies and analysis 1956   328
Article 14 of Convention No. 169: Rights of ownership and possession   237
 Adoption as a whole   260, 263
 Based on Article 11 of Convention No. 107   243
 Conference discussion 1988   248
 Conference discussion 1989   249
 Draft Convention 1989 (first)   251
 Explanation by the Secretariat   265
 Land claims   251, 255
 Law and Practice report 1988   244
 Multiple use and nomads   252
 Procedure for second discussion   249
 Proposed conclusions 1988   248
 Questionnaire 1988   245
 Replies and analysis 1988   245
 Restitution of lands   255
 Rights vs right   248
 Traditionally   246
 Working Party 1988   248

Article 15 of Convention No. 169: Natural
    resources   266
  Changes in final version   279
  Conference discussion 1988   272
  Conference discussion 1989   275
  First draft Convention 1989   273
  Final draft Convention 1989   275
  Law and Practice report 1988   267
  Meeting of Experts 1986   266
  Proposed conclusions 1988   270, 272
  Questionnaire 1988   269
  Recommendation No. 104   266
  Replies and observations 1989   273
Article 16 of Convention No. 169:
    Removal   280
  Adequate procedures   290
  Article 12 of Convention No. 107   281
  Conference discussion 1988   294
  Conference discussion 1989   299
  Final draft Convention 1989   298
  First draft Convention 1989   295
  Free consent   290
  Kinds of removals   289
  Lands of equal status   290, 292
  Law and Practice report 1988   288
  Limitations on removals   287
  Meeting of Experts 1986   286
  Proposed conclusions 1988   293
  Questionnaire 1988   290
  Replies and analysis 1988   291
  Right to return   295
  Temporary   288
  Working Party 1989   298
Article 17 of Convention No. 169:
  Transmission of Rights   236, 301
  Article 13 of Convention No. 107   301
  Conference discussion 1988   315
  Conference discussion 1989   317
  Law and practice report 1988   310
  Proposed conclusions 1988   314
  Proposed draft 1989 (first)   315
  Proposed draft 1989 (final)   317
  Questionnaire 1988   312
  Replies and analysis 1988   312
  Replies and analysis 1989   315
  Vote on adoption 1989   320
Article 18 of Convention No. 169:
    Intrusion   322
  Law and Practice report 1988   322

  Proposed conclusions 1988   324
  First draft Convention 1989   324
  Final draft Convention 1989   325
  Questionnaire 1988   323
  Replies and analysis 1988   323
  Replies and analysis 1989   324
Article 19 of Convention No. 169: National
    Agrarian Programmes   325
  Article 14 of Convention No. 107   326
  Law and Practice report 1988   331
  Proposed conclusions 1988   331
  First draft Convention 1989   332
  Final draft Convention 1989   333
  Replies and analysis   332
  Questionnaire 1988   331
As much control as possible   164, 197, 199, 267

Background to adoption of
    Convention No. 169   15
Belief   203

Citation of materials   10, Appendix IV, 380
  Preparatory materials   11
  Reports of discussions in the
    Conference   12
  Supervisory comments   11
Citizenship, general rights of   108
Civil liberties   152
Collaboration   152
Collective rights   52, 130, 231, 241, 248
Coercion, recourse to   110
Committee of Experts on Indigenous
    Labour   281
Committee of Experts on Native
    Labour   18
Committee on the Elimination of Racial
    Discrimination   183
Competence of the ILO   15, 18
  Competence to adopt Convention
    No. 169   38
    Meeting of Experts 1986   38
  Competence to adopt Convention
    No. 107   18
    Employers' group reservations   23, 34
    Support from governments   36
    Support from the UN system   21, 31
    Support from Workers' group   27, 32
  Competence to determine meaning of
    self-determination   78

INDEX 393

Consent 129
  Requirement would prevent ratification 168
  Meaning 173
  Not required in some cases 115
  Obtaining consent 169
  Removals 286, 291
  Seeking consent 168, 173, 177, 274
Consultation 148, 156, 164, 176, 334
  Authority responsible 193
  Development through supervision 334
  Effective 166
  Full 173
  General observation 2011 182, 188
  In good faith 175
  Meaning 173, 181
  Nature of consultations 193
  Pro forma 164, 176
  Subject matter 192
Contracts of Employment (Indigenous Workers) Convention, 1939 (No. 64) 44
Control over development 120, 162, 164, 165, 199, 206, 279
Co-operation 173
Coordinated and systematic action 120, 130
Co-ordinator for Indigenous Peoples' Rights 232
Coverage
  Convention No. 169 43, 57
  Meaning of 'indigenous' and 'tribal' 43
  Convention No. 107 45
    Conference committee report 1956 53
    Conference committee report 1957 55
    First discussion 1956 51
    Second discussion 1957 55
  Convention No. 169
    First discussion 1988 69
    Second discussion 1989 80
    Geographical coverage 73
      Own territories 74
      In independent countries 73
    Coverage beyond indigenous 102
Cultural identity 131
Cultural inferiority 63, 108, 120, 149, 163
Customs and traditions 131

Declaration on the Rights of Indigenous Peoples 1, 17, 60, 88
Decolonisation 164
Demarcation of territories 339
Democratic institutions 151
Development
  Right to 125
  Top down 163
Development plans and programmes 199
Documents consulted Appendix IV, 380

Elective institutions, participation in 174
Environmental impact studies 199, 204, 216

Flexibility of measures 108, 208
Food and Agriculture Organization 18, 22, 23, 24, 25, 26, 31, 32, 35, 60, 253, 254, 261,
Force, recourse to 110, 114
Four Directions Council 82, 268

Impact studies, social and environmental 199, 279
Inalienability 247, 302, 311, 313
Independent Commission on International Humanitarian Issues 168
Indigenous Peoples – Living and Working Conditions, 1953 18, 45, 62
Indigenous
  And tribal – distinction 43, 45, 59
  In Asia 59
  In Africa 59
  Discussion 1988 61
Indigenous and Tribal Peoples Convention, 1989 (No. 169) Appendix I, 345
Indigenous and Tribal Populations Convention, 1957 (No. 107) Appendix II, 359
Individual dignity, deletion 126
Individual rights 130
Integration
  As objective of Convention No. 107 54, 58, 64, 107
  As inescapable 109
  Outdated 118, 120, 156, 160, 162
Inter-American Commission on Human Rights 217
Inter-American Indian Congress 225, 304
Inter-American Indian Institute 78, 157, 267

International Covenant on Civil and Political
    Rights 78
International Covenant on Economic, Social
    and Cultural Rights 78, 119
International Indian Treaty Council 268
International Organization of Indigenous
    Resource Development 276
Interpretation requested by Switzerland
    90, Appendix v, 383
Introduction of new forms of life and
    work 150
Inuit Circumpolar Conference 83, 232, 249,
    268, 272, 294
Invasions of indigenous territory 338

Land claims 251, 255, 258
Land rights
    Article 11 of Convention No. 107 237
    Chapter 6 219
    Definition in Article 13 of Convention
        No. 169 236, 237
    Determining the lands 245
    Inalienability 247, 302, 311, 313
    Multiple use and nomads 252
    Ownership 237, 244, 260
    Possession and use 245, 247, 260, 262
    Explanation by the Secretariat 265
    Traditionally 246
    Transforming Indian *comunidades* 225,
        304
    Usufruct 238
Legal identity or legal personality 90, 96
Less advanced cultures 54

Mandate
    See Competence
Martinez-Cobo (Sub-Commission)
    study 155, 157, 160
Meeting of Experts 1986 6, 16, 38, 40,
    57, 59, 60, 61, 62, 63, 73, 117, 118, 120, 121,
    122, 124, 128, 154, 160, 161, 162, 163, 164,
    165, 166, 168, 196, 197, 198, 221, 243, 244,
    245, 246, 247, 255, 256, 266, 267, 269,
    286, 289, 290, 292, 296, 297, 310, 311, 313,
    316, 323, 331
Members of indigenous peoples 52
MINUGUA 145, 366
Motivation, mandate and competence of the
    ILO 15

National Agrarian Programmes 325
National Indian Youth Council 232
Native Labour Code 43, 164
Natural resources 266
    Compensation 274, 280
    Distinction between surface and
        subsurface resources 270
    Exploration and exploitation 274
    Indigenous control 270
    Meeting of Experts 1986 266
    Not related to land ownership 268
    Supervision 340
Nomadic 252, 254
    Recommendation No. 104 254
Nordic Sami Council 231

Orientation of Convention No. 169 120, 128,
    154, 161
Ownership of lands 239, 248
    Ownership, possession or use 251

Participation 122, 124, 128, 164, 170, 173
    Article 7 195
    Gaps in implementation 214
    General observation 2008 210
    In benefits of resources exploitation 280
    In elective institutions 174, 178, 179
    On an equal footing 170
    Policies and programmes which concern
        them 179, 199, 214
    To at least the same extent 176, 178
    To the extent possible 199
Penal Sanctions (Indigenous Workers)
    Convention, 1939 (No. 65) 44
Peoples or populations 57, 61, 66, 68, 71, 78,
    80, 82
    First Conference discussion 1988 69
        Different meaning from other
            international law 69, 70, 72, 81
        Legal Adviser statement to Conference
            Committee 71
        '(peoples/populations)' 73
        Statements by indigenous representa-
            tives 69, 70
    Second Conference discussion
        1989 77, 79
        '(peoples/populations)' 80
        Statements by indigenous
            representatives 82

Possession and use   245, 247, 260, 262
  Explanation by the Secretariat   265
Priorities for development   199
Property rights   239

Qualifying clause Article 1   79

Recognize land rights   240
Recommendation No. 104
  Decision to adopt separate
    Recommendation   27
  Nomads   254
Recruiting on Indigenous Workers
  Convention, 1936 (No. 50)   43
Religious institutions   341
Removals
  See Article 12 of Convention No. 107 and
    Article 16 of Convention No. 169
Representation   291
Resources
  See Article 15, natural resources
Rodriguez-Pinero, Luis   15

Self-determination   58, 66, 78, 154, 156, 161, 164, 197
  Decision not to mention   157, 164
  Internal self-determination   156, 161
  Sub-Commission study   157, 160
Self-identification as fundamental   67, 75, 92, 94, 99
Self-reliance   132
Semi-tribal   35, 48, 49, 60, 64, 68
Social impact studies   199, 204, 216
Special measures   125
Spiritual relationship to territories   119, 219, 222, 229, 230, 233
Spiritual well-being   101, 131, 158, 195, 203, 204
Standard of living   132
Standards, ILO
  Adoption   5, Appendix III, 370
  Process   6, 379
  Supervision   8
  Tripartism, influence on
    standard-setting   6
State within a state   81, 83, 164, 173
Sub-Commission (Martinez-Cobo)
  Study   155, 157, 160, 288

Supervision
  Complaint procedures   9
  Of ILO standards generally   8
  Regular supervisory mechanisms   8

Territories   202, 207, 208, 229, 231, 233, 236, 245
  Demarcation   339
  Explanation by the Office   321
To the extent possible   203
Top down development model   163
Traditional institutions   67
Transfer of populations   238
Treaty rights   125, 255, 257, 331
Tribal
  Meaning   46, 59
  Semi-tribal   49, 60, 68

UNESCO   18, 21, 22, 23, 24, 25, 26, 31, 32, 35, 78, 157, 197
United Nations   15, 18, 21, 24, 25, 26, 29, 31, 32, 33, 37, 38, 39, 41, 53, 58, 59, 60, 61, 63, 67, 71, 78, 82, 83, 125, 128, 156, 163, 165, 186,
  Declaration on the Rights of Indigenous
    Peoples   1, 17, 60, 88
  Special Rapporteur on the situation of
    human rights and fundamental
    freedoms of indigenous peoples   63, 183, 222, 256, 268
  Sub-Commission (Martinez-Cobo)
    Study   61, 62, 155, 157, 160, 288
  Support from the UN system for adoption   21, 31
  United Nations Verification Mission in
    Guatemala (MINUGUA)   145, 336
  Working Group on Indigenous
    Populations   38, 62, 268
Usufruct   238

Voting in the International Labour
  Conference   7

World Commission on the Environment and
  Development   168
World Conference on Agrarian Reform and
  Rural Development   253
World Council of Indigenous Peoples   160
World Health Organization   22, 24, 31, 32

Printed in the United States
By Bookmasters